Being Smart
Empowering Parents and K

"Matthews and Foster highlight the importance of an appropriate education for gifted and talented students with the concept of an optimal match between students and their learning environments... The ideas in this book represent an important conceptual framing that will help gifted and talented programs serve broader and more diverse populations of students."
—Frank Worrell, Ph.D., U C Berkeley,
American Psychology Association President-Elect, 2022.

"Drs. Matthews and Foster have given us a comprehensive, intelligently designed and brilliantly crafted book written with extraordinary understanding and compassion. Readers of all kinds—parents, grandparents, teachers, counselors—will recognize that the authors have "been there" and will be grateful for how smart about gifted learning they have become."
—Felice Kaufmann, Ph.D., Consultant on Giftedness and Creativity

"Being Smart about Gifted Learning is a brilliant book that empowers and enlightens parents with essential information about optimizing their child's educational, social, and emotional experiences. Drs Matthews and Foster provide a plethora of tips and strategies that lead to a winning formula: helping children and teens discover the right combination of safety and challenge to support life-long resilience and creativity."
—Mona Delahooke, Ph.D., Child Psychologist
and Award-winning Author

"Telra Institute illustrates Matthews & Foster's Optimal Match in practice, recognizing that learning is fluid and requires ongoing re-evaluation and appropriate levels of challenge.
—Michael Matthews, Ph.D., and Ronak Bhatt, Sc.D.,
University of North Carolina and Telra Institute, Charlotte, NC

"This comprehensive, thorough, all-encompassing resource dives DEEPLY into deconstructing the multiple facets of what the term "gifted" or "advanced learner" can mean in specific, reassuring, practical and helpful ways. Reading this book is a must for anyone who works with children."
—Nancy Kopman, Musician and Early Childhood Educator

Being Smart About Gifted Learning

Empowering Parents and Kids Through Challenge and Change

Dona Matthews, Ph.D., and Joanne Foster, Ed.D.

Edited by: Molly A. Isaacs-McLeod, JD, LL.M.
Interior design: The Printed Page
Cover design: Kelly Crimi

Published by
Gifted Unlimited, LLC
12340 U.S. Highway 42, No. 453
Goshen, KY 40026
www.giftedunlimitedllc.com

Dedications

I would like to dedicate this book to four brilliant thinkers who have inspired and guided me in my work in gifted education: Dan Keating, Rena Subotnik, the late Marion Porath, and the late Frances Degen Horowitz. I am grateful to each for their thoughtful wisdom and kindness along the way.

~Dona Matthews

To my wonderful and loving family—Garry, Eric, Cheryl, Aaron, Michele, Cara, Allie, Jake, Sari and Cooper. Each of you shows resilience, adaptability, kindness, and strength of character. You warm my heart, bring me joy, and encourage me to keep writing and learning. Thank you!

~Joanne Foster

Acknowledgments

Being Smart about Gifted Learning is a fully revised edition of its two predecessors, *Being Smart about Gifted Children,* and *Being Smart about Gifted Education*. We want to thank Molly Isaacs-McLeod at Gifted Unlimited for her faith in our vision for this book. She was generous in giving us autonomy, flexibility, and encouragement. We're delighted that Rena Subotnik wrote the foreword. She continues to be a guiding force for us, as for so many others in the field of gifted education. Nancy and Hal Robinson provided a conceptual foundation as well as just the right expression for the Optimal Match approach that we discuss throughout this book. Nancy's encouragement was instrumental as we extended the ideas and described broad-based applications for parents and teachers, and beneficial outcomes for children and adolescents. We also appreciate the dedicated efforts of Lisa Liddy who fine-tuned and executed the formatting of the book, and of Kelly Crimi whose creativity is reflected by the colorful cover design.

There have been many important mentors along the way for us both. Dona would particularly like to acknowledge Dan Keating, whose intellectual depth and breadth will always be an inspiration; Rena Subotnik, a loyal friend with a big heart, whose reputation for integrity and mastery of the field is well deserved; Marion Porath, a vibrant, generous, extraordinary teacher, researcher, and friend; and Frances Degen Horowitz, a pioneer in moving the field of gifted education toward a psychological focus on human development across the life span.

Joanne would like to acknowledge the many individuals who have provided guidance and support in the course of her teaching, consultancy, advocacy efforts, and writing over the years. This includes colleagues at schools and school boards across Canada, at the Ontario Institute for Studies in Education of the University of Toronto), and in collaborative settings elsewhere around the world; those who have published her books, chapters, and articles; and her parents, Clara and Nathan Stein, who instilled in her a lifelong love of learning that has served to underlie all personal and professional growth.

We appreciate the responses and feedback we've received from our readers, and thank all the educators, parents, children, and teens with whom we've worked over the past several decades. We're delighted to share some of their voices and viewpoints here. Several experts in the field of gifted education have also offered their perspectives, and we're pleased to be able to convey their wisdom within these pages.

A special shout-out goes to our friends and extended family members who cheered us on and gave us ideas as we worked on the manuscript of this updated version of *Being Smart*.

Our husbands, Stephen Gross and Garry Foster, have encouraged us in our research and writing, offering boundless support and patience, as well as humor, inspiration, comfort, and love. They've been right alongside us on this journey.

Finally, we want to thank our children and grandchildren. We continue to learn from them every day, and with each experience we gain perspective and immeasurable joy. We're grateful for these sweet blessings in our lives.

—Dona and Joanne

Table of Contents

Foreword

Dona Matthews and Joanne Foster provide us with a timely and timeless volume of wisdom for families of school age children. Gifted education is faced with two crises—one reflected in a lack of confidence and even outright hostility to the current form of gifted education in North America. The other is how to address educational service disruptions caused by the pandemic. These challenges need forthright response. On the pages of *Being Smart*, Matthews and Foster speak to the moment while providing accessible, evidence-based counsel that remains relevant across time and circumstances.

Although gifted education has always had supporters, it has operated in a region of the world that has been ambivalent about established hierarchies, revering tinkerers over the "egg heads." In response to the 1957 Soviet launch of Sputnik, fear provided a break in the pattern when funding from the U.S. National Defense Education Act of 1958 streamed to programs designed to find talent in science, mathematics, engineering, and critical foreign languages in post-secondary and even k-12 environments. Another rich period of support came in the mid-1980s as North America embraced not only corporate, but entrepreneurial and educational elites. The Reagan administration published *A Nation at Risk* (1983), decrying how our nation's brightest students were being underserved in school. During this period of funding and scholarly opportunities, classic volumes on gifted education like *Developing Talent in Young People* (1985) edited by Benjamin Bloom, *Conceptions of Giftedness* (1986) edited by Robert Sternberg and Janet Davidson, *Nature's Gambit (1986)* by David Feldman and Lynn Goldsmith, *Frames of Mind* (1983) by

Howard Gardner, and *Gifted Children: Psychological and Educational Perspectives* (1983) by Abraham Tannenbaum burst on the scene and influenced generations of scholars, including Matthews, Foster, me and most of our colleagues and collaborators. Notably, the two positive historical markers of our field's history did not concern fairness and equity, yet these books and scholars have continued the struggle to broaden our social responsibilities as educational professionals.

Especially since the 1990s, the general public and more specifically the education enterprise has become increasingly concerned about fairness and the efficacy of selective education, particularly when based on IQ. Questions about traditional identification processes increased as more research uncovered disconnects between high childhood intellectual prowess and adult outcomes. And more recent work by the National Center for Research on Gifted Education has demonstrated a lack of coherence between the implementation and goals of programs. Meanwhile, enrollment by racially and ethnically minoritized groups in gifted education has remained such a stubborn problem that more districts are resorting to lotteries over traditional approaches.

The pandemic, with its demands for at-home education, has provided parents with far more insights into the dynamics of learning experienced by their children. They have come to value the preciousness of excellent instruction and to understand the huge challenges faced by teachers needing to address wide variation in academic and social-emotional needs, even in selective programs. Many strategies used in talent development have been helpful in reconceptualizing how schools and particularly gifted programs might reorganize in the coming years. Dona Matthews and Joanne Foster promote rethinking how we identify students to focus on developing strengths in domains and by viewing children as embodying varying profiles over time. They also promote intelligent ways to parallel creative processes in the curriculum to serve as productive outlets for children's talent.

Finally, Dona Matthews and Joanne Foster have worked closely with children and their families in cultivating children's well-being. This is particularly important during this fragile period of transition back to school and some form of previous normality. My colleagues Paula Olszewski-Kubilius, Frank Worrell and I distinguish socio-emotional skills into two somewhat porous categories. One category includes those skills that are usually associated with the social-emotional learning literature and are essential for all students' well-being. The second category is associated with the needs of high performers including screening out distractions, as well as overcoming fears of public performances. Most important is to help students become secure enough to weather inevitable rejection of creative ideas. Matthews and Foster are uniquely skilled at conveying both categories with special insight into how important it is for children to feel comfortable in their own skins to enjoy learning, face obstacles, and engage the creative spirit with gusto.

—Rena Subotnik, Ph.D.

Introduction

Being Smart About Gifted Learning, the third edition of this book, emerges out of our decades of personal and professional experiences with giftedness, and also from a shared sense of the joys, challenges, and uniqueness of every child. In this book, we discuss ways to nurture children's learning and well-being across many dimensions of their lives.

We've written *Being Smart About Gifted Learning* with parents in mind, but also for grandparents, teachers, and others who want to encourage children's and adolescents' optimal development. One of the themes running through this book, as with the first two editions, is that there's no single formula to follow. The best place to begin is by reflecting on your child's uniqueness. Consider their emotional, social, intellectual, and physical interests, strengths, and challenges, and learn to empower them to engage more meaningfully with a wide range of learning opportunities.

We've revised and updated every chapter, introducing new research findings, theoretical perspectives, and stories of people's real-life challenges and triumphs. We pay close attention to the importance of diagnosing mismatches between your child's educational experiences and their level of functioning. We illustrate how an Optimal Match approach can open doors to gifted learning possibilities for diverse learners, many of whom are excluded from gifted programming because of test criteria they cannot meet, inequitable social and education policies, generational and systemic racism, or other reasons.

In this edition of *Being Smart*, we discuss topics that parents, educators, and policy-makers have asked us about, including some that are seldom covered in other parent-friendly books on gifted development. We devote an entire section of the book to tests, assessment, and identification issues. We offer insights on creativity as it relates to giftedness, and we provide extensive information on gifted programming, including recommendations on differentiation and other targeted learning options, best practice for teachers, and advocacy strategies for parents. We also discuss matters that affect children's well-being, including social-emotional, behavioral, and motivational issues, and key developmental aspects. Within this book, you'll read about the challenges, experiences, and successes of some of the adults and children with whom we work, as well as comments from experts across disciplines.

Over the years we've observed an accelerating paradigm shift in the field of gifted education. The Optimal Match approach that we champion here reflects that shift. Nancy and Hal Robinson wrote about the Optimal Match in 1982, and we're pleased to use the term they introduced, in a somewhat different form, within these pages. If you take just one thing from this book, we hope it's that the goal of gifted education should be finding and implementing the optimal educational match for your child's interests and abilities, remembering to keep it flexible because these targets change over time.

Our backgrounds in teaching, special education, developmental psychology, and educational psychology inform our work as we discuss the complexities, challenges, and wonders of gifted development. We continue to welcome readers' opinions, and hope you find these pages helpful in furthering your understanding of how giftedness develops. You will then be better able to make informed decisions that foster children's learning and development.

There's a double mission in gifted education. One is a focus on supporting exceptionally capable learners' development and education, the conventional role of gifted education. Equally important, however, is the second mission: using what's known about gifted development to encourage giftedness more broadly across the population, especially among those whose exceptional abilities might not be recognized. Each of us has a responsibility to give children what they need to follow their interests, affirm their strengths, and develop their capabilities.

Gifted education should be encouraging and inclusive, working to support the optimal development of all children, while at the same time ensuring meaningful opportunities for those with advanced learning needs. This book is about empowering children and adolescents so they can find a healthy balance in their lives, one that nurtures their abilities, and fosters their well-rounded development.

Poet Irving Layton wrote, "They who are driven dance best." Those words convey our passion and enthusiasm, and that which we observe in the parents, educators, and children with whom we work—the people we write about in this book. We're delighted to share our views, as informed by this rich collective experience.

Dona Matthews and Joanne Foster
Toronto, Canada
August, 2021

Postscript: A Bit about *Being Smart*, Editions 1 and 2

The first edition, *Being Smart about Gifted Children* (2005), was based on years of experience working with students with exceptionally advanced learning needs, and their parents and educators. We wrote that book out of concern for children's development because so much of what people were encountering about giftedness was misleading, or at the very least not helpful. We included the voices and viewpoints of different stakeholders in children's education, as we considered how to support optimal development in those who had been labeled gifted, and those who had not.

In 2009, we wrote the second edition, *Being Smart about Gifted Education* (2009), reflecting on what we'd written previously, and how the field was evolving. Parents and teachers had told us that our ideas helped them make sense of their problems and questions. Just as encouragingly, expanding research on brain development, expertise, and gifted education confirmed the importance of concepts we'd introduced about meeting children's learning needs. In that second edition, we reiterated our fundamental principles and positions, and provided more references and additional ideas based on our ongoing work.

We hope you enjoy reading this third edition, *Being Smart about Gifted Learning* (2021), as much as we enjoyed writing it.

Section I
Being Smart About Giftedness

CHAPTER 1

Perspectives and Paradigm Shifts

What Is Giftedness?

> *"Giftedness is not a thing in the mind to be found, but a form of excellence evidenced in many ways in a variety of domains and contexts… A paradigm shift in gifted education will make it more flexible, accessible, and responsive to challenges in the 21st century."*[1]

There's no such thing as a "typical gifted child." Each child with gifted learning needs is unique, with their own story and life experiences, their own profile of strengths and challenges. How a child feels and responds, and what they need in order to thrive, are individual and often unpredictable. Parents and grandparents who understand the diversity of individual experience, and who realize there's no single approach that works well for all children, are more likely to make good decisions for the children in their lives than those who think there's one right way to support the development of giftedness.

Throughout this book, we share our experience both as professionals in gifted education, and also as parents and grandparents of children who have had a variety of gifted learning needs and experiences with gifted education. In our time living and working with issues concerning gifted development and education, we've had countless conversations with other parents and grandparents. They often have mixed feelings, difficult questions, and worrying confusion about the term "gifted." Here are some of the concerns we've encountered:

○ *"How are gifted kids different from other kids?"*

○ *"My other son didn't make the gifted cut-off, even though he seems just as bright as his brother."*

○ *"If a so-called gifted student doesn't finish all her work, she isn't really gifted, is she?"*

○ *"My grandson reads chapter books to me, and he's only in Grade 1. Is he gifted? How can I help him?"*

Some of the most poignant concerns are those we hear from children:

○ *"If I don't understand the math, that means I'm not really gifted, right?"*

○ *"Why does everyone expect so much of me all the time?"*

○ *"I'd rather be cool than gifted."*

○ *"I'm embarrassed when people ask me about being gifted."*

If we're to understand exceptionally capable children and support them in their development—that is, provide them with the best possible guidance, challenge, and encouragement—it's good to start by reflecting upon their individual differences. From there, we can consider what to do about their giftedness at school, at home, and in the world. But first, let's talk about what giftedness means.

Understanding Giftedness: Mystery vs. Optimal Match

Some people describe "gifted children" as being obviously smarter than others, born with the ability to learn everything, or having a higher IQ. These perspectives reflect what we call the "mystery" concept of giftedness. From this standpoint, these children are born with high intellectual potential and score in the very superior range of intelligence tests, and once a child is identified as "gifted," they will always be gifted, no matter how well or poorly they do at school or anywhere else.

This way of thinking is implicit when children are simply categorized as "gifted" or "not gifted" without the label being tied to recommendations for changes to their educational programming. Using this mystery approach, children who achieve very high scores on intelligence tests can be placed together in a gifted program, even though the children's areas of ability differ greatly from each other. Some of the high-scoring kids might be unusually strong in mathematical or scientific areas but score close to average or below average in other subject areas; similarly, others may be extremely advanced only in social studies; still others may have exceptional linguistic abilities, with everything else at a lower level. A high global IQ masks the variations across areas of ability, which means that children selected for a gifted program vary at least as much in their learning needs as those in a regular class. The high scores are higher, but the lows are usually just as low.

While we celebrate the mysteries of life itself and respect the fact that there is much that we don't know about human development, we think that labeling a child as gifted without direct ties to educational implications is mysterious because, using this model, it's difficult to figure out what giftedness really is. Maybe it's simply the ability to score well on a test of intelligence. But when giftedness is thought of like that, some troubling questions arise about the content and process of the tests that are used. What does a high IQ tell us about a child's educational needs? And what if a child has high-level abilities in domains that have not been tested? Moreover, what if there are mitigating circumstances, or a student has not yet had an opportunity to learn in an area of potential strength? (We consider the answers to these concerns in Section II, "Being Smart about Diagnosing Mismatches.")

Now let's consider some children's comments about what being gifted means:

○ *"Smarter, at least in some areas."*

○ *"School is almost always boring, especially math."*

○ *"More curious. Needing to know stuff that other kids don't really care about."*

These answers are closer to what we call the Optimal Match concept of giftedness. From this perspective, the term "gifted" simply denotes a mismatch between a child's current level in a given subject area and the educational opportunities being offered.

The Optimal Match approach aligns well with best practices in special education, where the focus is on learning differences that require adaptations to the curriculum. From this point of view, a child might be considered gifted when their learning needs in a given subject are so advanced relative to those of their classmates that their learning will be stalled or impeded unless the subject area content is somehow modified to meet those learning needs.

There's no mystery about what giftedness means from an Optimal Match perspective: it's advancement at a certain point in time in a particular context, such that the curriculum requires adjusting in order to address the child's learning needs. You can see this approach applied in non-academic areas of achievement such as sports, music, and the arts more generally, where children are encouraged to progress at their own rate, and not held back because of their age.

Perhaps the best way to explain what the Optimal Match concept is all about is to compare it with the mystery concept:

○ **Origin.** Most educational practitioners now accept that genetic predispositions ("nature") and environmental supports ("nurture") are interactive influences on intelligence. Mystery proponents emphasize the nature or genetic component: giftedness is seen as innate, such that some children are born with superior brains. Optimal Match practitioners' understanding of superior intellectual ability, by contrast, focuses on children's opportunities to learn—that is, the nurture factor.

○ **Duration: Dynamic or Temporal Factors.** The mystery concept implies an intellectual superiority from birth and across the life span, and across all contexts, as expressed in the saying, "once gifted, always gifted." However, from an Optimal Match perspective, the only kind of giftedness that matters is that which requires current educational attention.

There are no assumptions about the duration of giftedness, because learning needs are understood as changing over time.

○ **Extent: Domain Strength.** Through a mystery lens, giftedness implies excellence across all tasks that require thinking, from reading a map, to explaining a Shakespearean sonnet, to learning advanced algebra. An Optimal Match perspective, on the other hand, recognizes that intellectual competence varies across areas. A person gifted in algebra is not necessarily gifted in map-reading or Shakespearean studies. Thus, a child might be described as gifted in mathematics, geography, English, or something else, and as functioning closer to average, or below, in other areas.

○ **Timing of Identification.** Using a mystery approach, the sooner in a child's life their innate giftedness is identified, the better, so it won't be squandered. However, because the Optimal Match view focuses on remedying educational mismatches, exceptional learning needs are identified as they develop, whether occurring at home or at school, and assessed on an ongoing basis to ensure a good match of instruction to learning needs.[2]

○ **Identification Measures.** Historically, the best mystery measure of giftedness has been IQ. For Optimal Match practitioners, though, the best way to identify giftedness is to use a combination of dynamic classroom assessments and high-ceiling tests of academic reasoning that provide teacher-friendly information about appropriate curriculum level in different subject areas. In some cases, IQ testing is needed to supplement these measures, but the real question concerns whether or not the child's learning needs are being well met, now how high they score on a test of intelligence. (There's a lot more on assessment measures and techniques in Section II, "Being Smart about Diagnosing Mismatches.")

○ **Identification Implications.** From a mystery standpoint, a child who makes the cut-off score is identified as gifted, and then invited to participate in whatever gifted programming is available, whether a full-time segregated program, a half-day enrichment class, or something else. Many jurisdictions still use some form of this approach, although increasingly, they're moving to an Optimal Match alternative—that is, identifying children who have one or more areas of exceptional strength, and need adaptations to what's normally expected, like subject-specific acceleration, participation in district-wide interest clubs, or some other form of appropriately targeted learning opportunities.

○ **Placement and Curriculum Implications.** For mystery adherents, the top-of-the-line program is usually seen as a fulltime segregated gifted class. Where that isn't available, gifted enrichment might be offered, where kids identified as gifted attend a program for a scheduled interval every week, or the regular classroom teacher provides more challenging or extra work. Unfortunately, and all too often, teachers implementing gifted programs receive little training or support in gifted development and education. (We discuss this in Chapter 11.) As more jurisdictions move toward an Optimal Match approach, a segregated gifted class might be one of many possibilities within a broad range of options, with the placement depending on a child's special learning needs.

○ **Coherence.** Under the mystery approach, there is no connection between having a high IQ and what happens in a gifted program. But the Optimal Match way of thinking focuses on a given child's educational exceptionality, and programming recommendations are based on understanding what that child needs in order to keep learning. This can be assessed through a multifaceted identification process designed to inform what level of instruction will be a good match for that student's ability in each subject area. In that way, definition, identification, and programming fit together coherently.

○ **Elitism and Political Implications.** From a mystery stance, gifted education doesn't meet an obvious educational need, and too often it leads to racially and economically disproportionate identification, which in turn leads to charges of elitism and unstable funding.[3] Alternatively, because an Optimal Match approach is clearly tied to addressing students' specific learning needs, it's much less likely to incur social, political, and funding problems, and it welcomes cultural diversity. When gifted program options are flexibly targeted to special learning needs, and include all those students for whom they are appropriate, gifted education is considerably less problematic.[4]

○ **Evaluation.** Evaluation of programming approaches has been a chronic problem in gifted education.[5] When definition, identification, and programming are disconnected, as happens with mystery thinking, it's hard to know if a program is working or not, much less what needs improvement. As a consequence, the usual gifted program evaluations are user-satisfaction measures. It's not surprising that people selected for an enriched educational experience generally like the program. Conversely, from an Optimal Match perspective, programs are responsive to what an individual child requires at a given point in time, so evaluation is more objective and meaningful. This leads to evaluation questions like, Does the programming match individual children's learning needs, on a subject-by-subject basis? Are students learning more, at a level and speed that is better aligned with their abilities? Are they more engaged in school and learning?

One Child's Story

The following two versions of a child's experience illustrate some of the differences between the mystery and the Optimal Match concepts. We show how these two ways of thinking play out so differently in the life of one young girl.

Raqi's Story, Version #1 (Mystery Perspective)

Raqi was an early talker and an early reader. When she entered kindergarten, she was fluently reading chapter books, and more than ready for what she considered "real schoolwork." She was lucky to have a kindergarten teacher who enjoyed her precocity and encouraged her to read books and complete workbooks while the rest of the class participated in reading readiness activities. Grade 1 was a good year for her, too, again thanks to a teacher who knew how to keep her challenged and learning, and who had flexible expectations.

Grade 2 wasn't so successful; there were no special accommodations for her advanced ability. Raqi frequently argued with her teacher, who tried to trap Raqi by giving her problems she couldn't solve, and who openly resented it when Raqi corrected a spelling mistake on the class whiteboard. Raqi survived second and third grade, not liking school very much, and following her own interests whenever possible. At the end of Grade 3, she participated in a system-wide gifted identification process. She was identified as gifted, and was happy she would be able to attend the full-time gifted program offered at a nearby school.

Raqi loved the idea that she'd be going to school with other kids who were as curious as her, who were keen to learn about everything, and who gobbled up books and wanted to talk about them. She waited impatiently all summer and strode off to school on the first day of Grade 4 with high hopes for a teacher who understood her, and friends she'd enjoy talking to.

But after just one day in the gifted class, Raqi came home dejected.

"Mom," she said, "I *hate* the gifted program. The teacher's nice but she talks in a little-girl voice, and she won't let us do *anything*."

Over the course of the next few weeks, Raqi's opinions of the gifted program and the teacher did not improve. She was even more dismayed to find that the kids in the class did not share her interests or enthusiasms. As if all that wasn't bad enough, she had some troubling experiences in which she discovered that other kids and teachers felt hostile toward the students in the gifted program. One day, for example, during lunchtime, a teacher walked past a group of kids in Raqi's class who were chatting in the hallway. He shouted at them for not picking up the litter, even though it had been dropped by other kids. "You're supposed to be gifted," the teacher said. "You should know better than to let that happen."

Raqi's mother went to the parent-teacher conference in October hoping to help Raqi's teacher deal with her daughter, whom she knew to be difficult when she felt her time was being wasted, but also to be positive and enthusiastic when she was learning and engaged. Raqi's mom discovered it was Miss Pinkerton's first year teaching. She had no training in gifted education, and no experience adapting the curriculum to meet special learning needs. Miss Pinkerton explained politely but firmly that she couldn't be expected to create a special curriculum for each of the children in the class, and that even if Raqi already knew the material they were covering, she would have to go through it with the class, doing all the homework and assignments. Raqi could do extra work if she wanted to, of course, although Miss Pinkerton wouldn't have time to mark it or to talk with her about it.

Raqi stayed in the gifted class, feeling a bit desperate. She'd hoped that once she was in a gifted program, she'd meet kids like her and have teachers who understood her hunger for learning deeply and broadly. Although that didn't really happen, she thought that staying was better than returning to what she'd experienced in second and third grades, and that maybe things would improve in the gifted program. It wasn't until high school that Raqi began to enjoy learning challenges at school again, and meet classmates who went on to become lifelong friends.

As with all of the stories we share in *Being Smart about Gifted Education,* this one about Raqi can be read in various ways. Like life itself, the story is complex, with different threads that can be pulled out for further consideration. We include Raqi's real-life experience (version #1) not to show how terrible fulltime gifted classes are, because, in fact, many parents and children have told us that such classes have been enormously important to them (as they were to one of our own children and now are to one of our grandkids). Rather we want to illustrate that gifted programs are not always the salvation that parents and kids hope they will be, and that a child's identification and placement does not ensure that their learning needs will be met.

Gifted education expert David Y. Dai shares the following idea: "Current thinking broadens our view of human potential, not as a fixed capacity, but as malleable and incremental, depending on multiple factors, exogenous [inner] as well as endogenous [outer], facilitative or inhibitive. This conception opens the door for new ways of thinking about strategies and provisions of gifted education."[6]

Let's replay Raqi's story as if her school district were providing gifted education designed to match her exceptional learning needs. We have the same little girl, a precocious talker and reader, keen to learn everything she can from her earliest days on, devouring mathematics and literature, foreign languages and geography.

We don't have to retouch the first two primary school years at all. Her kindergarten and first grade teachers did the right things by responding flexibly to what they observed and by providing opportunities for Raqi to keep on learning, even though she was advanced in so many ways when compared with her age peers.

Raqi's Story, Version #2
(Optimal Match Perspective)

In this second version of the story, Raqi's Grade 2 teacher realized that she was out of her depth and called in the gifted education consultant who did some assessments, and identified the nature and extent of Raqi's exceptional strengths. Together with Raqi and her mother, the consultant devised a plan for compressing the topics Raqi had already mastered, making time for Raqi to attend a weekly math challenge group working toward a district-wide math contest. Raqi was encouraged to be creative about assignments, and she was invited to chat regularly with the school librarian, who helped develop a meaningful reading plan for her. All of this made Raqi feel happy and motivated, and she often shared her creativity, reading assignments, and other products with her classmates.

The gifted education consultant worked with Raqi and her teachers for the next several years. Raqi accelerated through Grade 7, and she was ready for Advanced Placement courses in some subject areas by the time she finished Grade 8. She was looking forward to continuing to explore her interests at a large local high school with a wide range of subject area options, and a principal who was willing to oversee Raqi's program to help ensure that it would correspond to her particular learning needs. She was encouraged to explore university-based courses online, as well as courses at the local community college.

Through the sixteen years since *Being Smart* was first published, we've received hundreds of responses to the book from parents, teachers, and grandparents. They frequently mention the Raqi story, sometimes with annoyance because they think we're saying that fulltime classes don't work (and please note: we're NOT trying to make that point!), but more frequently with an "Aha! *That's* the difference between the two approaches." Here are a few of the comments we've received:

> *"The Raqi story shows me why I have so much trouble with gifted education. It's because I've been thinking of it from a mystery point of view. I prefer the idea that giftedness is fluid, and the aspect of domain strength is important, too. This way of thinking allows for growth and change, in addition to average achievement at certain times or in certain subject areas."*

> *"The mystery mode of thinking doesn't accommodate kids' subject-specific abilities. It's also not inclusive, so it's not defensible."*

> *"I never wanted my children to participate in gifted programs because I thought they were elitist, even racist. But when gifted education follows a more adaptable mismatch approach, I can see that it makes perfect sense. It's even necessary."*

Today, Raqi is a happily productive mother, wife, and novelist. She's politically active in environmental causes, and by any estimate, would be described as making a meaningful and vibrantly successful life for herself. She has no regrets, but in the context of this book, and given that story version #1 is the real one, we wonder what would have happened if her schooling had given her more support for developing her exceptional abilities.

Giftedness, Neurodiversity, and Neural Plasticity

> *"To our unique genetic profile, we add personal diversity through our memories, sensory processing, behaviors and actions, and our environmental influences. Together this*

creates a distinct brain, body, vision, nervous system, and one-of-a-kind individuality. No two humans are identical."[7]

Nicole Tetreault is a neuroscientist who writes about gifted development within the context of neurodiversity. In her recent book, *Insight into a Bright Mind: A Neuroscientist's Personal Stories of Unique Thinking*, she uses compelling stories to demonstrate the value of diversity in human brains and human experiences. She writes, "The brain is flexible, and we can guide children to reach their potential with the ability to learn at the level that suits them. The brain is a dynamic organ and has the ability to grow based on experience, environment, and genetics." This is an excellent description of neural plasticity, the mechanism that drives gifted-level learning, and that underlies the Optimal Match approach to gifted education.

The brain is malleable, and can grow under the right circumstances of experience and environment. Thus, supporting gifted development involves paying attention to your child's innate (perhaps genetically-influenced) interests, and helping your child develop those interests into strengths and talents. Increasingly, neuroscientists like Tetreault are affirming the remarkable brain plasticity that allows for extraordinary learning, given the right combination of interest, motivation, and environmental supports, most importantly parents and others in the child's world. Looked at this way, giftedness is not mysterious. It's a form of neurodiversity that should be respected and nurtured, as with all other individual differences that are in flux as children and adolescents learn and grow.

Shifting Paradigms

By definition, paradigm shifts are disturbances of the status quo. It's always difficult to identify when a paradigm shift begins to happen; it's easier to see in retrospect. With its focus on domain-specific abilities rather than general intelligence, the Marland Report[8] of 1972 laid early groundwork for the mismatch perspective. Another early and important influence in this paradigm shift was the work of Julian Stanley and colleagues at Johns Hopkins University, with the Study of Mathematically Precocious Youth.[9]

Similarly, Nancy and Hal Robinson's 1982 pioneering book chapter outlined their Optimal Match concept.[10] These authors argued for providing a range of options for gifted learners and matching programming to individual learning needs. We are most grateful to Nancy Robinson who, in January, 2021, graciously told us we were welcome to use their nomenclature to describe our approach.[11]

Then, in 1989, Jim Borland published *Planning and Implementing Programs for the Gifted*,[12] where he talked about gifted education in very similar terms to those that we use here. He described himself as "a special educator whose population of interest is gifted children." He enumerated seven underlying principles, and we find that his work continues to form a strong foundational base for ours. We applaud Borland's insight, and his foresight. Here are his seven principles, slightly amended to keep them up to date with changes in terminology since then:

1. Gifted education is a form of special education.

2. Children's current educational needs, not their prospects for future eminence, should guide our practice.

3. The nature of the students served will and should vary from one neighborhood to another.

4. No single program model can be appropriate for all children or all situations.

5. Gifted programming should be based on information gleaned from formal needs assessments, which can include informal measures.

6. The needs of gifted learners are best addressed in the company of their age peers.

7. Learning opportunities for gifted students should stress the acquisition of important and relevant knowledge.

Michael Howe's *The Origins of Exceptional Abilities* (1990) provided further evidence for a domain-specific developmental perspective on gifted-level ability.[13] About the same time, the inaugural issue of *Exceptionality Education Canada* (1991) contained several frequently-cited and thought-provoking articles along these lines.[14] Other approaches to gifted education that have gained traction are also consistent with important elements of the Optimal Match perspective. These include the talent development approach[15], the integrated curriculum model,[16] and Renzulli's enrichment triad model.[17] Recent findings on the importance and efficacy of acceleration further illustrate the paradigm shift toward the Optimal Match approach to addressing gifted learning needs, with its emphasis on ensuring a good match between a child's subject-specific developmental level and the academic challenges provided[18]. An increasing focus on expertise as a way to understand high level development provides yet another example of this shift.[19]

In *Mindset*,[20] developmental psychologist Carol Dweck pulled together findings in neuropsychology, developmental psychology, and education, that distinguish between a fixed mindset, where some children are categorized as inherently smart (mystery lens), and a growth mindset, where intelligence is seen as developing over time with appropriately scaffolded opportunities to learn (Optimal Match lens). The fixed mindset is associated with lower achievement and self-esteem, whereas the growth mindset is associated with greater confidence and risk-taking, and with higher academic and career success over time. Dweck has explicitly connected the growth mindset and the Optimal Match approach.[21]

In discussing his observations of a paradigm shift in progress, scholar David Henry Feldman wrote, "Recognition that the field of gifted education is holding an increasingly untenable position appears to be growing, perhaps to the critical point at which real change becomes possible, even necessary."[22] He posited (as do we in this book) that it's important for the ongoing viability of the field that educators pay attention to the developmental aspects of giftedness. Throughout these pages we provide a good way to do just that, and to simultaneously clarify the confusion that exists for many parents, grandparents, and teachers.

Origins: Nature or Nurture?

For decades, there was hot debate about the relative weight of genetic and environmental influences on intelligence. Experts weighed in on the percentage allocation to each, saying intelligence was 90% genetic, or 60% environmental, or assigning some other number to each side of the dichotomy. However, as neuroscientists have discovered more about how the brain actually works, virtually all experts today accept that high intelligence is built on a complex interaction of nature and nurture over time.[23]

The findings on high-level development come together in interesting ways, suggesting that high IQ most frequently results when a child feels listened to, cared about, and respected, and is provided with opportunities to learn and explore in age-appropriate ways.[24]

But giftedness can develop for other complicated reasons, too. For example, high achievement can be motivated by a drive to overcome some kind of obstacle (perhaps poverty, disability, or deprivation). In a book exploring influences on high-level development, Carl Simonton considered prevailing "common sense" notions and myths, as well as the research findings, including (among many others) genetic inheritance, gender, birth order, creativity, age, intelligence, personality, psychopathology, relationships, and opportunities.[25] Simonton concluded that the pathways to gifted-level achievement are as diverse and unpredictable as the achievements themselves.

Although some children exhibit high-level ability very early on, often, exceptional ability doesn't show up until middle or even late adulthood.[26] In fact, the majority of those who end up succeeding at very high levels in most real-world domains (with the exception of math, music, and sports) are people who weren't recognized as exceptionally advanced when they were children.[27]

So, if your child is not identified at school as gifted, you shouldn't conclude that you're a less effective parent than others, or that your child has less potential than others. Giftedness as seen from the Optimal Match perspective is about addressing mismatches as they occur. It is *not* about identifying who is naturally more intelligent than others, or predicting future success or possible eminence.

Domains of Competence

The concept of intelligence as multifaceted is not new and has been proposed by many people in various forms.[28] In 1983, Howard Gardner captured popular imagination and changed the way most educators think about intelligence with his theory of multiple intelligences.[29] He argued that a single measure like IQ is inadequate and misleading in describing a person's many different abilities. When trying to understand or assess a person's intelligence, there are different intelligences or ability domains that should be considered somewhat separately.

Gardner initially proposed seven intelligences: linguistic, logical-mathematical, spatial, bodily-kinesthetic, musical, interpersonal, and intrapersonal. (Subsequently, he added two more intelligences to his list: naturalist and existential.) It's possible that a given individual could have gifted-level abilities in one, two, or several of these domains, and not in others, but very few people have gifted-level abilities in all areas. Most parents realize that children's profiles of abilities vary greatly, and Gardner provides a model for thinking about that.

Among those who are identified as gifted because of a high IQ, most are not exceptionally advanced across all school subject areas. In fact, many children identified as gifted are quite average, or even below average, in some areas (sometimes called dual exceptionality or 2E). Discrepancies in ability across domains increases with the degree of giftedness in one domain or another.[30] The more exceptionally advanced a child is in one area or another, the less likely they are to be similarly gifted across other domains.

By the time a child reaches adolescence, being exceptionally good at everything is much more the exception than the rule. As kids get older, there are only a very few who can be considered gifted across most or all subject areas. Because of this, gifted education experts are increasingly advocating that educators consider multiple domains of ability, rather than simple global scores such as IQ tests provide.[31]

Is Learning Easy?

"I'm suddenly having trouble in math class. I guess that means I'm not gifted anymore."

"My homework takes me soooo long, and my friend does it in five minutes. Maybe I'm not gifted after all."

"I failed the geography test yesterday. Am I still gifted?"

Contrary to popular belief, being gifted does *not* mean learning is a breeze. A gifted learner might find it easy to exceed some age-normal expectations, but they experience the same challenges as anyone else in moving from their current level in a subject area to a higher level, although they may have some advantages in doing so. For example, gifted learners often have a larger and more conceptually complex foundation of knowledge than their age-peers, as well as the confidence that comes from previous learning successes.

However, real learning always involves effort and persistence. Investigations of the lives of the most highly gifted individuals virtually always include observations of the tremendous investment of time, energy, and attention to the learning process that has been made. The lives of Beethoven, Einstein, and Picasso all illustrate the fact that high level achievement reflects a huge commitment and countless hours spent mastering their respective domains of competence.

In their book *Cradles of Eminence*, Goertzel, Goertzel, Goertzel, and Hansen considered what childhood elements might have led to eminence in the lives of hundreds of prominent figures.[32] They found that personal strengths, abilities, and ambition were valued in the homes of most of the individuals described, and their homes were places where ideas and opinions mattered. In most cases, their love of learning was nurtured, and their parents respected and encouraged perseverance and achievement.

No matter how effortless learning might be for a given child, the moment always comes when something proves challenging. Some children experience this when they first attempt algebra or a second language; others become discouraged when they tackle philosophy or creative writing. If a child is lucky, they experience failure sooner rather than later. Sometimes when that first real difficulty is encountered, a child previously identified as gifted thinks they're no longer gifted. We do children a disservice if we allow them to go through years of schooling without experiencing the challenges that can help them learn how to work hard, persevere through challenges, and surmount obstacles. Resilience and persistence are not learned by managing easy tasks.

The most important component of gifted-level achievement in adulthood may well be hard work done consistently over many years with an attitude of problem-finding and problem-solving. Despite other strengths, every extraordinary contributor through history—even those like Mozart who got off to a very early start—had to learn and work very hard for an extended time (more than ten years) before they produced their first masterpiece. Exceptionally high-achieving adults have more failures than other people (as well as more successes) and also have a different reaction to them, specifically, a mastery orientation. They work to master the skills they're having trouble with, rather than deciding they aren't capable in that area.

We'd like to share two perspectives that were sent to us in response to an earlier edition of this book. A new teacher wrote:

> *"Without realizing it, I think I had adopted a mystery model perspective. I was struck by this as I read about how giftedness is domain specific and can change over time. I now recognize how important it is to engage in ongoing assessment and identification practices. The sentence 'The most important component of gifted-level achievement may well be hard work done consistently over many years with an attitude of problem-finding and problem-solving' jumped out at me. The emphasis here is on the interaction between the student's innate abilities and the nurturing and support required in order for them to develop. I'd always thought of giftedness as being more passive, as if it were bestowed upon someone. Engagement and effort really do matter."*

And an identified-gifted student wrote to us from university:

> *"Ever since I was young, I've had a tendency to back off from work, especially when it's difficult. Now, after reading this section, I understand why. I wish my teachers had challenged me more, and helped me to recognize that failure is an important part of learning."*

An important variable in all this is temperament, particularly as it interacts with the environment. You can reassure young people who are worried about losing their giftedness by telling them that the best way to stay smart is to work hard at things they're curious about, and that no worthwhile learning comes easily.

There's no real learning without failure; in fact, how we respond to failure makes the difference between achieving at a high level and being mediocre in our achievements.[33] As a colleague who's also a parent, says, "This is so important! It speaks to our impatient culture of instant success with minimal effort. So often, bright kids figure they should comprehend instantly, and they feel stupid if they have to reread something."[34]

Other Terms

"I don't believe in the term 'gifted.'"

We hear this comment frequently from parents, grandparents, teachers, and children. We always welcome it, because it usually means they're thinking seriously about what giftedness means. The term is controversial, and for good reasons.

Many who work in the field have trouble with the term gifted when it's applied to children because it implies that "the gifted" share certain characteristics, and it simultaneously establishes an implicit category—"non-gifted"—for everyone else. There's also a problem with the relationship between "gifted" and "gift:" the term implies that the gifted person is a passive recipient. The gifted label carries a risk of intellectual detachment, a feeling that accomplishments are handed out, rather than earned. It also bestows a burden of responsibility that the person has to use this gift wisely.

There are many other terms used to refer to high-level development. Here are some:

1. **Precocity** means *knowing ahead of time.* Precocious readers, for example, read sooner than expected. Doing something ahead of the age at which it's expected is commonly thought to be a predictor of exceptionally high-level achievement going forward. Although reading early does give a child a big advantage in independent mastery of the world of learning, not all precocious readers go on to become gifted learners. Similarly, not all of those who go on to gifted-level achievement are early readers.

2. **Prodigy** is a word used to describe a child whose *achievement in one area is truly extraordinary for their age*, at a level expected of a much older expert. Thus, a musical prodigy might play a violin solo with the kind of technical virtuosity of an older, already-accomplished violinist. A math prodigy might have skills usually exhibited by someone who has been studying mathematics for years. For various reasons, prodigies do not always live up to the promise of their youth, and not all of those who achieve prodigiously as adults were considered remarkable as children.[35] Early expertise in structured or formal domains like music and math has little to do with high IQ, and it does not guarantee future success. Ability, passion, temperament, and learning opportunities all fuel the fire for prodigious accomplishment.[36]

3. **Genius** is a term reserved for someone who has *demonstrated enormous achievement in an important field of endeavor*, such as Hawking, Da Vinci, Gandhi, Mandela, or Freud. A child is not usually described as a genius.

4. **Superiority** is a psychometric term meaning *at least one and a half standard deviations above the mean.* "Very superior" is the psychometric category used to refer to scores that are at least two standard deviations above the mean. We discuss these measurement terms more fully in Section II.

5. **Advancement** refers to *competence or achievement that is ahead of what is expected* for a child's age. It's similar to precocity, without implying any expectations of future achievement.

Of these five terms, advancement is closest to what we mean with the Optimal Match perspective. Because "gifted" is the term that's used in most educational jurisdictions, we occasionally use it (in conjunction with "learner" and "education") interchangeably with "advanced."

Talent Development

> *"Schools must take proactive steps to seek out students who need greater challenge right now, in a specific subject area, because they are performing ahead of the instruction their school provides."*[37]

Talent is typically associated with giftedness in the arts or sports. However, as Howard Gardner and others have pointed out, there are many ways to be intelligent.[38] The talent development approach to gifted education is consistent with the Optimal Match perspective for many reasons, including its focus on providing the right level of programming at the right time; supporting the development of individual strengths in domain-specific areas; and providing the psychosocial supports needed to stay productively engaged in the learning process.

Malcolm Gladwell, bestselling author of *Outliers* and several other books, has written extensively about factors that contribute to high-level development and successful outcomes. He makes this encouraging promise: *"If you work hard enough and assert yourself, and use your mind and imagination, you can shape the world to your desires."*[39] In other words, your child's mind and imagination are keys that—with effort over time, and confident self-assertion—can open many gateways to achievement and fulfillment.

Rethinking Giftedness and Gifted Education: A Proposed Direction Forward Based on Psychological Science is a seminal monograph, written by three leaders in gifted education, Rena Subotnik, Paula Olszewski-Kubilius, and Frank Worrell.[40] In a consideration of the science informing current knowledge about the development of giftedness and talent, and what that science means for parents and teachers, these authors make several points that support the Optimal Match approach to giftedness and gifted education:

1. **Giftedness develops.** According to Subotnik, Olszewski-Kubilius, and Worrell, "Giftedness is a developmental process."

2. **Giftedness is domain-specific.** "Different talent domains have different developmental trajectories that vary as to when they start, peak, and end."

3. **The development of giftedness depends on appropriately-targeted opportunities for learning.** "Giftedness must be developed and sustained by way of training and interventions in domain-specific skills."

4. **The child has a role to play in developing their own abilities.** "Opportunities need to be taken advantage of and committed to by the talented individual."

5. **Psychosocial strengths such as effort, risk-taking, perseverance, and motivation, are essential to gifted development.** "Psychosocial variables are determining factors in the successful development of talent."

Few people would argue that there are enormous individual differences in children's talents, personalities, developmental pathways, interests, experiences, attitudes, and ambitions. What is less well understood is that this is just as true for those who have gifted learning needs as for others. Supporting gifted development means attending to those individual differences and thinking beyond the misconceptions or mystery too often embodied in the word "gifted." For these reasons, we stay away from talking about "*the* gifted," and don't include lists of "characteristics of the gifted."

Historical Perspective

> "*For while we have our eyes on the future, history has its eyes on us.*"[41]

The concept of giftedness was not formally studied until the early twentieth century. In a longitudinal study called *Genetic Studies of Genius* (1925-1959), psychologist Lewis Terman examined the developmental characteristics of children he deemed to be gifted.[42] He believed that intelligence was genetically determined, and measurable using IQ testing. In spite of the many problems with this mystery-oriented approach (including elitism, racism, and other kinds of exclusivity), many educational jurisdictions continue to rely on IQ as a primary instrument for identifying gifted-level intelligence.

Leta Hollingworth made significant contributions to the fields of psychology and gifted education, stretching back to 1926. She focused on the guidance and counseling needs of gifted children. Rather than asking, "Who are the gifted?" (Terman's focus), she concentrated on finding out, "How can we meet the needs of gifted children?" [43] Her work is still highly regarded, and its impact is widespread.[44]

In the intervening years since Terman and Hollingworth conducted their studies, interest in giftedness has waxed and waned, and social and educational perspectives on it have varied greatly. One notable influence is the Marland Report (1972).[45] This document focused on problems resulting from discrepancies between children's abilities and educational program offerings, stating that children who are exceptional in one or more designated categories should be provided with special educational services. The Marland Report included these categories: (1) general intellectual ability, (2) specific academic aptitude, (3) creative or productive thinking, (4) leadership ability, and (5) visual and performing arts. These categories have been used by many educators for almost 50 years as a broad guideline for determining who might have gifted learning needs.

Today, many parents want to give their children every intellectual advantage, and a huge industry is thriving on marketing educational and technological toys, games, and programs that claim to make children smarter. Large regional talent searches, such as the Center for Talented Development at Northwestern University, and Center for Talented Youth at Johns Hopkins University, are popular throughout North America and around the world. These programs typically identify academically gifted children at early adolescence and support them into early adulthood.[46]

Even though there's great interest in supporting high-level development, in many places it's politically incorrect to even mention giftedness, much less to devote educational resources to addressing gifted learning needs.

Kids are often embarrassed to talk about giftedness:

"I try not to let anyone know I'm in a gifted program."

"It's not fun to be called a geek."

"Some kids 'dis' the gifted class, calling us nicknames like 'nerds' and 'smart people.' And sometimes they say we're really stupid."

Many educators who work in gifted education tell us their colleagues consider their work peripheral and elitist, and we have confronted this attitude ourselves. It's unfortunately true that much that's done in the name of gifted education is not only exclusive and racist, but also not evidence-based, and peripheral to what goes on in the rest of education. Gifted enrichment that focuses on random activities like building kites or drawing family trees might be interesting for some participants, but too often, little or no serious thought goes into connecting such activities with the curriculum. Students who describe this approach as unproductive are not wrong. There are, however, many inclusive and evidence-based ways to adapt curriculum for gifted learning needs. We describe these in detail in Section III, "Being Smart about Meeting Gifted Learning Needs."

If there's a bright future for gifted education (and we hope there is), the current problems in the field—such as categorization and grouping policies that embarrass children, or invite political sniping, or elicit charges of racism and elitism, or disregard mismatches between children's strengths and their learning opportunities—must be amended. This means ensuring that the learning needs of all children are assessed and met, diversity of all kinds is respected, and what's known about gifted-level development is shared widely.

Guidelines and a Definition

"All children are gifted."

"Neural plasticity is the brain's ability to form networks and pathways... This occurs through the brain's ability to develop neural patterns in response to repeated behavior and actions. The brain has the ability to grow and adapt over time."[47]

When people learn about our interest in giftedness, they sometimes inform us with a certain degree of judgment that all kids are gifted. We agree that every child has substantial learning potential, and that we ought to encourage the best possible educational outcomes in all children.[48] Using the Optimal Match perspective, those with gifted learning needs are those whose abilities are so advanced that they require a higher level of challenge in certain subject areas. That usually works to give pause to our critics: after all, very few parents want their child to be given harder work if they're not ready for it.

What do people mean when they talk about giftedness? One definition is, "A gifted pupil is one who has been identified as possessing an unusually advanced degree of general intellectual ability that requires differentiated learning experiences of a depth and breadth beyond those normally provided in the regular school program to satisfy the level of educational potential indicated."[49]

Here's another definition in use: "The term 'gifted pupils' shall mean those pupils who show evidence of high performance capability and exceptional potential in areas such as general intellectual ability, special academic aptitude,. and outstanding ability in visual and performing arts. Such definition shall include those pupils who require educational programs or services beyond those normally provided by the regular school program in order to realize their full potential."[50]

While both of these definitions have the advantage of being flexible and tied to appropriate programming modifications—and therefore much better than a simple "high IQ" definition—each is also ambiguous. What does "unusually advanced degree" mean? Or "general intellectual ability"? Or "potential"? Indeed, how can we possibly know with any degree of certainty who is going to accomplish what, or to what extent they'll excel?

The more that scientists learn about brain development (especially neural plasticity), the clearer it is that we have to be careful when setting limits on people's potential for learning. We're only starting to discover all that the brain can do, and its remarkable capacity for change. However, we do know that developmental pathways are as individual as fingerprints. After chronicling the lives of world-class performers in such diverse fields as neurology, mathematics, tennis, art, and concert piano, Benjamin Bloom (1985), concluded that "there is enormous human potential in each society [and] only a small amount of this human potential is ever fully developed. We believe that each society could vastly increase the amount and kinds of talent it develops." Certainly, we agree with Benjamin Bloom and others who have observed that there is a lot more human potential than is ever developed. Given that we cannot see into the future, however, we do well to avoid trying to identify which children might have more (or less) potential than others. Parents and others are on firmer ground when discussing gifted-level ability as a need for special education at a certain point in time.

With due regard to how the mystery perspective has shaped thinking about gifted education over the years, and with a sense that a paradigm shift is well underway, we've formulated a working definition of giftedness. It corresponds with the Optimal Match approach, recognizing that exceptionally advanced learning experiences should be aligned with individual special education needs. Our definition emerges out of the guidelines we've identified, based on current research findings[51] on giftedness and its development:

A definition of giftedness must

○ reflect what's known about individual differences in high-level cognitive development;

○ incorporate the domain-specific nature of intelligence;

○ respect the dynamic nature of the development of intelligence;

○ make no assumptions about differences in children's potential;

○ focus on a child's academic proficiency relative to others;

○ lead logically and directly to identification practices;

○ lead logically and directly to educational programming implications; and

○ minimize the categorical dichotomy between gifted and not gifted.

Working from the foundation of these guidelines, we suggest the following definition of giftedness:

Optimal Match Definition of Giftedness:

> Giftedness is exceptionally advanced subject-specific ability at a particular point in time, and in a particular context, such that an individual's educational needs cannot be well met without making significant adaptations to the curriculum, or providing other learning opportunities.

Note: Those familiar with special education for students with learning problems will recognize that this approach is consistent with adaptive instruction and best practices in special education.

We've observed that schools that use an approach that is consistent with the Optimal Match experience fewer problems (such as racism, elitism, political and funding tension, and parental pressure to get children into gifted programs). At the same time, academic curriculum for all students, including those who have gifted learning needs, is enhanced. When a program is focused on matching precious resources to clearly defined learning needs, there's less mystery to gifted education, and consequently less resentment and less sense of exclusion from resources from which all children might benefit.

What all students need are learning opportunities that challenge them sufficiently and appropriately, along with the right kinds of guidance and support so they can meet and enjoy those challenges, and feel good about themselves at home and at school. Since the first two editions of *Being Smart* were published (in 2005 and 2009) we've been gratified to have many respected colleagues discuss the advantages of the approach, and also to hear from parents and teachers who tell us about the difference it makes in their practice.

There's so much about human development that remains mysterious, so much we still don't know about what fosters expertise, exceptional accomplishment, and creativity, all components of gifted-level development. There's much we do know, however, about how to nurture interest into ability, and then to support ability into gifted-level achievement. That's what we emphasize in this book as we consider how parents can facilitate an optimal learning match for their child in order to help them thrive. In the next chapter, we consider creativity in the context of gifted education and development.

CHAPTER 2

Creativity and Giftedness

"Creativity...represents the future of humankind...It comprises a set of skills and attitudes that all people can develop."[1]

People often see creativity and giftedness as disconnected. They think of creativity as artistic ability, and giftedness as academic intelligence. We argue here, however, that these concepts are intertwined: creativity is an important component of actualizing giftedness in every domain, and gifted-level mastery is a prerequisite for high-level creative work. Rather than thinking of giftedness and creativity separately, our perspective is closer to that expressed by David Henry Feldman, a renowned professor of cognitive development:

> *"To be creative means to use your full set of capabilities for some valued and valuable purpose, the consequences of which make a significant difference to an established field of endeavor...Creativity is quintessentially a matter of devotion, mastery, patience, persistence, and talent... applied in full measure over a sustained period of time."[2]*

British historian Arnold Toynbee hailed outstanding creative ability as "mankind's ultimate capital asset." He argued that progress in confronting the problems of our world will be "spearheaded by some of the most advanced thinkers of our times," and that therefore, "to give a fair chance to potential, creativity is a matter of life and death."[3] When we consider the riches that humanity has created over the ages in every area—in art, science, philosophy, music, literature, and other domains—we see the achievements of those whose creative work has stood the test of time.

People are experiencing more rapid and profound transformations in their lives than ever before. This was true fifteen years ago, when the first edition of this book was published, but it's even more true today. The nature of the volatility, particularly in communications technology, suggests that the rate of change will continue to increase. One of the educational implications of living in these unpredictable times is that parents and grandparents who are interested in supporting gifted-level development should help the children in their lives learn how to adapt to changing circumstances. That's where creativity comes in: it's an essential tool for success and fulfillment in an unsettled and uncertain world.

What Is Creativity?

Over the years, many people have directed our attention to children's creative efforts. Here are some of the comments we've heard from kids and parents:

> *"I want to enter the creative writing contest but I'm just not creative, so I know I won't win."*

> *"Other kids call him weird. Even adults say he's weird sometimes, but he just looks at the world more creatively."*

> *"I don't want her to study too hard. I don't want to stifle her creative spirit."*

There are so many ways of understanding creativity, it's not surprising that people use the term in different ways. One way of thinking about it is to distinguish between big-C Creativity (eminence) and little-c creativity (everyday applications).[4] Big-C Creativity occurs only when a field has been fundamentally changed in a substantive way. Leonardo da Vinci, Martha Graham, Martin Luther King, and William Shakespeare would all be considered Creative by this definition. Nobody can be Creative in this big-C way until they've acquired mastery of a domain, which rarely (if ever) happens until the person has been working in that field for at least ten years. Only then is there a solid enough foundation of knowledge and skills that the potentially creative individual has the complex conceptual understanding required for important innovation.

On the other end of the spectrum, little-c creativity starts with the ability to generate novel ideas or unusual products. For example, suppose that a parent asks a child to depict a character in a story they're reading. If the child generates something that appears to onlookers as unusual, like a picture or a poem about a person with three heads, then the child and their ideas might be considered creative. Although it would be accurate to describe the picture or poem as representing divergent thinking, and to agree that divergent thinking has a place in creativity, from most perspectives, it would be a mistake to think that's all it takes. Divergent thinking is the ability to think of surprising ways in response to an open-ended question or problem; it is necessary but not sufficient for productive creativity.[5]

The Four C theory expands on the distinction between little-c and big-C creativity. At the lowest level, mini-c creativity is a new, personally meaningful insight, that with feedback, further effort, and guidance can evolve into little-c creativity, where the product is recognized by others as creative. Years of practice can move it up to Pro-c creativity, where the work is considered highly proficient in innovative ways. Big-C Creativity applies to work that is extraordinary to the point of changing a field, and being legendary over time.[6] In this way, the pathways of increasing levels of learning and creativity can be seen as interdependent.

For other perspectives on this topic, we look briefly at the work of four experts who have influenced the field of creativity. The first of these is Daniel Keating.[7] His position synthesizes many of the competing definitions of creativity, and was a direct precursor to the Optimal Match approach to giftedness.[8]

Keating argued that creativity builds on *content mastery, divergent thinking, critical analysis,* and *communication skills.* It requires a foundation of knowledge and skills, akin to what goes into gifted-level development. His theory recognizes divergent thinking as an essential component of creativity, consistent with most definitions, where thinking laterally or finding innovative solutions is an important component of creative work. People who are considered creative must be good at divergent thinking, but they must also be good at selecting their most promising ideas from the merely unusual or novel ones. As Keating argues, creativity requires people to analyze, synthesize, and evaluate their divergent ideas. They have to be able to think critically about which ideas are worth further time and energy. And, once an important idea has been generated and identified as promising, they must then be able to communicate it effectively enough for others to understand it or recognize its value.

When defined in this way, creativity applies to science, business, and other domains as much as it does to the arts. If a person cannot communicate their good ideas so that others can understand them, those ideas aren't very useful. Poorly written poetry, therefore, is *not* creative. It may show promise, perhaps, that with further work, the writer might be able to do something better, but, by Keating's criteria, a poorly executed poem is not in and of itself creative.

Another contributor to the field of creativity is Robert Greene. In *Mastery,*[9] Greene addresses the behaviors and creative processes of past and contemporary masters in various fields, discussing factors such as commitment, confidence, proficiency, and the importance of learning from others. He writes about the "dimensional mind" which he sees as being characterized by two essential requirements: "a high level of knowledge about a field and subject" and "the openness and flexibility to use this knowledge in new and original ways."[10]

A person with a dimensional mind is willing to explore, experiment, and learn; to be reflective, intuitive, and focused; to strive to perceive things from different perspectives; to make meaningful connections (even when these may not be evident); and to work hard and persevere. Greene notes that someone with a dimensional mind combines creativity and adaptability with insight and reasoning, and moulds ideas to current realities. The global pandemic, climate change, social inequities, and economic uncertainties are all crying out for attention by individuals with dimensional minds and the appropriate expertise.

Yet another approach to understanding creativity is by examining the lives and experiences of highly creative individuals. Psychologist Mihaly Csikszentmihalyi discusses how creatively successful people in a number of domains describe an experience of being so fully engaged in their work that their consciousness of time disappears, and they experience a profound sense of well-being. Csikszentmihalyi calls this sense of well-being and fulfillment in engaging in work "flow." Flow motivates further effort, and occurs when there's a balance between the challenges presented by a task, and the necessary level of expertise to succeed.[11] People in flow describe their experiences as "paying attention to a restricted set of stimuli—the artist to his canvas, the musician to her instrument, scientists to the problem they are tackling—and within that narrow field of vision they can achieve a sense of control as well as a feeling of freedom that is hard to achieve in ordinary life."[12] For all these reasons, creative flow is intrinsically motivating, and usually leads to further effort and achievement.

Csikszentmihalyi identifies the following essentials for a creative flow experience:

- ○ clear goals along the way
- ○ immediate feedback
- ○ a balance between one's challenges and one's skills
- ○ a merging of actions and awareness
- ○ full concentration, without distractions
- ○ no concern about failure
- ○ no self-consciousness
- ○ a distorted sense of time
- ○ a sense of an activity as its own reward

According to Csikszentmihalyi, these components combine in ways that are so fully absorbing that a person in a flow state can temporarily lose track of time and place, and even a sense of the world itself. A person in flow is motivated by a spirit of authentic inquiry, and their engagement in the activity is voluntary, often leading to emerging awareness wherein flow can evolve into surprising realizations. There may be no other purpose to flow than to inspire a person to keep on flowing,[13] thereby fueling intrinsic motivation and furthering creativity.

Humanistic psychologist Scott Barry Kaufman was the founding director of the Imagination Institute, co-founded *The Creativity Post*, and writes about creative fulfillment. He is particularly interested in incorporating creativity into daily life.[14] He discusses the complexities, contradictions, and messiness people encounter when engaged in creativity. Kaufman writes about a wide range of topics as they inform understandings of the creative process, such as the role of passion and purpose; the ways that adversity and constraints can be motivators; the neuroscience of creativity; the impact of personality; the power of positivity; the ramifications of education; and more.

As people everywhere confront challenges, it becomes evident that "being creative is not a luxury but a necessity in today's changing world."[15] The field of creativity studies is broadening, and its connections with high-level development continue to be strengthened, as Keating, Greene, Csikszentmihalyi, Kaufman and other experts across disciplines consider creativity from many different perspectives.

Can We Measure Creativity?

"How can I possibly grade students' assignments for their creative worth?"

"I don't think creativity is something that can be packaged, then put on a scale or placed alongside some kind of measuring grid to be given a mark."

We know a teacher who assesses creativity by observing her own reactions to her students' work. If she has what she describes as "spine-tingles," the student gets bonus marks for creativity. No tingles, no bonus. We suspect we're not alone in worrying about the reliability and validity of this measure, but we're often surprised by competent practitioners who think they can rank their students' creativity on the basis of their own intuitive responses to it, and decide in that way who is more or less creative than others.

Although many tests describe themselves as tests of creativity, it's rare that a test comes close to assessing creativity in a meaningful way. In order to fit easily into a paper-and-pencil, score-generating, group-administered testing format, most standardized tests of creativity focus on artificial divergent thinking tasks. For example, a child might be asked to do as many things as possible in a limited time period with a paper clip, or with a pencil and a page full of empty circles. There's no authentic challenge involved in such tasks. Those who accomplish truly creative work don't usually find such activities worth doing, and tend not to do well on creativity tests.

This story about Joel, a child we worked with who has many creative hobbies and interests, illustrates one of the problems with creativity tests:

A Parent's Thoughts on Creativity Testing

My son, Joel, is in Grade 4. He excels in math, sculpting, and building activities, but he was recently excluded from his school's gifted program because he failed a creativity test. He did exceptionally well on the academic ability and task commitment assessments, but his teacher told us that his score on the test of creativity was unusually low. As I see it, some people—like Joel!—can think in new and exciting ways, but may not be able to show it in a test situation.

Joel's Thoughts about Creativity Testing

I love Lego! It's my favorite thing. I also like to make stuff out of clay, and bubble wrap, and duct tape, anything I can manipulate into different shapes. Sometimes I build forts with the furniture. It drives my mom crazy.

The other day, the teacher gave our class this dumb assignment. She handed each of us a piece of paper with a bunch of circles drawn on it. She said, "Draw as many things as you can, all different." I looked at Sammy. We shook our heads and groaned. I drew some faces and a couple of bikes and a sun, just to make my teacher happy.

You're not going to believe this, but my mom says that circle thing was a test and it proved I'm not creative. Well, I think the test is not creative. Why didn't they just ask me to build something?

We agree with Joel and his mom that creativity is too idiosyncratic, too rooted in particular tasks and situations, to be quantified. If creativity shows up when a person generates a unique solution to a problem, how can that uniqueness be evaluated, and who should be the arbiter? Tom Balchin, a colleague of ours who has investigated creativity, wrote, "There is as yet no conclusive set of criteria for evaluating creative products."[16] That continues to be true today.[17]

Although most tests of creativity assess only decontextualized divergent thinking (like Joel's circle test), being able to generate many different ideas is only one aspect of creativity, and it does not necessarily translate into real-world creative problem-solving. Most creativity assessments are aimed at quantifying one of four targets: creative processes such as divergent thinking; personality and behavioral correlates of creativity, such as open-mindedness and flexibility; the extent to which a product might be considered creative; and attributes of creativity-fostering environments, such as support for open-mindedness and flexibility.[18]

Creativity testing is a topic of ongoing debate among researchers in the field. This is because of controversy surrounding what an ideal multifaceted assessment approach might look like, plus concerns around limitations, accuracy, usefulness, predictive validity, scalability for large groups, and more. Robert Sternberg points out that creativity testing often assumes that different kinds of creativity can be compressed into a single unidimensional scale; he cautions that this way of thinking is highly problematic.[19]

There are measures that can help educators assess specific aspects of creativity, enabling them to support their students' creative productivity. One such tool, Balchin's Creative Product Grid,[20] assesses products students have made, considering possible insights and risk-taking, as well as the potential functionality, uniqueness, well-craftedness, and attractiveness of the product. This kind of test doesn't pretend to rank students in terms of their creativity, but rather focuses on assessing creative dimensions of a specific product, in order to support students in further developing their creativity.

Another promising approach to assessing creative work is to focus on actual processes in an authentic context. Although creativity is too contextual, and too individualistic in essence and form, to ever be quantified by standardized tests, there are indications that creative and artistic potential in performing arts talent can be assessed with the *Talent Assessment Process* in dance, music, and theater.[21]

In general, though, creativity is too complex to be pigeonholed and quantified. It's too interconnected with psychological factors such as motivation, attitude, and the potency of perceived challenges, all of which resist reliable measurement.

As with giftedness, we agree with those who argue that it's better to foster creativity than to try and assign a numerical value to it. If we really want to measure creativity, the best we can do may be to assess Keating's four factors—content mastery, divergent thinking, critical analysis, and communication skills—in an authentic problem-solving context that has relevance to the individual test-taker.

Nurturing Creativity in the Learning Process

"Creative work can be incredibly difficult for students. I've found that I first have to establish a supportive and encouraging environment before their creativity emerges."

"Students who are told 'be creative' often give safe answers first. Only after seeing how far they can go without being called out as wrong do they begin to stretch their ideas."

"Creativity is important not only at school, but also in many workplace situations. Teachers need to adopt and model creative approaches to learning."

Over the years, teachers have expressed their concerns to us about how challenging and yet important it is to give a child's creative imagination room to grow. For example, a science teacher with whom we worked expressed serious concern that there's not enough creativity in science classrooms. She noted that too often, students are rewarded for memorizing or learning factual material, rather than for their insights or creative ideas, and that this is unfortunate. If we want students to become effective scientists, our colleague added, we need to help them develop their creativity right from the start.

Most creativity experts would agree. In a review of evidence-based best practices in gifted education, Ann Robinson, Bruce Shore, and Donna Enersen wrote, "Even as we admit that the complexity of creativity makes defining it difficult, there is agreement that creativity can be nurtured and developed in a person, or it can be repressed and even lost. For all children, creativity training and recognition of production is important."[22]

There are some excellent opportunities for educators to learn how to enhance children's creativity. For example, the University of Connecticut's Renzulli Center for Creativity, Gifted Education, and Talent Development offers professional learning through its online and on-campus courses. There are graduate certificates, Master's and Ph.D. programs, as well as many other resources. Other universities offer comprehensive programs designed to help teachers learn how to nurture students' creativity, as well as high-level learning.[23] Some university-based centers have programs for academically talented students, and their families as well. There are also websites promoting creative initiatives such as Future Problem Solving, Roots and Shoots, Odyssey of the Mind, and Destination Imagination.[24]

In the 1980s, North American educators invested considerable time, energy, and money in teaching creative thinking skills. However, research subsequently demonstrated that out-of-context creative thinking strategies don't usually transfer to real-world tasks. In spite of best efforts over the intervening years, it seems that we cannot teach people to "be creative"—or analytical—in a vacuum. Creativity is vibrant and meaningful only when it's applied in domain-specific areas, building on rich content knowledge.

Makerspace Programs

Makerspace programs[25] provide a great demonstration of supporting children's creativity by giving them real-world opportunities for exploration and innovation: *"To define a school makerspace by its purpose and simplest of terms, it is a place where young people have an opportunity to explore their own interests; learn to use tools and materials, both physical and virtual, and develop creative projects."*[26]

The Makerspace movement is focused on inquiry-based learning, and it brings together educators, students, and industry partners to collaborate, problem-find, problem-solve, and innovate. Makerspace opportunities invite students from all countries, socio-economic levels, and cultures to participate in activities that go beyond traditional classroom settings and explore different physical and virtual environments. Makerspace programs connect learners, experts, mentors, communities, tools, and resources. The emphasis is on making things that matter, through participation, play, hands-on involvement, and engagement in multi-disciplinary learning opportunities.

Award-winning Manhattan teacher Lou Lahana[27] credits the Makerspace program with his students' engagement in creating social change that improves their own and others' lives. Through innovative applications of art and technology, his students—half of whom are homeless themselves, and many of whom live in domestic abuse shelters—are tackling big real-world social problems like homelessness, domestic abuse, racism, and domestic violence. Sample projects from his Makerspace lab include hand-sewn pillows for homeless people, a documentary about Islamophobia, and an edible insect stand with the goal of raising awareness about animal cruelty and climate change. (Chocolate-covered crickets anyone?)

What's Involved in Nurturing Creativity?

> *"An opportunity most conducive to creative opportunity includes freedom for your child to do what he wants to do in a style that honors his uniqueness and capitalizes on his strengths."[28]*

Creativity doesn't come easily. It involves preparation, incubation, illumination, and verification. Researchers on high-level expertise suggest that creativity is built on the following actions and attitudes:

1. engaging actively in diverse kinds of learning and experimentation;

2. looking for tasks that match current ability levels, on a topic-by-topic basis;

3. progressively tackling higher-level problems; and

4. working hard over long periods of time (Practice, practice, practice really is the way to Carnegie Hall).

The importance of these actions and attitudes in generating high-level creativity have been demonstrated in a number of fields, and from several different angles, including talent development,[29] expertise,[30] equity and diversity,[31] and wisdom.[32] If you want your child to experience the fulfillment that comes with creativity, do what you can to encourage these ways of approaching learning.

Creativity is a Choice

Creativity expert Robert Sternberg has written about creativity as a choice.[33] He makes the controversial argument that we can decide to be creative, or not. Sternberg points out that as the world changes rapidly, people succeed only if they choose to acquire a flexible and creative attitude to their work, and also to life's other demands.

According to Sternberg, creativity can be developed, and creative decision-making processes can be taught. He lists twelve ways that people can decide for creativity. We present them here, accompanied by our own short explanations for parents, teachers, grandparents, and others who want to foster children's creativity:

1. *Redefine problems.* Help your child approach problems from different angles, staying open-minded, and looking beyond the usual ways of doing things. Many kids can do this better than adults, so if that applies in your family, do what you can to keep your mind open to your child's redefinitions of problems.

2. *Analyze your ideas.* Teach your child to think critically about their ideas. Help them figure out which ideas are worth pursuing now, and whether they need further work; which ideas can be set aside to work on later; and which are best abandoned.

3. *Sell your ideas.* When your child works toward having others accept and value their ideas, they become better able to analyze those ideas, and they also acquire other important skills, like persuasion and communication.

4. *Recognize that knowledge is a double-edged sword.* Expertise is essential to creativity, but it interferes with creativity when it impedes flexibility and open-mindedness. A person who believes they know everything about a topic can resist alternative approaches, whereas fresh eyes sometimes perceive new perspectives. Encourage your child both to keep learning, and also to stay open-minded to new ideas.

5. *Surmount obstacles.* Hurdles, failures, and rejections are inevitable in any creative enterprise. They may be external (such as the critical opinions of others) or internal (such as performance anxiety). Help your child realize that, as annoying as obstacles are, they're the best possible opportunities for fine-tuning and strengthening their ideas.

6. *Take sensible risks.* Teach your child to play it safe when necessary, to keep an eye on the long term, and to assess risks as they go. There are times when it's good for them to stretch beyond their comfort zone, and other times when it's best to take it slow, one safe step at a time.

7. *Encourage a willingness to grow.* Instead of concentrating on being right or clinging to a certain viewpoint, help your child seek new challenges and solutions.

8. *Believe in yourself* and your ability to produce creative ideas. Reinforce your child's faith in their own creativity and capacity for achievement. This will help them withstand criticism, rebound from errors, and appreciate creative possibilities in daily life.

9. *Tolerate ambiguity.* Help your child see that uncertainty, muddle, and "grey zones" are part of the creative process. Good ideas sometimes conflict with each other, leading to confusion, or even discomfort. Complexity usually includes some kind of ambiguity, and that's okay.

10. *Find what you love to do and do it.* Creativity is built on passion, aspiration, investment, and perseverance. People are at their most creative when doing what they enjoy. You'll be helping your child decide for creativity if you support them in discovering and exploring their passions.

11. *Understand the importance of delaying gratification.* Creativity can take time, and hard work and persistence may not be recognized for a long time, if ever. Sternberg says, "few serious challenges can be met in a moment." Most children need assistance learning "the value of making incremental efforts for long-term gains."

12. *Provide an environment that fosters creativity.* By modeling creative habits, and showing your child how these habits apply to all areas of endeavor, you can help them learn how to apply ideas from one area to another, enabling them to "cross-fertilize" their thinking, while also stimulating their creativity.

Sternberg observes that the impetus for creativity varies from one person to the next, so the factors that support its development also vary across children, and across different ages and stages. If one strategy doesn't work for your child, try another, or a combination of two or more.[34]

What about Children Who Struggle with Creativity?

Since creativity is a choice, it makes sense to consider why some children choose it and others do not. Creative expression can be fun, help kids solve thorny problems, and fuel their enthusiasm for learning. However, not every child knows this, and some need extra help to get to the point where they can engage freely in discovery, imaginative play, artistic activities, inquiry, or even brainstorming.[35]

Sternberg's strategies provide a great starting point for supporting your child in choosing for creativity, and here are some more suggestions for kids who struggle with expressing themselves creatively:

○ *Build on what you already know.* Your child can only be creative in areas where they've built a foundation of knowledge, skills, and competence. Help them see that when they extend their ideas, they feel more enthusiastic, self-reliant, and confident.

○ *Think purposefully.* Encourage your child to take control of their thinking and their creativity. That means learning to organize their ideas (including clarifying and revising them), forming solid work habits (including learning to focus, and tuning out distractions), and being persistent (including seeing things through to completion, without too much procrastinating). Model these attributes, and reinforce your child's efforts when they use some of the habits that support creativity. Point it out to them, so they can appreciate how they connect to being creative.

○ *Amplify the fun factor.* Have materials on hand that encourage your child to explore a variety of possible creative outlets. Art supplies, rocks and pinecones, a costume box, books with science experiments, a globe, recipe books for kids, writing material, musical instruments, anything that might invite your child to expand their ideas. Join them in their creative activities, if they want that. Stay open to wacky, spontaneous, and far-fetched ideas. And to sophisticated, eclectic, or puzzling ones, too.

○ *Encourage collaboration and idea-sharing.* Children who learn to listen to others' ideas, and to share their own, can become good at collaborative problem-solving, and find fresh approaches for tackling challenges. Creativity gets a big boost when kids work together to discover what they need or want to know.

○ *Encourage resourcefulness.* With a resourceful attitude, children can move beyond complacency, and discover their ingenuity.

○ *Co-create a safety zone.* Creativity involves pushing boundaries and looking at the world with fresh perspectives. That requires a willingness to take a chance. Many children find that daunting, and require extra support, guidance, and reassurance; they need a comfort zone in which their creativity can flourish.

○ *Be patient.* Creativity can't be rushed, pushed, or nagged into action. Respect your child's timetable. Give them the support and encouragement provided by these strategies, and then let them find their own way. Listen if they want to talk about their ideas or concerns, but don't criticize or micromanage them into being creative; it won't work.

○ *Welcome aha moments.* An aha moment occurs in a flash, but it's usually the result of long, hard deliberation. It's a sudden realization, typically pulling together disparate ideas into a surprising and meaningful fusion. An aha moment can be an inspiration; a springboard for adventure, acts of kindness, or personal growth; a great solution to a problem; or a creative idea for a project. Encourage your child to embrace their own aha moments, and to make use of the creative possibilities that open up.

What about Teachers Who Struggle with Creativity?

"Discernment comes from wisdom. Wisdom comes from experience. Experience comes over time when we are open to new approaches."[36]

Educator Brett Fischer has studied factors that develop and sustain creative processes among teachers.[37] He describes four interconnected processes that bolster teachers' creative experiences, and that work for students and parents, too:

○ *introspection*—thinking about aims and objectives

○ *reshaping the environment*—selecting tasks, maximizing collaboration, and promoting ideas;

○ *resistance*—overcoming obstacles, and being resilient when confronting adversity; and

○ *confidence-building*—increasing the scope and impact of projects over time.

Teachers who participate in creativity-focused professional development, including mentorships and partnerships, and who carve out opportunities to be creative in their teaching, as well as providing a creative classroom environment—whether individually or collegially—are better positioned to foster their students' creativity.

Creating an Environment that Supports Creativity

The optimal environment for fostering children's creativity is one that feels both safe *and* challenging. Whether at home, school, or elsewhere, such environments:

- ○ welcome diversity
- ○ characterize errors and obstacles as opportunities for learning
- ○ allow options for independent learning as well as collaboration
- ○ provide flexible tasks
- ○ enable time to listen, reflect, focus, and refocus
- ○ encourage children's input
- ○ invite children's questions
- ○ provide opportunities to work with varied materials under different conditions
- ○ reinforce courage and reasonable risk-taking

When your child experiences an environment that supports creativity, a world of possibilities opens up, and every member of your family benefits.

Creative Parenting: Twelve Practical Ideas

Creative parenting means looking at failures and setbacks as opportunities to broaden your own horizons, as well as your child's horizons. It means welcoming problems as possibilities, as ways of identifying what you can do better. It means pushing beyond your comfort zone, being open to new ideas, and inventing new ways of doing things. Here are some practical suggestions for integrating creativity into your child's life, and your own:

1. **Provide diverse experiences**. Encourage shared, independent, imaginative, unstructured, and hands-on play, games, and multisensory activities.

2. **Engage your child in role-playing**. When you want your child to understand something better, whether it's self-regulation, conflict resolution, rules negotiation, or something else, try creative role-playing. Take turns, each of you playing one of the roles in the situation, and then switching, so your child gets a sense of alternative possibilities and perspectives.

3. **Spend time with the arts.** Get the family involved in music, dance, theatre, writing, and other artistic activities, across a spectrum. This might include making art, sharing products with others, attending professional events, and going to museums.

4. **Go outside**. Taking time to enjoy nature will help your child appreciate the world around them, and open them to experiences and possibilities that feed their creativity.

5. **Get physical**. Sports, outdoor play, and other physically challenging activities (whether on land, water, or wheels), can strengthen your child's body, develop their motor skills, improve their energy, health, and well-being, and stimulate their creativity.

6. **Strengthen connections**. Creativity often emerges from collaboration, and from problem-solving together. Also, a strong network of social support is the biggest factor supporting your child's resilience, and is therefore important to their finding the courage to engage in creative self-expression. Think about chess clubs, reading clubs, library programs, learning centers, mentorships, community service, or other opportunities for you and/or your child to get together with like-minded others.

7. **Support your child's choices**. By providing diverse experiences, you encourage your child to find and develop their interests and abilities, no matter how different they might be from your own. These will change over time. Follow your child's lead as they decide where their interests lie.

8. **Get organized**. Help your child think about and get the information and materials they need for their creative expression. As they proceed, help them find opportunities to discuss their ideas or products, and take them further.

9. **Encourage questions**. Let your child know there are no stupid questions. Be available to listen, and to help them find answers. Show them how asking for help can open up possibilities that take them to next steps.

10. **Welcome curiosity**. Curiosity is often the first step on the way to discovery, investigation, effort, and eventually, creativity. Welcome your child's curiosity with enthusiasm and an open heart.

11. **Be positive.** Criticism and negativity destroy creativity. Approach your child's questions, curiosity, and interests from a positive perspective, and help them develop that outlook, too. Encourage an attitude of gratitude, and not of entitlement.

12. **Live as though creativity matters.** You are your child's best teacher of the benefits of living creatively.

Remember Daniel Keating's description of creativity as a combination of (1) high-level mastery in a domain, (2) divergent thinking, (3) critical analysis, and (4) effective communication.[38] These factors are as valuable in your own work and daily life as they are in supporting your child's creativity. Keeping all of these channels open can keep you fresh, eager to keep on learning, and enthusiastic about spending time with the children in your life.

Section II:
Being Smart About Diagnosing Mismatches

CHAPTER 3

Questions and Answers About Testing

*"Teachers and school staff must act as talent scouts, proac-
tively identifying students who are underchallenged. That
is, they should make it a priority to assess every student and
then review the data to find those who are performing at
a higher level than the material they are being taught.* "[1]

In gifted education, testing and assessment are controversial and can
be intensely anxiety-provoking. This problem has a lot to do with
the traditional Mystery Model perspective that "gifted" is a special
category of person that some people belong to and others don't, such
that it's possible to ascertain through testing who meets the criteria
(and therefore who "is" gifted), and who fails to meet the criteria
(thereby falling into the "not-gifted" category). Categorizing people
as either gifted or not-gifted is responsible for much of the confusion,
controversy, ambivalence, and anxiety concerning gifted education.[2]

Slowly, as the paradigm shifts from a mystery perspective to an
Optimal Match point of view, educators and parents are realizing that
the important questions are not about whether or not a child belongs
to the gifted category, but rather how their individual learning needs
might best be met.[3] The field is moving from a focus on categorization
to a focus on discovering and diagnosing educational mismatches.[4]

In this chapter, we address the *who, what, when, where,* and *why* questions that parents and educators ask, thinking about our answers in the context of mismatch diagnostics rather than the traditional focus on categorical identification. Next, in Chapter 4, we address questions concerning *how* to assess learning needs intelligently, and in Chapter 5 we think about mismatch diagnostics as applied to gifted education.

Who Needs Testing?

> *"I'm just not sure whether to put my son through the testing process."*

> *"I dislike the gifted label, but I can see that Adrianna is way ahead of her classmates and bored with grade-level work. Does she require the label to get the type of education she needs?"*

Parents and teachers often have questions about the educational testing enterprise, and nowhere is this truer than in gifted education.[5] People are uncertain about the tests themselves, the whole assessment process, and the cut-off scores that are used to designate giftedness.

The questions and uncertainties reflect valid concerns. Adults should think carefully before putting children through the time, anxiety, and trouble involved in the testing process, to say nothing of the expense incurred by parents or the school. Nonetheless, for exceptionally capable learners, test results can be important. They can show where areas of strength and weakness lie, and if used properly, provide guidelines for intelligent decision-making and programming.

In thinking about testing processes, it makes sense to begin by asking these two guiding questions:

1. "If this child is *not* tested, what is likely to happen?"
2. "If we *do* test, how will the information be used?"

Although these questions need to be considered on a situation-by-situation basis, there are a few basics that can help inform decision-making about testing in different situations.

The Child Who Is Unhappy

"I used to like school. Now I hate it. Nothing but blah blah."

"I was doing a math experiment in the school washroom. I was counting the number of flushes, but the toilets overflowed and then I got a week of detentions. It's not fair. I keep getting detentions just because I like learning new things."

If you observe that your child is chronically frustrated, bored, or unhappy at school, then it's time to consider an assessment. Guiding question #1 ("If this child is not tested, what is likely to happen?") is at the fore here because the unhappiness indicates they might have learning issues (possibly giftedness, as well perhaps as learning disabilities, or other concerns). These are better addressed sooner rather than later, in order to prevent more serious problems down the road. Guiding question #2 is also relevant ("If we do test, how will the information be used?"), because an assessment can help uncover your child's strengths and challenges, and lead to specific recommendations for productive learning.

The Child Who Is Doing Well

"I love spelling. But the words my teacher gives me are too easy, so I write them backwards."

If your child appears to be learning well at school, and if they appear to be thriving without needing any changes, testing may not be necessary. In this case, the answer to guiding question #1 ("If this child is *not* tested, what is likely to happen?") is probably something like, "Nothing. They're doing just fine as is."

Guiding question #2 might be more helpful: "If we *do* test, how will the information be used?" Do the teachers and school appear to understand your child's learning needs, at least reasonably well? Is your child getting what's needed in order to continue to learn and progress commensurate with their ability level? If so, then why bother going to the time, trouble, and expense of an assessment? If your child doesn't need an exceptionality label in order to get the education they need, it makes sense to wait until assessment information could be more useful—if problems occur with an aspect of their learning or school experience, for example, or if there are other indicators that they require a more (or less) challenging curriculum.

In some circumstances, however, a proactive assessment can be helpful. Sometimes a child appears to be doing just fine but *does* need something more in order to become fully engaged in learning. High-ceiling subject-specific reasoning tests (as discussed later in this section) can be administered informally in the classroom, and can be helpful in discovering gifted learning needs that might otherwise not be apparent.

The Child Who Is Different than Others

"He worries that others do not accept him for the way he is."

Schools vary widely in their readiness, willingness, and ability to consider and address individual differences, even if testing or observations have shown that a child is exceptional in one or more areas. An important factor in making a decision about whether to assess a child struggling with feelings of differentness is whether or not anything productive will be done with the results (guiding question #2). This is not always easy to know ahead of time. Some schools pay lip service to diversity and to "educating the whole child" but actually provide a "one size fits all" kind of education, with little or no adaptations for individual differences. These schools convey the attitude, "If you don't like what we provide, you can go elsewhere." Other schools welcome assessment information, and work actively to develop options that facilitate learning for each student, sometimes suggesting extracurricular activities as well as in-school options.

If you've observed that your child is significantly different than others, or your child has expressed concern about that, an assessment might help both of you understand the nature of those differences, as well as giving you ideas for moving forward productively.

Summary: Who Should Be Tested?

The strongest candidate for testing is a child who (a) attends a school where there's a reasonable likelihood that appropriate action will be taken on any recommendations that might come out of the assessment, (b) is having difficulties that can't be easily investigated or solved by parents and educators using their own knowledge of the child, and (c) exhibits problems over a sustained period of time, such as:

○ difficulty at school;

○ boredom or unhappiness at school;

○ anxiety or signs of other psychological stress; or

○ learning or other needs that may not be matched by the education being provided.

If your child doesn't meet these criteria as a strong candidate for testing, but you're still wondering if they'd benefit from an assessment, read on. By knowing more about tests and assessment processes, you'll be able to make a more informed decision about whether to proceed, and how.

What Are the Key Testing Concepts?

"There are so many different kinds of tests. I don't know what any of them are."

"How do we get the test results? Will someone explain them to us?"

"The school wants to test Maya, but I'm not sure if that's a good idea."

In this section, we provide definitions of several of the terms commonly used in the testing process.

Tests vs. Assessments

A *test* is a specific instrument, such as the *Stanford-Binet Intelligence Scale*, the *Wechsler Intelligence Scale for Children*, the *Woodcock-Johnson Psycho-Educational Battery*, or any of the academic achievement tests that are routinely given.

An *assessment* of a child's abilities is almost always much more comprehensive than any one test. They vary depending on the circumstances and the reason for the assessment, but typically include several different measures. A full psychoeducational assessment usually includes an intelligence test; one or more academic achievement tests; various measures of learning styles, self-concept, and attitudes toward school; and a consideration of the child's functioning at home, with friends, and at school. It may include observations of the student at school, and interviews with the parents and teachers. Parents are usually asked to provide medical and other relevant history, and to comment on the child's interactions with siblings and friends.

Standardized Tests

Standardized tests are designed to allow reliable comparisons of individuals with others of the same age or grade level. They are standardized in both the administration of the test, and in the scoring procedures. There are detailed rules about how to administer and score each item, so that the test conditions are as close as possible to identical or "standard" for each person who takes the test. The big advantage of these tests is that they provide an age or grade-level standard against which to measure an individual's ability. You know how well your child is doing relative to others of the same age or grade level who take the test. The disadvantage is that they allow no flexibility in administration or scoring. Through the rest of this chapter, and the next two chapters on assessments, we'll discuss more about why that can be important.

Percentiles

A percentile designates where one person's score falls relative to other people's scores. If a child scores at the 60th percentile, it means they have scored as high as or higher than 60% of others who have taken the same test and are included in the comparison group. If someone scores at the 98th percentile, they have scored as high as or higher than 98% of others. These percentiles do not mean that the child knows 60% or 98% of the information being tested, but rather that they've done better than that percentage of the comparison population.[6]

Standard Scores

As with percentiles, a standard score shows a person's functioning on a given test as compared with other test-takers, usually of the same age or grade. Intelligence and academic test results are usually reported as standard scores, which are based upon a normal, bell-shaped population distribution, with 68% of the population falling within one standard deviation of the mean. For many tests, including most IQ tests, the standard score is based on a test mean of 100. A score higher than 100 is above average (or above the 50th percentile); scores higher than 115 are above the 84th percentile; and scores higher than 130 are above the 98th percentile. However, since tests always have some possibility of error, IQ scores are usually expressed as belonging to a range. The Average range typically includes IQ scores from 90 to 109, the Above Average range includes scores from 110 to 119, the Superior range includes scores from 120 to 129, and the Very Superior range includes scores above 130.

Standard Deviation

Standard deviation is a statistical term describing the distribution of scores around the test mean. With intelligence tests where the test mean is set at 100, the standard deviation is usually 15. Most people (68% of the population) score within one standard deviation (that is, 15 points) above or below the mean (that is, between 85 and 115). The farther from 100, the more exceptional a standard score is. Developmental delay is usually considered when scores are more than two standard deviations below the mean (70 or below). Giftedness is usually considered when scores are more than two standard deviations above the mean (130 and above).

Intelligence Quotient (IQ)

Historically, the "quotient" in IQ referred to the relationship between a person's so-called "mental age" (as determined by their score on the test) and their actual chronological age. While that computation is no longer used, the term intelligence quotient (IQ) remains, and is widely used to designate a standardized measure of intelligence. The two most valid and reliable tests that yield IQs and that are used for school-aged children are the *Stanford-Binet Intelligence Scale* (currently in the fifth edition, with the sixth edition coming soon) for ages 2 to 90, and the *Wechsler Intelligence Scale for Children* (WISC) (currently in the fifth edition) for ages 6 to 16.

Group vs. Individual Tests

Group-administered tests can be given to many people at once, in a classroom setting, for example. They are time- and cost-efficient to administer, although they provide little or no opportunity to consider individual differences in response styles or reasons for making errors. Their administration does not usually require specialized training.

Individual tests are administered privately, one-on-one, by a highly trained and experienced test administrator (a psychologist or psychometrist). Individual tests are significantly more expensive than group tests but provide much better opportunities for observing a child's individual learning style, attitudes, strengths, and problems, and therefore yield much richer information for assessment purposes.

What Purpose Does Testing Serve?

> *"Robert's test score was 129, so he's not considered gifted. His friend got 130, and he is supposedly gifted. That doesn't seem right."*

Tests can provide valuable information about exceptional learning needs. Or not. The value of test scores lies in the way they're interpreted and used to inform educational programming and decision-making. The numbers are meaningful, but they can easily be misinterpreted or misunderstood. One of the most confusing aspects of an assessment report is the number of scores provided; figuring out which ones matter and how they all come together is one of the most sophisticated demands of assessment interpretation. The value of a thoughtful and experienced interpreter cannot be overstated.

Typically, a psychoeducational assessment report is several pages long and includes (a) scores of several subtests and tests (reported in percentiles and in standard scores, or in ranges), (b) verbal descriptions of the child's areas of strength and weakness, and (c) recommendations for home and school.[7] Although jurisdictions vary in what specific cut-off score is used for gifted identification, there is usually a requirement that certain scores be above the 98th percentile.

Whether or not the official label of "gifted" is used, when major scores[8] are above the 98th percentile (or standard scores above 130), parents and educators should consider the child's educational and other needs, as it's quite possible that the school program is not sufficiently challenging. An unusually high intelligence test score should be seen as an indicator, a warning flag, that caring adults need to investigate the match between the child's ability and the learning opportunities they're being given.

It's also important to realize that if your child's IQ is below 130, or below your school's gifted cut-off, your child may still have gifted learning needs. A child may achieve a lower-than-accurate IQ score for many reasons, such as fatigue, distractions, poor motivation, medical reasons, and more, which we'll discuss later. This means that careful test interpretation is essential. Test scores can be useful, provided they—as with other information generated—are wisely considered, and carefully communicated.

When to Test?

There are many ways to answer the *When?* question. We consider the child's age, comfort with testing situations, retesting, the time of year, and whether advance preparation is required.

Age

"We've been told that our four-year-old is showing signs of giftedness. Should we have her tested?

"Do schools typically test smart kids in the primary grades?"

"My son is 13 and has never had an IQ test. Is it too late?"

Although intelligence testing can be done when a child is as young as two and a half, it only makes sense to test that early when there are reasons for concern. If your child's development is generally proceeding well, and they seem happy and interested in learning, there's no reason other than curiosity to think about testing.

There are huge individual differences in several dimensions of maturation, which make it hard to score test behaviors in standardized testing situations, particularly at younger ages. For example, some independent and inquisitive youngsters are not much interested in complying with a stranger's requests that they manipulate some blocks in a certain way. They'd rather invent their own block designs than copy the ones the examiner shows them. Alternatively, they might rather play with the puzzle pieces than put the puzzle together as quickly as possible, which is necessary to score well on many standardized tests. Although gifted assessments are sometimes conducted in the preschool years, they have poor test reliability until about age seven.[9]

We discuss these issues more fully in Chapter 5 in connection with early identification, and we illustrate some of them with this story in the form of a parent's question, followed by our response.

When to Test: A Parent's Question

Jay is six years old and in Grade 1, and I'm wondering if he should be tested. He's currently reading chapter books at the Grade 4 level. He's also starting to write his own chapter book. He's well into Chapter 2 already, and he has a storyline and his characters are well described. His teacher is supportive, encouraging him to do this during class while the other children are learning to read. She also goes out of her way to find interesting materials and activities for him.

Jay has always been very verbal. He's extremely focused and intense. He gets frustrated, but at the same time, he has a lovely sense of humor. Socially, he's friendly and well adjusted, but we're beginning to notice that a lot of his friends don't have the same desire to remain at various activities for the length of time he does. He appears to be strategy-oriented (he likes chess) and looks for patterns everywhere. He has taught himself many things, particularly in the sports world—names and other info of all the players, as well as the ins and outs of baseball and hockey. He is very self-challenging (for example, with computer games, he won't rest until he has completed each level of difficulty), and he loves it when he's successful.

Since Jay is our first child, we don't know if he's that different from others his age. So far, he's happy and loves school. However, he is quite mature for his age in some areas. He can reason like someone much older, and he's always thinking ahead. He's also the multi-tasking king. He can follow a hockey game (or two) on television while playing on the computer, and he can still carry on a conversation. If you could shed light on any of this it would help.

Our Response

Jay sounds wonderful. Although he might test at the gifted level, we do not recommend testing at this point. As long as his learning needs are being met and he's doing fine in other ways (and he sounds like the kind of child who goes more than halfway to ensure that!), our position is to leave things as they are.

As he gets older, if you notice signs of unhappiness, boredom, frustration, aggression, or depression, consider testing then. In the meantime, it seems like your instincts are excellent and that Jay is in home and school environments that are meeting his needs very well. So, keep doing what you are doing! You also might want to take a look at some of the resources we provide on our websites and consider joining a gifted association or local parent group for bright children.

Although we have focused predominantly on young children in this discussion, there is no upper limit to the appropriate age for testing. Adolescents are not too old. Even adults who perceive a mismatch between their abilities and learning or career opportunities can sometimes benefit from assessment information.

Comfort with the Testing Situation

"I had a fever on the day of the test, but I never told anyone I felt sick 'til later."

"I wanted to make sure the stupid test was done in time so I wouldn't miss lunch."

"When I got tested last time, the lady had an accent. I couldn't really understand her."

A child who is sick or distracted, or who decides to rush through the testing in order to do something they really want to do (lunch, gym, recess, photography club, a music jam session, or maybe math) is not going to perform as well as they are able, and their test scores will be lower than they would otherwise have been. A child who is uncomfortable with the test administrator, feels pressured, or has trouble understanding the instructions might also have difficulty doing well in such a testing situation. Standards of professional assessment practice include that a child should be physically and emotionally comfortable, and that they understand the instructions. Unfortunately, that doesn't always happen.

Retesting

"Can we have Christopher retested on the WISC?"

"Emily took the Stanford-Binet six months ago. She has matured a lot since then, so we want her to redo it."

"Sanjay took an IQ test when he was six. That was eight years ago. He's going to high school next year. Does it make any sense for him to do it again now, or will the results be the same?"

Intelligence tests are not tests of academic content mastery, such as mathematics or English language, or science. Instead, they are designed to provide information about a child's cognitive processing, including reasoning ability, when faced with novel puzzles and problems. In order to provide valid scores, the tasks must be new to the child, and because of this, the same test cannot be given too frequently. In many cases the rules governing test practices actually prohibit re-administering a given test before a minimum of one year. Some jurisdictions are more conservative than that and will accept the results of a retest only if it has been at least two years since the previous testing using the same instrument. This prevents giving a scoring advantage to children who have been recently tested.[10]

If children are assessed when they're young, it's sometimes necessary to repeat the testing later. Generally, assessments that are two or more years out of date are not considered adequate for making current programming decisions. Children grow and develop in ways that cannot always be predicted, and children's test scores (including IQ) can change over time, occasionally dramatically, sometimes rising, sometimes falling. At the same time, there is rarely a good reason to do "regular" intelligence testing or to retest a child at all unless there is an important decision to be made that requires new information.

Time of Year

> *"Should children be tested at the beginning, middle, or end of the school year?"*

The best time to test a child is when the need for it is recognized. Experience has shown us that in schools that use a September-June calendar, the two peak months for testing are October and May. If classes begin in September, problems tend to surface in October, so parents and teachers identify reasons for assessment at that time. In the spring, people begin thinking about and planning for the next school year. There's enough lead time then to incorporate any necessary changes into educational planning for the fall.

If testing is being done by the school rather than by a private practitioner, parents don't usually have any say in scheduling, unless there are special considerations such as illness. There tend to be waiting lists for individual assessments, particularly if the referring issue is giftedness, which is often given a lower priority than other assessment referrals.

Advance Preparation

> *"What can we do to make sure our child doesn't 'fail' the gifted test?"*

> *"Are there practice tests our son can work on?"*

> *"How can we reduce test anxiety?"*

Sometimes parents ask how to prepare their child for testing. Our answer: "Make sure they get a good sleep the night before and eat a nutritious breakfast." There is little that one can study that helps prepare for an intelligence test.

Intelligence tests are designed to assess a child's reasoning ability and knowledge in several areas. Preparation is what has occurred all through the child's life up to the time and date of testing. A child who feels loved and listened to, whose curiosity has been encouraged, and whose questions have been addressed, is as ready as they can be. If their learning has been supported and they have been exposed to a variety of situations and learning opportunities, then they have done the best homework or preparation possible.

In fact, studying for an intelligence test is more likely to make a child anxious and so reduce the score rather than improve it—that is, unless an unscrupulous person who has access to the test is coaching the child in the actual test items or similar tasks. Even when parents are willing to collude in this unethical practice and find someone willing to prepare their child in this way, they do the child no favor. If this practice succeeds in artificially boosting the child's score into the gifted range, the child is likely to find themself struggling to keep up with others in a gifted program, going from being one of the most competent members of a regular class, to being the least capable learner among those who are more advanced. Even though tests and scores are problematic in many ways, if they are the standard that all children are being held to, it's not usually an advantage to be the least competent in the group at meeting that standard. This kind of situation can seriously damage a child's self-esteem, learning, and eventual achievement.

Another concern about test preparation relates to test anxiety. Some children become anxious just because they're being tested, or as soon as they see a stopwatch being used to time them. Parents can help prevent or reduce anxiety (and its possible score-lowering effects) by making sure that their child is comfortable, rested, and well-fed on the day of testing. They can also help by modeling a calm and curious attitude toward the assessment session.

Parents can help their child do as well as possible in an assessment by explaining the reasons for doing the testing. It can be helpful to chat with the child in a reassuring manner, ensuring there's not too much emphasis placed on performance outcomes. One way to talk about the testing process is as an exploration of how the child learns in order to think together about the best educational plan going forward.

When parents ask us what to tell their child about what they will be doing during an assessment, we suggest saying something like, "The psychologist is a learning detective who needs your help to find some clues. The learning detective will ask you to do some puzzles, thinking activities, and quizzes. You'll be working together to figure out how you learn best. We want some ideas about that, and some information that we can share with your teachers." Most children like the idea of working with the psychologist to help figure themselves out.

In our experience, most curious and intellectually engaged children love assessment tasks, and many of them ask their parents on their way out of the testing if they can come back another day or do this instead of going to school. Generally, the only children who dislike the process are those who have had bad testing experiences already, who are experiencing too much pressure to do well, or who feel that their weaknesses are being investigated and exposed.

Life itself is the best preparation for an intelligence test, and being fresh and relaxed helps, too.

Who Should You Consult?

"Are the tests done by the school the same as the ones done by private consultants?"

"Jill was tested two years ago, and the school psychologist concluded that she had emotional problems. Since then, none of her teachers has even thought about her giftedness. Instead, all they do is focus on her so-called emotional issues."

"Does it matter where he takes the test? Will the scores be part of his school record?"

In some school settings, parents who want an assessment for their child have no choice other than to hire a psychologist in private practice. In other settings, there are school psychological services available, at no charge to the family.

Some parents have concerns about testing that's conducted through the school, because once the testing has been done, test results become part of the child's permanent school record, and may be used to support programming that the parents don't believe to be appropriate. This can happen, for example, in the case of a child who has more than one exceptionality (sometimes called 2E), perhaps gifted learning needs, and also learning, emotional, or behavioral issues. In many jurisdictions, the school will address only one of these special needs, and it is usually not the gifted learning needs. In other jurisdictions, a special education consultant will assist in designing an individual education plan that addresses the multiple exceptionalities.

If you have any concerns about what the assessment results will be, or how they will be used, discuss this ahead of time with the teacher, special education consultant or school psychologist.

Choosing a Professional in Private Practice

"Are there people who specialize in counseling gifted kids? If so, how do I find them?"

Just as very few of us have the expertise required to set a child's broken bone, or even to know that a bone is broken, few parents have the training in child development and exceptionality that is sometimes required to make it happily through a child's growing up years. If you decide to consult a psychologist privately, look for someone you think will work well with your child. Choosing a competent and caring professional requires some patience and effort, as well as some knowledge about what to look for.

There are many possible avenues of professional help, depending on the nature of the problem a family is experiencing. Fees vary considerably, as does health plan coverage, and availability of professionals. In general, as with other areas of specialization, the more exceptional the situation (for example, a highly advanced adolescent with emotional problems and truant friends), the more likely it is that appropriate specialists will be found only in larger urban areas.

If the problem requires tutoring or educational advocacy, parents can contact an educational consultant with experience working with gifted learners. This person might be an educator with graduate training in special education. Or, it might be a psychoeducational consultant with a master's degree or doctorate in some aspect of educational psychology or special education, working either within or outside of the child's school system. Ideally, it is someone who understands giftedness issues, and has a successful track record in dealing with exceptionally capable learners.

If a psychoeducational assessment is required, the best consultant is usually a psychologist with training and experience in giftedness, or a psychoeducational consultant, someone with both educational and psychological training, as well as expertise in assessment. This professional should have a doctorate in psychology or education. If it is a matter of meeting gifted identification criteria, the services of a psychometrist may be sufficient. This is someone with a master's level certification in test administration, but not in interpretation or synthesis of findings.

In situations requiring counseling help for family dynamics or emotional issues, there are counselors with graduate degrees in clinical psychology or social work who have experience working with high-ability learners. When there are serious emotional or psychological problems, a psychiatrist with expertise working with giftedness may be the right professional to consult. Psychiatrists are medical doctors specializing in psychiatry, and they can prescribe medication if needed.

With such a wide range of possibilities, in combination with a scarcity of gifted education specialists, it's no wonder that parents can find it daunting to find someone able to help their child and their family. Parents who understand the Optimal Match approach, including the idea that giftedness develops over time, with the necessary supports and opportunities to learn, are well placed to choose professionals who share their positive perspective.

When to Consult?

Many of the parents who consult professionals about gifted issues feel the same kind of uncertainty that Luke's mother expresses here:

A Parent's Request for Help

Luke's reading is coming along slowly; he is showing no great interest in it. This would not concern us very much—he is only in Grade 2, and lots of his friends aren't reading any better than him—except that the school has made it clear that acceleration is impossible unless his reading and writing skills keep pace with his math reasoning skills. I must admit that at times I wonder whether Luke's learning ability is as advanced as the test results indicate.

We've sought the assistance of a psychiatrist because of Luke's argumentativeness. Things seem to be improving, but my husband and I wonder whether boredom at home and at school contribute, at least in part, to his acting out. Would it be helpful for Darren and me to meet with you once again before the school's next review meeting? When we met with the principal, the special education resource teacher, and Luke's teacher last December, the school administration stated they wouldn't consider acceleration or out-of-level instruction, at least not yet. I'm concerned that Luke's academic needs will not be adequately addressed at that meeting. Would it be possible for you to contribute your opinions and interpretation of his assessment results to the hearing? I think we'll need an advocate!

This message illustrates the confusion and turmoil that many parents feel as they try to navigate their way through a gifted learner's childhood. In this case, we had previously done a psychoeducational assessment in which Luke had scored exceptionally well on an intelligence test and extremely well on mathematics achievement tests, but had scored in the average range in both reading and writing. We responded to this parent's message by affirming the school's current position on full acceleration, pointing out that it is quite reasonable and sensible not to do a whole-grade acceleration at this time. We wrote, "If Luke isn't reading and writing at least at a moderately high level in the grade into which he would be going, we would not be helping him by accelerating him there."

We also affirmed the parent's concerns about Luke possibly having problems because his learning needs were not being met, while at the same time cautioning a balanced perspective, saying, "School is not the only place where a child's learning needs can be met. There are extracurricular and other options we can discuss." We agreed with the parents about the importance of working with the school, and we set up a meeting to discuss ways to facilitate that.

This story shows one of the situations where expert consultation can be helpful. Luke's parents had concerns in a number of areas, including their son's problems with boredom, anger management, and argumentativeness, as well as his exceptional educational needs. They understood that the social/emotional concerns and giftedness needs might be interacting and reinforcing each other, and they chose to try to address them both at the same time. They met with a counselor for the social/emotional needs, in this case a psychiatrist, and they consulted us for help with educational planning.

Other parents in similarly complex situations may choose to tackle one problem at a time (and in fact, this would be our usual recommendation), in the hope that as one problem area is solved, others will diminish. In many cases, once a child's learning needs are being well met, the argumentativeness (or boredom, or frustration, or other problematic behavior) does in fact diminish. In more serious cases, however, it can be a good idea to address several issues simultaneously, as this family did.

Giftedness is truly an individual developmental differences phenomenon. Each story is unique, and therefore each situation must be looked at in its own context. The simplest answer to the question of when or why to look for professional help is to pay attention to the child's development, and to seek sound advice when things aren't going well.

When families have to deal with exceptional circumstances such as parenting a gifted learner, they often find that other people's notions of "common sense" fails them. They discover that what they read about child development, what their friends and family tell them about parenting, and what educators recommend based on experiences with other children and adolescents don't apply very well to their particular situations. Often, they just need some help understanding the exceptional developmental needs of their own child. Sometimes they simply require reassurance that their sense of the situation is right, and that they *do* know how to proceed in the best interest of their child.

Very often, consulting a giftedness expert means having one's parenting instincts confirmed. It can also mean finding support, strategic approaches, and targeted assistance for sorting things out and responding to the unique challenges a child presents.

Pre-emptive Counseling

One of the problems with seeking professional help is the risk of pathologizing a situation that is not pathological; that is, making a child feel that there is something wrong with them when in reality everything is developing as it should be. Depending on the circumstances, there are usually ways to provide counseling help that will not make the child feel they are somehow defective. For example, a focus on the arts can be used "as a therapeutic intervention as well as a creative and expressive outlet."[11]

Career counseling is another good idea for gifted learners. This can provide a forum for self-discovery, opening up interesting possibilities for current and future investigation. If this is not offered at an adolescent's school, parents might consider looking for outside assistance.

Parents might want to talk to a giftedness expert when they have concerns that their child is unhappy, is hiding their abilities, is being singled out as a behavior problem for acts of mischief or boredom, or is not making good academic or career decisions. Just as there are medical specialists available to deal with specific physical problems, parents can take comfort in knowing that there are professionals who can help them if they run into trouble with parenting issues related to giftedness. Such professionals can be hard to find, and you might have to settle for someone who is good enough (not perfect). The most important criterion is that your child feels a sense of connection with the expert. not whether or not the expert has the gifted education credentials you were hoping to find.

Why Test?

"I know my son is smart, but his grades are terrible."

My daughter's really creative, but she's always getting in trouble at school. The teachers just don't seem to like her."

"Becky is so curious, and I think that's a good thing, but her teacher says she's driving him nuts with her questioning. And

she keeps helping other kids with their work, before she's done her own. Apparently, she's becoming a behavior problem."

Most teachers have little or no training in gifted development,[12] and so their personal biases and assumptions influence their perceptions of what giftedness looks like. Their preconceptions can prevent them from recognizing gifted learning needs in their classrooms. Testing can provide helpful information in these situations, as long as the results are presented in teacher-friendly language, and the teacher is supported in implementing any recommendations.

Under the Mystery Model (which we discuss in Chapter 1), there are often students in a given classroom who are exceptionally advanced in one area or another, but who don't qualify for gifted programming. Some of the most capable learners are so bored and frustrated by what they're asked to do at school that the last thing they appear to be is keen, curious, task-committed, or high-achieving—attributes that are often regarded as typical characteristics of "the gifted."[13] Some advanced learners' grades are appalling except when the child happens to like the teacher, the assignment, the subject, or is motivated by an extrinsic factor like grades or recognition.

The best way to answer the "Why?" question concerning testing for giftedness is that test scores can show what kind of gifted learning needs a student might have. As researchers David Dai and Joseph Renzulli write, "In static models of gifted education, assessment (identification) and educational provisions are separate processes, but in dynamic models of gifted education, they inform each other and thus become an integrated system."[14] From an Optimal Match perspective, which is a dynamic approach, standardized academic test scores can show your child's areas of strength, as well as their challenges, and testing will indicate whether or not your child is experiencing mismatches. Once that's been determined, it's important to integrate that information into the educational plan, and the question to ask is, "What learning opportunities does my child need in the mismatched areas?"

Here are examples of children's experiences of testing for gifted identification. Although each of the following students was identified as gifted, the reasons for testing, the procedures used, the children's responses, and the consequences of the assessments were all quite different.

Dana

Dana was a lively and energetic ten-year-old who had always achieved at a high academic standard at the private school she'd been attending since kindergarten. Her parents believed that a full-time gifted program in the public school system would be comparable to the program in the private school, but at considerable financial savings, as well as being within walking distance. Accordingly, Dana's parents arranged for a psychologist to administer the *Stanford-Binet Intelligence Scale* during the summer. In talking to Dana about the testing ahead of time, her parents treated it as an entry exercise, allowing her to go to the public school. She met the criteria for her public school's gifted program, and once she started her new school, Dana loved the new environment.

Mariana

Mariana was a hesitant, soft-spoken fourth grader who described herself as "mostly bored" at her local elementary school. She was involved in a weekly program that provided enrichment to a group of children on a pull-out basis, and she said she enjoyed her half-day in that program. The special program teacher believed that Mariana was a suitable candidate for full-time gifted programming and nominated her for testing. Mariana took part in assessment procedures, and on the basis of a WISC score above the 98th percentile, she was identified as gifted. As far as Mariana was concerned, she was ready to "start fresh," and after careful deliberation, her parents decided to enroll her in the gifted class. From fifth grade onward, Mariana went from being mostly bored to being happily challenged. She compared work demands, reporting they'd become "a lot harder and much better than before." When we spoke to her after a year in her new program, she was livelier, and more communicative.

Corey

Corey was a feisty, fast-moving nine-year-old who described school as "yawwwn, zzzz, ahhh! Boring, exhausting, and far too much work." His report cards were a spatter of As to Ds, with comments about problematic work habits. He loved mathematics and all things to do with computers, although his school grades did not reflect that. In fact, his lowest scores were in mathematics. Corey said he had almost no friends, and he perceived school as a place he was obliged to attend but which served little purpose socially or academically. "I like school because it ends," he told us. Corey's gifted identification procedure consisted of a group intelligence test at school. After a long wait, the school informed Corey and his parents that he had been selected for placement in a gifted class. He was hopeful that being in a full-time gifted program would make school more interesting and enjoyable; however, a year into the gifted program, he told us that nothing much had changed. He hadn't made any friends, and his advanced abilities in math and computers were not being addressed at school. He said, "The only place I learn anything worthwhile is at home in front of my computer."

Although intelligence test scores are not always used intelligently (as in Corey's case), when they are seen in the context of other information, they can help parents and educators understand a child's learning strengths and any problems they might be experiencing. It is important to keep in mind that the only good reason to test gifted learning needs is to figure out how to better meet those needs, putting the focus on diagnosing possible mismatches, rather than on categorizing children as gifted (and not). Testing merely to discover an IQ score does not help a child, parent, or teacher understand precisely what kind of educational programming a child needs.

Now that we've considered the "Who, What, When, Where, and Why" of testing, we look at the "How?" question—that is, how to understand assessments and tests.

CHAPTER 4

Assessments And Tests

In Chapter 3, we introduced many of the terms, concepts, and issues involved in assessing gifted learning needs. Here, we discuss the way assessments are actually done, the various tests and measures that are used, and how to make sense of the results. Again, we emphasize the shift away from the Mystery Model's focus on identifying children as gifted or not-gifted, toward the Optimal Match focus on diagnosing mismatches, for the purpose of addressing them.

It Starts with the Parent or Teacher: Dynamic Assessment

> *"Madeline whips through every activity. She's ready for more. Where do I start?"*

> *"All the students in my class have been identified as 'gifted.' What math should I teach?"*

Whether learning happens at home or at school, or somewhere else (e.g., a museum, a playground, a music studio), it's deeply influenced by the learner's relationships with the parent or teacher, as well as by the other students, and the child's personal history, interests, and abilities. A good place to begin to identify academic and other needs is with an ongoing dynamic assessment. This is because *"learning is a dynamic process that happens in a particular context or environment."*[1]

In dynamic assessment, the parent or teacher engages with the child or adolescent as an active partner in an ongoing, cyclical process:

○ informally assessing the young person's learning needs
○ teaching to the individual's optimal levels
○ assessing learning outcomes
○ teaching to the individual's optimal levels
○ assessing learning outcomes
○ and so on, in a continuous loop of learning and growth.

In this way, instruction and assessment inform each other, and each is grounded in a clear understanding of what the learner already knows and can do. Once a student has mastered a section of curriculum or skill, they are given (or can help the adult discover or design) new and ever more challenging material. By keeping close track of learning in this way, adults and kids can work together to make informed decisions that match curriculum demands to learners' developmental levels.

This approach has obvious benefits for all students, but it's particularly important for gifted learners, whose exceptional learning needs might otherwise go unnoticed by the parent or teacher. By enabling young people to confront new and appropriate challenges, this strategy both encourages students' ongoing growth, and also helps to prevent boredom, frustration, and tuning out.

Dynamic assessment minimizes the need for formal testing, labeling, or withdrawal of children from the regular classroom. There are several advantages to using ongoing dynamic assessment with gifted learners:

○ It significantly reduces the cultural and socioeconomic status biases inherent in standardized testing;[2]

○ Learning assignments can be more readily tailored to a learner's temperament, personality, motivation, and interests;

○ It provides a more targeted indicator of ability in specific areas (such as math reasoning or reading comprehension); and

○ Dynamic assessment is directly related to each student's learning needs at a given point in time, providing specific implications for where and what kind of instruction or intervention is appropriate.[3]

The Student Portfolio

> *"Over the past few years, portfolio assessment has become the most pervasive and prominent alternative assessment approach. Although portfolios take different forms and serve different purposes, they share in common the ongoing selection and collection of work as evidence of learning and development over time."[4]*

One dynamic assessment approach involves the use of portfolios, or compilations of students' efforts that demonstrate their progress in one or more areas.[5] Students are responsible for putting samples of their various efforts in their portfolios, in collaboration with the parent or teacher; the degree of student responsibility depends on age and other individual factors.

A portfolio might contain work samples, journals, tapes, pictures, test results, parent assessments, teacher assessments, or descriptions of achievements and learning experiences, including self-ratings and reflections. The collection chronicles the student's learning processes, strategies, progress, and achievements over a designated time period. In planning for and assembling the portfolio, the student manages their own work and sets personal goals, both important life skills. They learn to take ownership and pride in their accomplishments, moving away from a dependence on outside evaluation from teachers or parents.

Portfolios generally reflect responses and tasks that are authentic; that is, they are personally meaningful to the individual, and connected to some kind of real-world outcome. For example, a typical student portfolio might contain initial plans for a project; several written drafts; self-evaluations; feedback from peers, teachers, parents, or other experts; finished products; resources including information from across different subject areas; and possibly plans for subsequent activities. These materials can be kept by the parent, the teacher, or the student, depending on maturity level, and can always be revisited. By sixth grade or so, a child should be fully responsible for assembling, maintaining, and updating their own portfolio.

With the portfolio approach, students, parents, and teachers are able to observe an individual child's or adolescent's growth in particular areas over time. Increasingly, portfolios are being recognized as useful for motivating and assessing student learning, for tracking guided independent studies and project-based learning, and also for showcasing students' progress for parent-teacher conferences.[6]

Performance Assessment

> *"Performance-based assessment...represents an indispensable approach for assessing gifted learning."*[7]

> *"Performance assessment offers the most meaningful evaluation of higher order thinking."*[8]

Performance assessment is embedded in what students are actually doing or creating in their learning activities. Such assessments "focus on challenging open-ended problems that require high-level thinking and problem solving."[9] The emphasis is on the learning process, not on whether the child can find the answer quickly. A parent or teacher starts by identifying the learning goals or outcomes along with the student, working from there to create a scaffolded structure for the learning process.

One popular approach to performance assessment is "Understanding by Design"[10] or backward planning. It's a three-stage approach to designing authentic and dynamic assessment: (a) identify desired results, (b) determine acceptable evidence, and (c) plan learning experiences and instruction. Architectural metaphors are often used when this model is applied to education, with the teacher seen as an architect who starts with a vision of the completed building, and carefully works backward from there, thinking about content, scope, process, and coherence, and how these might be authentically assessed.

In addition to being a good way to implement dynamic assessment for all learners, performance assessment (like portfolio assessment) is an excellent way to include more diversity in gifted programming. Some of the features of performance assessment that contribute to its being more inclusive are that it rewards fluency and complexity rather than speed; acknowledges multiple right responses rather than one right answer; involves manipulating materials as a pathway to solution-finding; employs pre-teaching; encourages students to be planful; focuses on higher level thinking and problem solving; and incorporates self-reflection.[11]

Day-to-Day Diagnostics

Effective teachers (whether they're parents or school-based teachers) can understand a lot about where students are in their learning through meaningful daily interactions with them. There are four key aspects to day-to-day diagnostics: careful observation, active listening, open dialogue, and reflective responsivity.

Parents and teachers can pay attention to how a child reacts in various learning situations (for example, working in small groups, large groups, or independently), and how they respond to certain teaching methods (such as direct questioning or written assignments). By observing them in action—not just looking but *seeing*—and also recognizing what works and what doesn't, adults can get a better sense of how a child learns and what they know.

Listening carefully to what children say to each other, to the parent or teacher alone, to the class as a whole in the context of classroom activities, and within small group settings, can also be illuminating. Active listening is an art, and it starts with a willingness to really hear what children are saying. There's no better way to learn about others than to listen attentively to them.

Communication that involves open discussion and two-way dialogue is another informal but highly informative assessment method. Talk with children, engage them in meaningful and respectful dialogue, remain observant, and be emotionally available and open to their questions. This will encourage them to demonstrate what they're thinking about and what they're learning, and to discover what they don't yet understand.

Finally, reflection is an integral component of informal day-to-day assessment. Students can be encouraged to be reflective, to think about what's being taught, and to ask questions as they engage with the material, thus providing another meaningful indicator of where they are conceptually. And adults who reflect on children's questions and learning needs are in a better position to respond with appropriately targeted curriculum and assessment.

These processes—observation, listening, dialogue, and reflective responsivity—are perhaps the best assessment tools available, giving parents and teachers a heightened attunement to the individual, and allowing them to gather considerable information about the young people with whom they work. Employed on a daily basis, these informal child-focused methods provide a solid and authentic foundation for understanding and identifying many gifted learning needs.

Standardized Tests

"Tony loves school and does really well, but I'm not sure whether he needs harder work."

"I'd like to know the actual benefits of achievement tests."

Unlike dynamic assessment methods that teachers can use in their classrooms, standardized tests are not flexibly responsive to a single individual or context. By their very design, they cannot reflect the authentic, interactive, and dynamic nature of learning. What they do accomplish, however, is important: the ability to consider the child's current functioning relative to others of a defined age or grade level. This is essential information when considering the appropriate level of instruction to provide. If a child is in third grade and functioning in the top one or two percent of a third-grade test, it shows a need to consider modifying their instruction and homework demands. In that case, it would be even more useful to find out how the child is achieving relative to higher grade levels: is that third grader able to manage sixth grade instruction, or ninth? Standardized testing is a very good way to figure that out.

There are many different kinds of standardized tests, and we discuss a few of the most relevant here.

Academic Achievement

Standardized academic achievement tests measure how well a student is mastering school curriculum, as compared with others at their age or grade level. Used wisely, they can be an important supplement to classroom-based assessment, providing a reference point and source of accountability for parents and educators.

Standardized academic achievements tests are typically pencil-and-paper tests administered to one child, or to an entire class group at one sitting. They might be scored electronically or by a parent or teacher. They measure how well a student is learning, and they indicate grade level of content mastery and reasoning ability, by subject area.

Because of the time, effort, and expertise that go into their construction, standardized academic achievements tests are generally much more reliable in their design than teacher-made tests. They can yield useful information about where a teacher ought to be targeting instruction, showing for example, if a given student has already mastered most of the grade-level math curriculum, or if their reading comprehension is well below grade level.

These tests are also useful for comparing schools and programs, and for providing standards of accountability. For example, if a school discovers that 75% of its fourth graders are scoring below the fourth-grade mean in mathematics, the school has important information for thinking about possible reasons for this, and for encouraging improvements in the fourth-grade (and first-, second-, and third-grade) mathematics curriculum.

In theory, and provided academic achievement scores are interpreted carefully, they can indicate what a child knows about a certain subject area. But because these tests are standardized, they may or may not be directly related to what a given student has been taught in a particular school. A student's low score on a standardized test is not always a good measure of how well they've learned what they've been taught, because they haven't necessarily been taught what the test is measuring. As with other kinds of assessment, there are many reasons for a child to score poorly on these tests, reasons that have nothing to do with the child's actual ability. Nevertheless, standardized academic achievement tests can be a useful information source for thinking about how to match individual learning needs and educational programming.

High-Ceiling and Above-Level Testing

"Juan needs more challenging work in math. How far should I advance him?"

> *"I think Zaria is capable of doing sophisticated reading comprehension activities. But she's only in Grade 3!"*

When academic achievement tests are used to assess giftedness, they must be able to differentiate between those students who are excellent grade-level students from those whose abilities are far beyond the current grade level. If a child scores the maximum possible score on a test, they're said to be scoring at the test ceiling (sometimes referred to as "topping out" on the test). When that happens, one can't tell how much more the child knows, because the test doesn't have enough items that are sufficiently difficult to measure the upper extent of their ability.

Academic achievement tests that are designed to assess students' mastery of one grade level of curriculum can't be used to identify whether students should be placed at higher grades, or at what level. For example, if a child is in third grade but is functioning at the tenth-grade level in reading comprehension, they'll score very well on a third-grade reading achievement test, topping out at the ceiling. They'll achieve the same score as a child who is working at an early fourth-grade level. Top scores on a third-grade achievement test don't allow a teacher to distinguish between the student who has gifted educational needs (the one who reads at a tenth-grade level) and the one who is doing very well at or slightly above grade level and does not likely require any significant modifications.

However, there are achievement tests that assess a wide enough range of grade levels that they're useful for identifying the actual grade level at which a student is functioning in a given subject area. The Stanford Achievement Tests are an example of a set of measures (sometimes called a test battery) that satisfy the three essential properties of such tests:

○ *very high ceilings*, which means they have enough very difficult reasoning items to allow for differentiation between excellent grade-level students and those whose ability would be better matched by considerably higher grade-level curriculum;

○ *norming flexibility*, so that students can be compared with their age-peers and also grade-peers; and

○ *assessment of reasoning separately from content knowledge,* providing information about a child's level of conceptual mastery somewhat independently of their opportunities to learn the actual content.

High-ceiling tests can provide useful information about which students have gifted educational needs and what curriculum level matches their learning abilities. Tests that focus more on reasoning than on content knowledge can help identify a younger child who has not yet been exposed to curriculum at higher grade levels but who can master it conceptually.

Another approach that is sometimes used for the same purpose is above-level testing, using tests that are aimed at a higher grade level than the child's age would normally suggest. Consider, for example, the two children described above who score very well on a third-grade test of reading achievement, but who are widely different in their actual learning needs. If they were to take a fifth-grade, or seventh-grade, or even a ninth-grade reading achievement test, the difference between their scores would become evident. This kind of information enables educators to differentiate curriculum effectively.

For curriculum planning purposes, a teacher needs to understand the extent of a child's development in order to provide appropriate learning opportunities. This prevents children languishing in classrooms where they already know the material being taught. Here is an example of this.

Above-Level Testing: Felix

Luc Kumps was concerned about his son, Felix, who was exceptionally advanced in his academic development, but seriously unhappy at school. The school seemed blind to 7-year-old Felix's advancement, and was focusing instead on his behavior, a result of boredom and frustration. (A situation we encounter too often, and something we discuss in Chapter 10.)

Luc gave Felix some questions from a Grade 3 math test, the grade above his own, which Felix handled easily. With a series of increasingly advanced questions, Luc discovered that Felix enjoyed Grade 5 math in a way he didn't enjoy his Grade 2 work, which was just too easy for him. Luc suggested that the school test Felix on Grade 3 math, and at the very least, allow him to do that math instead of forcing him to do math classes and assignments at his age level. With advocacy help from some teacher friends, Luc managed to get Felix tested on above-level math, and to receive the differentiation he needed to better match his ability level, at least in that subject area.

Felix's teacher was surprised at the difference it made. Felix was happier at school, and his behavior improved dramatically. The above-level testing gave the teacher the necessary information to provide Felix work that was challenging and didn't feel like a waste of his time.

From an Optimal Match perspective, children's learning needs are best understood by using a combination of dynamic assessment approaches and standardized high-ceiling or above-level subject-specific achievement tests. Each child can be encouraged to study, learn, and progress at their own pace, going through the curriculum as quickly or as slowly as works for them. When teachers have the training and support required to implement this approach, many of the problems associated with giftedness and other exceptionalities disappear.

Intelligence Testing

"Justin is good at everything he tries. I know he's really bright, but I have no idea how well he'd do on an IQ test."

"Katelyn used to be smart. She had a high IQ when she was five years old, but I sure don't see signs of that anymore."

Intelligence as measured by intelligence tests is a much more limited concept than the name of the test suggests. Forty years ago, Stephen Jay Gould wrote compellingly about the limits of intelligence testing and the changeability of IQ scores.[12] Many scientists since then have confirmed his findings, including the fact that people's IQ scores can change quite dramatically over time.[13]

How much emphasis should be put on intelligence tests? Most important aspects of successful careers and lives are not measured by intelligence tests. These aspects include motivation; social/emotional development; creativity; leadership; musical, athletic, and artistic ability; decision making ability; and independent thinking.[14] Rather than seeing IQ as a true measure of a person's intelligence and as some kind of "real" indicator of a person's innate and permanent general cognitive ability, it's more accurate to see it as describing an individual's functioning at a certain time on a certain number of specific tasks. When asked to think about the intelligent use of intelligence tests, Carol Dweck wrote:

> "The real danger of these [IQ] tests is that many educators come to believe (erroneously) that they are a good index of how intelligent children are and what their intellectual potential is. The public needs to be educated; the fact is that nothing can measure intellectual potential. It is something that unfolds as children work hard and learn. Moreover, scientific research is showing that many of the most basic parts of intelligence can be changed with training.[15]

Intelligence tests can be a good interactive tool for assessing how well an individual learns in many important areas. Although they certainly have limitations and miss much of what is important about gifted development, when used in conjunction with other measures of academic achievement and observations of social and emotional functioning, these tests can provide useful information. By using a combination of assessment approaches that includes intelligence testing, it's possible to identify a child's or adolescent's learning styles, strengths, and weaknesses in a way that informs both short- and long-term educational planning.

Group-Administered Intelligence Tests

> *"I'm confused about all the different kinds of intelligence tests."*
>
> *"Is a group test as good as an individual one?"*

Examples of group-administered intelligence tests are Raven's Progressive Matrices and the Canadian Cognitive Abilities Test. Such tests often include the words "intelligence" or "cognitive ability" in their names. They attempt to measure an individual's abstract reasoning ability, differentiated as much as possible from academic learning. Group intelligence tests have the usual benefits of tests that are administered in a group rather than individually: they are cost- and time-effective.

However, group tests aren't very useful for identifying gifted learning needs. To begin with, there's no direct connection to academic curriculum, and they provide little information about a curriculum mismatch for a given child. They provide no opportunities for the child to interact in a dynamic way with the material or the test administrator. Therefore, these tests miss the capable thinker who looks at questions differently than others, or who thinks in more complex ways than the "right answer" requires. Because of the paper-and-pencil format, they miss the child whose reasoning ability is exceptionally advanced but whose reading or writing skills haven't developed as far as their reasoning. These tests almost always miss the child with double or multiple exceptionalities, like the child who is both gifted and learning disabled.

Group intelligence tests can sometimes be useful for preliminary screening, as long as educators realize that some exceptionally capable children won't show up as high scorers, and will need to be searched for below the cut-off score. We discuss these issues in the remaining pages of this chapter, and in Chapter 5.

Individual Intelligence Tests

Individual intelligence tests have several of the same validity problems as group-administered intelligence tests, in that they primarily measure the ability to do well on intelligence tests. And these tests suffer from some of the same diversity-fairness issues as group intelligence tests, such as cultural differences in opportunities to learn. No matter how a test is redesigned or the scores adjusted for life experience, children will not do well if they do not know the material being tested, or if they have not had a history of learning opportunities that prepare them for effective test-taking. Although test developers have worked hard to overcome such criticisms, many observers are concluding that trying to make conventional intelligence tests culture-fair may not be productive, and that gifted identification itself is fraught with serious problems.[16]

At the same time, however, individual intelligence tests do have strengths. Individual intelligence tests are interactive in their design. The test administrator has an opportunity to observe a child's learning in a novel cognitive performance situation. Extensive training is required in order to administer individual intelligence tests, and an experienced clinician takes careful note of the child's approach to receiving, manipulating, and communicating information. The testing process takes an hour or two (depending on the child and the subtests administered). It consists of oral questions as well as tasks requiring manipulation of different objects and puzzles, with several subtests measuring various kinds of abilities. Throughout the process, the examiner's role is to observe the test-taker's response style, noting relevant dimensions of cognitive and emotional functioning. When considered along with the test scores, these factors can be used to inform placement and programming decisions.

Another important benefit of the major individual intelligence tests is that they are highly reliable measurement instruments. If the scores are interpreted carefully, taking individual and cultural factors into account (such as tiredness, illness, test anxiety, language spoken at home), they can provide an effective indication of a student's exceptionality.

When an IQ is extremely high, some kind of exceptionality exists that implies special educational needs. Exactly what cut-off designates exceptionality is contentious and frequently debated. However, when a student's score is more than two standard deviations above the mean (an IQ of 130, at the 98th percentile), there is good reason for parents and educators to examine the nature of the learner-learning match.

And an IQ score above 145 (three standard deviations above the mean) is even more compelling in its suggestion of a probable mismatch.

There are two major individual intelligence tests in use, both of which have excellent test design and normative properties: the Wechsler tests, and the *Stanford-Binet Intelligence Scale*. Wechsler tests currently in use include the *Wechsler Preschool and Primary Scale of Intelligence* (4th edition, WPPSI-IV), designed for children ages 2 to 6; the *Wechsler Intelligence Scale for Children* (5th edition, WISC-V), designed for children ages 6 to 16; and the *Wechsler Adult Intelligence Scale* (4th edition, WAIS-IV), for age 16 and over. The *Stanford-Binet Intelligence Scale* (5th edition, SB-V) is designed for ages 2 to 90. Tests in both systems are in a constant state of revision, which is why their names include designations like "4th edition."

Individual Testing: Zachary

Five-year-old Zachary was taking the Stanford-Binet Intelligence Scale. His parents had sought an assessment to find out if there was something wrong with their son's cognitive processing that might lead to his problems at school. At home and elsewhere, they observed an insatiable curiosity and appetite for learning, in combination with an extraordinary intensity of focus when he was interested in something. However, his kindergarten teacher described him as unexceptional intellectually, and a behavior problem in her class.

On one of the early items of the intelligence test, Zachary was asked to put together a puzzle that depicted a person's face. He did very poorly on this item, getting very few of the puzzle pieces in the right place. The test-giver was dismayed. Was the child's visual/spatial perception distorted? Did he have some kind of emotional problem that led him to misperceive human faces?

The little boy, however, seemed quite pleased with himself as he declared, "I made a face like Picasso would do it!" He then went on to discuss in some detail Picasso's work, including listing his reasons for preferring the work of Camille Pisarro to that of Pablo Picasso.

Through Zachary's conversation with the test administrator on this and other test items, it was obvious that he was extraordinary in his knowledge and interest in a wide range of areas. If a group-administered test had been given instead of the individual test, he would probably have had the same kind of fun thinking up interesting answers. But items in such a group test would simply have been marked wrong, and Zachary wouldn't have had anyone with whom to discuss his answers. In that case, his parents would have been informed that the teacher was right, and his intelligence was average (or perhaps below) and that his problems were emotional, maturational, and/or behavioral.

Although his score on the Stanford-Binet was considerably lower than he was capable of achieving, it was possible—because the test was administered orally and one-on-one—to provide an intelligent assessment of his exceptional curiosity, knowledge base, and inventiveness. It was also possible to make a strong recommendation for gifted programming for Zachary. He needed more challenges and he would continue to create his own.

Update on Zachary

Zachary is now almost thirty. His education was as bumpy and idiosyncratic as you might have guessed, with highly variable grades through high school. He took a couple of years off as gap years, spending one year working at a ski resort, and another riding across North America on a motorcycle, stopping to work as a waiter when he needed money. He studied art history at university, and then switched over to an applied arts and design program, where for the first time in his life, he flourished at school. He graduated with top grades, winning major awards in his college program.

Since then, Zachary has been teaching at that college, as well as doing his own painting, mostly large colorful mixed media abstract pictures. Zachary is beginning to make a name for himself as an artist. His early test scores (and many of his elementary and high school teachers who were inflexible or inpatient) completely missed everything that would lead to his later success: his curiosity, artistic passion, independent thinking, and drive to do his own work.

Nonverbal Tests

The most widely used nonverbal tests in gifted identification are *Raven's Standard Progressive Matrices*,[17] the *Naglieri Nonverbal Ability Test*,[18] and the *Universal Nonverbal Intelligence Test*.[19] These are tests of figural or visual/spatial reasoning and working memory that require test-takers to solve matrices, mazes, and other figural and spatial tasks.

There has been considerable controversy concerning nonverbal tests when they are being used to identify giftedness. Its proponents[20] have argued that nonverbal tests are more inclusive than other measures, and should be used in gifted identification in order to address concerns about under-representation of students from minority, English as a second language, and low socioeconomic status families. This argument has been challenged from both an empirical and a theoretical point of view.[21]

From an Optimal Match standpoint—where the emphasis is on addressing mismatches between a student's learning needs and their educational provisions—it makes no sense to use a test of visual-spatial reasoning to identify learning needs, unless the curriculum on offer is map-making, geometry, mechanics, or other activities based on visual-spatial reasoning abilities. Even if a child does exceptionally well on a test of nonverbal intelligence, but is not doing advanced level academic work, what kind of advantage is it to attend a program where they receive advanced level academic work?

Advocacy for nonverbal tests in gifted identification rests on two Mystery Model assumptions: (a) that intelligence is innate (and thus can be measured if only we find the right tool, the one that transcends prior learning and other cultural advantages); and (b) that the goal is to identify and categorize children as gifted (and not-gifted). A shift to the Optimal Match perspective is particularly valuable for those children who come from the diverse backgrounds that nonverbal test advocates say they are concerned about.[22]

Creativity Testing

Pencil-and-paper tests purporting to measure students' creativity are not useful long-term predictors of their creative talent, ability, or achievement.[23] The best judges of creativity are experts in a particular domain.[24] If we want to know if a child is artistically creative, for example, the optimal way to find out is *not* to ask the child to do a creativity test, but rather to assemble a panel of experts in that area (such as sculpture or painting) and ask them to comment on the child's work, just as a teacher might evaluate an academic portfolio. The same goes for musical, scientific, and other forms of creativity. The extensive literature on this topic shows that domain-specific ratings by experts are the best predictors of subsequent achievement.[25]

Creativity assessment has very little place in an academic assessment of gifted learning needs, except perhaps as a trait to note if apparent, as in Zachary's case described above. As we discussed in Chapter 2, although creativity is an important component of high-level real-world achievement, it does not make good theoretical or practical sense to attempt to quantify it as a component of gifted identification for placement in a program for gifted learners, unless creativity is going to be an explicit focus of that programming.[26]

Career Interest Inventories

> *"Monique isn't sure what she wants to study after high school. There are so many options open to someone with her talents and abilities. How can I help her decide what to do?"*

> *"Cole wants to be a lawyer. But he also wants to be a musician. AND he wants to be a scientist. Now he has to make course choices that will eliminate one or more of these possibilities. Help!"*

A student with multiple and diverse interests and abilities can have difficulty figuring out which future directions to choose and which areas of interest to sideline. As highly capable children become adolescents and young adults, choosing a college major or a career path can be complicated and potentially troubling. Consider for example the dilemma faced by a student who loves chemistry and is being encouraged by their science teachers to become a pharmacist or scientist, but who also loves writing and has been told by their English teachers that they have the makings of a fine journalist. At the same time, their drama teacher has suggested they think about becoming a professional actor because of their thespian talent and passion. Such a person often experiences a serious quandary, because they must choose high-level courses and focus their attention more narrowly in an area of serious interest, at the same time losing out on further exploration of other areas.

There are career interest inventories and other tests designed to help with this process, starting at age fifteen. Although they tend to be limited to somewhat conventional career paths, and typically don't include highly specialized or less-common occupations such as biochemical engineer, neuropsychologist, or international investment banker, they can provide a framework for thinking about options and interests. These inventories are most valuable when used in combination with other experiences that encourage career exploration, accompanied by guidance from someone who understands high-level development. Some of the ways adolescents who exhibit multipotentiality can get the support they need in order to make informed decisions include mentorships, career days, job-shadowing, and part-time opportunities in their areas of interest.

Parents and educators can help by encouraging students to explore unconventional options, and to think and talk about ways to combine two or more areas of ability. Career education is recognized as an integral practice within gifted education, but the focus is on helping students learn about the career itself and develop the self-awareness and self-regulation skills that go into good decision-making rather than on career interest inventories.

Nonstandardized Measures and Other Information Sources

> *"Jordan has been failing math all semester. I'm afraid his attitude is creating a block for new learning."*

How a student approaches learning tasks can be more useful than test scores when diagnosing a learning mismatch. Error analysis (noticing where a child is making errors and why) and reactions to various kinds of tasks can be especially informative. Some reactions to pay attention to include how a child handles easier and harder tasks, their responses to timed tests, and their preferences for different kinds of activities. Some children perform much better on the harder items on some subtests, and make careless errors on the easier items. Even though this pattern can lead to a low or mediocre test score, it clearly indicates a need to be intellectually challenged.

Surveys and Inventories

There are many kinds of surveys, questionnaires, and inventories available to help educators learn more about students' learning needs. These include measures of self-concept, orientation to learning, school attitudes, past experiences, and learning styles. There are questionnaires that include questions about hobbies and extracurricular activities, preferred school subjects, and various aspects of daily school life. These kinds of inventories are informal and not designed to provide reliable scores. Nevertheless, used in combination with other assessment tools, they can be important and useful additions to understanding a child's learning needs in order to make good academic recommendations.

School Reports

"Corinne's poor marks are becoming a regular thing. How can we break the cycle?"

"I can't wait to see my daughter's report card. It lets me know how well she's doing in school, and how I can help her improve in some subjects."

"I got a B on my science project because my teacher had a problem with one little part of my presentation, but Dean got an A just for trying! It's not fair. I think teachers play around with report card marks, and parents don't even know it.

Report cards are another source of potentially useful information about whether or not a child is experiencing a learning mismatch at school. Sometimes they're helpful as written, but other times they require a parent to have advanced decoding skills. It's not unusual for parents of gifted learners to see report card comments like, "fails to complete his homework," or "is often disruptive in class," or "spends her time daydreaming." Knowing that the child in question is competent, such comments can signify that they may not be sufficiently challenged by school tasks and would benefit from adaptations to the curriculum.

Teacher-assigned school grades can indicate gifted-level ability, as in the case of students who consistently achieve extremely high marks. However, one problem with using high academic grades in identifying gifted learning needs is that (like grade-level achievement tests) they don't differentiate high achievers working at grade level from children who are working way beyond grade level. It's important, too, to remember that children who already know most of the material being presented in class or who are exceptional in other ways as well as giftedness (such as gifted/ADHD) are often disinterested, bored, or frustrated. As they get older, these students may put less and less effort into their schoolwork. They may not even pass their courses, much less demonstrate gifted-level achievement. We have known many highly gifted learners in middle and high school who received below average or even failing grades. Still others drop out of school entirely, feeling it is just too irrelevant, a total waste of their time.

The use of high academic achievement and high task commitment as criteria for gifted programming can trap students who need to demonstrate motivation in order to have their learning needs met, but who aren't motivated *because* their needs are not being met. (We discuss issues with motivation in Chapter 8.)

Consider the comments of classroom teachers who have argued against gifted programming for some exceptionally able children:

"She doesn't do her schoolwork, or her homework."

"He never pays attention to what we're doing in class."

"She never finishes anything. She'll start a project and then lose interest halfway through."

"He needs to learn good work habits before he goes to a gifted program."

Rather than showing that the child should *not* participate in a gifted program, these comments could reflect a desperate need for gifted educational adaptations. In each of the above cases, for a variety of reasons, we had evidence that the child could pay attention for long periods of time, and had all the necessary skills to work very hard when they were given appropriate intellectual challenges. However, their report card marks and teachers' comments did not reflect this.

Another concern about report cards is that although a grading system does provide a kind of yardstick enabling parents to know how a child is performing at school in comparison to other children (which can be useful), grades can be highly subjective. The underlying message of teachers' comments can be difficult for parents to figure out. And marks are inevitably and directly tied to teacher expectations, which can be quite variable. For example, what exactly is an excellent mark? A? A+? Does a child have to *exceed* grade expectations to earn A or A+? Moreover, many comments are generic, selected by teachers from a list of alternatives they're given to use as written, without changing to fit the child, and that may not reflect what actually needs to be said. School reports, like every other measure, can provide useful information, but have to be interpreted carefully.

The nature of the report card is in flux. Today, most parents have online access to student progress throughout the school year, allowing them to stay informed about their children's work and achievement levels. Some schools use process portfolios in place of report cards. Such portfolios show the learning and efforts of a child over time and don't lend themselves to being ranked or compared because each student is competing against their own past achievement record. A student participates in determining the criteria by which their work is evaluated, and then uses that to reflect on their performance, and how they might improve it. Teacher-documented descriptions of a child's progress through the stages of the learning process usually supplement the portfolio. A teacher can prepare this using notes from discussions with the child, and observations on processes, final products, and celebrations of successes.

While process portfolios can provide a lot of descriptive information, they can be heavily time-consuming for teachers, and can also leave parents blind to problems or challenges their child is experiencing. The most useful and easily understood school reports for parents include some process descriptions, but also some form of ranking or grade allocation. Too many times, we've seen families who'd been receiving report cards with no grades, only positive process comments like, "Wanda is learning to read and write sentences," or "Jonas is learning coping skills for his abundant energy," only to discover much later than would have been ideal that Wanda couldn't read or write, or that Jonas was experiencing behavior problems.[27]

Aptitude Testing

> *"Aptitude implies a readiness to learn or to perform well in a particular situation. This means that the person not only is capable of performing well in the situation, but actually is in tune with it. There is a beneficial match between what the situation demands or makes possible and what the person brings to it."*[28]

Aptitude is a much broader concept than intelligence or ability. It includes extracognitive factors such as motivation, drive, interest, and persistence in a particular domain, as well as the cognitive strengths such as reasoning ability and prior knowledge that are required to succeed in that domain. It also takes into account the context in which learning takes place, including the kind of teaching (instructional or problem-based, emphasis on rote memorization or critical thinking, etc.). "The term aptitude does not refer to a personal characteristic that is independent of context or circumstance. Indeed, *defining the situation or context is part of defining the aptitude.* Changing the learning context changes in small or large measure the personal characteristics that influence success in that context. Aptitude is thus inextricably linked to context."[29]

It's important to include drive, motivation, and persistence, as well as cognitive ability and context when thinking about giftedness. An aptitude perspective is consistent with findings in developmental psychology and cognitive neuroscience that demonstrate the importance of these extracognitive dimensions in the development of high ability.[30] This perspective also aligns with the Optimal Match approach, in putting the emphasis on the attitudes and habits of mind that foster giftedness, rather than on a mysterious inherent superiority that some children have (and others supposedly do not).

An aptitude approach to assessment makes sense for a lot of reasons, including that the variables that predict academic success are the same for children from all families, across race, culture, and socioeconomic status.[31] These variables are domain-specific, and include prior learning and achievement, and ability to reason, as well as determination and engagement. In order to assess students' aptitude for mathematical giftedness, for example, and their need for advanced mathematical programming, the best predictors are mathematics achievement measures (standardized test scores and grades), scores on tests of quantitative reasoning, interest in mathematics, and teachers' ratings of motivation and persistence. This is true whether or not the students fall into one of the under-represented categories (such as Black, Hispanic, low socioeconomic status, English as a second language).

Like the difference between assessments and tests, it's important to distinguish between an aptitude *approach* and an aptitude *test*. We advocate an aptitude approach to assessing giftedness (that is, taking into account the extracognitive and cognitive factors that lead to successful learning outcomes), but not the pencil-and-paper "aptitude tests" that include a mix of reasoning and content mastery test items. These tests are similar in their format and appearance to academic achievement tests and group-administered intelligence tests; they are standardized in administration and scoring; and teachers can both give and score them. However, aptitude tests don't test aptitude in the broad sense of the term, or incorporate meaningfully the defining features of the aptitude approach—domain-specific motivation, drive, engagement, persistence, and context—all of which require different kinds of assessment tools that together go into the multiple measures approach that has become an official standard of practice in the field.[32]

A Synopsis

The following chart provides a synopsis of the benefits and challenges of the various kinds of tests we discuss.

Table 4.1. Synopsis of Assessment Tools

	Benefits	Challenges
Dynamic Assessment	Cyclical; collaborative; responsive; diversity-friendly	Time-intensive; non-systematic; subjective
1. Student portfolios	Cumulative; authentic; purposeful; evolving; student-created	Time intensive; non-systematic; subjective
2. Performance assessment	Supports student engagement; embedded in action	Parent or teacher as architect requires planning and time
3. Day-to-day diagnostics	Heightened attunement to individual learning needs; child-focused; highly individualized; authentic	Time-intensive; non-systematic; subjective
Standardized Tests	Norm-referenced (allows comparisons with others); reliable; objective	May be little or no connection to students' learning context or content; anxiety-inducing
1. Academic achievement	Subject-specific and targeted information for curriculum decision-making (if sufficiently high ceiling)	Test items may not reflect what has actually been taught; no interaction with material or test administrator
2. Intelligence—Group	Cost and time effective; can be useful for screening	No connection to curriculum; no interaction with material or test administrator

	Benefits	**Challenges**
3. Intelligence—Individual	Interactive; opportunity for observations of attitudes and approach to learning; information on reasoning ability is tested separately from content	Questionable utility for academic decision-making; diversity and culture fairness issues; very expensive; tend to be over-weighted in decision-making processes
4. Intelligence—Nonverbal	Appear to be more inclusive and culture-fair than other intelligence tests	Measure spatial reasoning rather than constructs of greatest educational concern (language and quantitative development)
5. Creativity	Affirm that creativity is valued	Not indicative of creative or academic talent or ability
6. Career interest	Starting point for thinking about possible career paths	Need to be combined with guidance; tend to include conventional careers
Other Information Sources	Criterion-referenced; responsive to individual differences and contexts	Unreliable; subjective; compromised comparison across settings
1. Surveys and inventories (for example, attitude, self-concept and orientation to learning)	Provide information on learning preferences, experiences, outlook, interests, and motivators	Static measures of dynamic constructs; limited information; questionable reliability of self-report data
2. School reports	Information on actual school performance and work habits	Subjective; variable in format; variable across teachers and settings

	Benefits	Challenges
3. Aptitude approach (not aptitude *tests*)	Reflects context and extracognitive as well as cognitive factors that lead to successful learning outcomes; multidimensional; includes multiple measures	Similar concerns as with dynamic assessment approaches, because assessing many of same attributes (motivation, persistence, etc.)

We conclude this chapter with a reminder that the real value of test scores is in their interpretation. Only when assessments and test interpretation are conducted with sensitivity to an individual child's particular situation can scores be used intelligently to diagnose an educational mismatch and inform educational decisions.

CHAPTER 5

Mismatch Diagnostics: Labeling Learning Needs, Not People

"By all means, use tests to diagnose what children need to learn, but not simply to label them or to place them into fixed categories."[1]

As much as possible, the Optimal Match approach avoids categorizing some children as gifted (and some therefore as not gifted), and instead focuses on identifying individual children's subject-specific gifted learning needs. Parents and teachers using this model pay attention to what a child already knows, and where they might require differentiation for gifted learning needs, or for learning problems. We call these parents and teachers mismatch diagnosticians, because they're diagnosing mismatches between a child's needs and the academic challenges they're being given.

The Way It Ought to Be: Diagnosing Mismatches

"I'm sure I know more about my daughter than any tester could ever know. Yet it seems to me that schools value 'official test results' more than what parents have to say about their child's abilities."

"Why doesn't someone tell us more about these tests before they give them to us? It would be nice to know what to expect."

When giftedness is understood as exceptional subject-area advancement that requires adaptations to the curriculum at a particular point in time, that means looking for academic mismatches on an ongoing basis. One way to think about it is to focus on finding the "zone of proximal development" (ZPD) for each child, in each subject area. The ZPD is that learning space where an individual's learning experience is both *challenging enough to be interesting* and *familiar enough to be mastered with some help.*[2]

In practical terms, that means finding those children who are working so far above the learning zone within which the teacher is teaching that they're learning little or nothing from the normally assigned activities. When a child's day-to-day learning experiences aren't providing much educational value, then it's time to consider a change. This can be hard to figure out unless you know what to look for, and how to look for it.

For every learner, the best assessment approach occurs in a comfortable place, in a manner that's sensitive to their individual differences and developmental levels. It is an ongoing process, by subject area, clearly integrated with the curriculum.[3] There are clear and measurable educational benefits of assessing students' zones of proximal development in each subject area, and then offering guidance and learning opportunities accordingly. Looked at in this way, the identification process—ongoing diagnostic assessment integrated into the classroom—is formative, practical, and an integral part of the learning process.[4] With this kind of practice, there is a natural match between a student's developmental level and their education, and therefore, in many cases at least, no need for formal labeling as gifted.[5]

In order to diagnose learning mismatches, teachers need to (a) be very familiar with the domain or subject being assessed, (b) have a good understanding of content and procedures across several years' worth of curriculum, and (c) have access to excellent diagnostic measures, or (d) receive support and resources that can provide this kind of knowledge and expertise. Sadly, however, it is too often the case that even when (a), (b), and (c) are in place, teachers are faced with administrative hurdles that make it impossible to implement these policies. We acknowledge that it can be extraordinarily difficult in some settings for a teacher to differentiate for gifted learning needs. At the same time, our experience suggests that there is usually a window of opportunity, something we discuss in Chapter 11 in connection with teacher development.

Typical but Inadequate Identification Processes

"I never perform well on tests. I get nervous and tense, and I have mental blocks, even when I know the stuff being tested."

"We recently moved, and our daughter is no longer eligible for gifted programming That makes no sense! What should we do?"

"Demarco was tested in Grade 6 at his new school, and they want to place him in a gifted program. Did he suddenly become gifted? Now we wonder what educational opportunities he's been missing."

In many jurisdictions, gifted identification procedures take place at one age or grade level for all students. Children who achieve the designated cut-off score become eligible for special programs, and others do not. This one-time-only identification identifies as "permanently gifted" those children who test better than their peers at that point in time. Such snapshot assessments miss all those whose need for advanced programming is not evident at the time of identification for any number of possible reasons, including:

○ domain-specific (rather than global) ability, such as mathematical or linguistic giftedness;

○ maturational differences;

○ poor test-taking skills;

○ test anxiety;

○ learning or attention problems;

○ motivational factors, including a desire not to be identified as gifted;

○ environmental test-taking factors (such as heat, crowding, or noise);

○ personal factors (such as hunger, tiredness, or illness);

○ differences between a child's first language and the language spoken in the assessment;

○ poor personality fit with the test administrator; and

○ cultural differences in answering a stranger's questions, with no apparent goal.

Sometimes cut-off scores or identification methods differ from one school district or jurisdiction to the next, so that children "become" gifted or lose the label as their families move. Losing the label can feel like a serious problem to a child or their parents when it's seen as designating something real and innate (as happens with mystery model thinking). Even within a single jurisdiction, gifted identification practices can change over time, leading to situations in which a child might be moved in or out of program eligibility for political reasons such as changing financial priorities and educational philosophy, as well as other factors that have nothing to do with whether or not the child requires educational differentiation.

Although there is evidence that things are changing,[6] the typical gifted identification process happens once or perhaps twice in a child's schooling and goes something like this:

○ The child takes a preliminary screening test—usually a group-administered cognitive or academic abilities test, or a spatial reasoning test—along with their classmates, most commonly in the third or fourth grade.

○ If the child achieves above a designated score on the screening test (e.g., above the 95th percentile), the next step is usually further testing, often a more complex, individually administered intelligence or cognitive abilities test.

○ If the child achieves the necessary score (usually a standard score of 130 or 135, or above the 98th or 99th percentile), they are usually designated "gifted." Other measures may be included in the determination, such as parent inventories, teacher checklists, creativity tests, etc. In practice, however, these additional measures are rarely used for decision-making or programming purposes, but rather to demonstrate that multiple broad measures have been included in the process, consistent with Public Law 94-142 in the United States, and standards of professional practice.

Following the school's formal identification process, the child has the required "ticket" for admission to enriched academic learning opportunities, whether those opportunities match the child's advanced learning needs or not.

Some schools have an official anti-gifted policy rooted in a well-meaning but misguided belief that *all* children are gifted and that they do not want to show favor to some children over others. Other schools—usually private schools—have the attitude that children's high-level learning needs are met by the excellent education they provide for all their students. In these situations, schools take an explicit or implicit (and often uncompromising) position that they don't need to assess or provide accommodations for gifted learning needs.

In other situations, there's a gifted identification policy and process in place that works against meeting the learning needs of some of the most advanced students.

We include here a true story about a situation that cost a lot of time, dedication, and effort, on the part of the parents and educators involved.

A Gifted Education Tribunal: Logan

Logan had always been fascinated by numbers, shapes, and building activities. Although he was only in Grade 4, his math abilities—both conceptual reasoning and calculation skills—were at the Grade 10 level. His parents were concerned that his learning needs weren't being met at the local public school, but he'd failed to make the 130 IQ gifted programming cut-off score, and so was deemed ineligible for gifted programming. As far as Logan's teacher and principal were concerned, Logan's IQ score meant he wasn't gifted, and therefore he didn't need any kind of gifted education.

The legally-mandated definition of giftedness in the jurisdiction (Ontario, Canada) was (and still is at this writing) "An unusually advanced degree of general intellectual ability that requires differentiated learning experiences of a depth and breadth beyond those normally provided in a regular school program to satisfy the level of educational potential indicated."[7] It was obvious to Logan's parents that he needed differentiated learning experiences, at least in mathematics.

Logan's parents discovered that the official policy on gifted identification[8] required the following:

1. Evidence indicating a student's functioning to be at an advanced academic achievement level (at least two years or two grades higher than chronological age).

2. The possibility of nomination by the child's parent, a peer, or a teacher.

3. Evidence of strengths in areas other than those measured by an IQ score (such as social perceptiveness, or advanced social interaction skills, or athleticism).

4. Demonstrated creativity.

5. Task commitment, as related to persistence in activities or pursuits (academic or otherwise).

Because this policy had not been followed (only one criterion was used for gifted identification in Logan's district, a minimum of 130 on an IQ test), Logan's parents objected. They advocated for Logan's right to suitable programming, and against the use of IQ scores as an exclusionary criterion. The school denied their request, so they hired a lawyer, as well as a gifted education consultant (Dona Matthews), and took their case all the way to a provincial tribunal where a panel of judges listened to both sides of the case.

Logan's advocates argued that, under the law guaranteeing special education adaptations as needed (including giftedness as one of the designated exceptionalities), Logan needed special educational accommodations. They described an approach consistent with the Optimal Match perspective, reflecting current knowledge about intelligence and gifted education, and maintained that Logan needed advanced mathematical learning opportunities to match his highly advanced mathematical ability.

The lawyer argued that, under Ontario special education law, a single test should never be used as the basis for a decision about a child's educational placement and that gifted identification should be a multifaceted process.

The final decision was in Logan's favor. The school board provided a gifted specialist to help the staff at Logan's school design a program that supported his gifted learning needs. They did not want another expensive and embarrassing tribunal, and so embarked on a total revamping of their gifted education policies. Following this tribunal, this school board became one of the most progressive in the province, and a leader in gifted education policies and practices.

Most jurisdictions don't have laws supporting the right to gifted education, or a legally mandated system leading to a tribunal to handle grievances (as in Ontario), but there are usually policies in place that do support children's rights to an education that meets their learning needs. Logan's story encourages our optimism that educational institutions are in the process of becoming less tied to outdated mystery model practices, and more attuned to the needs of individual learners, in ways that are consistent with Optimal Match recommendations.

Labeling

> *"The gifted label that many students still receive, and that their parents relish, may turn some children into students who are overly cautious and challenge-avoidant lest they make mistakes and no longer merit the label."*[9]

> *"Why do I have to be gifted? I was happier when I was normal."*

> *"Am I really different than other kids?"*

The gifted label can cause a child to question their identity and abilities. It can trigger uncomfortable self-awareness or worries that someone has made a mistake about their abilities.

Some children react to the label by working hard to prove their intelligence. Others worry they won't be able to manage the academic expectations associated with being gifted, or that kids will tease or ostracize them. An open, honest, and careful response to your child's questions, made with sensitivity to their level of understanding, can be helpful—even essential—to their healthy self-concept and continued joy in the learning process.

Children are not the only ones who worry about the gifted label. Parents also have concerns:

> *"Does this mean that my daughter is smarter than I am?"*

> *"Now that Jesse is officially gifted, I guess we'll have to sacrifice everything for him, right?"*

> *"I wasn't a good student. The gifted gene must come from my husband's side of the family."*

And here are some comments we've heard from teachers:

"I'm not gifted. The kids in my class are way smarter than me."

"I've two kids in my class who are so smart, it makes me nervous."

"If he's really gifted, he'll do fine without extra consideration from me. I have students who need a lot more help than he does."

Parents' and teachers' self-doubts, questions, and concerns can interfere with their ability to support the children in their lives. Adults should keep in mind that every child is unique and needs help growing into a healthy adolescent, and ultimately into a happily self-sufficient adult. No matter how apparently smart or confident, each child is a child first and foremost, with all the difficulties and anxieties that go with being young, vulnerable, and inexperienced in life. Having gifted learning needs doesn't change that.

In "Rethinking How We Identify Gifted Students," researchers Scott Peters, James Carter, and Jonathan Plucker discuss some of the problems with labels.[10] The authors emphasize that the focus should be on individual learning needs and services, not labels: "The point isn't to identify talented students (stamping them with that label in permanent ink), but to identify talented students in context and to match them with appropriate services that will benefit them in the moment."

Challenging activities that don't require a gifted label are great ways to provide the learning opportunities a child needs without the problems associated with the label.[11] Examples include mentorships, advanced music classes, contests, clubs, and other extracurricular activities. (We discuss many options in Chapters 6 and 7.)

The Label: A Mixed Blessing

Labeling certain children as gifted is troubling for several reasons, including the implication that other children are *not* gifted. At the same time, some school districts make it difficult to build the case that a child requires special academic accommodations unless they're given a label that designates the nature of their special needs. When there is no official label, too often the necessary programming adaptations are just not provided.

All labels carry awkward connotations. Labels designating learning problems have their own issues, but the gifted label is particularly provocative for many parents and educators. It implies that the majority of children (all those who are *not* in the gifted category) lack special abilities or gifts, and so it can evoke negative reactions from peers, teachers, and others. Just as troubling, getting labeled as gifted leads too many children to believe they don't have to work hard at school, or to choose simple courses so they can succeed easily.

Children are often unsure what to expect once they've been given the gifted label. Responses include pride, confusion, embarrassment, excitement, and fear. Many children worry about social implications. Others are apprehensive about academic workloads. Some feel vindicated or relieved to have a "name" for their differentness, yet don't know what to expect going forward. Parents often have similar concerns and uncertainties. Here are some students' points of view:

> *"It's cool to be gifted."*

> *"I don't think like other kids, but I know I'm not 'gifted.'"*

> *"If I hadn't been identified gifted, like my friends, I might have considered drugs."*

> *"I feel embarrassed when people ask if I'm really gifted."*

Now let's consider some parents' views on their child's being identified as gifted:

> *"All I care about is whether or not my son works hard, learns lots, is kind, and happy."*

> *"I was extremely proud of her. I always knew she was special."*

> *"We had a number of questions about the whole testing thing, and no one to put them to."*

> *"I hope the gifted label opens doors in the future."*

Many people think of giftedness as a good thing, such that the gifted label is an enviable achievement. However, giftedness is not an endowment or "gift." Nor does it reflect a once-and-forever quality. Instead, giftedness is fluid and changeable depending on motivation, effort, and opportunities to learn. However, like a beautiful rose with surprisingly sharp thorns, the gifted label can be accompanied by unexpected difficulties.

A parent might have many possible reactions to the label, including worries, questions, confusion, reassurance, expectation, and pride. It's important, however, that they deal sensitively and patiently with their child by listening to and communicating honestly with them. Knowing what the child's concerns might be and how to find appropriate resources can make a big difference in how positive the gifted labeling experience is for a given child.

Most children experience a mix of pluses and minuses to being labeled as gifted, a mix that can change over time with shifting circumstances, opportunities, and maturation. The following benefits came to light in a series of in-depth interviews with children and their families about their reactions to the gifted label and its consequences:

○ validation of abilities

○ reduced boredom and frustration due to programming modifications

○ enhanced learning opportunities

○ bolstered self-confidence

○ a confirmation and affirmation of feelings of differentness

○ opportunities for interaction with intellectual peers

There were also many problems identified by the children and their parents. Here's a sampling:

○ the need to change schools to get gifted programming

○ programming uncertainties

○ controversy about the label

○ unhappiness with the elitism and exclusivity sometimes associated with the label

○ dealing with the stereotypic views that others have of giftedness

○ intensified demands imposed by oneself, or by parents, family members, or teachers

○ inflated self-confidence

○ scorn and/or misunderstanding from peers

○ envy and rejection from old friends

Each child and each situation is unique. In addition to the educational opportunities that can result from the gifted label, a child's personal experience can vary depending on their age, resilience, sensitivity, maturity, social competence, family support, personality, domain(s) and degree of giftedness, siblings who are (or are not) labeled as gifted, attitudes of teachers and peers, and the presence of any other exceptionalities.

Here are some of the troubling experiences the children shared with us, along with examples of their comments:

○ misconceptions about the label: *"Is being gifted like being super smart in everything? I think they made a mistake, because there are LOTS of things I don't know!"*

○ ridicule or lack of support: *"The teacher made fun of me today. She asked the class a question that NOBODY knew, and then she turned to me and said, 'Let's see how gifted you really are. What's the answer to the question?'"*

○ concerns about developmental issues: *"I wonder if I'll outgrow being gifted."*

○ conflicting expectations: *"My teacher says there'll be a lot more work in my new class. My mom says I won't have to worry about it because I'm gifted and I can handle it. But I AM worried."*

○ confusion about roles and responsibilities: *"I bet I'm going to have to give talks to the whole class and lead study groups. I won't be able to do that!"*

○ fears that the test scores were wrong, that they're not really gifted, or that they won't be able to measure up in the gifted class: *"I think they messed up when they scored my tests. I won't be able to keep up with all those smart kids!"*

Although there are certainly cases where children and their parents believe that the gifted label is essential for the child to find a good educational fit, in general it's best if a child can be in a challenging learning environment that matches their learning needs without the gifted label. The label's meaning and value reside only in its practical consequences. It should be pursued or accepted only when it's required for entry to the educational programming a child needs in order to keep learning appropriately.

A simple and effective alternative to the practice of labeling students that emerges out of the Optimal Match approach, and that is consistent with current best practice in special education, is to label educational services instead of students. This involves offering a variety and range of options to those who are interested in and capable of taking advantage of them.[12]

Parents and Children Need to Know What's Happening and Why

"Now what?"

For some parents and teachers, a child's identification as gifted suggests strengths and abilities that are beyond the child's actual competence, leading to unreasonable expectations or responsibilities. Adults can prevent possible future problems if they are attuned to the child's actual strengths, as well as their challenges, and if they remain sensitive to the child's needs and feelings about labeling and program experiences.

Children benefit from being informed about their learning strengths and challenges so they can enjoy developing their exceptional abilities, and strengthening their areas of weakness.

Here's a conversation between a mother, who has just found out that her daughter has been identified as gifted, and her nine-year-old daughter.

A Conversation about the Gifted Label: Amber and Gennifer

"So, Amber, what did you think of that test you took a while back?"

"Do you mean the gifted test?"

"Yes, the intelligence test."

"It was fun. I liked doing the block patterns. Did you get the scores yet?"

"Yes. That's why I was asking you about it."

"SO…HOW DID I DO? MOM!!! DID I PASS?"

"You did very well, Amber, but it isn't a test that you pass or fail. It helps with educational planning. In fact, the school is suggesting that you might like to go into the gifted program."

"WOW! Wow. Oh. Wow. That is actually sorta scary. I don't know if I want to."

"Okay. Let's talk about it later with your dad. We don't have to decide right now. We can think about it for a couple of weeks and chat about the pluses and minuses."

"I don't want to leave Jessica and Lynn's class. Are they gifted too?"

"I don't know. Maybe we should make a chart with all the positives and negatives, and also any questions you might want to investigate."

"Does that mean I'm smarter than the other kids?"

"No, not really. It does mean that you can solve puzzles and figure things out, and that you have the brainpower you need to do lots of wonderful learning. All kids have things they're good at, and things they're not so good at, and you happen to be good at the kind of thinking that that test measures."

For several reasons, this is an encouraging way to tell a child they've been identified as having gifted learning needs. Amber's mother, Gennifer, is low-key. She's not too enthusiastic nor does she push one attitude or another. Rather, she allows Amber to think about her own questions and concerns. Gennifer listens to Amber's questions, and then reassures her that they can work together to address them carefully and patiently. This kind of dialogue helps Amber understand what the test scores and any other gifted assessment indicators do and do not mean. The high scores indicate that she is particularly competent at certain kinds of intellectual tasks that help her do well at school, but they don't mean that she's superior to other kids in all things.

Here's another conversation between a mother and her son.

A Conversation about the *Not*-Gifted Label: Matt and Michaela

"So, Matt, what did you think of that test you did a while back?"

"Do you mean the gifted test?"

"Yes, the intelligence test."

"It was fun. I liked answering all those questions. Do you have the scores yet?"

"Yes. That's why I was asking you about it."

"SO…HOW DID I DO? DID I PASS?"

"You did very well, Matt. You scored higher than most kids your age."

"But did I pass? Am I gifted?"

"It's not a test that you can pass or fail. You definitely did great in a lot of areas, but overall, you didn't quite make the score for the gifted class. That does NOT mean that you aren't very capable, only that there were some things you didn't do quite as well as you'd have to do to get that label."

"I failed it."

"No, Matt. You did NOT fail that test—not at all! Let's take a look at the scores, and I'll show you where you did really well, and where you didn't do so well. Actually, there were no bad areas, and there were some amazingly good areas. Look how well you did on the verbal reasoning area: 98th percentile!"

"What does that mean?"

"What do you think it means?"

"Maybe I'm good at figuring things out with words?"

"Sounds like it. And 98th percentile means that you did better than 98% of kids your age on that part of the test."

"Verbal reasoning is pretty important if I want to be a lawyer, isn't it?"

"My guess is that it's pretty important in practically everything. Definitely including practicing law."

"So maybe I didn't do so bad after all."

"Exactly. These scores show that there are some areas you're especially good at. For example, solving puzzles and problems, and you have the brainpower you need to learn in lots of areas. All kids have areas they're strong in and some they're not so strong in, and you happen to be good at many things that this kind of test measures."

"Yeah. Yeah. But I'm not gifted."

"You're great at all sorts of things that are *not* on that test—you're a dynamite hockey player, a fabulous big brother, a caring friend to a lot of people, and you play the piano beautifully. If there were scores for those things, I think you would have been through the roof on all of them!"

"Maybe. But I'm not gifted."

"You're gifted in stuff that matters a lot more than what that test measures."

"Oh, Mom."

There are many things to note in this conversation that make it an effective way to talk with a child about not making the gifted cut. As with the previous example, the mother—Michaela—has parked her own emotional responses off to one side, understanding that Matt needs to process this news for himself, and that her emotions (one way or the other) will only get in the way of that. She is available and responsive but she does not express her own disappointment, if that's how she feels. As with the previous example, she helps her son see what the scores do and do not mean. She emphasizes his strengths, as well as the fact that people vary in how well they do on tests like this.

Unfortunately, many schools don't tell children and parents very much about the test results or their implications, let alone how to make sense of the news.

Everyone benefits when policies and procedures are widely and easily available in parent-friendly terms, as well as kid-friendly terms. Most parents find it helpful when schools hold information sessions so they can ask questions about gifted education, including testing and programming processes. When a teacher, principal, or school psychologist is readily available to discuss parents' and children's concerns, there is considerably less speculation, misinformation, and misunderstanding.

There are also other benefits when schools make gifted education information more accessible. As teachers become more familiar with the principles and practices of an Optimal Match approach, and think collectively about how to implement them, they become more attuned to and supportive of children's needs for differentiated education. Many schools find it useful to open up their gifted education practices for school-wide discussion. They notice positive changes not only for gifted education, but also in the overall learning climate for every student.

New Directions vs Entrenched Ways

"Historically, many schools have failed to provide advanced opportunities for most students who need them. However, past failures need not predict the future. Schools can help all students meet their potential, but only if they commit to taking proactive steps to seek out students who need greater challenge right now, in a specific subject area, because they are performing ahead of the instruction their school provides."[13]

There are indications that identification practices are becoming more aligned with the Optimal Match approach. In a recent comprehensive study of gifted education practices in two states, researchers found that educators were "aligning identification and programming practices to meet the needs of gifted students identified in mathematics and/or reading/English language arts."[14] We don't yet know how widespread such policies are, but we are encouraged to see movement in this direction.

Another indication of progress toward an Optimal Match approach is that more assessment processes are using multiple sources of information.[15] This allows for assessment processes that take into account the facts that (a) intelligence is domain-specific, and *not* best represented by composite test scores such as IQ; (b) giftedness is dynamic, not a static attribute of a person; and (c) for educational programming to match a child's real learning needs, a range of individual, contextual, and developmental issues must be considered.

On the downside, however, the current reality is that gifted identification is often a one-time-only test. This should NOT be the case. As children mature, there should be regular (perhaps yearly) re-evaluations of their emerging abilities,[16] as well as opportunities for children to be evaluated at any other time if teachers or parents notice something that might warrant it.

Although ongoing assessment is an important part of program standards and recommended practices, unfortunately it is rarely implemented in any real way in typical gifted education identification practices. Instead, once a child is labeled gifted, they're usually considered to *be* gifted for the rest of their school career, unless serious problems develop in their grades or behavior (which may then threaten programming eligibility, not necessarily the label itself). And, in situations where a child doesn't meet the gifted criteria at the time of initial testing, they're unlikely to have any gifted learning needs considered in subsequent years unless the parents take action, such as seeking professional testing outside of the school system.

Thus, many gifted learners are lost in the very identification system that is supposed to discover them, and it can be difficult for them to get the educational adaptations they require. School districts that do offer ongoing testing and assessment opportunities are better positioned to identify high-ability learners, including those who are later in maturing or who don't test well at earlier stages.

Diagnostic Emphasis

Because the identification process should be used to assess individual children's learning needs or degree of educational mismatch, it should be seen as diagnostic—that is, test data should be used to find children's areas of weakness, as well as areas of exceptional strength, for purposes of specifying adaptations to programming. It is unusual, however, to find school-based gifted identification practices that are, in fact, diagnostic. More often, the assessment for school-based gifted identification provides a summary report consisting of scores or ranges of scores. This is accompanied by a simple statement about whether or not the child has met the gifted criteria. and therefore "is" or "is not" gifted, which perpetuates the "one size fits all" Mystery Model approach. This is in sharp contrast to the Optimal Match focus on understanding an individual child's areas of strength and challenge, and then matching the curriculum and other learning opportunities accordingly.[17]

As the paradigm continues to shift, however, more educators are arguing that it is programming that should be labeled gifted (or challenging, or advanced) rather than individual children.[18] When there is a range of learning options available (including many kinds of acceleration, enrichment, and extracurricular learning) which allows educators to match an individual to a learning option at a particular point in time, the need to label children as gifted disappears.

Early Identification

> *"Our 22-month-old daughter is advanced for her age. Her vocabulary is amazing, and she prefers to associate with older kids. But the daycare teachers won't place her in a group with older children. Should I have her tested?"*

Although one of the most contentious areas in gifted education concerns early identification, there is very little research on this topic.[19] Even in jurisdictions with gifted identification policies and practices, such policies often do not come into play until third or fourth grade. Although many children come to school having mastered basic literacy and numeracy skills quite well, and may appear to need gifted programming as early as four or five years of age, there are other skills that are at least as important to their future success. Prior to age eight or nine, much of the learning going on in children's lives concerns their physical, social, and emotional development. Research on high-level development emphasizes that for most children who go on to exceptionally high-level achievement and healthy adult lives, those early years of learning are better characterized as play than as work.

Another important concern about early identification is the high degree of developmental variability and the low reliability of test scores before age seven.[20] When a gifted labeling process is begun too early, children are at risk of being inappropriately placed in a program where they may have trouble keeping up with the learning of the other students: "The majority of primary-level children who obtain high scores on an ability or achievement test generally do not retain their status for more than a year or two. Each year, new children excel. Others whose accomplishments were unusual at one age may show less precocity a year later."[21]

From this perspective, parents who are anxious that their young child could be learning more are not necessarily doing them a favor by advocating for gifted identification. As long as the child is not actively unhappy in the regular classroom, a parent's energies might be better spent ensuring they have extracurricular and other activities that engage their enthusiasm for learning, including lots of opportunities for spontaneous unstructured play, creative expression, and exploration.

There are some young children however, who, because of their advanced ability in combination with their temperament, find it difficult to handle a regular classroom and curriculum. Some are impatient with or feel insulted by a teacher's insistence on their doing work they find too easy. If, for example, a child is already reading at a level markedly higher than other children in the class, a solution might be to provide single-subject acceleration or enrichment through more materials at the child's level of interest and challenge, without changing anything else. In other situations, it can be beneficial to accelerate the child to a higher grade, which we discuss in Chapter 7.

Despite widespread notions to the contrary, the research is strongly supportive of the benefits of early entrance to school or whole-grade skipping, in some cases, for certain children.[22]

For most children, however, the research on high-level achievement shows that when parenting or working with young children, what is most important is listening and responding sensitively to the child.[23] Play is an essential ingredient, and much more likely to lead to giftedness than forced application to academic tasks like reading or arithmetic.

Parents' Roles

"What parents typically know about their children is worth a thousand standardized tests. Parents are constantly observing their children under a variety of changing conditions and over a period of years. Testers, on the other hand, see kids in only one setting: the school."[24]

Children display their learning progress and the richness of their individual growth experiences in different ways, many of them not at school. Parents who work collaboratively with their child's teachers can help them identify learning needs, and even become involved in planning appropriate programs and instructional strategies. Parents can also assist in assessment processes. Many abilities and accomplishments can be demonstrated through non-testing assessment approaches that provide valuable information about a child's learning.[25] We offer the following suggestions for parents:

○ Encourage your child's teacher to use a variety of evaluation methods besides tests—methods that reflect day-to-day diagnostics and that provide information about your child's grasp of subject matter including where they may need help. (Examples include portfolios, checklists of skills, conferencing records, and work samples.)

○ Keep a record of your child's learning activities outside of school, and share your concise observations with educational professionals.

○ Create a scrapbook or home-based portfolio of photos, paintings, written material, tape-recordings, etc. that illustrate your child's abilities in different areas and at different ages. Include videotaped or otherwise documented special events, presentations, demonstrations of effort and persistence, and learning outcomes.

○ Encourage your child to become involved in self-assessment; that is, to keep a record of their learning experiences and personal accomplishments that can be shared with teachers. This is also a useful strategy to help your child develop self-confidence, solid work and organizational habits, and self-reflection skills.

Recognize that some educational environments are toxic for certain kids, and such situations can only be fixed by finding an alternative placement. Assessment information—whether it's collected at home or at school—is useful only if interpreted and used intelligently. This means matching learning opportunities to an individual's level of readiness and ability on a subject-by-subject basis.

We discuss how to do that in Section III.

Section III
Being Smart About Meeting Gifted Learning Needs

CHAPTER 6

Differentiation: Meeting Gifted Learning Needs in the Regular Classroom

"All I want is an education, and I am afraid of no one."

Every child we've ever known wants to learn. They yearn to be engaged, and to have their time in school feel useful and relevant. Not all of them are as fearless as Malala Yousafzai, whose words appear above, but all of them share that hunger for real learning. Each child arrives at school with their own unique learning needs, and those who arrive already knowing big chunks of the curriculum won't be doing much learning without some kind of change to what's normally taught, or how it's taught.

Many advanced learning needs can be met by a homeschooling parent or in a regular classroom by a teacher who is well-trained and well-supported in working with exceptionally capable learners.[1] Because children with gifted learning needs are diverse in their abilities, interests, attitudes, and backgrounds, the "best approach" can vary from one child to another, and from one context to another. Meeting diverse learning needs involves ongoing assessment,[2] and providing a range of different learning options.

At face value, providing diverse gifted learning opportunities, whether at home or in the regular classroom, may sound too simplistic, too complicated, or too idealistic, even though these options are more powerful and closer to possibility than many people realize. We recognize that most teachers have neither the training nor the support they need to bring this into reality, except maybe on a limited basis or from time to time. However, we have seen schools make it happen as required, and we know it can work brilliantly, with benefits for all kids, as well as teachers.

The first step to providing diverse and meaningful learning experiences in the regular classroom is an attitude shift, a realization of what giftedness really is, and what it isn't (which we address in Section I). The next step is understanding how best to assess gifted learning needs (Section II). Now, in Section III, we ask, "What educational options can meet gifted learning needs?" We consider how to use these various options to support high-level development on an as-needed and ongoing basis, in ways that are consistent with the Optimal Match perspective.

A Wide Range of Learning Options

> *"It is often said that in an ideal world, special education, including gifted education, would not be necessary, because curricula would be sufficiently responsive to individual differences to make separating children into exceptionality categories unnecessary."*[3]

Before outlining what a wide range of learning options might include, we define some of the basic concepts involved for those who aim to provide an effective education for children with gifted learning needs.

NAGC 2019 Programming Standards

The National Association for Gifted Children has formulated programming standards that focus on six specific areas, with separate frameworks detailing best practices and student outcomes for each.[4] Here are their brief descriptions of what each area embodies:

1. *Learning and Development*: "Educators understand the variations in learning and development in cognitive, affective, and psychosocial areas between and among individuals with gifts and talents, creating learning environments that encourage awareness and understanding of interest, strengths, and needs; cognitive growth, social and emotional, and psychosocial skill development in school, home, and community settings."

2. *Assessment*: "Assessments provide information about identification and learning progress for students with gifts and talents."

3. *Curriculum Planning and Instruction*: "Educators apply evidence-based models of curriculum and instruction related to students with gifts and talents and respond to their needs by planning, selecting, adapting, and creating curriculum that is responsive to diversity. Educators use a repertoire of instructional strategies to ensure specific student outcomes and measurable growth."

4. *Learning Environments*: "Learning environments foster a love for learning, personal and social responsibility, multicultural competence, and interpersonal and technical communication skills for leadership to ensure specific student outcomes."

5. *Programming*: "Educators use evidence-based practices to promote (a) the cognitive, social-emotional, and psychosocial skill development of students with gifts and talents and (b) programming that meets their interests, strengths, and needs. Educators make use of expertise systematically and collaboratively to develop, implement, manage, and evaluate services

for students with a variety of gifts and talents to ensure specific student outcomes."

6. *Professional Learning*: "All educators (administrators, teachers, counselors, and other instructional support staff) build their knowledge and skills…to ensure quality professional learning experiences in pre-service, initial, and advanced educator preparation programs."[5]

The NAGC programming standards are thoroughly consistent with the Optimal Match approach, and provide a good foundation for the practical applications we discuss in this section of *Being Smart*. In this chapter, we discuss classroom-based differentiation to meet gifted learning needs. In Chapter 7, we extend the range of options, some of which take the child out of the regular classroom full time or part time.

Differentiation

"Even though students in a classroom may be chronologically the same age, one-size-fits-all instruction will inevitably sag or pinch as surely as single-size clothing would. Acknowledging that students learn on different timetables, and that they differ widely in their ability to think abstractly or understand abstract ideas, is no different than acknowledging that students at any given age aren't all the same height. It is not a statement of worth but of reality."[6]

Parents who understand the basic principles of differentiation, as well as some of the options available for creating an optimal learner-learning match, are able to support their children's education. As described by the NAGC programming standards, learning options for gifted learners should be developed, adapted, modified, or replaced as required. Instructions should be flexible and suitably paced, allowing for accelerated learning opportunities that are fitting and fair.[7] Teachers should be supported in having access to a continuum of curriculum options, instructional approaches, and resource material.

Classroom-based differentiation capitalizes on all of this, and it can be transformative.

"Differentiation" is a term used to describe the proactive and fluid process of matching educational expectations to individual students' learning needs. In its application to giftedness, it's about challenging advanced learners appropriately. In its application to prevailing concerns about learning loss or deviation due to the pandemic, it provides a way to help children catch up in areas that have not been sufficiently supported, and/or extend those interests that have been newly ignited.

Educators wanting to differentiate their teaching to meet diverse learning needs can think about this process on different levels. For example, working with *curriculum planning* (think big-scale and broad–based, over several weeks or months), suitable modifications might entail

○ Removing unnecessary or repetitive chunks of content,

○ Enhancing existing units of study by reorganizing or intensifying content, or

○ Connecting a unit of study to other subject areas or disciplines.

Working with the *program* (think smaller scale, more focused, such as daily instruction within a classroom), teachers might adopt one or more of these ideas:

○ Using flexible grouping practices, based on students' strengths, interests, and weaknesses;

○ Increasing breadth (more choices, learning style variations); and

○ Increasing depth (different levels of content for different ability levels).

All of these approaches come under the heading *differentiation*. When differentiating experiences for diverse learning levels, these practices can and should be combined. "Differentiation is not something to do from time to time—it is a way of thinking and should pervade what a teacher does in the classroom."[8] From looking at curriculum development, to adapting daily lesson plans, the teacher's goal in differentiation is to engage students fully in their own learning, as much as possible at their individual ability levels.[9]

An inclusive classroom is one where the teacher differentiates effectively for every learner. It is a welcoming and opportunity-rich environment, one where diversity is respected, where the teacher responds to the needs of individual students by offering instructional supports, and where students are systematically encouraged to master their individual learning objectives. An inclusive classroom not only keeps advanced students engaged, but it can also meet the needs of students with various kinds of learning challenges.

Most simply, differentiation can be thought of as ways of altering students' learning environment, process, product, or content. But that's certainly not all it entails. Carol Ann Tomlinson, an expert on differentiation, offers these principles of a differentiated classroom:[10]

1. Learning experiences are based on diagnoses of a student's readiness, interest, and/or learning profile.

2. Content, activities, and products are developed in response to the varying needs of learners.

3. Teaching and learning are focused on key concepts, understandings, and skills.

4. All students participate in respectful and engaging work.

5. Teachers and students work together to ensure continual engagement and challenge for each learner.

6. The teacher coordinates use of time, space, and activities.

7. Flexible grouping ensures consistently fluid working arrangements, including whole class learning, pairs, triads and quads, student-selected groups, teacher-selected groups, and random groups.

8. Time use is flexible in response to student needs.

9. A variety of management strategies (such as learning centers, independent study, collegial partnerships, tiered assignments,

learning buddies, etc.) is used to help target instruction to student needs.

10. Clearly established individual and group criteria provide guidance toward success.

11. Students are assessed in a variety of ways appropriate to demonstrate their own thought and growth.

It makes sense to think about differentiation as a good way to implement an Optimal Match approach. Some basic principles for successful differentiation:

○ Assessment data should reflect the nature and needs of the child.

○ The program should match what the assessment results indicate.

○ The teacher should have the necessary support in order to implement that match.

○ Students' and teachers' expectations should align so the child can succeed.

○ And, helping parents understand what's happening with their child's learning reinforces their ability to encourage and support the child's educational journeys and outcomes.

Ideally, a differentiated curriculum satisfies each of these requirements. Knowing how this works gives you an important tool in advocating for your child: "Remember, no one knows your child as well as you do. Advocating for their academic needs to be met is not pushing or demanding, it is a reasonable expectation."[11] (We discuss advocacy in Chapter 11.)

In fact, many gifted learning needs can be met with adaptations to the basic instructional program, working from a child's placement in an age-appropriate regular classroom. This approach has some obvious advantages, such as preventing problems associated with labeling and elitism, and allowing for more teacher creativity. And, perhaps most importantly, this approach allows teachers to respond to changes in a child's development and circumstances; their learning preferences and personal interests; their choices; and their engagement in the learning process.

Optimal Match in Practice in the Regular Classroom

"Have you ever spent time in a classroom? Do you have any idea how hard it is? I have kids coming to school in the morning without breakfast. They can barely function. Now you're also expecting me to think about providing a smorgasbord of possibilities for the extra bright ones?!?"

"I can't do everything! It's enough just to keep on top of the mandated curriculum and all of the paperwork. I cannot individualize a program for every child in my class!"

On their first encounter with differentiation principles, teachers sometimes express concern, dismay, dismissal, or even anger. We often hear comments like the ones above that focus on the real and difficult challenges that teaching presents, without adding differentiation to the burden. We're not suggesting that teachers provide an individualized version of every lesson, targeted especially to each child's developmental level. As teachers ourselves, we fully appreciate the impossibility of that demand. However, we also know from our professional experience that a differentiated approach can go a long way toward matching exceptional students' learning needs, while simultaneously easing the teacher's burden, not increasing it.

We've observed and experienced how differentiation can enliven the learning process for teachers as well as students. Effective differentiation is built on and enhances solid teaching practices. Of course, it requires training and support, including time, tools, and professional development. We discuss that in Chapter 11, but we consider foundations of best practice here.

In every classroom, there are certain principles of best practice that encourage high-level learning outcomes. We characterize these as the five R's of teaching to support gifted development: being *resourceful, reasonable, receptive* to changes, *respectful* of students' feelings and abilities, and *responsive* to their questions. The best activities are designed or adapted for children's learning interests and levels of readiness.

Whether teaching preschool or graduate school, developmentally delayed, learning disabled, exceptionally advanced students, or students with multiple exceptionalities, teachers working within the Optimal Match framework are sensitive to their students' individual levels of subject-specific competence, at a given point in time.

1. Effective teachers co-create with their students clear expectations and goals, aligned with children's areas of strength and weakness in different domains.

2. Effective teachers open channels of communication, and enable them to stay open, by listening; showing a willingness to entertain creative and sophisticated ideas; and encouraging growth in reading, writing, and the use of technology.

3. Effective teachers network with other teachers, become familiar with available support services, tap into a wide range of community resources and learning provisions, and seek information about gifted education from multiple sources.

4. Effective teachers strengthen children's learning spirit by being proactive, motivating, supportive, nurturing, well-informed, and attentive to diversity in all its forms.

Those four points all reflect an Optimal Match approach, and here are fourteen options for supporting the development of giftedness.

Choice

> *"Our limit should be the world. But then again, it should be the stars!"*
>
> *"The strongest principle of growth lies in the human choice."*[12]

Perhaps our single most important recommendation for the regular classroom is that educators provide as wide a range of learning options as possible. Although the highly visible gifted programs (pull-out or self-contained) are often the ones that parents want, and that educators think of as the gold standard, the less visible differentiation that happens in the regular classroom can often be more powerful and effective, given that it incorporates flexible pacing, choice, and continuous progress.

Thanks to current technology, classroom walls are no longer constraining. Students can take part in online math, science, and language arts programs offered at facilities around the world, such as the Weizmann Institute in Israel, the Virtual School for the Gifted based in Australia, and NASA Aerospace and Science Programs in Florida. We know adolescents who have networked and participated in summer learning programs in Greece (archaeology), in the United Kingdom (English literature), in Italy (art), in Costa Rica (biology), and elsewhere. Many of these programs are affiliated with universities.

These online programs can be great ways to learn, and to acquire academic credits. When educators and parents work together to take advantage of what's new, accessible, and interesting, they greatly increase the likelihood of keeping students engaged. The supplementary learning activities we propose in this chapter are only a sampling; there really are no limits to the possibilities.

As teachers come to understand giftedness, matching, and differentiation, and acquire the tools they need to provide a range of curriculum options and choices, they are usually surprised to find (after the initial learning investment) that their workload decreases. Like their students, they usually enjoy school more.

Curriculum Compacting

> *"Students can 'recycle' their time for enriched or accelerated learning...Always allow students to capitalize on their strengths through activities that extend their exceptional abilities."[13]*

Advanced learners can often master the important facts, concepts, and skills of a given curriculum unit with a minimum of instruction and practice. The practice of carefully assessing a student's subject-area mastery, and then condensing curriculum areas so that they can be covered more quickly, is called curriculum compacting. For example, a child who has high proficiency in a unit of mathematics can demonstrate a solid grasp of the necessary principles and skills by answering a few representative questions, and have extra time they can invest more happily and productively elsewhere.

Shortening the amount of time needed to cover a section of curriculum accomplishes several objectives:

○ It reduces the boredom of unnecessary repetition for students who have already mastered the concepts and related skills.

○ It frees up time and energy that can be directed toward other interests and more relevant learning outcomes.

○ It allows children an opportunity to delve further into the material and thereby intensify their content mastery.

Curriculum compacting shows respect for students' prior learning, and is a prerequisite for many of the other strategies we describe that adapt basic instruction to gifted learners' needs, without radically changing programs or schools. It must be done with care, however, so that important foundational skills are not omitted from the child's program, and so they don't feel rushed in their learning. Several steps are required for successful implementation of curriculum compacting:[14]

○ Identify the essential learning outcomes of a particular unit of study.

○ Develop a pre-test to assess how much of the essential learning the student has already mastered. Pre-tests can be informal or formal, varying from a discussion with the child about what they already know, all the way to a score on a standardized test.

○ Establish the criteria that will be used to designate mastery of the essential outcomes. That is, should the child know 85% of the required material? Maybe 75% is enough? Or perhaps 95%? Make plans for using the time that's gained by compacting or eliminating the already-mastered material.

And this is where the other instructional options and strategies come in.

Project-Based Learning (Sometimes Called Problem-Based Learning)

"A key to successful project-based learning is to give students a choice in the area in which they would like to work."[15]

Many learners enjoy opportunities to explore their own interests, or are keen to pursue challenges somewhat independently of normal classroom constraints. Project-based learning, or PBL, can be done individually or in a group, and is focused on a target product (the project). The value of project-based learning is enhanced when the area of exploration—or the problem—is relevant, when tasks are varied, there are self-directed and collaborative experiences, and there is opportunity for some kind of end product or completion. Modification of PBL for gifted learners might involve advanced content, multi-disciplinary connections, and more complex concepts. Teachers can encourage students' use of high-level reasoning skills, reflective habits of mind, and grappling with conflicting ethical issues.[16]

Children's motivation in the learning process is greatly enhanced when their activities have real-world relevance, as they can do with PBL. This learning option is designed to engage students, to give them a sense of ownership, and to broaden and deepen their knowledge base. The process begins with identifying a problem or question that motivates them to work at solving the problem or answering the question. This might involve developing critical and other higher order thinking skills, including predicting, designing experiments, researching, managing data, drawing conclusions, and reporting. Learning might culminate with the creation of artifacts or products that address the initial problem or question.

Project-based learning can be used in any subject area. For example, it can incorporate scientific methods and concepts (involving, for example, a consideration of purpose, hypotheses, methods, observations, conclusions, and implications), which makes it an excellent way to teach science topics in a meaningful and engaging manner.

Simulations are a form of PBL. Students interact with one another in a situation that replicates reality and promotes skill-building, with help from the teacher.[17] Examples include planning a children's playground, or role-playing confrontational situations that require conflict resolution, or solving community-based issues. There are many intriguing game-based simulations available online.[18]

Experiences that simulate real-life circumstances or engage children in a thought-provoking study of issues have benefits for diverse learners, including but not restricted to those with gifted learning needs. However, sometimes teachers assign a project, and expect the student to do it whether or not they're interested, or to pursue it to completion without any further guidance. The learning outcomes in situations like this are typically unsatisfactory. To be worthwhile, project-based learning should be chosen by the student, challenging, and enjoyable, and accompanied by ongoing monitoring, scaffolding, and guidance.

Portfolio assessment is a great way to assess project-based learning because it is process-oriented, and it encourages children to build ongoing connections across their learning, rather than focusing exclusively on the end product. The process of developing a portfolio that records their progress helps students become organized, reflective, and explicit about what they're learning. They can showcase their efforts, engage their creativity, and use a variety of expressive and illustrative means to record and chart information (such as conferences with the teacher, interviews, and any resource material they've gathered). Portfolios have the advantage of being flexible in design and orientation, and can be used in a variety of learning situations, including guided independent study, which we discuss next.

Guided Independent Study

> *"I love school because work is fun; it's fun because I learn new things!"*

> *"Diversity: the art of thinking independently together."*[19]

Guided independent study is an umbrella term, often used to describe project-based learning, as well as other activities in which students identify and explore interests beyond the regular curriculum, while working somewhat independently of a teacher. Examples include learning a foreign language or a new computer program, or studying environmental issues or local history. Guided independent study goes best when a teacher, parent, or mentor is actively involved with the student in devising and monitoring the study, providing ongoing constructive feedback.

Although a given learner may be able to work at an advanced level and produce complex products, they might not have the skills necessary to successfully complete an independent study project. They might need to learn some research skills, like identifying good questions for investigation or selecting interview subjects; or they might need help with technology or synthesizing their findings. The teacher, parent, or mentor can provide the necessary help along the way to support the student in meeting their own learning goals.

The independent study process should be based on a framework that reflects the child's interests, background, and skills. Independent studies are used by many homeschoolers.

Implementation steps might look like this:

○ *Introduction.* Define the process and describe a plan for managing it, including a proposed timeline for completion; the target audience; and an evaluation framework.

○ *Topic selection process.* Consider a school or community problem the child wants to solve, an issue to debate, a perspective to prove, a new activity to try, or something unusual, useful, or exciting the child wants to learn more about.

○ *Organization.* Map out the project; determine how to gather information; and look at logistics such as comparisons, and causes and effects.

○ *Inquiry.* Develop and ask good study questions of varying levels of complexity.

○ *Study method selection.* Consider an experimental, descriptive, or action research approach; use of primary and secondary sources; and methods to ascertain authenticity.

○ *Information-gathering.* Investigate as appropriate and as related to the study questions, including observing, reading, interviewing, hands-on activities, surveys, brainstorming ideas, using online sources, doing experiments, or going on a field trip.

○ *Product development.* Create a report, song, diagram, diorama, video, interview, game, poster board, debate, collage, dramatization, poem, graph, speech, model, computer program, or something else entirely.

○ *Information-sharing.* Communicate for improvement, support, and evaluation purposes; the sharing process should be planned out, practised, and delivered.

○ *Evaluation.* Base this on what the child has learned, using both formative (process oriented) and summative (product oriented) methods.

Assessment of an independent study project should be ongoing and flexible, and it can be informal. Ideally, it occurs before, during, and after the learning activities, for the purpose of modifying the process and for extending the child's inquiry and development experiences. "Formative assessment with appropriate feedback is the most powerful moderator in the enhancement of achievement."[20] Information acquired from children about their progress can motivate future learning, and help teachers strengthen learning initiatives.

Many parents and teachers think that guided independent study is for older students only, but even for younger children, it can be an exciting way to learn, provided there is sufficient guidance. A resource teacher or librarian can provide additional assistance as children pursue topics and engage in various research and thinking activities.

Reading

> *"Effective educators acknowledge the importance of literary rich environments for young learners. Ready access to books and other print materials and accessible writing materials for composition give students a learning advantage."[21]*

Reading can provide an endless source of intellectual and creative stimulation for people of all ages and should be encouraged (and modeled) whenever possible.[22] Books can nurture, enrich, inform, stimulate, and soothe. They can be used as a basis for sharing, thinking, learning, dreaming, inspiring, and exploring.

According to current understandings of teaching, learning, and brain development,[23] there are numerous reasons why reading is beneficial:

○ stimulates reflection and high-level thinking

○ increases engagement in relevant, self-directed learning

○ broadens and extends children's knowledge and understandings

○ contributes to a feeling of connection to different communities and cultures

○ alleviates loneliness, especially for children who feel different or experience social isolation

○ offers an escape from stressful or troubling circumstances

○ inspires and motivates

○ provides models for experiences in various circumstances and contexts

○ stimulates thinking about values and life choices

○ provides relaxation

○ expands vocabularies

Through reading, children can develop and extend their studies and interests. As children get older, more of their learning is presented in written format, until they reach graduate school, where most academic programs are reading-intensive.

A final word for avid readers: librarians know a lot about books and where to find good ones. Librarians are usually pleased to offer suggestions on topics kids are curious to know more about, and to discuss new books, classics, and the varied resources on the shelves or in digital archives. For children engaged in independent study, and others, this can be especially helpful.

It should be noted, however, that (as with independent study) reading isn't a replacement for what goes on in the classroom. Rather, it can be an excellent choice within a range of options for enriching children's learning in personally relevant and purposeful ways.

Cross-Grade Resources: What Are the Possibilities?

"No-one, no matter how advanced or independent, lives in a vacuum, and everyone, regardless of age, can benefit from supportive others... Those who reach out to others and embrace life collectively become enriched through experience."[24]

Gifted programming options can often be discovered by thinking creatively, considering the diversity of locally available teachers, classes, materials, and students at different levels, from pre-school through college. For example, a ninth-grade student, gifted in language arts and a keen writer, might find their learning needs met by meeting once a week with an interested English teacher who sets up a workshop for serious writers across several grade levels. The creative stimulation, support, and discourse, combined with writing time allocated to substitute for attending regular English classes, may accelerate their interest in writing and learning about writing. Or, a fourth-grade student who is outstanding in both math and science might be introduced to advanced algebra by a math teacher in the nearby middle school. If the student has a particular interest in, say, lab experiments, they could work with a middle school or high school science teacher, setting up and conducting research.

There are innumerable similar possibilities, each of which is embedded in the local context. These options cost little more than creative flexibility on the part of educators and parents, who can start by identifying the individual's learning interests and needs, and then ask the question, "What provisions might be available in our local environment that will help meet those needs?"

This is a "What are the possibilities?" approach. The best gifted programming often emerges serendipitously from parents and educators working together creatively, and staying open to opportunities for collaborative solutions.

Single-Subject Enrichment

> *"Sometimes a task that lacks challenge for some learners is frustratingly complex for others... Teachers who differentiate understand the need to help students develop agency as learners... In a differentiated classroom, it's necessary for learners to be active in making and evaluating decisions that benefit their growth."*[25]

Parents and teachers often think that a child with gifted learning needs requires advanced level instruction in all subject areas. Sometimes that is the case, but other times, focusing on just one subject area at a time can be the best way to foster a child's love of learning and meaningful engagement with school. Single-subject enrichment can be implemented within the classroom, or on a pull-out basis. It can be coordinated by the classroom teacher, a resource person, or a parent.

Here's a story from Nanci Wax Pearl, a teacher who participated in one of our professional development sessions:

A Teacher's Plan for an Enriched Math Group

I selected a small group of students on the basis of their math proficiency to participate in an enriched math program. They'd worked together in the classroom on a variety of different math activities designed to extend the regular fifth-grade curriculum so they were eager to participate. They were open to ideas and investigations, and their parents were supportive and happy that I was establishing this enrichment option.

The concept has been working, but I want to refine the process. I realize that some of these students have exceptional ability in one area but not others, even within math. For example, some show tremendous proficiency in number sense and numeration, but not in geometry. Then, within number sense and numeration, they might demonstrate strong computation skills, but struggle conceptually with fractions and percentages.

I've learned several things that I will apply to future implementations of enrichment grouping. 1) I have to keep the group of more able learners open to constant change in order to accommodate individual strengths and weaknesses. 2) The block of time I set aside has to be flexible. 3) I need a more specific set of criteria to show which students might benefit from enrichment grouping in particular units of study because I want to choose the right students without leaving anyone out. 4) I have to strive for better communication with the parent body as a whole about the program.

Single-subject enrichment makes excellent sense for a child who has one or two areas of exceptional advancement, and is closer to average, or below average, in other areas. It can give them a sense of engagement in in-depth learning that carries over to enthusiasm for school more generally.

Single-Subject Acceleration

Acceleration is a topic we discuss at greater length in Chapter 7, but we introduce single-subject acceleration here, because it can often be done within a regular classroom. The following story is an example of how it can work.

Accelerating Ben

Ben was assessed in fourth grade. He scored in the gifted range (above the 99th percentile) on the Wechsler Intelligence Scale for Children, and in the highly gifted range mathematically, operating at the tenth-grade level (six grades above his own) on tests of math reasoning.

Although he was eligible for the gifted program at the local public school, his parents decided to send him to the nearby private school that his two siblings attended. There wasn't a gifted program at that school, and no accommodations were made for his exceptional ability. Things went along pretty happily for him until the end of sixth grade, when he began to be described by his teachers as a behavior problem. His parents and teachers were concerned and arranged for an updated assessment during the summer, with a follow-up meeting to be held early in the next school year.

In early October of Ben's Grade 7 year, a team meeting was held that included the school principal, Ben's parents, his homeroom teacher, and a gifted consultant hired by the parents, along with Ben himself for the first part of the meeting. By then, the behavior concerns were getting worse, and Ben's teacher described his attitude as disruptive in class.

The team members listened thoughtfully to Ben's concerns, suggestions, and opinions, and promised to discuss any plans with him. In subject areas other than math, his teachers agreed to enrich and extend the curriculum and assignments for him, as well as for a small group of other highly capable seventh graders. However, Ben's mathematical ability and interests were so advanced that they knew they would need something else for him in that subject. His impatient personality meant he was at serious risk of dropping math altogether if he didn't feel he was progressing as fast as he wanted without wasting his time.

On the recommendation of the gifted consultant, Ben was allowed to take the seventh-grade end-of-year math exam to demonstrate his competence. Because he did well (the criterion was set at 85%), he was excused from attending all seventh-grade math classes. Instead, Ben was provided with a combination of independent study and some tutoring, to work his way through the eighth-grade math curriculum, and he was encouraged to participate in regional and national math competitions as well. He was excused from classwork that provided no real learning for him and that he found deadly boring. He could finish the eighth-grade math curriculum at his own pace, free to move to higher-level or enriched mathematical work as he wished.

The math teacher who tutored Ben spent a couple of hours a week mentoring Ben's progress to ensure he understood the material. For a time, Ben thought he'd been given a "spare" for math class, and he let his classmates know what a good time he was having while they were working furiously. However, after his parents told him they could withdraw the privilege, the taunting stopped. Before long, Ben moved from being noticeably bored and unhappy at school, and causing trouble there and at home, to being happy and keen. He felt respected and committed himself to making the single-subject acceleration program successful.

Postscript on Ben

Ben went to a competitive high school where he continued to accelerate mathematically, and he learned to thrive on challenge. He attended university, and completed a double major in math and music. Another interesting outcome: after seeing Ben's success, the schools he attended made similar accommodations for other exceptionally capable learners, and became known as excellent schools for high-ability students.

Optimally, an elementary or middle school will have enough flexibility and a strong enough relationship with a local high school or community college that arrangements can be made to grant high school credit for courses that a highly competent student completes ahead of time. The student may need an advocate to negotiate on their behalf. As the student gets older, they might be helped to find advanced placement courses and other university-connected high-level options that will allow them to continue to pursue subject-specific learning interests at their own pace. School administrators typically have to be on board with that.

With mathematically gifted learners, subject-specific acceleration is particularly important for a number of reasons. First, the subject itself tends to build more sequentially than most other curriculum areas. It's harder with math than with other subjects to create enrichments that do not also move beyond the child's age/grade level. Second, there is solid research evidence supporting this approach, grounded in the widely renowned Study of Mathematically Precocious Youth (SMPY) conducted over the course of several decades.[26] Third, most important breakthroughs in the field of mathematics are made by individuals in their twenties. For students who are truly gifted in mathematics, appropriate early acceleration is necessary for them to build the foundation of skills and knowledge they will need to make their contribution to the field while still young.

Flexible Grouping

"The greater the commitment to serving gifted students, the greater the acceptance of advancing and grouping them appropriately."[27]

Flexible grouping refers to the practice of having children work in groups for different purposes, and in different subject areas. It might be for part of a school day or for particular classes. The purpose is to foster children's learning, while encouraging them to build community and learn from one another.

Grouping might be based on students' individual strengths, interests, learning preferences, or needs (academic, social, emotional, behavioral, or motivational). Group composition is often determined by a teacher's perception of what is fair and most suitable. Thus, gifted learners may be grouped with others who are similarly advanced, or not. Groups may be fluid; that is, they could change depending on how tasks match with each members' subject-specific needs, so that grouping and regrouping might occur as deemed appropriate by the teacher (or students). There is also the option of enabling students to self-select their groups.

It's important for groups to have clear goals, a collaborative spirit, and learning activities that align with children's development levels. Within groups, no two students will be alike. They may be risk aversive, innovative, extroverted, or enthusiastic. They will have different skill sets, talents, content knowledge, dispositions, feelings, and expectations. Part of the learning process involves building the skills required to work with diverse others, and then succeed.

A responsive learning environment is one that encourages collaboration. Here are several tips for successful flexible grouping:

○ Ensure enough space for children to move about and comfortably engage in activities together.

○ An open-ended approach allows students to contribute information and ideas in various yet meaningful ways.

○ Social skills should be taught, modeled, and reinforced by the teacher.

○ Different groups may choose to focus on different activities, with a range of resources, study methods, complexity level, and end-products.

○ Groups might be composed of students across grade levels or combinations of in-class and online members (for instance, homeschoolers, or students in other schools or different countries).

○ Consider group size. It should be manageable, perhaps three or five members. (Decision-making tends to be more effective when groups consist of an odd number of people.)

○ Some children prefer working in groups, while others prefer independent learning. A way for a child to ease into group work might be to start with a partner, or to independently complete a portion of a group task, and then bring it to the others for discussion and input on a final product.

Keys to any group endeavor include flexibility, choice, patience, and appropriate challenge. This should be combined with thoughtful planning, preparation, and monitoring on the part of a teacher who recognizes and appreciates children's areas of strength and weakness, blends personalities thoughtfully, promotes cohesion, and encourages discovery.

Career Exploration Built into the Curriculum

"When we travel as a family, I take my kids to explore the local university campus. They've seen Fashion Institute of Technology, University of Toronto, Bowdoin College, University of Iowa, McGill, and others. It helps them keep their eye on intellectual places beyond high school, reminds them that school is a long process and, through university catalogues, exposes them to non-typical fields of study."

"Last fall, a lady from the Humane Society came to school and described how they look after the animals. I've been volunteering there twice a month ever since. I want to become a veterinarian."

"A forensic diver described his underwater diving job. It was awesome!"

As kids discover and develop their interests and strengths, they benefit from support in investigating career opportunities. Students with exceptional ability should be encouraged to explore a wide range of possibilities, including unconventional ones. This should begin early in their education to increase the likelihood of their choosing the appropriate high school or elective courses and, in some cases, prevent them from dropping out of school.

Students who have talents in many areas need adult help prioritizing their interests and activities, and examining possibilities for combining two or more of these—for example, studying bioengineering as a way of melding strong interests in both math and science, or medical engineering for combining medical research, math, and science. Students can read about the lived experiences of different medical professionals, such as surgical technologist, paramedic, clinical psychologist, veterinarian, emergency medical technician, and others who have chosen exciting vocations.[28] Material such as this can inspire and inform kids about requirements, specialty areas, research options, and help with decision-making processes. Teachers can also discuss the value of subjects like computing science, the kinds of careers that are open to individuals with these skills, and areas that might be closed to those without such skills.

Another reason to encourage career exploration in exceptionally capable learners is to support their understanding of the relevance of schooling. Interest in a possible career path can promote academic engagement, making learning feel meaningful and worthwhile. Sometimes people can endure high school better when they see that it can take them to a better place.

Students with diverse exceptional abilities can derive great value from learning about wide-ranging and atypical career possibilities. The learning can take various forms, both in the classroom and outside of it. Ideas that work well include the following:

○ Career days, where representatives from various occupations talk with students and answer questions

○ A career resource center located in the school library or elsewhere, where students can acquire information and discuss ideas with others

○ Student visits to career sites, including job shadowing

○ Career exploration options infused into course work

○ Internships, mentorships, co-op placements, and other opportunities for authentic exploration

○ Informal chats with people engaged in diverse kinds of pursuits

○ Skills-based personal growth plans, designed in consultation with guidance counselors, parents, mentors, or teachers

○ Critical analysis of occupation-related media stereotypes built into curriculum

○ Simulations and role-playing

○ Biographies of eminent people in different career paths

You can encourage your child or teenager to participate in these kinds of activities, and think with them about other ways to learn about career options and pathways they find appealing.

Leadership Opportunities

> *"Leadership often takes active shape by the time young people reach adolescence... The roots of leadership are being nurtured during this formative time, through a young person's relationships and life experiences."*[29]

Greta Thunberg is a teenage activist who set out to make a difference. In her efforts to address climate change, she has galvanized people all across the globe, not only increasing awareness about critical issues threatening the planet but helping to establish action-oriented plans as well. Thunberg said, "You are never too small to make a difference." Her motivating story continues to be shared in classrooms, over dinner tables, and among millions of children and teens. Anyone can engage in efforts that contribute to the greater good or take a leadership role in facilitating positive change. It might have to do with homelessness, cyber bullying, social reform, or other pressing concerns. Children are raised differently, and have different experiential backgrounds.

We started this chapter with a quote from Malala Yousafzai, teenage winner of the Nobel Peace Prize, who was determined to acquire an education, despite serious obstacles, including having her life threatened. Her fervent energy and courage set a remarkable example and, as a result, countless young girls have had opportunities to learn—opportunities that they would otherwise not have had. Yousafzai has said, "One child, one teacher, one book, one pen, can make a difference."

Children and teens who have areas of high-level ability, and are willing to exercise hard work, persistence, and passion, are well positioned to become leaders. They can also inspire others to set meaningful goals, take on leadership roles, spearhead change, solve problems, and experience personal and collective triumph.

Parents and teachers can help kids commit to whatever causes inspire them, encouraging them to gain voice and vigor, to use their strengths, and to take on increasing responsibility. Marilyn Price-Mitchell refers to young leaders as "tomorrow's changemakers." She emphasizes the importance of reinforcing core attributes that can empower kids to become caring, strong, and successful. Adults can teach children about empathy, resourcefulness, resilience and more.

Here are two examples of children who have been supported in making a powerful impact.

Examples of Youth Leadership

When Jahkil Naeem Jackson was eight years old, he founded a non-profit organization called "Project I Am" to help feed the hungry.[30] He is now 13, and he and his family have created and distributed tens of thousands of care packages ("blessings bags") to homeless people around the world. He is also a motivational speaker "on a mission to influence kids around the country to get involved in their communities."

Meagan Warren was reading by the age of two, and she loves books. In 2014, when she was eleven years old, she created the non-profit organization "Books for Bedtime"[31] with the support of her grandparents. The goal: "To give as many books as possible, to as many children as possible, in as many places as possible." As of February, 2021, 101,129 books have been donated to children in need.

Theologian Albert Schweitzer said, "Example is leadership." Children on every continent are demonstrating how to raise consciousness and lead the way. At home and school, the adults in their lives can help them continue to do just that. (We discuss this further in Chapter 12.)

Peer Coaching

"I believe that the best way to learn is to teach."

"Peer coaching gives my gifted learners a chance to see how other children think. It should make them grateful that learning comes so easily to them, rather than resentful that they have to do it."

Sometimes, and in some settings, a peer coaching experience can consolidate a student's' knowledge, encourage high-level discourse, and support the development of both intellectual and social skills. Working together with others in a group of mixed strengths can encourage respect for diverse kinds of ability and facilitate the development of alternative skills.

Often, however, when teachers without gifted education training are faced with an advanced-level learner in a regular classroom, they ask that student to work with someone who is having difficulty. These teachers think they are not only giving better learning opportunities to the child who is behind in their work, but they are also providing the gifted student with an opportunity to develop social and communication skills.

As might be expected though, if the gifted learner is neither a natural teacher nor unusually altruistic, or if peer coaching is used too frequently, the student becomes a resentful teacher's helper. When this happens, the peer coach may come to think of the responsibilities as an irritating annoyance. Many advanced learners are unable to explain to someone else how they "get it" when completing some tasks—they just do. There is also a risk that the coach will end up completing the work rather than going to the trouble of guiding someone who is having a hard time getting through something that seems easy and obvious to the peer coach. Nobody gains when that happens.

Alternatively, the student who is asked too frequently to be a peer tutor may identify with the teaching role and take that as an unexamined career path, coming to see the helper/mentor role as their place. They may learn to downplay or even hide their advanced abilities out of sensitivity to others. Worse still, working with struggling students may reinforce concerns they might have about being abnormal.

For peer coaching to work well, each participant must be gaining something from the activity, and must perceive that that's the case. The teacher should have private preliminary discussions with each prospective participant to ascertain their interest in participating, what the responsibilities, obligations, and benefits are, and what the teacher's role will be. It's essential, too, to discuss procedural basics such as how to respond in various situations, how to recognize when the peer teaching is not working, and what to do if that occurs. In some jurisdictions, students can receive course credit for doing peer tutoring under a teacher's guidance, which can help make it worthwhile to the tutor. Peer coaches in such settings can function like a teaching assistant by planning, helping with some administrative duties, preparing materials, and working one-to-one monitoring seat work.

As with all of the strategies we discuss here, and perhaps even more so with this one, peer coaching must be undertaken carefully and appropriately, with the teacher available to step in quickly if requested. Peer coaching must be tailored to individual learning needs and to the personality profiles of the students involved, as well as to the learning objectives of the task. When conditions and supports are in place to ensure that it works for everyone concerned, peer coaching can satisfy some gifted educational needs.

Online Learning

"Every learner can, at his or her own choice of time and place, access a world of multimedia material…Immediately the learner is unlocked from the shackles of fixed and rigid schedules, from physical limitations…and is released into an information world which reacts to his or her own pace of learning."[32]

"We will not march back to what was, but move to what shall be."[33]

"What shall be" cannot be known in all its detail, but there is little doubt that the future of education includes technological know-how. Increasingly, different learning styles, curriculum requirements, and educational objectives can be met online by anyone at any time. Kids can navigate discussion threads, gain access to far-ranging resources, and supplement material that's being covered in class, deepening and broadening their knowledge and understandings. Students can join global communities of learners, communities without borders.

Online learning options include interactive educational activities, software programs, web-forums, courses, collaborative groups, and networks. Children can become facilitators, or work independently, all at a pace that works for them. Computer-based options can be exciting supplements to classroom instruction, extra-curricular activities, or homeschooling, by enabling children to explore their interests, seek answers to their questions, develop new understandings, or motivate one another across cultures, age, time, and space.

In some cases, online learning opportunities can replace in-class learning—even more so since the onset of the COVID pandemic. Hybrid programs (mixes of online and in-class instruction) have also become increasingly common.

Online activities have some serious risks, in addition to their benefits. Not every child has access to high-speed connections, or even a computer. Parents and teachers should discuss their concerns from the beginning, along with working together with the child to establish rules, limits, and monitoring guidelines. Online discussions can be a great enrichment for a child, but they shouldn't replace real-time face-to-face interactions. Children need to be taught about online etiquette, including what plagiarism is, why it's wrong, and what the consequences are for doing it. Kids need to learn how to distinguish good sources from questionable ones, and be given guidance about establishing the credibility of online sources.

Parents and teachers should also consider the broader picture relating to children's online activities, including secure computer outreach, and safe digital practices. Although technology can serve us well, there are serious issues regarding intrusions on privacy, excessive and meandering use, and cyberbullying. (We discuss other computer-related concerns, including cyberbullying, in Chapter 9.) Children require guidance about how to use hardware, software, apps, platforms, and social media responsibly. They also have to learn self-discipline. "With appropriate thoughtfulness—dispassionately identifying the undesirable elements of technology and championing its advantages—our choices can lead to positive outcomes and mitigate the negative ones."[34] Goals for students include meaningful engagement, digital skill-building, and increased knowledge and networks.

Most schools offer families membership in a dedicated webforum where they can see online resources, information, and notices about their child and school activities. Posts might include educational resources, technical support, library catalogues, study skills and tips, classroom agendas, a virtual reference desk, web-adventure-learning experiences, instructions for building web pages, and more. We are witnessing a quickly growing range of innovative learning and teaching possibilities. Online venues can provide powerful options for developing new practices and relationships, and for contributing to children's advanced learning needs on an increasingly expansive scale.

Learning about the Brain

> *"Human neurodiversity is like the spectrum of light, each of us illuminating at our own wavelength, with some of us even in the UV range. …Neuroscience studies show that no two brains are alike, and each brain has a distinctive signature, like a fingerprint[35]."*

Exceptionally capable learners—like others—are intrigued by questions such as: What does my brain look like? How are synapses and neural pathways formed? What is neural plasticity? How does the brain respond to different emotions and activities? How does the body respond to different kinds of brain activity?

Parents and teachers can explain some of the brain's inner workings, differentiating in accordance with children's levels of interest and comprehension. They might describe how certain regions are more involved in attention, music, or language; or how greater processing speed or quicker reaction time reflects increased neural efficiency, because of better coordinated neural networks.

Most children are fascinated to learn that at its peak the brain has 100 billion neurons, and can process 1000 signals per second per neuron, with a total brain capacity of 100 trillion basic operations per second. Mind boggling! Students can find out about executive functioning, and learn how using skills like organizing, prioritizing, planning, and self-monitoring builds a more efficient brain. The value of learning becomes clear when young people come to understand that the more associations they consolidate, the more they learn. All children benefit from knowing the importance of brain health, and that the brain is influenced by factors such as physical well-being, nutrition, rest, sensory stimulation, and emotional nurturing.

Encourage your child or adolescent to learn about their brain and increase their brain power with these suggestions:

○ Practice high-level thinking skills such as analysing, interpreting, elaborating, applying, and synthesizing newly acquired information in conceptual frameworks.

○ Draw connections across different people, subject areas, and interests.

○ Reinforce a growth mindset, helping your child realize that their intelligence develops over time, with effort and opportunities to learn.[36]

○ Ensure that learning is engaging, and that it fosters your child's curiosity and creativity.

○ Seek multisensory experiences.

○ Balance social/emotional and intellectual activities. A stimulating conversation, a walk in nature, an informative book—a balance of different activities and experiences keeps the brain fresh and engaged.

○ Get creative. Ask your child to think about imagery to illustrate the workings of the brain, such as spaghetti mazes, intricate highways, or electronic circuitry. Neuroscientist Nicole Tetreault uses this analogy: "Brains have their own unique lands of Oz, crisscrossed with distinct yellow brick roads....As parents and educators, we have the power to directly impact the roadways in our children's brains."[37]

○ Discuss processes like consolidating information; different kinds of memory (relational, working, short-, and long-term); and detecting patterns.

○ Encourage open-ended problems with many possible responses; manipulation or structuring of objects; chess; classification of data; orienteering; graphing or concept mapping; analysing information for conflicting aspects; or complex word analysis.

Children can learn about cognitive diversity and how to actively control and build their own intelligence, at home and at school. For kids who are exceptionally capable in one or more areas, knowledge about how the brain works helps them put their exceptionality into a healthy perspective.

Systems of Differentiation

"Identifying students' specific academic needs only adds value if schools actually do something with that information, providing each student with an appropriate course of study that offers the right level of challenge. Because learners—including gifted learners—are diverse, no single instructional model will serve everyone."[38]

There are several systems for differentiating curriculum that can help parents and teachers extend children's learning opportunities in ways consistent with the Optimal Match perspective. Each of these systems provides a framework for differentiating programming to meet gifted learning needs, and to expand the range of learning options in a given classroom or school. A school that wants to go slowly into gifted education can make a good start by implementing just one of the 14 options described in the previous section, "Optimal Match in Practice in the Regular Classroom." An educator who is ready to differentiate for gifted learners and who wants to consider a more systematic approach may be interested in learning about and adapting one of these systems.

We review briefly here three different systems. Each one offers flexibility, is evidence-based, and respects that abilities develop over time across intelligences and talent areas. Each also has a strong track record of effectiveness.

The Schoolwide Enrichment Model—SEM

A longstanding and much-used approach to differentiation is the Schoolwide Enrichment Model (SEM). First proposed by Joseph Renzulli, the SEM is a continuum of enrichment services. On the basis of a comprehensive assessment process (that can include achievement tests, parent and teacher nominations, student-created talent portfolios, and other measures), teachers make decisions about who might benefit, and proceed to next steps with curriculum compacting and differentiated enrichment experiences. Students are encouraged to engage in activities at one of three different levels: Type I, general exploratory experiences; Type II, group learning and training activities; and Type III, individual and small-group investigations of real-world problems.[39]

In this model, under-challenged students are given targeted enrichment opportunities, and various areas of giftedness and talent development are addressed. Learning involves academics, but also music, art, drama, leadership, social service, interpersonal skills, creative writing, and more.

SEM offers enriched learning experiences and higher learning standards for *all* students, and its objectives are threefold: 1) to develop children's talents, 2) to provide a broad range of enrichment experiences, and 3) to provide advanced follow-up opportunities based on children's areas of strength and weakness. SEM has an impact on the regular curriculum through *compacting* (content modification), *in-depth learning* (content intensification), and *enrichment* which is integrated into regular curriculum activities so as to build upon students' abilities that are above and beyond the norm.

Information on SEM is readily available,[40] including online at the Renzulli Center for Creativity, Gifted Education, and Talent Development.[41] There are plentiful resources, videos, and presentations, and scores of articles addressing SEM particulars such as planning and implementation, research and evaluation, subject-specific topics, and more.

The Integrated Curriculum Model—ICM

For the past several years, Joyce Van Tassel-Baska and her colleagues at the Center for Gifted Education at the College of William and Mary have investigated ways to integrate differentiated learning experiences into the regular curriculum, so that gifted learners receive the accommodations that they require, while systematically mastering the regular curriculum in alignment with educational standards.[42] An important contribution of this research group is the development of an integrated curriculum model for gifted learners. They have developed flexible approaches to enrichment and acceleration, as well as comprehensive field-tested curriculum resources across subject areas and grade levels.[43]

The Integrated Curriculum Model is based on differences in children's learning rates, problem-finding and problem-solving abilities, and their capacity to manipulate abstract ideas and make connections. The role of the teacher is to accommodate individual differences by increasing or loosening the planned learning experiences, thereby meeting children's diverse needs.

The Integrated Curriculum Model is focused on three distinct but overlapping dimensions: a) *Advanced Content*; b) *Process/Product*; and c) *Overarching Concepts/Themes/Issues*. When blended together they provide a coherent and balanced approach comprised of meaningful clusters of activities designed to complement what a regular educational program might be offering gifted learners—a program that may otherwise be insufficient or inappropriate for their needs.

The strategies employed by the teacher are the "instructional glue" that holds the ICM approach together. Areas of importance include (but are not confined to) opportunities for individual and group learning; problem finding and solving; critical thinking; creative thinking; information-gathering and application; and assessment based on determined goals and purposes. The ICM is a fusion of sorts. It works across all subject areas, emphasizes intra- and interdisciplinary connections, is appropriately challenging, and is predicated on student engagement in authentic and active learning.

For example, in a recent school-wide intervention designed to change teachers' perceptions about giftedness in low-income learners, a team of researchers used the ICM to help teachers in a Title 1 school differentiate for their students in Kindergarten through Grade 5. After two years, the teachers understood high-level curricula and instruction, saw their students as more talented, and gave them more appropriately challenging work.[44]

The ICM's design restructures the curriculum for gifted and other learners by differentiating content, process, and conceptual bases, and by offering enriching challenges. There are many online resources that describe aspects of the ICM in greater detail.[45]

The Parallel Curriculum Model—PCM

Developed by Carol Ann Tomlinson and colleagues, the Parallel Curriculum Model layers four curriculum areas: core, connections, practice, and identity. [46] Tasks, lessons, and units of study revolve around these four parallel layers that can be used singly or be combined by blending and modifying them in accordance with learners' needs.

The Parallel Curriculum Model is subtitled "Design to Develop Learner Potential and Challenge Advanced Learners," and that is precisely what the PCM strives to do. The underlying premise of "ascending intellectual demand" rests on enhancing the incremental stages of advancement from novice through to expert in a particular domain, by scaffolding tasks and content toward higher levels of difficulty, while focusing on students' abilities, interests, and preferences.

The core curriculum of a particular subject or grade (the first parallel) is the basis for the other three parallels. The curriculum of connections supports students in exploring relationships between and among disciplines of knowledge. The curriculum of practice promotes applications for learning, including authentic problem-solving, skill-building, and grouping. The curriculum of identity encourages students to reflect, and to develop understandings of how a discipline is personally relevant. PCM support material encourages online presentations, distance learning, discussion forums, and other forms of expression.

All elements of the multifaceted PCM are matched to individual students' needs over the course of their learning, helping them embrace challenge, and appreciate the importance of collaboration, effort, and their own place in the world.

Optimal Differentiation: Tying the Ideas Together

> *"For decades, gifted educators have noted the need for differentiated instruction in recognition of the fact that students enter the classroom with different levels of knowledge and skill, different past experiences, different goals, and different learning modality preferences. This recognition has been an advocacy success for the field of gifted education, as the concept of differentiated instruction has been widely embraced in both special and general education, although implementation remains spotty at best."[47]*

For parents or teachers who want to reflect further on evidence-based possibilities for supporting giftedness, we conclude this chapter with a foundational framework that reflects a multi-tiered way to think about appropriately differentiated instruction. The focus is on flexibly connecting four cornerstones of teaching that are consistent with the Optimal Match approach: planning, meaningful assessment, activities, and motivating learning environment. Here are key aspects of each:

○ *Planning* involves looking at objectives (the teacher's and/or parent's, and the student's); cultivating supports (such as administrative, consultative, and technical); developing, sourcing, and sharing resources; and becoming familiar with solid educational practices, such as those we describe throughout *Being Smart* and elsewhere.[48] This also includes engaging children in the planning process themselves.

○ *Meaningful assessment* can be woven into your child's learning experiences to ensure a steady increase in challenge levels. This includes identifying their areas of strength and weakness on an ongoing basis; enabling your child to ask questions about the assessment process, and what they're learning, thinking, still have to learn, and why; encouraging them to evaluate their own progress; and seeing setbacks as stepping-stones for further learning.

○ *Activities* include all of the approaches and possibilities for exploration and learning described throughout this section, as well as anything else that interests your child. Activities can incorporate a wide range of options that align with the child's knowledge, talent areas, learning preferences, and interests.

○ *Motivating learning environments* are friendly, accepting, and collegial, welcoming every kind of diversity. Once your child's abilities and challenges are known, learning processes can build from there by way of multiple teaching strategies, flexible grouping, technological means, and clear criteria for learning outcomes.

By flexibly bringing together the elements in this foundational framework, there are no limits to strengthening differentiated experiences and learning engagement. You can help your child plan goals, stay on track, pursue their passions, seek resources, and reflect upon never-ending possibilities for growth across domains. You can also support teachers by advocating for educational policies and professional development opportunities that support the development of giftedness and differentiated leaning opportunities.

Some circumstances call for system-wide applications, and others would benefit from one or more of the many classroom-based differentiation approaches we review within this chapter. Still other circumstances require moving beyond the general education classroom altogether. The boundaries between the various possibilities for gifted learners are not distinct, and implementing one approach almost always means incorporating important aspects of one or more of the others. The wider the range of learning opportunities available, the more likely you are to find a meaningful educational match for your child.

CHAPTER 7

Other Options: Stretching The Boundaries

"Educators should keep in mind that to create an equitable education, they don't have to teach all students the same way on the same day, any more than providing equitable medical care means writing the same prescription for every patient."[1]

Although many gifted educational needs can be met in a regular classroom by a teacher who is well-trained in working with gifted learners, sometimes children require alternative options which may take the child out of the regular classroom. These approaches include acceleration, full-time and part-time gifted programs, second language immersion and dual track programs, specialty subject focus, specialized and alternative schools, private schools, and home schooling. They also include early entrance to college, extracurricular possibilities, mentorships, and more.

We've seen how a little creativity and a resourceful attitude can stretch a child's learning boundaries and lead to other exciting opportunities for high-level learning outside the more conventional approaches to schooling. In fact, sometimes all that's required to meet the gifted learning needs of a particular child at a given point in time is for a parent, teacher, or the child to take a curious look around, and see what's out there waiting to be explored. And, sometimes the best course of action is to combine or reimagine educational alternatives. We offer several different ideas to consider.

Acceleration

> *"Whole-grade acceleration is the practice commonly known as grade-skipping…A decision to whole-grade accelerate a student is one of the more difficult and controversial issues that educators and parents encounter…However, a great many gifted and talented children clearly need additional educational challenge that can only be obtained by allowing them to advance at least one grade, sometimes two or more."*[2]

> *"What on earth were they thinking when they decided to skip Jon? He may be smart, but his behavior is completely inappropriate, and the other kids in my class don't like him. His social maturity is WAY behind his intellect."*

Acceleration enables advanced learners to move through school more quickly than usual. Some people perceive it as rushing childhood, potentially leading to gaps in knowledge, and forfeiting the benefits of interactions with age-peers. On the other hand, though, the research evidence on acceleration is strongly positive. When important factors are taken into account—such as a child's readiness and willingness to accelerate, their level of advancement in subject-specific areas, and the necessary planning and support from parents, teachers, and administrators—then acceleration can work well and merits careful consideration for those who are significantly ahead of their grade-peers.

There are many forms of acceleration, including advancing by one or more full grades, or in a single subject area; entering higher-level courses earlier than usual; telescoping grades (as when a child completes three grades in two years); and mentorships. In order to make wise decisions about which option might be most suitable in a given situation, teachers and parents need to consider not only the learning needs of the child, but also the potential social ramifications, and the emotional aspects of tackling advanced-level challenges.

Is Acceleration Right for Your Child?

"I don't like to hear the word 'skipping' used to refer to moving children ahead in school. It sounds frivolous, when in fact it's a serious decision for parents and children."

How do you know if your child is a suitable candidate for acceleration? Here are some fundamental points to consider:

○ Extent of the advancement in specific subject areas

○ Child's motivation, feelings about accelerating, and maturity level

○ Attitude of the receiving teacher; their willingness and ability to support the process

○ Child's social-emotional adjustment history, including a consideration of other changes happening in their life, resiliency, and overall health

○ Timing (a natural transition juncture is preferable, such as the beginning of a school year, or entry into a new school)

○ Curriculum flexibility and attitudes toward acceleration within the school, district, or board

○ Opportunities for collaboration with teachers, parents, and other stakeholders, in the decision-making and change processes

○ Accessibility of counselling and psychological supports

The *Iowa Acceleration Scale 3rd Edition,*[3] is a research-based guide for educators and parents that facilitates systematic analysis of the pros and cons of acceleration for an individual student. Targeted to children in kindergarten through Grade 8, the IAS includes case study examples and descriptions of key elements for decision-making. It emphasizes the importance of discussion, planning, and continued monitoring.

Over the past several years there has been much discussion and research on acceleration, including practical issues, best practices, and process monitoring both during and following grade-skips.[4] When done thoughtfully, and with attention to children's physical, social, and emotional development, in addition to their academic levels, acceleration can be an effective way to provide a match for a child's learning needs.

In *A Nation Deceived: How Schools Hold Back America's Brightest Students,*[5] the authors explained why many educators and parents rejected the idea of acceleration, in spite of fifty years of evidence that supported it. Based on their research, they cited the following reasons for the negative attitudes toward accelerating kids:

○ lack of familiarity with the research;

○ the belief that it's better for children to spend time with their age peers than with older kids;

○ the idea that acceleration "hurries" children;

○ political concerns about equity; and

○ a concern that other students and their parents could be offended if one or more students are accelerated.

Other potential concerns included putting children at risk of social isolation or rejection, or alternatively at risk of conforming to more mature social norms than they're ready for (such as moving into dating behavior before being emotionally mature). And, when whole-grade acceleration hasn't been well-planned or well-chosen, children are at risk of failing to thrive at the advanced grade level, resulting in a previously successful student experiencing a sense of failure. Although educational placement decisions are not irrevocable, and a child can go back to their original class where the teacher can try another approach, this can undermine the child's self-confidence and self-concept.

A Nation Deceived[6] generated lively discussion about acceleration processes, policies, and beliefs, and provided the education community with a comprehensive perspective on what acceleration entails, its effectiveness, and why it should be seriously considered as one option in a range of options for advanced learners.[7] Subsequently, *A Nation Empowered: A Ten-Year Follow-up to the Important Nation Deceived Report* was published in 2015.[8] Interestingly, the subtitle is *Evidence*

Trumps the Excuses Holding Back America's Brightest Students, which sums up the gist of this report. It is informative, debunks myths and misconceptions, and includes an extensive resource list, all of which is accessible online.

Acceleration: Cost-Benefit Analysis and Strategies

> *"The goal of acceleration is to position the student where there is appropriate challenge on what is being learned with the possibility of enhancing the student's work ethic and reducing the time necessary for traditional schooling... This means that the student is not wasting time with curriculum already mastered, and supports moving toward arenas with more satisfying and long-term academic involvement."*

There has been a substantial increase in the number of children who are accelerating, as well as greater acceptance of acceleration practices across North America and elsewhere. The heightened awareness draws attention to the need for more research, policy initiatives, and information for purposes of intelligent decision-making about gifted learning needs. Although whole-grade acceleration is still controversial, there is considerable evidence that when it is done carefully, acceleration practices can have positive long-term effects. In fact, it's the gifted educational option with the strongest and most robust research validation.[10]

To help in the decision-making process, parents and teachers can do a cost-benefit analysis for a particular child. The costs to the child of *not* accelerating may be increased boredom, frustration, alienation from school, and behavior problems, as well as reduced learning achievement. Possible benefits include a faster and more appropriate pace of learning, less time wasted in classes where content has already been mastered, a level of challenge that's better matched to a child's capacity to learn, and renewed excitement about learning.

Generally speaking, a student who is self-directed; achieving well beyond grade-level; comfortable working ahead of age-peers; and socially, emotionally, and physically mature for their age, is an excellent candidate for full-grade acceleration. One or more teachers should be available to monitor and guide the process, crafting an ongoing match between the child's ability in the different subject areas, the curriculum content, and the pace and depth of learning. It's important that both the pre- and post-acceleration teachers work together to make the process as smooth as possible, and monitor any problems that may later compromise the child's knowledge or skill-building. For example, prior to a grade skip, the pace of learning can be faster for a time, so the child masters grade-level content and skills systematically, but more quickly than usual. This helps to eliminate gaps in knowledge once the child is placed in the higher grade. As we emphasize throughout this book, children's learning trajectories are highly individual, and even the most advanced learners can have gaps in foundational knowledge or skills and, if they're not addressed, these gaps can cause difficulties down the road.

Schools can facilitate a successful whole-grade acceleration experience by providing teachers with the professional development and support they need to make the process successful, and by creating a school climate that respects individual differences. Some schools choose to develop non-graded or multi-grade classes which allow for a seamless acceleration where appropriate, with children moving through the curriculum at their own pace.

Whole-grade acceleration works best when arrangements are made for a group of students to go through the process together. An obvious advantage of the group approach is that, as students move quickly through the curriculum, they do so with a network of peers. This is beneficial in every way, from academic support and discourse, to friendship-building.

There are certain times in a child's life when acceleration is simpler and less disruptive. Examples of potentially easier transition times include entering kindergarten or first grade a year early; advancing a grade when a child is changing schools anyway, whether because of moving or entering middle or high school; and early entrance to college. Full-grade acceleration must be considered on a case-by-case basis, paying close attention to educational objectives and to the individual—including assessment information, learning profile, attitudes about school, motivation to learn, other stressors in the child's life, social and physical maturity.

In the end, acceleration may or may not be the best option for a particular child. In general, though, this approach is an evidence-based way to support the development of advanced learning needs, and certainly warrants careful consideration.

Early Entrance to College

"Calendar age is only one criterion to consider when seeking an optimal educational and social match for a gifted student who is ill-served by the ordinary high school curriculum. Programs that allow students to enter college or university early provide options to better meet the needs of highly gifted students."[11]

Some students in high school (or even the middle grades), are so advanced in one or more subject areas that it makes sense to investigate college-level courses to see if they might provide a suitable learning match. A teen who has already mastered material being offered at school in one subject area or another, and who is keen to keep learning, may be ready both academically, and in terms of their organizational skills and emotional maturity, to take on the extra responsibility. Many colleges welcome exceptional learners who are highly motivated and want to pursue post-secondary credit courses early on. Students don't need a high school diploma to be accepted to take courses at some colleges, and homeschooling is an acceptable entryway. Local community college courses can also be good stepping-stones for early entrance to university.

Taking advanced-level courses early may be enough for some kids, but those who need even more advanced learning opportunities can consider accelerating quickly through high school and enrolling at university two or more years earlier. Nancy and Hal Robinson designed and administered a highly successful program at the University of Washington, which acted as a model for subsequent similar programs, like the Transition Years program at the University of British Columbia.[12] A program that leads to early admission to college must be well-administered and carefully thought out. Here are a few factors for parents and students to consider:

○ *Financial costs.* There will be application fees, tuition, books, and possibly costs for commuting or accommodation.

○ *Hurdles that may require parents' help.* There are multi-tiered application processes, including transcripts, interviews, work samples, and more, demonstrating that prospective students not only meet the entrance criteria, but that they'll also be able to hold their own in a college milieu.

○ *Adolescent stressors.* Early entrance to college is a transition that presents a new set of challenges, on top of the normal stressors of adolescence. Can this pressure be managed?

○ *Self-advocacy.* Students are expected to work independently with professors and college administrators. This requires enough confidence to navigate the system on their own, and to speak up when need be.

○ *Social implications.* Most social interactions will be with older students who will be physically more mature, engage in adult behaviours, and may not be interested in socializing with a younger classmate. It can be tough being out of step in this way. There's the risk of not fitting in, or even of being rejected.

○ *Supports.* In addition to possible maturational and social issues, there will be increased academic demands. Investigate the support systems available on campus, such as counsellors, advisors, peer groups, or others.

○ *Executive functioning skills.* Students should be emotionally mature enough to manage the necessary self-discipline, study habits, planning, self-monitoring, time management, prioritizing, report writing, and more.

○ *High school hallmarks.* Teens who enter college early often miss out on high school team sports, student council and other leadership opportunities, dances, band, valedictorian selection, and other events.

○ *University activities.* If a student is too young to live on campus it can preclude participation in some on-campus activities, and perhaps options to study abroad.

○ *Loss of star status.* There's the likelihood of no longer being the most competent pupil in the class. Are they emotionally ready for that?

○ *Need for open communication.* Teens will require support through unfamiliar and sometimes stressful circumstances. Do you have an open honest relationship that will allow for help to be requested, and then provided as necessary?

Consider carefully whether or not early entrance to college is a viable option. You are looking for access to appropriate levels of challenge that facilitate intellectual growth, while at the same time meeting other needs as well. It won't be perfect, but according to Nancy Robinson, "This synthesis of student readiness and educational response is called the 'Optimal Match.'"[13]

When thinking about acceleration, investigate it as thoroughly as you can, and take time to learn about the experiences of those who have taken that route. For example, Felix (who we discuss in Chapter 4 in regard to above level-testing) was bored and frustrated at school for most of middle school and high school, and ultimately started college at sixteen. His social life actually improved (contrary to the commonly held belief that early college entrance leads to social isolation), and he completed a Master's degree in philosophy. He's now completing a Master's degree in anthropology, he's happy, and he enjoys going on nature treks with friends he's made at university. In "Turn on the Power," Noel Jette explains how she got a Ph.D. in educational psychology at the age of nineteen, and Haley Taylor Schlitz describes her college journey beginning at thirteen, graduating with a Bachelor of Science in interdisciplinary studies at sixteen. She is currently in law school.[14] Reading about the experiences of students like these, and those of their parents, and discovering what families have found to be challenging and rewarding, can be informative and inspiring.

For another perspective on radical acceleration leading to early entrance to college, you can watch a compelling movie that follows several kids through university and into adulthood: *Superkids2*.[15] This was based on the University Transition Program established by Marion Porath, an educational psychologist, at the University of British Columbia. According to the interviews with the students themselves (now well into adulthood), as well as several experts interviewed on film,[16] there can be intellectual advantages to radical fast-tracking, but there are also serious costs to contemplate, including the necessity to compress emotional and social development. Some of the students accomplished this more successfully than others.

Gifted Classes

> *"Finally, I found a class where I can learn what I want to learn, with others who want to learn cool stuff, too!"*

> *"By the time I get home and finish all my work, there's hardly any time left to relax or do other things like skating or swimming or playing the piano."*

> *"Betsy used to be what her teachers called a 'lazy learner.' But once she joined the gifted class, she began working harder and enjoying it more."*

> *"It seems as if the gifted class has revved Rob's learning a few notches, but he doesn't seem any happier. He's just more—I don't know—'driven.'"*

Full-Time Gifted Classes

Many parents and teachers believe that self-contained classrooms are the best way to provide gifted learners with appropriate intellectual stimulation, as well as opportunities to meet and interact with others of like mind and interest. In some places, there are entire schools for gifted learners, sometimes affiliated with university campuses and teacher education programs.

At the same time, there can be problems with full-time segregated gifted classrooms. One particular concern has to do with labeling, as we discuss in Chapter 5. In a self-contained class, the gifted label is made explicit on a daily basis, exposing the child to possible experiences of social ostracism from students who don't have that label, friends, siblings, other kids' parents, and sometimes even teachers. Another potential problem is transportation. Participation in gifted classes may require commuting to a new school outside of the home neighborhood, which cuts into the time and energy a child has available for other activities, including before- or after-school activities, sleep, play, and leisure, all of which are essential to optimal developmental outcomes.

There are some additional concerns. When considering a self-contained gifted class, parents and educators should remember that within each such class, half the students will be below the class average. A child who moves from being at the top of the class to being below average, or even the bottom, can suffer serious blows to self-esteem. On the other hand, such challenges, when accompanied by the necessary understanding and support, can provide students with opportunities to learn about the resilience and persistence that are needed for high-level achievement.

Another possible social/emotional problem identified with participation in full-time self-contained gifted classes has been called the "hothouse effect."[17] A segregated gifted class is an artificial environment in some ways, and may not provide sufficient opportunities for children to learn to cope effectively with the broad variety of people and situations they will have to learn how to interact with sooner or later.

An academic concern with full-time gifted classes is that individual domain-specific learning needs are not usually taken into account, unless the teacher has the necessary training and support. For example, a child who is exceptionally gifted in math is unlikely to be provided with a mathematics curriculum appropriate to their ability, which is highly advanced relative to their classmates, whose areas of advancement may be in language or science or other areas. Another often-overlooked fact is that sometimes exceptionally gifted children are deeply disappointed to discover that they do not fit in, even within the gifted class, that their interests are still not understood, and that their exceptionally advanced learning needs are still not being met. This can increase the burden of feeling different and somehow wrong.

Despite these concerns, many children find that full-time placement is both socially comfortable and academically stimulating. An important benefit of this option is the probability that the teacher has had at least some training in gifted education. There's also the increased likelihood of students finding intellectual peers, and this can be both invigorating and reassuring. There's less likelihood of kids feeling bored or having to bide their time while others catch up. In addition, some schools organize their self-contained gifted classes so that the academic classes occur in the self-contained format, but other classes (music, physical education, etc.) are organized more heterogeneously, encouraging more diverse kinds of interactions among students within and across grade levels, which can help reduce the potential hothouse effect. And, interactions can occur in other ways as well through school-wide activities like school plays, clubs, sports teams, and various shared interests.

A child's learning needs may be better met on a consistent basis in a self-contained gifted class, facilitating a higher level of motivation to learn, and subsequent personal achievement. Many parents have told us that the full-time class is a good way for their child to receive the challenges they need, and the depth, breadth, and pacing of learning experiences that make school more enjoyable for them. They can also supplement learning further by means of mentorships, online opportunities, early college programs, and extracurricular activities.

However, as with all placement decisions, the emotional, social, academic, and motivational implications of joining a full-time gifted class—where one is available—have to be weighed carefully by parents, teachers, and students working together during and after the decision-making process.

Part-Time Gifted Enrichment Classes

> *"I'm not gifted just on Tuesdays from 2-3 P.M."*

> *"I can teach Cassie perfectly well! My strongest math students do not have to leave my classroom in order to be challenged."*

For a number of reasons, part-time gifted placements are rarely a good option. Children's gifted learning needs are not restricted to the day on which their pull-out gifted class is scheduled. Some children tell us that their regular classroom teachers penalize them for their absences by planning special activities during the time when the kids have gone to the gifted program, or by giving tests or assigning work they're expected to make up later.

An additional problem with part-time programs is that the home-room teacher can resent the pull-out teacher taking the strongest students out of class. Most problematic, perhaps, is that typically, the work in the pull-out program is not differentiated for individual learners' special needs, or well-integrated into a child's other learning experiences. Too often, pull-out programs do little to meet gifted-level learning needs other than to reduce boredom for a few hours a week, and to bring together for short periods of time those who are more likely to be intellectual peers.

Teachers of gifted pull-out programs are not necessarily trained in gifted education. Classes may be taught by resource teachers, or subject area specialists. These classes also can involve more work for students who will have follow-up assignments due from one week to the next, in addition to their regular class work.

Because gifted education from an Optimal Match standpoint is about matching curriculum to advanced learners' specific academic needs on an ongoing basis, it's hard to justify a part-time gifted enrichment class as doing much to support the development of giftedness.

Second Language Immersion and Dual Track Programs

> *"Opportunities to learn more than one language should be provided to all students in an increasingly smaller world with the concomitant need for communication across languages and cultures."*[18]

> *"Miguel is able to talk fluently with his grandparents now!"*

> *"I had hoped that the immersion program would challenge Zoe. Instead, she became even more bored."*

Learning about other cultures and languages can enrich a child's life immeasurably, and dual track and language immersion programs can offer opportunities to do that. In an immersion program, instruction is predominantly or completely in the language of focus, across all subject areas. In dual track programs, students learn to speak two or more languages over the course of several years. Typically, dual track programs provide a compacted version of the regular age-appropriate curriculum in one part of the day, with a separate course of studies for the remainder. For example, students might spend the morning on the general studies curriculum of math, language arts, science, and history; and the afternoon working on various aspects of religious studies or humanities, and on alternative language learning. In both immersion and dual track programs, children develop second language fluency, beginning at the preschool level and continuing on through high school.

In some jurisdictions in Canada, the United States, and elsewhere, parents can choose to have their child enrolled in a language immersion class starting at kindergarten, and many parents of high-ability children choose such classes as a way of enriching their child's learning. Sometimes learning part or all of the core curriculum in a second (or third, or fourth) language provides sufficient additional challenge to keep a student interested in school, while at the same time developing another area of skill (the language itself, such as French, Spanish, Hebrew, or Mandarin).

Such programs, however, are not always good choices for meeting gifted learning needs. Consider, for example, a child whose strengths are philosophical and scientific, and who thrives on high-level discourse. In a French immersion program, it will take years before their knowledge of the French language is well enough developed to keep pace with their ideas and concept formation. This can impede meaningful discussions with the teacher and classmates until they've acquired fluency in the new language. This can make school frustrating and boring rather than stimulating and challenging, especially for the first few years in this kind of program.

When instruction is being provided in a foreign language, the general conceptual level is typically significantly lower in science, geography, history, etc., than what is provided in first-language classes. With children whose reasoning skills are exceptionally advanced, it is often better to provide second-language instruction as a subject area on its own, rather than as a medium for learning in other areas, at least until a high level of second-language proficiency has been acquired. This is particularly true for children who are not really interested in second- and third-language acquisition.

Another concern with using language immersion to address gifted educational needs is that it may put the child at a disadvantage in standardized testing, at least for a few years. Because the student will not have the same depth and breadth of discussion in the first language as they might otherwise have, test scores are unlikely to be as high. While this disadvantage evens out over time, and is eventually converted into an intellectual advantage, this can be an important consideration if a language immersion program is being considered as a temporary enrichment measure until the child is old enough to qualify to participate in another program that requires high scores on standardized testing.

Educators in dual track and immersion programs often argue against additional provisions for gifted learners, suggesting that the programs themselves are challenging enough to meet gifted learning needs. Additionally, because of the time pressures involved with such an intensive curriculum structure, they often question the practicalities of adapting instruction for gifted learners, even if it were deemed desirable or necessary.

A dual track program can work well for children who are keenly interested in the particular focus of the second track, and who don't mind spending less time on other subject areas. However, for those who are less interested in the second-track focus or who experience some difficulty with it, such programs can be seriously problematic. The sheer breadth of the curriculum leaves little room for in-depth study of areas of interest (math, science, English literature, etc.), and often less time for extra-curricular pursuits. Curious and highly motivated learners often experience frustration due to the narrowness of focus necessitated by the amount of material being covered. However, when teachers are given the professional development opportunities and support they need to adapt instruction for individual differences, they may be able to meet gifted learning needs in these programs. (We discuss teacher development in Chapter 11.)

Specialty Subjects

"Joey amazed everyone after he joined the Drama Club. He hadn't been doing well at school, and had trouble reading. But once he discovered drama, he had a reason to become an excellent reader. English has become his favorite subject."

"Last year, when Collin joined the school band, he had no friends and no interests outside of academics. Now he has discovered a talent for music, a much broader set of interests, as well as a group of kids to do things with."

Throughout this book, we are concerned primarily with students who are so advanced academically that their time will be wasted in school if little or no accommodations are made for their exceptionality. Not only is there tremendous diversity in patterns of gifted development within the core academic areas, but there are also children who have gifted learning needs in one or more of the specialty subject areas such as art, music, drama, leadership, or alternative language study.

In much the same way that programming can be differentiated for the more traditional academic subjects, gifted programming can be designed in subjects such as drama or dance. It can be used both to support gifted development in those who show evidence of talent in certain specialties, and also to provide high-ceiling learning opportunities for those whose academic giftedness is not otherwise being addressed.

Consider, for example, a highly accomplished young pianist, or a child who is mathematically advanced and also interested in music. Such students can be given opportunities to hear, play, and perform advanced pieces, to compose their own work, and to incorporate music into school projects and activities. There are also online composition and recording opportunities, collaborative and support networks for sharing and critiquing melodies and performances with others around the globe, and awards and scholarships, too. There are myriad possibilities for parents and educators interested in finding challenging learning opportunities in the arts. We know of young students who have played solos with orchestras, and others who have had featured parts in movies, theatre productions, and ballet. Children may find vehicles to develop their talents, interests, and love of learning through community-based theater, studios, You Tube, conservatories, extra-curricular bands, or festivals, rather than in traditional classrooms.

Parents and teachers can encourage children who might otherwise focus too narrowly on their area of expertise to explore their abilities and interests more extensively. For example, someone who is passion-ately engaged by science but unremarkable in the arts might enjoy role-playing a scientific discovery in drama class, drawing an invention in art class, or creatively graphing physical responses to athletic activ-ities, as an independent study project. A cross-disciplinary attitude invites children to bring their enthusiasms into their learning, and broadens their scope, discoveries, and understandings.

Other strategies that work well in specialty subject areas and that are useful for supporting talent development more broadly include:

○ flexibility in program design, allowing for individual differences;

○ open-ended assignments that encourage high-level exploration;

○ student participation in planning and choosing learning options;

○ tapping into new technology, thereby amplifying outreach and connections;

○ availability of a variety of resources, with openness to finding more; and

○ authentic collaborations that are carefully planned, guided, and facilitated.

Specialized and Alternative Schools

Many large jurisdictions establish schools or programs within schools that specialize in a particular area such as the performing arts, applied sciences, technology, languages, or the International Baccalaureate. Sometimes, alternative schools are established in which the approach to learning is more flexible and individualistic or, alternatively, more structured and traditional, than is usually the case. These kinds of schools vary greatly across jurisdictions. Most are aimed at the high school level, although there are increasingly more specialized and alternative programs for younger students, too.

These facilities frequently operate on a magnet basis, attracting those who demonstrate their interest, and their ability to participate in the programming offered. There's almost always an audition or application process involved and/or other prerequisites for admission. We've seen cases in which a particular alternative school has provided exactly the right educational match for a particular student.

Although specialized and alternative schools can sometimes address gifted learning needs and support high-level development, there are questions to consider. One is the possibility of prematurely narrowing a child's interests and focus. For a child with diverse intellectual enthusiasms, a challenging traditional school may be the best learning environment in which to hold their options open for as long as possible. While specialized or alternative schools may provide a high level of challenge and stimulation in the targeted areas, they are not always as strong in other areas.

Schools for the performing arts, for example, are sometimes less demanding in the traditional academic subjects, which can pose problems for intellectually gifted learners. And, while some students thrive on the competition that's often part of specialized schools, others find they do better in a more collaborative atmosphere. Finally, there's almost always extra travel time and other commitments required in order for children to commute to and from the school, and to engage in the practices and rehearsals that are typically part of such programs.

Private and Independent Schools

> *"I won't send my child to a public school. She'll get a much better education at a private school."*

Many parents think private or independent schools are more prestigious, or offer a better education than public schools. Whether or not that is the case, the best school for your child is the one that provides the most suitable match.[19]

A private school that provides academic support, and values achievement and excellence in a wide variety of areas can be the most suitable option in some circumstances. For example, good Montessori or Reggio Emilia-type schools can work very well for independent, intrinsically-motivated, young learners. These approaches encourage and respect children's unique learning needs and interests within a context of independence and structure. Children have opportunities for sensorimotor experiences, manipulative play, social skills development, and leisurely pursuit of learning activities. The theoretical framework of both of these methods are strong foundations for nurturing young children's individual and developmental diversity, including supporting their gifted-level abilities, but the actual schools vary considerably in how well they translate that excellent theory into practice.

Sometimes private schools publish expensive brochures or have impressive websites promoting exciting or unusual learning opportunities such as rock-climbing excursions, ski trips, archeological digs, museum visits, foreign trips, state-of-the-art athletic facilities, and so on. Such opportunities can sound enticing. Many independent schools do provide wonderfully supportive learning environments, but parents must do the necessary research to find out if a particular school will actually be a good fit for their child. We suggest that parents take the time to visit the schools they're considering; ask lots of questions and listen to the answers; notice what's happening in the classrooms, school yards, and hallways; and find out what might be available for children with the needs, interests, or abilities that are of particular concern to them. Each family has different priorities, and private schools vary a lot in how well they adapt to individual children's learning needs.

We did some informal field research, asking hundreds of parents, teachers, principals, and students to consider what factors they thought mattered most for supporting children's optimal development.[20] Here are ten areas of focus that our respondents told us were their top priorities in deciding whether or not a school (private, public, or other) "measured up." You can use this list as a starting point, supplementing it or creating your own list of important factors, based on your child's learning needs:

○ safe and secure environment

○ challenge across subject areas

○ possibilities for meaningful learning

○ reinforcement of effort and intellectual risk-taking

○ clear and attainable goals

○ dynamic grouping practices

○ open communication

○ inclusive and collaborative school climate

○ respect for diversity (including high-level development)

○ well-trained teachers (including training in differentiation practices)

Regulations concerning teacher qualifications in independent or charter schools are often different than those governing teachers in the public sector. Therefore, parents should inquire about teachers' certification and experience, including specialized training in gifted education, gifted consultation and support network availability, and professional development opportunities.

Homeschooling

"We don't think the educational system can provide our son with the opportunities we can offer by teaching him at home. But how do we design a curriculum?"

Thomas Edison, Florence Nightingale, and Agatha Christie were all taught at home, as were countless others who have achieved at exceptionally high levels in one or more areas. There are many reasons to consider homeschooling. Some children are too advanced or are otherwise unsuited to the available classroom options. Others who miss the cut-off for acceptance into a gifted program consider homeschooling as an alternative. Still other children are homeschooled because of circumstances that make it necessary; COVID-19 restrictions and school closures immediately come to mind. Some families choose homeschooling for religious reasons. Others want to be more directly involved in their child's education. Some may have tried to collaborate with their child's school and found the experience unwelcoming or disconcerting.[21] And some parents who homeschool object to public school practices as too permissive or too constraining.

Additional concerns that lead parents to consider homeschooling revolve around safety issues in school, frustration with the educational system, wasted time, and children's special learning needs.

The Nature and Benefits of Homeschooling

"A child who learns quickly will not be held back by lockstep curriculum; a child who has deep and wide interests will be exposed to a banquet of learning experiences; a child who has specific interests and passions will be provided time and resources to pursue them."[22]

Homeschooling enables a child's education to be enriched, individualized, and accelerated. Sometimes homeschooling is a full-on endeavor, and other times it occurs in concert with classroom-based instruction on a more temporary or hybrid basis, as we've seen throughout the pandemic. If parents are willing and able to invest the necessary time and effort, and if they have the inclination to provide homeschooling, then it can be a viable educational alternative for some children. However, there are a number of factors to consider.[23]

Homeschooling is implemented in a variety of ways, and part of that variability reflects local regulations, which vary dramatically from place to place. As with education generally, homeschooling regulations are under constant review and revision. Parents who wish to teach their own children, or to hire an education professional to do so, should start by investigating government policies in their jurisdiction. In order to meet local requirements, parents may simply have to inform local education authorities of their intent to homeschool, or they may have to provide ongoing and extensive evidence of curriculum development and evaluation processes, and perhaps evidence of their own pedagogical qualifications.

There are active support groups and online networks providing information about all aspects of homeschooling—from establishing goals, expectations, and limits, to legislative issues, curriculum, and extracurricular options, as well as providing a way to interact and share resources with others.[24]

As might be expected, there is a continuum of approaches to learning used in homeschooling practice. This ranges from mirroring what might go on in a typical classroom, and across the spectrum to extremes of various kinds. For example, homeschooled children might learn about snakes by doing book or Internet research and then going to the zoo, or they might be involved in actually buying and caring for a snake. What goes on in a homeschooling program is as individual as the children, educators and parents who design it, which can be the biggest advantage of this educational approach, as well as its biggest drawback: "On the one hand, parents frequently will have deep insight into the educational strengths, weaknesses, and needs of their child. On the other hand, their lack of specific expertise in gifted education may result in them overlooking useful pedagogical strategies and curricular resources."[25]

Depending on parents' values, teaching expertise, and personality, a homeschooling program can be nurturing, motivating, and directly targeted to a child's domain specific strengths and weaknesses—or it can be rigid, narrowly focused, and authoritarian. Technology, and ever-increasing resources are making homeschooling more attractive than ever. "Around the world at the moment, we have children learning from home—on the backs of horses, in tractors, at dining tables, and on balconies. They have more flexibility and freedom than in their regular school day."[26]

The benefits of homeschooling include efficiency; self-selected scheduling; safety; warmth and nurturing; expanded curriculum; accommodation of special circumstances; accommodation of special needs; continued learning for the parent or teacher; discovery of like-minded others; and academic achievement.[27]

The curricular flexibility and academic effectiveness of homeschooling are big draws. Also, the barriers that traditionally have existed between homeschooled students and public schools are now far fewer than was previously the case. In many districts, homeschooled children can participate in bands, theater productions, excursions, sports, clubs, and other activities. Parents often work collaboratively with one another to co-create meaningful programs, to advocate on behalf of their children, and to share ideas and concerns.

Online homeschooling programs can complement other learning options that parents provide. For example, Athena's Advanced Academy[28] offers courses for gifted and talented learners (as well as those with other exceptionalities) in the form of "interactive, a la carte online classes" across multiple subject areas and grade levels. Options include live webinars, study projects, virtual classrooms, individual enrichment offerings, tutoring, and online communities. Remote schooling opportunities accelerated during the COVID-19 pandemic, and more and more homeschooled students are enrolling in such programs.

Concerns about Homeschooling

Concerns include financial implications (such as textbooks and other supplies, and loss of other income, or hiring a teacher), record-keeping, goal-setting (short, medium, and long-term), academic credentials (important especially as children get older, if they hope to attend postsecondary education), transitioning into or out of home-schooling, and progress assessment and evaluation. Some parents worry that their kids will not have enough interaction with age-mates or will feel isolated at home.[29] Children may benefit from a hybrid approach, where they're homeschooled part of the time, and also have opportunities to attend a local school part time. They might attend one or more classes or participate in extracurricular activities so they can interact regularly with others. Homeschooling support groups often provide opportunities for social interaction, and students can also become involved in community and volunteering pursuits.

Parents who opt for homeschooling because of their child's boredom or waning motivation can provide learning opportunities and curricular options that are more engaging. Home learners "may exhibit exceptional motivation to learn at home, especially if the homeschool environment encourages self-efficacy, self-pacing, enjoyment of learning for its own sake, challenging explorations in the areas of strength, and consistent hard work in areas of weakness."[30] However, motivation problems may persist or even be exacerbated if parents take too much responsibility for keeping their child challenged, thus robbing them of the chance to become self-sufficient and intrinsically motivated. Boredom can be a good thing if a child learns to become accountable for their own learning and intellectual stimulation.

Parents who homeschool need to pay attention to their own needs and to monitor whether they're becoming too stressed by the responsibilities of managing and implementing an educational program, in addition to the other responsibilities in their lives. There can also be negative judgments from parents whose children are in mainstream schools, or from homeschooling parents who have different values or priorities. A sampling of parents reported, "Some elements of the homeschool community do not appear to have embraced the subpopulations of gifted homeschoolers or their parents."[31]

Homeschooling can be taxing, although with some children it's actually easier than one might expect because they become self-directed learners. Consider the following letter, sent to us by a parent.

Homeschooling: A Mother's Perspective

Home schooling is going very well for us. There are days when I feel like pulling my hair out, but then I had days like that when Derek was still in school! The real difference now is that if something isn't working, we can just sit down, talk it through, and try something else.

I found a discussion group under my district's educational services umbrella. It's very interesting to read and exchange e-mails with other homeschooling parents. There's something refreshing about the been-there-done-that advice/comments, even when you know each kid is unique. The group is also extremely useful for getting advice and evaluations of book and curriculum alternatives since there's almost always someone who has had some relevant experience.

Derek is soaring ahead. He loves being able to focus on topics in as much detail and for as long as he wants (at least until he has exhausted his mother for any single sitting). We quickly evolved an approach that is quite eclectic, with a flexible structure for day-to-day planning. One of my biggest challenges is finding the appropriate balance of a predictable schedule and routine for a kid who loves many things, while at the same time letting him pursue a specific topic rather than shutting it down simply because it's time to do something else. A well-rounded education is like a well-balanced diet: you don't have to have something from each food group every meal to remain healthy, so long as you don't go too long without spending some time with each group.

Derek wants to continue homeschooling until he's ready to go to college. I'm keeping an open mind, although I'm not sure if a school exists that can accommodate his wide range of skill levels.

Homeschooling Tips

"A child's own interests and goals are as important as their aptitude."[32]

"Gifted behaviors blossom according to your child's unique self—what interests him and how he opts to spend his time and direct his interests. In the dynamic learning environments you create and encourage, he can enjoy a degree of stylistic wiggle room that in all likelihood is unavailable to him in the classroom."[33]

Here are a dozen practical suggestions we've gleaned from parents who homeschool gifted learners. This is just a sampling. Talk to homeschoolers. They're generally happy to share their experience as well as useful information:

1. Maintain up-to-date records of your child's progress. This can be especially important when navigating entrance requirements for various advanced or college level courses.

2. In addition to academics, encourage your child to pursue their other passions. This might be anything from chess to building ships in bottles. Learn alongside them. Also consider mentorships, volunteerism, and leadership opportunities.

3. Tap outside agencies such as museums, galleries, and science centers from all around the world. Most promote virtual learning experiences and have ready-made resources.

4. Join one or more online homeschooling discussion forums; for example, GHF (Gifted Homeschoolers Forum) Discussion Group on FaceBook. Ask questions. But don't get too worked up about other people's programs or advice. Do what's best for your own child.

5. Look for digital resources that build depth and complexity into the learning activities.

6. Organize learning around themes and integrate it across subject areas. This can help your child make meaningful connections and build on previous knowledge.

7. Take advantage of anything and everything. Discarded appliances can be rebuilt, electronics can be repurposed, boxes and packaging material can provide the foundation for structures. Whatever can be reimagined can also ignite a learning opportunity.

8. Think of homeschooling as a privilege, and let your enjoyment shine through. Remember the *home* part (versus its more institutionalized counterpart), and relax. Cuddle, make blanket forts, and get outside when the mood strikes, so nobody gets bogged down.

9. Some homeschooling parents find it helpful to connect with a local or online consultant. Such a consultant can help you find resources, including information about attaining college credits while still in high school. There are books, apps, catalogues, and programs galore, so guidance can be beneficial.

10. Embrace trial and error. Mistakes are part of the learning process.

11. Look beyond your child's areas of strength. Someone who is exceptional in math (or languages or science) may be just as interested in trying golf, yoga, sculpture, karaoke, or baking—or all of that, and more.

12. Try to envision each day as an opportunity to learn new things together so there is a sense of adventure and anticipation in your home school. Set reasonable goals but don't worry if things go off track. It's just another part of the adventure.

Lisa Rivero created a homeschooling guide for parents of gifted learners that has stood the test of time. It contains a wealth of guidelines and practical ideas. Rivero says, "Homeschooling is certainly not for everyone but for us and for thousands of other families, homeschooling offers a respite from sometimes inappropriate education, or in some cases, a long-term or near-permanent alternative to formal education."[34]

We're also reminded of psychologist Angela Duckworth's words, "All children really need the same thing: *appropriately demanding challenges* in combination with consistently warm and respectful support."[35] That is the crux of the Optimal Match approach, whether at home, school, or elsewhere.

Extracurricular Enrichment

"We should no longer even be thinking about "a program" in gifted education for which testing is required to "get in." Rather, we should be thinking about how to collect a variety of information on individual children in order to best match their demonstrated needs with any of a variety of options…"[36]

"How can I supplement what's going on in my daughter's school?"

Extracurricular enrichment activities can help keep children intellectually challenged and developing. At the same time, however, it's important to remember that children and adolescents also need time to find out more about who they are, and what it is they want to do with their time and their lives. Here are some extracurricular ideas as a starting point:

○ *Music:* playing an instrument, participating in a choir, band, or orchestra, composing music, creating vocal harmonies

○ *Theatre:* costumes, makeup, acting, clowning, script development, sets, lighting, and puppet plays

○ *Dance:* ballet, jazz, modern, ethnic, hip-hop

○ *Performance appreciation:* professional concerts and showcases in different artistic media

○ *Art:* painting, drawing, sculpture, photography, cartooning

○ *Crafts:* woodworking, sewing, pottery, model-building, knitting, jewelry design

○ *Recreational reading:* anything of interest, including comics, magazines, graphic novels, nonfiction, travel literature, biographies, fiction of any genre

○ *Writing:* stories, poems, articles, for pleasure or submission for publication

○ *Second or third language learning:* classes, tutoring, online study, summer experiences

○ *Math and science:* business, engineering, research labs, or other specialized programs

○ *Technology:* computer design and programming, interactive media networks, software design, videogame design

○ *Community service:* veterinary clinics, youth organizations, global causes, political activities, faith group activities

○ *Leadership opportunities:* tutoring, interest groups, cultural activities, religious and community organizations

○ *Competitions:* local, regional, national, and international levels, in different areas

○ *Clubs:* chess, astronomy, cooking, photography, photo-journalism.

○ *Summer programs:* talent development programs of various types, run by museums, other cultural organizations, universities, and talent searches

○ *Distance learning:* unlimited possibilities and options

○ *Camps:* summer and/or weekend recreational or specialized by area of interest, such as sailing, dance, language immersion

○ *Sports and physical activity:* gymnastics, martial arts, baseball, hockey

There are countless possibilities for extracurricular involvement that can provide stimulation and learning opportunities for your child. As with everything else, it's important to remember that while learning and stimulation are good, over-programming kids can be counterproductive. The key is to find a healthy balance that provides enough stimulation, and also affords opportunities for relaxation and enjoyment.

Mentorships

"Mentoring makes a difference in lives. In their simplest form, mentoring programs can begin with one child working with one adult. From that simple beginning, the possibilities are endless."[37]

"Our 14-year-old daughter worked with a doctor who helped her design an experiment on pediatric testing for chicken pox. She learned how to structure a research study, and her results were compatible with findings from other studies. Her work is being sent to a medical journal for possible publication."

Mentoring is a supportive relationship that can be established wherever there is a learner and someone with more experience who has the time, patience, and willingness to support, challenge, and guide the learner to greater knowledge and understanding.[38] It is a dynamic interaction that can include the transmission of values, attitudes, and passions, as well as knowledge, skills, and practical connections. Mentors can have different roles in students' lives, and "may serve as intellectual sparring partners, emotional supporters, or providers of professional contacts."[39] Strong mentorships are built on foundations of shared interests, and are mutually respectful, responsive, and gratifying.[40]

The term "mentor" comes from Greek mythology; Odysseus' son Telemachus was entrusted to the care of Mentor, a wise advisor. History and literature from classical times to the present abound with examples of mentorships in politics, business, science, the arts, and education. Aristotle benefited from his mentorship under Plato, as Mickey Mouse benefited from his (with some resistance and turbulence from time to time) in *The Sorcerer's Apprentice*.[41] Mentorships aren't always smooth sailing and do require work.

Benefits of Mentorships

> *"Apprenticeship and mentorship are concepts underappreciated in the current model of education: we tend to forget how beneficial it is to learn from other people and experience the undivided attention of those who simply know more."*[42]

Mentorships offer potential benefits for both parties. Benefits to students include:

○ enriched perspective on a topic or area of interest

○ increased competence

○ encouragement and guidance for self-directed learning

○ new connections between one's learning and the real world

○ discovery of resources beyond the classroom

○ personal growth (confidence, persistence, empowerment, self-efficacy, autonomy)

- career path awareness
- respect for expertise
- relationship-building experiences
- model for enjoyment and accomplishment in the chosen area
- introduction to other individuals who might provide insight and support
- increased exposure to and visibility within a field of interest
- preparation for taking on roles within society, especially important for students from under-represented communities[43]

Benefits to mentors include:
- continued learning
- rejuvenation of spirit
- sense of fulfillment
- sense of respect and being valued
- fresh perspective
- involvement and enjoyment
- vicarious satisfaction through accomplishment of the protégé
- contribution to skills and expertise of those entering the field
- connection to the educational system

Mentorships are an excellent way of providing students with gifted level challenges and are one of the most highly and frequently recommended, though under-utilized, practices in gifted education.[44] They can be particularly important for students from culturally diverse and economically disadvantaged backgrounds, providing positive role models, and contributing to an understanding of the components of and pathways to high achievement.[45]

Mentoring should not stand alone. It's more likely to be successful and mutually rewarding if it's seen as an integral component of a student's overall education. It can be even more effective when academic credit is granted.

Mentorship Models

Though the format of mentorship programs vary, all involve a student as well as an adult whose work the student respects, and who can inspire and guide the student. A good starting point is a discussion about each person's hopes and expectations of the relationship. In formal academic situations, it's good to prepare a written agreement that specifies the intent and responsibilities of each party, including the right to withdraw from the arrangement. Periodic review of this written "contract" helps to ensure that expectations are being met by both parties.

There are many models for and levels of mentorships. They can take the form of job-shadowing, in which students prepare at school for the mentorship, and then spend a certain number of hours in the career setting of their mentor. Alternatively, mentorship programs can consist of visits to the school from community experts who increase the depth of programming that classroom teachers are able to provide. Under the guidance of the teacher, a mentor and student can co-create an individualized program. Parents, teachers, or a guidance counselor can assist in finding potential mentors in the educational or broader community who are (or have been) actively engaged in working productively in areas of interest to the student. Mentorships also work well in elementary schools, although they require even more careful monitoring.

To encourage the formation of such learning partnerships, teachers and parents can network with one another, asking for nominations for possible mentors, thinking about people working in a particular area, or who have retired. We have seen such drives recruit musicians, actors, doctors, chefs, professors, business people, artists, artisans, architects, and others, each of whom was willing to help a keen and able student explore and develop particular interests and abilities. A good mentoring relationship is built on mutual respect. Ideally the mentor is someone who possesses good communication skills, is comfortable working with young people, has a flexible attitude, and is prepared to invest the time, effort, and patience required to make the mentoring relationship work.

Structuring Mentorships

A student and mentor share a commitment over time, and work together to develop and advance guided independent and in-depth learning. When developing a framework for a mentorship arrangement, there are a number of questions to consider:

○ What is the student's current level of expertise? What can they do independently, and what kind of help do they need?

○ What are the student's interests?

○ Is the student receptive to the learning opportunity, and willing to commit the necessary time and energy?

○ How does the student learn?

○ Are there any special issues to be aware of (for example, personality, resilience, emotional or social issues)?

○ Does the student demonstrate a high level of motivation? Self-management skills? Task commitment? Responsibility?

○ Is there a safe and comfortable space available for learning, or can such an environment be created?

○ What community resources have already been used?

For those thinking about implementing a mentorship program in a school, there are important time and energy factors to consider. Organizing, maintaining, and monitoring mentorships are time-consuming activities. Teachers who want to support mentorship activities must think about the form that they want these experiences to take, and what their own roles will be in the context of their other duties. School mentorship programs are often most effective when the major responsibility for coordinating them is assumed by a member of the special education or administrative support staff working in collaboration with teachers, parents, students, and mentors.[46]

Female and minority mentors do triple duty; they challenge gender and cultural stereotypes and serve as alternative role models, in addition to providing the mentorship experience itself. Bringing nontraditional minority professionals such as female Black and

Hispanic mathematicians, scientists, and other experts into the classroom as mentors is an excellent approach to enriching and accelerating education while providing authentic connections to important domains of competence, and simultaneously expanding students' understandings of diversity and possibility.[47]

In the end, after finding each other and agreeing to their goals and expectations, the student and mentor figure out a way forward. They find a shared focus for their mentorship activities and, in the most successful mentorships, have a rich and mutually productive experience.

Travel

> "...it was a beautiful map, in many colors, showing principal roads, rivers and seas, towns and cities, mountains and valleys, intersections and detours, and sites of outstanding interest both beautiful and historic. ...He closed his eyes and poked a finger at the map. "Dictionopolis," read Milo slowly when he saw what his finger had chosen.... Suddenly he found himself speeding along an unfamiliar country highway.... "Welcome to Expectations," said a carefully lettered sign on a small house at the side of the road."[48]

> "MOM! I just looked up the route from Rome to Paris on Mapquest. It's only 875 miles and the total driving time is thirteen and a half hours! I'm going to plan a trip, in case we ever want to go!"

Travel is a springboard for extending and supplementing more conventional learning methods. Whether it's actual, virtual, or whimsical, travel is an exciting way to learn. Although long trips to foreign lands are not possible for most families, any kind of travel stimulates children's intellectual development and broadens their horizons. Family excursions can cover short or long distances, and may last a few days, a semester, or a year, depending on individual circumstances and constraints. You can take a day hike in the mountains, a weekend in a nearby city, or visit a museum or historical site in your community. The learning happens more in the participants' engagement, attitudes, and perspectives, than in the duration, cost, or destination of the trip. All the ideas we mention here can be implemented by a family touring a faraway continent, taking a daytrip to a town a few miles away, exploring their own hometown, or embarking on a virtual vacation.

Before You Go

- ○ Include everyone in family decision-making regarding places to visit.

- ○ Encourage all family members to look at atlases, maps, or travel websites, tracing possible routes.

- ○ Buy or download travel guides.

- ○ Arrange times to discuss information, observations, and ideas.

- ○ Spend time online, or browse travel magazines or newspaper travel sections, investigating what might be interesting and what each person might like to explore. If one child is enthused about a particular activity or phenomenon, whether it's stargazing in the countryside, visiting baseball stadiums, browsing magic shops, or swimming with dolphins, look for opportunities to share and enjoy such experiences on your trip.

While You Are Away:

- ○ Encourage everyone to notice and discuss differences they see in food, weather, clothing, farms, houses, scenery, and other sights, sounds, smells, and influences.

- ○ Think about what captures your own interest in the new environment. Demonstrate engagement in discovery and exploration.

- ○ Ask questions that stimulate higher-order thinking about the experience and environment. For example, if your family spends a weekend at a cabin on a lake, discover what everyone likes the most about this new place. What do they like better at home? What aspects of life in the new environment would they like to take home?

○ Encourage everyone to keep a diary or sketchbook or to take photos to record their impressions. Do that yourself.

○ Look for ways to make the experience alive for others. For example, during or after the excursion, write articles for a website, a local newspaper, or for a school assignment.

○ Create a collaborative travel document or scrapbook. Consider compiling a photo journal. Perhaps one or more members of your family can take pictures of personal interest, while someone else takes responsibility for writing, and another person puts together the final product. This can be assembled upon returning home, to be shared with others.

Travel offers a world of opportunities to learn and acquire fresh perspectives on other places, cultures, and languages. Some children love the detailed organization involved in planning a trip (doing the research, deciding on the itinerary, thinking about the budget, and so on), whether or not they'll be taking the trip anytime soon. Just planning a get-away can be a motivating and invigorating learning experience—and if you actually take the trip, well, so much the better!

Do-Nothing Times

"I've got way too much to do!"

"I never have time just to think anymore."

"Mom, I'm BORED!"

These comments are typical of children and teens who need some down-time. In encouraging their optimal long-term development, it's important that they experience periods entirely free of scheduled stimulation. Everyone needs some unprogrammed time and space in their lives to explore the scope and shape of their interests and pleasures, figure out what they enjoy doing, and consider and reflect upon their experiences, successes, failures, and preferences. If they don't invest in this kind of reflection, they may eventually find themselves out of touch with their goals, hopes, and dreams. One of the most important tasks of childhood and adolescence is discovering a sense of self, and this requires an investment of time that's not otherwise required for homework or participating in scheduled activities.

From another perspective, parents should try not to rescue their child from boredom. Children need unscheduled time in order to learn to set priorities and develop time management skills. Figuring out what they want to do with their discretionary time can be a valuable learning experience in and of itself. Many conscientious parents, in an attempt to provide appropriate stimulation, take responsibility for keeping their children engaged and happy and organized. However, too much programming can deprive children of something vital: it can prevent them from learning what it is they enjoy doing and who they really are. As with adults, children whose lives are micromanaged lose their zest and enthusiasm, and those who are over-programmed can get stale and stressed.

As we wrote in *Beyond Intelligence: Secrets for Raising Happily Productive Kids*, "There's growing evidence of the value of time being left free for imagination, exploration, collaboration, invention, and even boredom. Depriving kids of these experiences robs them of essential opportunities for developing important skills such as managing their feelings, moods, time, behavior, and intellectual focus."[49]

And So...

> *"No matter where you've come from or where you're headed, your thirst for adventure never ceases. It's an insatiable desire to experience the unknown, to test your own limits, to explore further than your imagination has ever ventured."*[50]

The range of options that can nurture high-level development is without limit. Some of these options can be made available in regular classrooms, while others happen in specialized learning environments. What works well for one child may not work for another. When selecting or constructing a program for your child, the main task is to find what's most appropriate at that time in their development, given the challenges, constraints, and opportunities inherent in the situation. The objective is to find a good match between the learning needs of your child, and the range of learning opportunities that are available, thinking as broadly and as carefully as possible.

And so, having considered many of the available learning options, it's now time to think about motivation and achievement issues. What makes a child or adolescent want to learn? And what can you do to nurture that?

Section IV
Being Smart About Gifted Development

CHAPTER 8

Motivation and Achievement

"Motivation is the art of getting people to perform necessary tasks they might not otherwise do."[1]

"Motivation is the study of why people think and behave as they do."[2]

"There are almost as many theories about what motivates people as there are theorists to think them up."[3]

Motivation: The Heart of Learning

Every healthy baby starts out as curious, intrinsically motivated to learn and acquire practical skills.[4] Some children retain that curiosity and engagement in learning; that high level of motivation to learn is at the heart of gifted development. A major longitudinal study[5] showed that some children experience what the study's authors called "gifted motivation" at an early age. They found that keen learning motivation was more important than cognitive ability in the children's achievement outcomes, both short-term and long-term.

One of the most urgent questions teachers ask is how they can stimulate and sustain their students' motivation to learn. High school science teacher Chris Healey, reflecting on this question, responded,

"Students need to know where they stand relative to expectations... Teachers must effectively set goals for their students based on their individual needs and motivation levels...

> *This may require creativity and resourcefulness on the part of the teacher, but consistent, constructive feedback is especially important for maintaining interest, and keeping their situation in perspective."*

Chris Healey's experience-based recommendations aligned with the results of an informal study designed by Martin Choi, a new teacher. In order to inform his own professional development, Choi asked one hundred teens, "How can teachers motivate their students?" Three distinct themes emerged. As far as these high schoolers were concerned, the best ways for teachers to motivate students are to (a) encourage their expectations of success, (b) facilitate their understanding of the importance of the learning, and (c) maintain and enhance their self-esteem. These themes apply to younger students as well, and are valuable not only for teachers, but also for parents, grandparents, coaches, mentors, and others who want to nurture children's and adolescents' motivation to learn.

Another perspective on motivation is to see it as tied both to an individual's valuing of the task at hand ("Do I want to do it?"), and to the person's expectation of success ("Can I do it?").[6] For example, a child who doesn't value an assigned math task is not likely to invest much effort, if any, in doing it, even if they're fully competent to handle it. And one who believes that math is important, but also believes they cannot do it, may skip class, avoid doing homework, or give up easily when asked to solve a difficult math problem. All these self-defeating behaviors contribute to poor performance, which in turn will reinforce the person's low expectation of future mathematical success.

On the other hand, a student who feels confident about their ability, and who also values a particular activity is more likely to persevere and be successful. Children who experience the motivation that results from a combination of self-confidence and personal engagement are more inclined to meet or even exceed high academic and other expectations.

Recent research[7] points to three major recommendations for motivating continued engagement in learning:

1. *Match tasks to each child's ability and interest.* Children's learning tasks should be both challenging and manageable, so they feel they're learning, and their time is well spent. (This is the essence of the Optimal Match approach.)

2. *Support students' autonomy.* Encourage them to define problems they think are worth solving, and to engage in learning opportunities they experience as intrinsically valuable and authentically relevant.

3. *Create an environment that's warm, welcoming, inclusive, and accepting.* This means nurturing a growth mindset, where children's, teachers', and parents' failures and mistakes are treated as learning opportunities. Social interactions and competence are key components of the motivation to learn, so work to prioritize, build, and sustain positive relationships.

Throughout this chapter, we provide many other recommendations for supporting children's motivation to learn in different contexts and circumstances.

Purpose

> *"Finding purpose fuels the emotional energy required to work through adversity."*[8]

Whether navigating through tough times or everyday circumstances, having a sense of purpose can empower people to get moving. Literally: in fact, the word "motivation" comes from the Latin "movere" which means move. Purpose is modifiable; that is, with enough motivation and commitment, an individual can alter their sense of purpose. Having a sense of purpose is linked to better health and well-being, and can help to safeguard cognitive abilities, even protecting against cognitive decline in older adults.[9]

Scott Barry Kaufman suggests that instead of looking at intelligence in relation to processing speed or reasoning, it's better to look at it "through the lens of expertise, wisdom, and purpose."[10]

Purpose motivates persistence, resolve, and commitment. It knows no age restraints, and it can apply to any domain at any time. An infant trying to reach a toy, a young child determined to learn how to skate, a teen studying to get a driver's license, or a parent learning more about gifted education—each of these illustrates purpose in action. Whether a person's interest is math, karaoke, astronomy, photography, or something else, a sense of purpose can propel them to the next level of learning and achievement. Parents can demonstrate how to become more purposeful by modeling goal-setting, a strong work ethic, and resilience, and also help their kids find meaningfulness in everyday learning.

Psychologist Angela Duckworth writes about grit.[11] Being "gritty" involves effort and commitment over time. Luck, talent, and good intentions matter, too, but it's essential to remain purposeful. Duckworth refers to the "ferocious passion" of highly successful people, describing these individuals as being "unusually resilient and hard-working" and knowing "in a very, very deep way, what it is they want."[12] Grit is a combination of passion and perseverance, and it stems from purpose. High achievers are often characterized by their drive to improve, and their sense of purpose. They don't give up. The stick-with-it-ness that typifies people with grit translates to intensified engagement, and sometimes, the experience of flow. That is what we describe next.

Flow

"Flow state: feeling so fully immersed in an activity or experience that it transforms our sense of time."[13]

Leonardo da Vinci said, "Learning never exhausts the mind." A person experiencing a flow state is deeply focused, and may feel disassociated from external pressures. (In Chapter 2 we discuss the work of Mihaly Csikszentmihalyi and the connection between flow and creativity.) The concept of flow is also being embraced by practicing clinicians in the field of positive psychology.[14]

How does flow relate to motivation? Research shows that flow can enable relaxation and greater acceptance of the present moment, contribute to well-being, and have a beneficial impact on productivity and performance. This can be especially helpful when students are struggling to meet deadlines or scholastic demands. Flow helps children and teens distance themselves from their fears, rigidity, and expectations. It allows them to give themselves up to being immersed in an activity or task, and to embrace the effort that goes into achievement. While flow has many benefits, it's also important to balance flow activities proportionately with the rest of life.

Praise: A Complicated Relationship with Motivation

"Praising children's intelligence harms their motivation and it harms their performance."[15]

Parents are sometimes surprised to learn that praise can not only strengthen a child's motivation, but it can also undermine it. Praise has more in common with criticism than many people realize: both offer potentially constructive feedback, showing a child what they're doing well, and where their work might benefit from more effort. And both praise and criticism can take the wind out of a child's engagement in the learning process.[16]

Experts on praise and motivation usually recommend praising children's efforts rather than their achievements, praising a child for running quickly and staying alert to the ball in a soccer game, for example, rather than being part of the winning team. This is often called "process praise." It's specific, focused on effort or on something the child feels they can change.[17] Toddlers who receive process praise learn to think of their ability as incremental, something that develops over time with hard work; they do significantly better than others academically right through elementary school.[18]

Process praise can be contrasted with global praise, which targets a global attribute such as athleticism, intelligence, or appearance. Most people think of global attributes as permanent and innate, something they either have or don't have, and over which they have little or no control.

It may seem counter-intuitive, but adults have to be most careful when they're praising children with low self-esteem.[19] Praise that's global ("You're so smart!") or inflated ("You're the smartest kid ever!") lowers children's self-esteem, motivation, and ability to overcome setbacks, especially if they have self-esteem issues already. Inflated praise makes the child feel they must be truly bad at the task in question to be getting such obviously false feedback.

Although process praise can improve children's learning motivation, it also has limits, possibly even backfiring in adolescence. Adolescents can experience process praise as a suggestion they need to work hard because they have low ability.[20] That doesn't mean you should avoid process praise with teenagers, just that you have to be careful, and make sure they know you value them for their authentic selves.

In a study with children from seven to eleven years old, among those with high self-esteem, parents' inflated praise led to an over-blown sense of their abilities and worth. It had the opposite effect, however, on children with low self-esteem, reducing their sense of self-worth. Objectively accurate praise neither inflated nor deflated children's self-esteem.[21]

What is the effect of parental praise on academic achievement and psychological health? The best outcomes in terms of academic grades and psychological well-being are experienced when parents' praise is honest and accurate, or slightly inflated. Parents and teachers should pay careful attention to children's perception of the praise they give them.[22]

When and How to Praise?

"I work really hard because I want to, but I hardly ever hear a word of praise. It's like they expect me to always do things really well and so they don't bother telling me when I do."

Whether it's a warm compliment or a boisterous "Hooray!" punctuated by a fist pump, thumbs-up, or high-five, children almost always appreciate enthusiastic acknowledgement of their successes. What they really need, though, is praise for the hard work along the way that leads to that success.

The best time to praise children and teens is when they've earned it, whether in the process of working toward a goal, or the end result. The most valuable praise is for effort, persistence, commitment, collaboration, self-regulation, smart prioritizing, and sound decision-making.

That kind of praise supports forward momentum, providing information about what will lead to further successes and achievements. The most effective praise is immediate, direct, and relevant to the task at hand. It doesn't have to dazzle. But it should be meaningful.

Praise: Strategies and Examples

○ *Show enthusiasm for your child's work by noting aspects that are striking or that show creativity.* For example, "I really like the color, texture, and shape of that blue unicorn! What should the background look like? (Where do unicorns live?)"

○ *Provide praise that emphasizes resilience.* "It's hard learning something new, and I love how you keep at it. You know the great thing about making mistakes? You have the challenge of figuring out something new."

○ *Help your child extend their work, and take it farther.* "That's an exciting story! Can you draw a picture that illustrates it?"

○ *Ask your child to share their opinions about what they're working on or what they've accomplished.* This can help them validate their abilities and boost their self-confidence. Instead of saying you like their poem ask, "What do you like most about that poem?"

○ *Validate your child's efforts and achievements by helping them find others who share their interests.* You might say, "That's a colorful nature collage. The conservation center has a workshop next month. Maybe you'd enjoy going, and you can collect more specimens with other nature enthusiasts."

When you offer constructive, specific, and accurate praise, you're supporting your child in their continued engagement in play, exploration, and learning. Provide praise while showing respect, valuing their interests and agency, and being careful not to impose your own preferences. Appreciate your child's personal "brand" of movement, design, musicality, language, numeracy, or artistic expression, without setting unnecessary limits or reservations. Reaffirm their growth, enjoyment, and effort; make positive, honest comments on how they manage demands and tackle challenges; and celebrate their pursuit of passions, learning opportunities, and creative outlets.

As a parent, you are uniquely positioned to make suggestions, offer praise, and shape your children's learning trajectories, from infancy onward.[23] There are others in your child's life like grandparents, coaches, and mentors, who can also offer productive praise and help to support your child's learning motivation. This can empower them to invest more effort, prevail under difficult circumstances, be creative, learn, and feel confident and capable.

Strategies for Motivating Learning

> *It's time "to rethink old assumptions about what it means to be gifted, how to identify and serve students who need gifted programming, what those programs are supposed to accomplish, and how to measure their success."[24]*

Children with gifted learning needs are too often expected to motivate themselves. However, they're children, and they can't do it alone. To that end, here are several recommendations for parents, educators, and other stakeholders who want to motivate gifted learning in children and adolescents.

○ *Generating Suspense, Intrigue, and Curiosity*
   Give children opportunities to connect uncertainty and effort with the joy of discovery. This is particularly effective if a question is an authentic one for which you don't have the answers. For example, you see a picture or observe, "It's a hot summer day, but there are hailstones and prickly ice pellets! How can this happen?" Kids may not know the answer but if you ask the question at an opportune moment, they may become curious and begin to generate hypotheses. Together you can think about how to find answers. (We discuss curiosity in Chapter 10.)

○ *Using Guessing and Feedback*
   Guessing (or, in more scientific language, hypothesis-generation) and feedback are complementary partners in high-level learning. Suppose you start a science investigation with the

question, "What are the basic human survival requirements?" Guesses can whet your child's appetite for knowing more, and motivate further learning. Your appropriate and timely feedback can guide and stimulate additional inquiry, ensuring that it's channeled productively.

○ *Connecting to Previous Knowledge*
When introducing new ideas, draw links to what children already know. Connecting new learning to already consolidated knowledge increases the likelihood it will be accessible later. For example, if you want a child to learn about the discoveries of the Perseverance rover on Mars, you might start by talking about circumstances that are similar in some way, and that are somewhat familiar, such as a desert terrain, a dried-out riverbed, or uninhabited countryside. This will help give the faraway exploration meaningful perspective.

○ *Resolving Controversy and Contradiction*
Controversies can be great motivators for learning. You might ask about the relative importance of one thing as compared to another. For example, "Which is a better form of transportation, a car or a bicycle?" Or, "Should dogs be allowed in restaurants or is that unsanitary?" Help children consider alternative perspectives, gather information, and engage in reasoning, critical listening, and refutation. Older kids can participate in debates or create flow charts that illustrate different perspectives on a given issue.

○ *Creating a Conducive Learning Climate*
A conducive learning environment is one where a person is comfortable, confident, and supported in their skill development and personal growth. If a learning environment is uncomfortable, unwelcoming, dreary, or full of distractions, it's not as motivating as one that's welcoming, richly stimulating, and well-organized.

The most favorable environment has an atmosphere of challenge and support, where adults encourage children's persistence and goal-directed activity, respect their interests, and foster their curiosity. Children usually enjoy opportunities to participate responsibly in program planning and evaluation processes, where expectations and timelines are reasonable, and where they feel safe enough to risk making mistakes. This allows children to "work on the edge of their competency."[25] Although success and high achievement are not guaranteed, this kind of environment can lead to increased momentum and improvement.

Finding a Balanced Approach to Online Learning

Across the globe, COVID led to more remote learning activities. Children's screen time increased considerably, partly for digital learning, and partly because families were at home more. With parents working from home in many cases, screens often became go-to babysitters. Additional time online works well for some children, but not at all well for others. Too much digital instruction and interaction can be boring, exhausting, enervating, or distracting. Parents can support their children to a certain extent by paying attention to the online content, drawing real-world connections to it, creating a social interaction component, and eliminating distractions. (We discuss computer-related issues in Chapter 9.)

Author James Lang writes about student distraction, suggesting that adults monitor their own online behavior. This includes thinking about what draws them in, what they can learn from their experiences, and how they can share that with their children, translating online learning into a more "attention-filled" and conducive learning environment.[26]

Innovative and Expansive Approaches

"Every action needs to be prompted by a motive."[27]

"Ability is what you're capable of doing. Motivation determines what you do. Attitude determines how well you do it."[28]

A discussion of how to motivate students would be incomplete without mentioning innovative educational approaches. Countless educators nurture their students' confidence, generate excitement about what's happening in their classrooms, and try out new and creative ways to engage their students in learning. (Creative teaching is also mentioned in Chapter 2.) We address some innovative options in the following paragraphs, and we encourage parents to consider these approaches, and to explore other innovative possibilities as well.

Arts-based Learning

A promising innovative model is arts-based learning, where meaningful collaborations between classroom teachers and artists (songwriters, musicians, writers, fabric artisans, and others) inspire students to do their own creative work. Programming designs use art, music, or drama to complement academic subjects, including math, language, science, and social studies, in all cases incorporating creativity and interactive thinking into the curriculum. Children and teachers participating in these experiences report they enjoy integrative approaches in which the arts are not peripheral but are woven into the curriculum's foundational subjects.

Gifted Education Centers

Many educational innovations of the past began with educators' attempts to address gifted learning needs, and some of these have evolved into exciting and information-filled educational offerings. A good example of this is the Renzulli Center for Creativity, Gifted Education, and Talent Development. The Center has post-graduate programs in talent development and giftedness, and holds an annual conference so educators can learn more about engagement and enrichment opportunities for students. The Center has grown over the course of several decades, applying emerging research findings (their own and that of others in the field). Educators (and parents, too) can discover ideas for augmenting and individualizing children's learning. The Schoolwide Enrichment Model (which we discuss in Chapter 6) has been implemented by thousands of schools, enabling teachers to match students' gifted learning needs with advanced-level learning experiences. (In Chapter 12 we discuss the range of resources and programs offered by other university-based gifted education centers.)

Technology-Based Programs

Countless educational programs are being created and marketed, some of them excellent, and some a lot less so. It can be a challenge to know where to "plug in," so people have to do some investigative work to find a good match for their needs of the moment. Internet-linked software can support students as they construct knowledge, build on their ideas and questions, and connect with others around the world. These programs can motivate students to become part of a global community of learners, and to experience the joy of sharing their ideas, while they're learning. (More on smart and safe use of technology-based learning in Chapter 9.)

Slow Schooling

Yet another educational technique is "slow schooling," where it's argued that learning is not a race, and that more information and intense rapid-paced instruction is not necessarily the best way to teach children. Proponents of this approach have observed that too much pressure on children to perform or to acquire facts and figures can be counterproductive, and can take the joy and motivation out of learning. As educators consider how to infuse excellence and enjoyment into the learning process, some are advocating taking a slow route. Slow refers to a different way of learning, "exploring something deeply and thoroughly, learning how to learn, how to ask questions, how to understand, how to apply that understanding to other areas of study."[29] Students use nonstandard resources; seize opportunities to learn as they arise, without curricular constraints; take time to think about matters; experience learning rather than studying facts; and receive ongoing support to sustain enthusiasm and engagement.

Inquiry-Based Learning

Makerspace programs (which we describe in Chapter 2) are great examples of inquiry-based learning opportunities.[30] Activities like this encourage student involvement in projects that fuse creativity and innovation, facilitate broad-based community outreach, and use technology to help fuel real-world problem-solving efforts. Programs like this encourage children to become collaborators and proactive learners as they strive toward invention, positive change, and possibly entrepreneurship, too. This can be highly motivating because students can pursue their personal interests while putting their ideas, knowledge, skills, and creative energy to good use.

Gift-Creation

Emerging from the living theory approach,[31] some innovative educators advocate a gift-creation approach, whereby educators assist students in finding and developing their own talents and abilities. The possibilities are endless. The gift-creation approach makes room for individual differences among students in their speed of learning, mastery of content, cultural background, economic circumstances, extent and quality of supports, and more. It also reflects emerging understandings about giftedness and diversity: "Even within gifted programs, some students need more challenging material, or to move through material more quickly than others."[32] This approach is a way to support every student in getting the gifted learning experiences that will enable them to thrive. The emphasis shifts away from identifying a select few students as gifted, and toward fostering giftedness more diversely, in teachers as well as students. This approach is a strong example of the growth mindset, and reflects current knowledge about neural plasticity.

Extrinsic and Intrinsic Motivation

> *"As they explore and learn, very young children are the most nearly perfect examples of intrinsic motivation— the type of motivation that encourages them to ask and answer questions without worrying about the "One Right Answer"—and the kind of motivation that often goes to sleep when the thrill of learning is replaced with classroom regimentation and rote learning."[33]*

With a shared focus on engaging students in the learning process for its own sake, each of the approaches we discuss in this chapter puts the emphasis squarely on helping children discover and reclaim their intrinsic motivation to learn. Intrinsic motivators are internal to the person experiencing them. They include feelings of curiosity, competence, pride, autonomy, self-actualization, and satisfaction from achievement that has required persistence and perseverance.

Extrinsic motivators are external to the person, factors put in place by the individual or by others to encourage the completion of a given task. They include grades, scholarships, praise, money, gifts, trips, and other kinds of treats, awards, and prizes. In order for an extrinsic motivator to be effective, the student must value it, and believe they can be successful in attaining it.

Extrinsic rewards have to be treated carefully because they can have unintended and counterproductive consequences. For example, grades are regularly used to motivate children's learning, and are highly valued by most parents, students, and teachers. However, what if a child wants to earn high grades and the praise that typically goes with them, but doesn't believe they have the necessary ability? They might choose to take easy classes rather than more challenging ones, or decide to achieve the high grades they want (or feel they need) by cheating. Rewards are two-edged swords that can stimulate a desired behavior, but paradoxically, can also work to undermine rather than motivate effort, achievement, and real learning.

When parents or teachers use extrinsic rewards wisely, they can facilitate intrinsic motivation to learn. Although extrinsic motivation is generally short-term (that is, once the reward disappears, the desired behavior may cease), a reward can act as a bridge to intrinsic motivation. For example, a child who is told they will earn some kind of outing if they do all their piano practicing for the week may, in addition to collecting the prize, find pleasure in musical achievement, and want to continue practicing the following week, whether or not they get an extra outing. Extrinsic rewards can provide opportunities to experience the joy inherent in a sense of growing competence and mastery, and so support a movement toward intrinsically motivated learning. Parents support a powerful form of intrinsic motivation to learn when they encourage children and adolescents to think about who they uniquely are, and then guide them in finding good pathways to advance their enthusiasms.

Once a value like honesty, diligence, kindness, or integrity has been internalized, it becomes an intrinsic motivator, and extrinsic rewards or punishments are no longer needed to sustain them. A child who internalizes the value of diligence may find pleasure in working hard at school and become intrinsically motivated to read and study. It should be noted, however, that valuing hard work is unlikely to sustain itself through self-reinforcement alone, and it usually needs to be supplemented by other motivators, such as feelings of competence and mastery.[34] This usually happens naturally, but parents and educators are wise to pay attention to it.

Increasing competence leads to experiences of success and enhances a person's self-esteem. Providing children with opportunities to experience the pleasures inherent in developing competencies— from proficiency with mathematical calculations, to mastery of a second language, to computer keyboarding skills—encourages their intrinsic motivation to learn. If a task is perceived as being *too easy* (that is, the individual already knows the material or skill), then the task will have little value, and there will be little or no intrinsic motivation to complete it. (This is one of the reasons exceptionally capable learners can have problems completing assignments.) On the other hand, if a task is perceived as *too difficult*, then the individual will not expect to succeed, and so once again will not feel intrinsically motivated to attempt it.

As one might expect, the research on motivation to learn shows that individuals learn best when levels of challenge are calibrated to match their learning needs. If a child isn't enthusiastic about completing a task, consider the design and intent, and check to make sure it's appropriately targeted to their interests and prior learning.[35]

Solving Problems of Motivation and Achievement

We've considered several of the factors that nurture children's motivation to learn and achieve, and now we'll consider some of the obstacles.

Academic Mismatch

> *"If unchallenging scholastic environments produce underachieving gifted students, then providing intellectual challenge and stimulation at all grade levels should decrease underachievement."*[36]

The simplest and most obvious reason that a capable learner might lack motivation and get low grades is that there's a mismatch between the curriculum being offered and the child's learning needs. In some instances, a child may be asked to do tasks that are so easy that they're not learning much, so see no point in doing them. In other situations, demands entail more work or harder work with no perceived benefits, and again, the child sees no point in investing the necessary time and effort. In yet other situations, the work may be targeted reasonably well to the child's ability, but they see no connection with their life and interests. Academic mismatch and ways to address it are discussed throughout this book.

However, what if curriculum match and relevance are addressed as carefully as possible and a child is still not doing well at school? The possibility of cognitive processing problems (such as a learning disability or problem with attention), or psychological problems, or something else that interferes with learning and achievement, should be considered.

Low Motivation to Succeed at School

"He seems to resist learning. I know he's smart but why isn't he a better student?"

Not all highly capable learners are highly motivated to do well on their schoolwork. Gifted education expert Del Siegle says, "We choose where we place our energy."[37] In the same way that people are sometimes content to walk even though they're able to run, some highly capable low-achieving students are going as fast as they want to. A person's motivation to attend to schoolwork or succeed at school depends on a number of interconnected factors, including their emotional and physical well-being; the suitability of the classroom or learning environment; their relationship with the teacher; their family situation; and other influences. There's always a reason for a child's disengagement, and adults should never assume that an unmotivated but capable child doesn't care, or is lazy, or uncooperative.

Just because children CAN do something doesn't necessarily mean they will. A child might need guidance, a more welcoming emotional environment, greater challenge, less busy-work, fewer distractions, an extended timeframe, a different kind of space, more time in nature, physical activity, less interference, or something else entirely. When a child deems a task to be important, or appropriately challenging and intellectually stimulating, they may choose to become more motivated straightaway or over time.

Sometimes kids have to gain confidence or self-efficacy in one or more domains where they're feeling less inclined to "run." Clear, fair, and attainable expectations, and a sense of the value of a task, can invite involvement. Research by Lannie Kanevsky and Tacey Keighley suggests the importance of the five Cs: Control, Choice, Challenges, Complexity, and Caring. [38] Kanevsky says, "Students with an extraordinary capacity and craving for learning need rich, challenging opportunities to learn that are tailored to their passions, preferences, and strengths."[39]

Parents who consult with us sometimes have serious concerns about their children's grades. These concerns might center on a recent drop in interest in a particular subject area, or they may be broader and more pervasive, including failing an entire semester or year. There are many reasons why students do not do well at school or have difficulty with certain approaches, like e-learning, classroom learning, or homeschooling. "Children not only have varying interests and abilities, but varying modes of desired instruction, too."[40]

Low academic achievement does *not* necessarily mean laziness, willfulness, or lack of ability. Nor do low grades always indicate a problem. Sometimes they simply reflect a temporary and intentional disengagement of self-directed learners who find themselves in learning environments they don't find stimulating. Alternatively, however, sometimes low achievement results from home situations, peer pressure, anxiety, or other sources, and kids decide they need a break and choose to wind down. There are also times when gifted learners, just like others, require educational or psychological interventions.

Motivation is always in flux. It can be driven by dreams and desires, and be negatively affected by anxiety, influences, and stressors. We discuss emotional issues including anxiety, as well as offering additional coping strategies, in Chapter 9.

Underachievement

> *"Student performance that falls noticeably short of potential, especially for young people with high ability, is bewildering and perhaps the most frustrating of all challenges both teachers and parents face."*[41]

> *"To what extent are some of these students set up to fail by their placement in gifted programs where there's increased competition and task-orientation?"*

People typically use the term "underachiever" to describe a child who is not doing well at school but is perceived as very capable, but it's rarely, if ever, used to describe a child who is achieving similar grades but is perceived as not so capable. The child who is deemed capable but underachieving is apt to feel confused and criticized by the "gifted underachiever" label. Frequently, the child actually wants to do well and, when told they're "not working up to potential," feels even more pressure than before. Conversely, for the student in the same school environment who is not given the underachiever label but who has similarly poor grades, there's an implicit conclusion being made that low grades are the best they can do (that is, they're not so smart), and a cycle of low expectations is thereby reinforced.

This selective designation of some children as requiring attention as underachievers while others are just fine because they are inherently low achievers is problematic for three reasons:

○ It assumes that school grades are relevant motivators for all learners;

○ It assumes that methods of assessing intellectual potential are reliable enough to distinguish the underachiever from the low achiever; and

○ In addition to the fact that these assumptions are questionable, neither the underachieving nor the low achieving student benefits from the concept. The underachiever often feels confused about what's expected and why, as well as unsure about how or if they can meet the higher expectations. The low achiever feels they're not expected to achieve academic success, so why bother to work harder? Categorizing children in this way does nothing to enhance anyone's learning experiences or achievements, and in fact works against their academic confidence and success.

Linda Edwards, a colleague of ours, was described as an underachieving gifted learner when she was a student. Upon becoming a secondary school teacher, she designed an action research project, and field-tested it with a group of advanced high school students she wanted to motivate—kids who "regularly arrived in a disheveled manner, flopped into their seats, and read novels, regardless of what was requested of them." Parents and teachers alike can learn from various aspects of her creative approach.

Edwards' learning program featured content that met the following criteria:

○ relevant, current, and significant to outside-of-school life

○ not traditionally presented in schools

○ technology-based

○ immediately accessible, but offering challenging breadth

○ targeted to the development of effort and specific skills rather than achievement or evaluation

Students were asked to do these activities:

○ listen to and interpret the song lyrics of twentieth-century music *(auditory note-taking skills)*

○ decode text-messaging poetry *(literacy skills)*

○ look at cell-phone copyrights to make detailed descriptions and diagrams of objects *(observation, language, math, drawing skills)*

Edwards observed that students were engaged and cooperative. She reported, "The 'cool' factor was way up, and the output blockades were gone." She said the teens were motivated, and they agreed to try more traditional activities such as web quests on study skills, personal surveys on time management and learning styles, and readings on study habits. Edwards suggests the following strategies for motivating learners:

○ Offer non-motivated, low-achieving kids acceptance, be patient, and gently guide their learning by exposing them to relevant, concrete subject matter that connects to their own lives and current interests.

○ Ensure a relaxed, non-judgmental environment. Let intellectual sparks fly as kids willingly engage with challenging material.

○ Provide content that focuses on learning positive attitudes and behaviors, and as much choice and freedom as possible.

○ Be creative because standard rewards and motivational tools are not potent enough for those who reject achievement-based rewards like praise and grades.

Lecturing low-achieving students, telling them to work harder or to rise to their "intellectual potential" doesn't work. Some kids endure school bitterly or opt for invisibility by skipping classes or dropping out. (Edwards told us, "I know. I did that.")

Edwards says that underachievers can drain motivation from parents, teachers, and peers, and spark frustration and anger as others try to motivate them. They often reject things that others value (e.g., education, direction, goals, rules, evaluation). The challenge for adults is to avoid taking this rejection personally. Rather, they must make themselves available for patient personal connection and support, and be flexible about the non-essential elements of academic learning, like perfect attendance, conformity to hairstyles and uniforms, and handing homework in every day. Low motivation and low achievement *can* be turned around.

Learned Helplessness

"The work is too hard. No way I can do it."

"Our daughter has trouble dealing with pressure, disappointment, or big challenges."

Sometimes a child decides to avoid work that is difficult and chooses to tackle only work that is "safe." Children who are uncomfortable with open-ended tasks, or who demonstrate a lack of initiative in problem-solving, or who will only put effort into safe learning activities, may have learned to be helpless. These children believe that they might as well not try something that appears at first glance to be difficult, because failure is probable.

Learned helplessness is characterized by an avoidance of anything new or challenging. It becomes a self-fulfilling prophecy, and increases the likelihood of mediocre performance and failure. When confronted by an unfamiliar or challenging task, children who have developed the learned helplessness pattern shut down and think, "I can't do this!" and then find a reason why. They might complain of a stomach ailment or too much other work, or insist that they can't do math, aren't athletic, or are otherwise incapable. You might recognize the fixed mindset at work here.[42]

Individuals with a growth mindset, or mastery orientation to learning, on the other hand, tend to welcome and even thrive on challenge. Like the brave little engine in the children's story *The Little Engine that Could*,[43] they take on challenges and are far more likely to risk failure.

They look for opportunities to expand their range of skills and knowledge, and expect to encounter difficulties along the way. Those with a mastery orientation believe that learning is incremental, and that intelligence develops systematically over time through effort (growth mindset).

However, those with the learned helplessness pattern tend to believe that people are either smart or not smart, and that everyone is born with a fixed amount of ability or intelligence (fixed mindset). Many intellectually competent children develop this pattern. They can combat it by

○ learning to define success in terms of improvement and progress instead of grades and prizes;

○ viewing errors as a normal and essential part of the learning process rather than as unacceptable embarrassments to be avoided;

○ orienting themselves toward the process of learning, rather than the products that are a result of it; and

○ finding pleasure in learning itself rather than in doing better than others.

Here are three aphorisms that illustrate the growth mindset in action:

1. "When life gives you lemons, make lemonade."

2. "Some people see stepping-stones where others see stumbling blocks."

3. "You can see the glass as half full or half empty."

All children should be encouraged to welcome their errors, false starts, and failures as constructive learning opportunities, remembering that learning happens incrementally, one step at a time, and that no one is exceptional in everything. Mistakes help people understand something about what they need to learn. Children suffering from learned helplessness need guidance putting these ideas into practice.

Frustration and Boredom

"My daughter does well in school, but she says she dislikes it. I want learning to be exciting for her, not a heavy task that weighs her down."

"I can't be bothered. It tires me out! It's boring."

Academic instruction that is far above or below a student's ability induces frustration, boredom, and alienation. When students are encouraged to demonstrate their competence and are given appropriately targeted learning opportunities, they're more prone to be engaged by school and learning. When previously keen learners show signs of being bored or frustrated, the first thing to determine is whether there's an appropriate educational match for their ability. Allied with this is the question of relevance. Authentic learning experiences can

be absent from academic programs, and it's up to teaching professionals—or parents—to bridge the gap between the official school
curriculum and the vitality of real life.

Sometimes a child's degree of exceptionality is beyond the school's
capacity to address their learning needs. Albert Einstein was considered a genius as an adult, but he found much of his schooling deadly
boring. He failed courses, was deemed a mediocre student by most of
his teachers, and was not accepted into the university programs of his
choice. The nature and degree of his giftedness was almost certainly
a major reason for his lack of engagement in class. A school would
need to be truly extraordinary to recognize and meet the learning
needs of such a person.

In addition to creating a better educational match, a good way
to address boredom and frustration (and sometimes alienation) is
to help a child find engaging extracurricular activities, such as those
we discuss in Chapter 7. It can be motivating for a child to participate in extended learning opportunities with other kids who are as
enthusiastic as they are about particular areas of interest. Finding one
area of shared enthusiasm can infuse other areas of life with renewed
vibrancy, improving a child's feelings about learning and achievement,
and even life itself.

Sometimes all a child needs is the encouragement to figure things
out independently. Sara Blakely (a billionaire entrepreneur) attributes
much of her success to the way in which she was raised.[44] Her mother,
Ellen Blakely, believes in "creative free time" and she encouraged
her children to be bored so they could determine what they might
want to do. Not just to keep busy or to be entertained, but to find
meaningful outlets for their creative ideas and energy, and to create
their own fun, too.

It makes good sense for students to make time to explore fields
that will be critical for the future, such as science, engineering, and
economics. Kids who are at a loss for something to do could explore
possibilities for learning more in these areas, or others. Countless teens
and young adults avert boredom by starting with an interest, hobby, or
small community project (for example, designing masks, handcrafting
jewelry, or helping the homeless), and then building upon it.[45] They

investigate further, determine next steps, take matters into their own hands, and make their mark. Successful ventures and outcomes are the result of self-reliance, initiative, a good work ethic, and perhaps an enterprising spirit. Such attributes can be demonstrated, and instilled in children at a young age.

Study Skills and Work Habits

> *"Nobody ever taught me how to properly organize notes or how to write a composition. Now I'm in high school, and even when I know the subject matter, I can't put together a decent essay!"*

Capable learners often have trouble with study skills and work habits. When learning comes too easily for too long, children can manage to get by with minimal effort, and acquire little in the way of good work habits. At some point in their education, however, they will almost certainly find they have to invest some effort in acquiring the habits and skills (organization, time management, note-taking, etc.) that less capable learners may have long since mastered. It's easier sooner than later, but that doesn't always happen.

When the day comes that a lack of study skills or work habits catches up with a student, it's time for action. As with everything else, what works for a particular person depends on age, temperament, and context, as well as other individual factors. For some, a private tutor can help on a one-on-one basis, addressing the student's unique issues and concerns, and adapting support to meet changing needs over the school year. The tutor might be an older student with expertise in the necessary skills, a retired teacher, or a professional tutor or other instructor.

Sometimes a peer study group works well. Groups can be organized according to what the group members think will be most beneficial. A structured approach is usually helpful in the process of acquiring study skills, if only as a model for learning what organized structure looks and feels like. Meetings can be more or less formal, weekly or as desired, depending on the circumstances. Occasionally study sessions include teachers, parents, relevant experts, or other students.

Some learners prefer to develop their own approach to studying and then work independently, perhaps with some guidance from others. They might use study skills workbooks or resources they find on the Internet,[46] in libraries and at reputable bookstores. One highly effective tool is to break difficult work down into smaller, more manageable portions, with simple frameworks and achievable schedules for completion. Adults can guide a child's effort by offering tailored assistance. They can also facilitate collaborative learning, encourage goal-directed motivation, and provide constructive feedback that promotes self-monitoring and persistence.

Another motivational strategy has been called "habit stacking." This involves linking new or daunting activities or changes with already set routines. For example, if a child or teen requires more physical exercise but isn't motivated to do that, they can add a few minutes of stretches to the front end of something they do routinely every day—perhaps before doing their homework, having an afternoon snack, or brushing their teeth. Health and wellness coach Mitzi Weinman advises, "Habit stacking makes it much simpler to ease into something new. The key is to start off small with one step and devote a short amount of time."[47] Existing routines become triggers for the new habit, and as long as expectations are reasonable, grouping activities together like this can lead to positive change.

Procrastination

> *"Being too quick to label someone a procrastinator can further impede productivity, erode self-confidence, make a person feel less capable, and even devalue accomplishments. It may make more sense to think of procrastination not as a way out but rather a way around, or another way altogether."*[48]

Some children and teens procrastinate, and there are various and often legitimate reasons for it. For example, they might be confused, risk-aversive, disinterested, fearful, distracted, fatigued, disorganized, or overwhelmed. They might avoid tasks occasionally, or only in certain situations or timeframes, or it might be habitual. Task avoidance can interfere with an individual's learning, relationships, and self-confidence. It can dampen motivation and trigger worry, guilt, shame, and anger.

Procrastination doesn't always result in inefficiency, however, nor is it always problematic. In times of adversity, or if a child feels a situation is uncomfortable or onerous, procrastinating may be a self-help mechanism that provides a measure of containment or control. Putting things off can free up time to think matters through and let ideas percolate. By modifying the pace and timing of actions, a child may feel calmer, and this may be beneficial, especially if circumstances feel overly demanding or stressful.

Procrastination is willful avoidance. Doing something–or not doing it—is a matter of choice. People choose whether to use their capacities, create, act, step up, or put forth effort.

Children who procrastinate may feel discouraged, anxious, or rebellious. They can overcome their procrastination—if they want to do that—by paying careful attention to their attitudes, preferences, influences, and behaviors. They may need assistance becoming more focused, purposeful, patient, or whatever else it might take to develop the strategies and strengths they require to be more productive.

Parents and teachers can help children learn to manage their responsibilities, perceive possible setbacks, and manage their stress. Adults can encourage kids to figure out what might motivate them to overcome the procrastination. They can also support them in acquiring good time management skills, and learning how to build on their strengths, empowering them to move forward with more self-assurance.

Bust Your BUTS [49] is a resource for kids that will encourage them to think about what underlies their procrastination tendencies, and how to resolve the issues so they'll be more motivated and productive over the short, medium, and long haul. [50]

Academic Overload

We had many voices to choose from about the prickly topic of academic overload. We finally settled on six. The first three are from students, and the others are from parents:

"Watch out for the homework!"

"It's a lot of pressure. Everyone expects so much of me. I HATE IT! And if I make one mistake, I never hear the end of it."

"I've got way too much work! The pile goes up to the ceiling!"

"He was expecting different work in the gifted program, not more work."

"Complete tension. Our whole family is feeling it. She comes home stressed about the homework."

"I see her struggling with the amount of work. I wonder if it's fair."

Schoolwork should be engaging and appropriately challenging, but it has to be balanced with other activities in a person's life. Just as with adults, there can be negative consequences when a child's work becomes too burdensome or all-consuming. Academic expectations are so arduous in some settings that kids and parents are stressed, and the quality of family life is adversely affected. When academic overload happens, it's time for teachers and parents to pay attention to children's balanced development and adapt their demands accordingly. For example, staggered due dates or interim goal-setting might help.

Sometimes it's not the academic program itself but rather a child's extracurricular commitments that cause the overload. Some children juggle school with lessons, practicing, games, and social, family, community, and religious activities. One way to address this is to pare down the extracurricular commitments so that the child has some breathing room.

A sense of academic overload may accurately reflect the demands of school and other obligations. However, a sense of overload can derive from other sources. For example, parents who derive a sense of pride and accomplishment from their child's achievements may have very high performance expectations. These expectations can have a positive effect on the child, supporting their achievement and contributing to their confidence, but that's not always the case. The child might be experiencing a heavy burden of having to achieve so as to continue to please their parents in order to enhance their self-esteem, and earn their approval. Parents must seriously consider the child's well-being, and disentangle it from their own hopes and egos. If your child is experiencing a burden of overload, take a step back and ask yourself if you might be contributing to that with your desire for them to succeed.

Undue stress and overload can also result from demands that children impose upon themselves. Some children tend to be too self-critical or search too relentlessly for complexity, perfection, or order. Others have learning problems, and experience academic overload in situations where their classmates might not. Children and adolescents need help from the adults they trust in order to put the demands in their lives into healthy perspective.

Although it can be rewarding to pursue excellence, it's unhealthy to pursue it to extremes. Students who are trying to handle an oppressive workload may begin to lose their sense of initiative, doubt their capabilities, or become alienated from school altogether.[51]

Sometimes children choose to avoid being challenged in order to concentrate on activities that showcase their areas of strength, thereby lightening their load, and circumventing disappointment or tasks that might expose their areas of weakness. Helping students develop a growth mindset is an important step in enabling them to feel good about themselves and to experience a higher degree of motivation and, subsequently, success.

Children who wrestle with academic overload may also experience social problems if their anxieties and concerns interfere with their ability to relax and interact with their classmates and friends. Parents and educators who live or work with children who feel overwhelmed by work, push themselves too hard, or avoid their responsibilities, should be sensitive to signs of overload. Some things to watch for include:

○ a drop in grades or markedly lower levels of academic achievement

○ procrastination, reduced initiative

○ tension, stress, short temper, mood swings

○ anxiety, worry, nervousness, sleep problems, lack of communication, change in appetite

○ fear of failure, fear of success

○ power struggles with those who set expectations

○ academic burnout, which may include giving up and extreme exhaustion

Like children who are low achievers, those who exhibit learned helplessness, or those who are disenchanted with learning because of boredom or frustration, children who are distraught due to heavy workloads can learn to regulate their responses to the demands of school and home. Parents and teachers can assist children and adolescents by showing them how to pace themselves, set learning priorities, relax, break tasks down into smaller parts, and establish reasonable goals—all of which will enable them to feel more comfortable about whatever learning demands come their way.[52]

Other strategies your child can use to cope with academic overload and sustain their motivation include the following:

○ Pause and step back from work now and again in order to get a healthy perspective on what really has to be done, to what extent, and when.

○ Think carefully about what can be accomplished within a given timeframe.

○ Maintain a sense of humor, especially when things get tough.

○ Develop better organizational and study skills.

○ Share the load and work alongside others to meet demands.

○ Create a personal system of guidelines and strategic work plans (such as checklists, periodic rewards, or interim finish lines).

○ Increase your emotional intelligence in order to learn about ways to handle stress.[53]

○ Aim for good enough, not perfect.

○ Talk to teachers and/or guidance counselors about your concerns, and ways to manage, reduce, or rearrange academic loads.

When it comes to academic overload, as with other school problems, open and regular communication between home and school can make all the difference. Parents and teachers should be ready to intervene as necessary, remembering there are times and situations that require professional counseling.

Motivating Students Who Have Extra Burdens of Responsibility

Here's another example of motivation, again shared by Linda Edwards. It puts motivation in context, and illustrates the reality of kids trying to keep up with school assignments while holding down jobs, looking after siblings, or taking on additional responsibilities at home. This kind of lived experience became more prevalent during the COVID pandemic, which rocked economic stability and transformed the employment landscape.

When Other Demands Interfere with School

I had a really bright student who was always tired in class because he worked the night shift in order to help his family pay the rent. I think in cases like this, we have to modify classroom requirements as much as possible. Beyond that, we can acknowledge the value of a student's work experiences.

I praised this young man's work ethic and told him I was impressed by his attitude and perseverance amid tough circumstances. After I had given an assignment, I always went over to him to make sure he had heard and understood it, and I made a point to show him ways to work smarter rather than harder. I showed him—and other students— how to be precise with effort.

Efficient time and work management are helping him stay motivated and get through the very heavy load he has to carry.

We'd like to note that Edwards' caring attention and valuing of this student's efforts on behalf of his family also supported him in staying engaged at school. She gave him not only some valuable coping techniques, but also emotional support—and that's the most powerful motivator for all learning.

Additional Ideas for Maximizing Motivation

Here's a checklist of practical strategies, many of which we've touched on elsewhere. We wrote the checklist originally for teachers, but they're also helpful for parents who want to motivate their children's engagement in learning. You'll see we've divided the strategies into three categories: the nature of the tasks, children's involvement, and evaluation processes.

Nature of Academic Tasks

1. Are tasks appropriately challenging and also achievable?

2. Are tasks multidimensional?

3. Are they open-ended?

4. Are different kinds of skills valued?

5. Is there a recognition of the dynamic nature of learning, of development over time?

6. Do activities have real-world significance?

7. Do learning opportunities invite active participation?

8. Do tasks invite exploration, experimentation, or hands-on learning?

9. Is there an element of surprise or wonder?

10. Are activities linked to children's interests, curiosities, and experiences?

11. Is the pace of learning suitable for each child?

12. Is there enthusiasm in the learning environment?

Children's Involvement

1. Can children make choices in their day-to-day experiences?

2. Are children's perspectives valued?

3. Are their opinions welcome?

4. Are there rewarding and meaningful activities for those who complete their work quickly?

5. Is it safe to ask for help?

6. Is creativity encouraged?

7. Are new or abstract concepts connected to familiar or concrete ones?

8. Are there problems and questions that challenge those with the highest level of mastery?

9. Do children have as much discretion and autonomy as they can handle?

10. Do children have opportunities to collaborate and share ideas with each other?

11. Do children belong to a community of learners—using resources, exchanging information, taking courses, and reading books?

Evaluation of Learning Processes

1. Is there attention to children's effort and improvement?

2. Is there a specified and reasonable standard of achievement?

3. Are timelines clear and fair?

4. Are children given timely and constructive feedback?

5. Can children participate in the design of their tasks?

6. Can they help decide on the level of difficulty?

7. Are there self-evaluation questions throughout the learning process?

8. Are children involved in personal goal-setting—short and long term?

9. Are learning and understanding monitored?

10. Are children accountable for their efforts?

11. Are errors treated as a natural and important part of learning?

12. Do children feel that not knowing something is no reason for embarrassment?

13. Are "wrong answers" incorporated into discussions as productive contributions to the learning process?

14. Are biases, priorities, and viewpoints checked?

15. Are successes attributed to effort and perseverance, not innate ability?

At the end of the day, motivation is just a beginning. *Doing* something is what makes a difference. "You don't just find a paved path of education with a sign next to it with your name on it…That's not how life works. You must be willing to do the proverbial work. You cut the vines, trim the trees, and pave the road yourself. You make a path where there was none."[54] That observation takes into account the importance of children's investment in their own education, and it aligns well with the next chapter, where we focus on responding to children's social, emotional, and behavioral issues.

CHAPTER 9

Social, Emotional, and Behavioral Considerations

Being academically advanced isn't a problem in and of itself, but being different than others can be socially and emotionally challenging, and can lead to behavior problems. In this chapter, we address some of the social concerns associated with giftedness, as well as emotional considerations and behavioral issues. As throughout this book, our focus is on providing the support that parents need in order to understand what's happening, and address it in ways that optimize their child's likelihood of thriving.

Social Concerns

"Why won't they be friends with me? I'm like yanking my hair out!"

"He wants friends more than anything, but he doesn't know how to go about it."

"The children in Megan's class are VERY hard to handle. They tend to form cliques, and lately she's been the odd one out."

Humans are social animals. Our needs for acceptance and belonging are hard-wired, a survival adaptation that continues to stand us in good stead. For children, peer pressure or rejection can be particularly brutal. A gifted labeling experience can trigger uncertainty, dismay, or other concerns. (See Chapter 5.) Although giftedness results from cognitive or other strengths, it doesn't predict social competence, and it can sometimes interfere with peer acceptance.

Your child's social milieu is the classroom, the playground, the places they go outside of school, and the people they encounter each day. Are they a valued member of their various social groups? Do they have a sense of belonging? Of being seen and heard? Over the years, many children have talked to us about their social experiences. We've listened to them discuss problems making friends and keeping them, and how their giftedness (or a gifted label) can sometimes separate them from others.

Social competence varies from one individual to the next. As with adults, some children attract friends like magnets, easily and effortlessly, while others do not. Some children have trouble socializing in certain situations and manage fine in others. And there are those who try very hard to get along with their peers but just can't seem to make it work in any environment, and decide they don't want or need friends after all. In the first section of this chapter, we address problems associated with moving to a segregated gifted setting, family relationships, and strategies for nurturing children's social intelligence.

Moving to a Gifted Classroom

In order to better understand the lived experience of gifted identification and programming, we asked a sample of children, their parents, and their teachers to tell us about it, from their points of view. One of the lines of questioning concerned the social aspect of the gifted experience. The children's responses varied dramatically:

> *"I didn't like my regular class, and I so much wanted to go to the 'smart' class."*

> *"Mean kids who aren't in the gifted class tease me."*

> *"I'm definitely more comfortable in the gifted class."*

> *"My friends are my friends. I don't care if they're gifted or not."*

> *"It's made me a happier person. Finally I've found kids who think like I do!"*

The parents' views also varied considerably, and were sometimes disturbing.

> *"After viewing the gifted class, we came out frazzled. Did we do the right thing by enrolling him here?"*
>
> *"She's gained personal confidence in social situations."*
>
> *"She carries a weight on her shoulders."*
>
> *"Before she had to fake a little bit just to blend in. She came back from the gifted class glowing that first day, and she's been happy ever since."*
>
> *"We had no idea it would be this hard. He left his school, classmates, teachers, and a set of rules that he knew, to go to a distant neighborhood into an already established pecking order with no support."*
>
> *"Even now in the gifted class, he still doesn't have a close friend at school."*

The teachers' comments confirmed the need to pay attention to children's social concerns when they make a transition from a regular classroom into a segregated gifted program:

> *"I have a whole class of gifted learners. It's a jumble, emotionally and socially."*
>
> *"I have several students who don't want to participate in group activities. They're kind of isolated. It's sad, and it's frustrating for me, but it's their choice."*
>
> *"The kids in my gifted class don't socialize much with kids in other classes. There's not a whole lot of opportunity for that, I guess."*
>
> *"There's a group of kids in my class who are super keen. They seem to feed on each other's talents. Others are reserved and prefer to work independently."*

It's not possible to predict how a child will respond to a new classroom or social situation. However, it is possible to provide an environment where individual differences are accepted, diversity is seen as a strength, and students are helped to understand themselves and others. In this kind of social environment, all children feel welcome, respected, and appreciated, and have ample opportunities for positive interactions with others.

Classroom Cultures that Support Children's Social Development

Parents are sometimes surprised to discover that academic changes such as moving into a gifted program, can involve social and emotional challenges that are harder to manage than the changes in curriculum. Children can feel uncertain, confused, or anxious when they join a full-time gifted class, often in a different school. Parents may feel that way as well.

School culture and valued attributes (such as appearance, social skills, family wealth or social status, clothes, intellectual abilities, or athletic prowess) vary from one school setting to the next. Sometimes a child will find it easy to fit in within a certain setting. Other times, fitting in requires a child to think about adapting to the new milieu. In some cases, kids feel a need to adjust their vocabulary, take more (or less) care with their dress or personal grooming, or think carefully about how often they give answers in class. Some children find such adjustments difficult. Others perceive the change in culture and expectations but refuse to conform. Still others see the social adjustments as temporary inconveniences, or even interesting challenges. It's comforting for all concerned when a child quickly feels at home in a new learning environment. At the same time, it's not the end of the world when that doesn't happen.[1]

Changes in educational programs bring hidden and unexpected social adjustments. By being responsive to a child's concerns, adults can help them anticipate and manage change in ways that increase their resilience and sense of competence.

Psychologist Marilyn Price-Mitchell discusses sociability—the capacity to create and sustain relationships, to collaborate, and to be together comfortably—and its importance for learning, emotional well-being, and life success. She says children need to feel respected, and be able to communicate freely.[2] She writes, "Some kids express their abilities in quieter, introverted ways, while others interact in more energetic, extroverted ways. Neither path is superior to the other. They are merely different paths toward the same goal."

Taking a longer view, change can be positive. Sometimes it works out so well that everyone wonders why they were ever worried. Other times it proves to have been a mistake, in which case wise parents and educators begin to problem-solve about how to proceed.

Children, like adults, want to feel accepted, to be affiliated with others with whom they share something, and to be recognized for their accomplishments. This may take time, effort, social skills, support, compromise, and self-confidence, all of which can be encouraged and reinforced by parents and teachers who care. Adults can help by recognizing when children feel anxious; by taking their emotions, observations, or experiences seriously; and by modeling reflection, mindful habits, and kind social practices.

Friendships

Child psychologist Eileen Kennedy-Moore writes, "There are many different kinds of friendships: friends you play with, friends you laugh with, friends you work with, friends you talk with…Good friends make happy times more fun and hard times more bearable. But friendships aren't always easy."[3]

Kennedy-Moore's suggestions for children who need help with social learning include being open to friendship; taking the first steps (such as giving simple greetings, and finding common ground); showing kindness to others; being a good sport; and taking things slowly. Children who are shy or socially anxious, or who purposely distance themselves from others (for example, by immersing them-selves in music, books, computer activities or independent projects), can learn to feel good about their roles in the classroom, the schoolyard social milieu, or during sports and other extracurricular activities.

Social Skills Problems

> *"I don't know why, but I don't seem to have friends over at my house anymore."*

> *"Those who are different in some way have an advantage on the distinctiveness side of the ledger, but a big strike against them in the "fitting in" department."*[4]

About ten percent of children are born with a difficult temperament, meaning they have intense reactions, avoid new people and situations, and are frequently irritable, impatient, and negative. Parents often need assistance helping such children develop social, emotional, and behavioral skills. There are terrific resources and supports available for you if you're raising a child with a difficult temperament.[5]

In other circumstances, regardless of their temperament, there are children who have trouble with social activities because the nature and degree of their exceptionality is such that their age peers don't understand their enthusiasms or language use. This is sometimes misdiagnosed as a social skills deficit, but no amount of social skills training will fix it, if that's what's going on.

When a person's interests are profoundly different from others', and their communication skills are several years ahead of their grade-mates, it can be difficult to forge meaningful friendships with age-peers. In these situations, it's best if their individuality is respected, and they're encouraged to find interactions outside of school. They may find it easier to interact with adults or older children whose interests they share. "Parents have important roles in guiding their children, so they come to have positive perspectives on their ways of being different. It helps when youngsters understand that intellectual ability is a long- term strength: although high intelligence can sometimes feel like an albatross, that's usually temporary."[6]

Well-meaning educators and parents sometimes exert pressure on socially awkward children to take socials skills training so they can learn how to behave more "normally," or so they can fit in better with their age-peers. This can be a dismal failure or even traumatic, an experience in which the child's self-perception as a hopeless misfit is only reinforced, and their social skills are further eroded rather than enhanced. It's usually more productive to invest that energy in ensuring that the child's learning needs are well met, and that there are ample opportunities for high-level engagement in their areas of interest and strength.

We're sometimes contacted by parents who want to know about resource groups or programs for children experiencing social issues. We start by recommending that parents be wary of social skills programs that focus on "niceness," which often means trying to fit a wonderfully individualistic square peg into a conventionally round hole, where the child may come to think there is something wrong with them because of who they are. If a child seems satisfied with their social situation, then social skills groups can be seriously counterproductive.

A good question to ask is whether the child is actually experiencing their social situation as a problem. A child who is unhappy about their social life may want some help figuring out the rules of social interactions, just like some kids benefit from extra help learning to read. For these children, a well-run social skills group can be beneficial.[7] If a child strongly desires to know more about how to make and have friends, there can be something gained by participating in such a group, as long as there's a good personality fit with a leader who respects and values each person's individuality.

If, however, the problem is that the adults in the child's life (parents, teachers, or relatives) think the child should have (more) friends, then it's time to step back and think carefully about the child's personality and authentic interests. When a child's age-peers don't understand or share interests with them, this won't be rectified by social skills training, unless the child decides to "dumb down" in order to fit in. It's better for their long-term development to look for opportunities to engage with people who share their interests and curiosities, no matter their age.

There are strategies for building social skills that parents can use at home. Here are a few suggestions to help make your child's social experiences more positive:

1. Consider your child's social preferences and tendencies. Some children do not need or want more than one friend, and that's perfectly healthy.

2. If your child has no friends, help them find one person with whom to share a common interest. It could be a grandparent, librarian, or neighbor.

3. Offer reassurance. Help your child realize that each person is unique, and so will fit better into some environments than others. Exceptionally advanced thinkers often don't find same-age intellectual peers until they're in high school or college, or even into adulthood.

4. Reinforce positive social behavior whenever you see it. Do this privately, however, so as not to embarrass your child publicly.

5. Increase your child's confidence in social situations by looking for promising opportunities for successful interactions, such as clubs or interest groups where people can share their ideas and be engaged intellectually.

6. Encourage participation in extracurricular activities, cooperative play and learning, and shared activities within the community.

These suggestions apply to all children, and can be especially helpful for those who are cognitively advanced, and have trouble fitting in because of that. In situations in which children have more serious social skills deficits, such as Asperger's Syndrome and Nonverbal Learning Disabilities, other approaches may be required.[8] For all children, and from early days, home is the best place to learn social skills.

Family and Sibling Relationships

"The sun looks down on nothing half so good as a household laughing together over a meal."[9]

"When they told me I was gifted, I felt happy but also uncomfortable."

"I'm just average. My sister was identified as gifted, but when I took the gifted test, they said I didn't make it."

When parents create a healthy home environment where each child feels loved and valued, this not only supports each child's optimal development, but it also strengthens the bonds among the family members, and reduces the likelihood of problems from sibling rivalry.

Sometimes one child is identified as a gifted learner and one or more siblings are not. The following reflection was shared by Laressa Rudyk, a teacher.

On Being the Gifted Sister

I was identified as gifted in Grade 4, but my sister Taryn, who is exactly one year older than me, was not identified as gifted. Three years ago, both of us now in our thirties, Taryn told me, "Nobody understands how hard it was to have a sister like you."

I recalled my extreme sensitivity to Taryn's feelings when we were kids. I deliberately "dumbed down" my abilities as early as age five in front of our parents to protect her feelings. Our father was insensitive and treated my sister and me differently. Our mother, a psychologist, was aware that I was scared of hurting Taryn's feelings, and we discussed it in private regularly.

Taryn's and my birthday happen to be on the same day. On my fifth birthday and her sixth, our father gave each of us a book: hers was Cinderella and mine was Mensa puzzles. When Taryn saw my book, she started crying, dropped her book, and ran out of the room. I guiltily dropped my book, picked up hers, and went after her. Ever since, our father has given us exactly the same thing for our birthdays, probably at my mother's insistence.

On my tenth birthday and Taryn's eleventh, our father made us a birthday cake and put the numbers 10 and 11 on the cake. In binary. He put the cake in front of us and told us to figure out what the candles represented. I recognized the numbers immediately but pretended that I didn't. He eventually said to me, "Come on. It's binary. You know that."

Last week, I asked Taryn if she remembered the binary birthday cake incident. She certainly did. "It was so mean to put the candles on our cake in binary when he knew that I didn't know binary. I asked him to explain it and he just waved me off, telling me not to worry about it. That was pretty awful because it was supposed to be my cake, too."

Laressa and Taryn talked about their painful memories, so many years later. Such conversations can help to strengthen relationships, but siblings have happier, healthier childhoods when their parents are sensitive to their differences.

The dumbing down that Laressa described happens not only in families, but also in schools and other circumstances where a child feels uncomfortable about being or feeling different than others.

Here's another story about family dynamics.

Triplets: Two Gifted and One Not

Julie Stoyka, a teacher, told us about some long-time friends of hers. They were triplets, three girls, two of whom were identified as gifted, and were offered a special program at school. Their parents were unsure whether to accept the gifted placement for two of their three daughters, but ultimately decided to accept because they realized they had distinct learning needs that might be better met in a gifted program.

As an adult, the sister who was not identified as gifted told Julie, "I was the only one who wasn't smart. Now I can say that I have a more positive view of it, but it was really hard back then. I sometimes felt that everyone else was feeling sorry for me, so I started doing different things, and succeeded." Cohesiveness prevailed, and each sister thrived, all of them ultimately attending university.

The parents supported their daughters by encouraging their involvement in activities outside of school, and also by taking care not to put too much emphasis on any one child's strengths. They recognized that scholastic attainment is just one facet of development. As one of the identified-gifted sisters said, "Emphasizing life skills, communication skills, presentation skills, thinking skills, and entrepreneurial skills is more important than marks."

Parents who reinforce and maintain a strong and healthy family dynamic empower each of their children to forge a unique identity and pursue their own strengths and passions.

Different Children, Different Treatment

"My dad loved quizzing me, and we'd have long philosophical discussions. It made me feel sort of embarrassed because it was obvious that he thought I was more interesting than my sister."

"My brother was a math whiz. When we were growing up, my parents said they couldn't afford summer camp for me, but somehow they could always afford special trips, contests, and activities for him."

Two children in the same family can experience what appears to be the same environment very differently. Parents don't always treat each child the same, and siblings do not react in the same ways to parental pressures to perform, or to other aspects of family life or parenting style. Factors influencing children's responses include their temperament, personality, interests, birth order, birth spacing, sex, relationship to each parent, and perception of parents' treatment of their siblings. Because of these differences, parenting approaches that work well with one child may not work with another. Although it's important to be fair, it's sometimes essential to treat children differently.

The needs that all children share is that their parents provide love, structure, respect, a variety of stimulating learning experiences, and encouragement for their developing competence and responsible independence. How parents provide this can vary across individual children in the same family, depending on each child's particular needs and age level, but when parents do a good job with these factors, their children are free to thrive, each in their own individual ways.

Conflict happens from time to time within all families. Although some people have difficulty handling conflict, it's an important part of a healthy family dynamic.[10] Children need examples, guidance, and instruction in order to learn how to settle things constructively, responsibly, and creatively. They need to experience conflicts in order to learn how to resolve them, and it's best if that happens at home, under the loving guidance of adults who care about them. You want your child to learn to express their opinions honestly, and disagree with others productively and respectfully. These are valuable assets in all relationships.

Optimally, each of your children will learn how to contribute positively to the family dynamic, buoying up one another's weaknesses, feeling comfortable demonstrating their own strengths, and celebrating each family member's success as a shared success. You can model this behavior, explaining what you're doing and why you're doing it as that's appropriate. Although differences of opinion are to be expected, everyone is more likely to thrive if the overall family climate is warm and generous.

Strategies for Nurturing Your Child's Social Intelligence

Here are some strategies for creating a home environment that fortifies family bonds, and nurtures each child's social intelligence and abilities:

○ Show that you respect and value each child's abilities. Celebrate every victory and achievement as a win for the entire family.

○ Help each child know that everyone has strengths as well as challenges, and that profiles of abilities vary, none being better than another. For example, if one child is mathematically gifted and another is good at sports, help each child respect the other's abilities or interests as well as their own.

○ Avoid comparing your children with each other, or with others.

○ Provide each child with learning experiences that align with their interests and capabilities.

○ Look for activities for each child that will allow them to shine.

○ Don't allow the pursuits of one child to take precedence over another's, or to consistently disrupt family leisure time.

○ Be sensitive to possible friction relating to the gifted label.

○ Don't refer to one child as *being* gifted (and another not), but rather emphasize that different people have different strengths, challenges, and learning needs.

○ Stay alert to signs of a child feeling inferior or superior relative to their siblings.

○ Consider family counseling if you're concerned about the interactions between siblings, and if these recommendations don't help.

When one or more children in a family is identified as gifted, parents should anticipate the possibility of different reactions and responses, and for that to change over time. You can reduce the chances of problems with jealousy, rivalry, and provocation if you pay attention. Make sure each of your children feels competent, valued, and supported, and be prepared to act quickly at the earliest sign of trouble.

Understandably, siblings who are not labeled as gifted will be looking out for implications that they're less capable than those who have been identified as gifted, and so may feel a need to prove their worth. They may feel underappreciated, and might challenge the ability of designated gifted family members, become sullen, or perhaps choose another domain of achievement for themselves. Siblings of one or more children designated as gifted or talented can feel incompetent or even stupid, even though they may be highly capable, too.

Some parents give giftedness more weight than it deserves. Yes, it's important to recognize and address exceptionality where it occurs, but no, a child who scores above a certain IQ (or demonstrates gifted learning needs in some other way) is not more deserving of parental time and other family resources than lower-scoring siblings. For everyone's sake, it's important that parents realize that each of their children has unique abilities, and needs to feel equally loved and accepted. When each child feels capable and confident, and is given opportunities to extend their learning reach, every member of the family is strengthened.

Self-Concept

> *"Contrary to stereotypes, gifted students are not socially isolated misfits. Their social self-concept is similar to that of their peers…Attempts to enhance self-concept will require examining an individual's communication with significant others, comparisons with reference groups, experiences of success, and perceived ability across various domains."*[11]

How people feel about themselves influences how they approach the people and situations in their lives. Those who feel confident about their competence are more likely to experience successes than those with troubling self-doubts.[12] A person's sense of self is constructed in an ongoing and complex process. It incorporates perceptions of the opinions of others, available support mechanisms, personal history, and developmental maturity.

As with intelligence, self-concept can be domain-specific: people generally see themselves as competent in some areas but not others. Children have different levels of self-concept in the academic, social, behavioral, appearance, and athletic dimensions of their lives, all of which come together in different weights to inform their global self-concept.[13] Global self-concept, which reflects the level of self-concept in the dimensions that are most valued by the individual, is the most important predictor of emotional well-being. This is very much affected by a person's age and developmental history.

Although there's considerable research on giftedness and self-concept, the results are not consistent.[14] Giftedness can be both a *risk* factor and a *resiliency* factor when it comes to self-concept. Although being exceptional increases the likelihood of being rejected by peers or feeling isolated because of that difference, most studies show that advanced learners tend to have a stronger self-concept than others.[15]

However, there is a contextual factor: a child's academic self-esteem may be reduced when they enter a full-time gifted program or a larger school. When comparing oneself with others who do as well as or better than they do academically, a child who was previously the best student in their class can experience a loss in academic self-concept. "Students report more negative academic self-concepts when exposed to learning environments with relatively higher-achieving students."[16]

If you're concerned about your child's self-esteem, consider the observation made by child psychologist Eileen Kennedy-Moore, who writes that it's important to help kids "find their voice, figure out what matters to them, and connect with something bigger than themselves."[17] She encourages children to be kind to themselves and to make an effort to avoid self-criticism. She also suggests that kids practice mindfulness, formulate their own ideas about what matters most to them, and take pride in their uniqueness and self-worth.

How these various considerations and possibilities play out in the life of any one child depends on individual circumstances and situations, and on the supports that are in place to help that child adjust to challenge and change, gain confidence, and find their own way forward.

Emotional Considerations

> *"Maleke welcomes change as an adventure, an opportunity for learning and exploration. My other two kids need lots of advance warning, preparation, and reassurance."*

> *"High academic intelligence is no guarantee of high emotional intelligence, and all children—no matter how smart they are—need help learning to cope with the complexity and intensity of their feelings."*[18]

What matters in our lives is not so much what happens to us, as the way we experience what happens, how we feel about it. What are some of the issues that are more likely to cause problems for gifted learners than for others?

We discuss some serious problems in this section (fear of failure, fear of success, perfectionism, arrogance, anxiety, and suicide), and in each case we provide some general recommendations and suggestions. If you're having problems, however, that can't be solved in this way, you may need professional help that takes into account the complexity of your personal situation.

Fear of Failure

> *"There's no way I'm going to enter that Math Olympiad. What for? Just because I'm good in math? I'll have to work myself to death, and I won't win anyhow."*

Somewhat paradoxically, high-ability learners who experience consistent success can develop a fear of failure. It's human nature to fear the unknown, and people who never learn how to cope successfully with failure come to fear it. Conversely, those who've fallen flat on their faces and who've had the support and resources to pick themselves up again discover they can recover from failure, and they usually learn something, too.[19]

You know your child is becoming afraid of failure if they resist trying new activities or select only safe tasks that will lead to easy successes. Children who opt out of challenging opportunities and competitions are at risk of developing a fear of failure. They may worry that failure will show them up as incompetent, or that they'll experience rejection or criticism. As a result, they may develop habits that reinforce the desire to stay within their comfort zones.

If not remedied, the fear of failure can be debilitating. Although choosing to jump low hurdles and take easy courses can result in a child achieving strong academic grades, it minimizes their real learning and reduces the likelihood of successes at higher academic and professional levels. A key to high competence in any area is purposeful and meaningful engagement over time in that area, with an understanding that risks, explorations, and failures are essential to the learning process. It's helpful when kids appreciate that abilities develop incrementally, and that failure can usually be overcome. This realization helps them persist over and beyond the stumbling blocks that are inevitable in every area of life. Children who purposefully tackle challenges and welcome setbacks as learning opportunities can achieve successes that those who are afraid to fail cannot.

However, fears can be serious. If your child has a deeply embedded fear of failure or is profoundly or recurringly afraid of making mistakes then, as with other problems, a suitable course of action involves seeking professional advice.

Fear of Success

> *"He does his homework so beautifully, and then he forgets it, or loses it, or doesn't hand it in. It's almost like he's afraid to excel."*

Doing well can lead to ever-increasing expectations from others and (often worse) from oneself, sometimes to ridiculously high or unachievable levels. Sometimes it feels easier just not to try. Not infrequently, highly capable learners pre-empt their own possibilities of success by not submitting their work, not studying for a test, not investing much effort in a project, or not applying for an award that they might win. Sometimes, just when they get close to proficiency, they opt to redirect their energy elsewhere.

Although fear of success might appear to be the other end of the spectrum from fear of failure, it's actually similar. Successful experiences can lead an individual to doubt they've merited the achievements with which they've been credited, or whether they'll be able to achieve at that level in the future (sometimes called the imposter syndrome). In cases like these, success can be more anxiety-provoking than average achievement so that, over time, people develop a fear of doing very well.

A fear of success usually shows itself in self-sabotage. This can be in the form of procrastination, pessimism, forgetting essential tools or deadlines, or laziness. At its root, it's usually an unconscious fear of future possible changes. Other reasons for fear of success include harboring a belief that there will be an increased burden of responsibility; that once they reach their goal that will be the pinnacle and they won't find further joy; others will be jealous of their success; or success will disappear. Such concerns can be real to a child, and sometimes fear of success (as with fear of failure) becomes so debilitating as to require professional help.

Encourage healthy self-awareness and self-acceptance, so that defense mechanisms do not get in the way. Chat with your child about their concerns and aspirations. Share your own experiences. Discuss how to manage changes and responsibilities that might accompany high-level accomplishment. Offer reassurance about the perceptions of others. Talk about the pursuit of happiness, too. Successes do not vaporize, and achievements can be good starting points for other worthwhile dreams and goals.

Perfectionism

> *"Sylvie always has to get a 100 on every assignment. Last week, she got 98% on a test and asked if she could rewrite it!"*

The desire to get things right is conducive to high achievement. Some children, however, establish unrealistically high standards for themselves, and become anxious, dissatisfied, and discouraged when they don't meet them. They may be more concerned about avoiding mistakes than they are about learning. As with all dimensions of well-being, the objective for children or adolescents who have perfectionistic tendencies should be to find a healthy balance in which there's enough challenge that there's growth, but without undue and debilitating stress.

Perfectionism is associated with an emphasis on order, precision, and perseverance, which are also associated with healthy achievement motivation. When, however, there's an overemphasis on these tendencies, or when individuals focus too hard on their deficiencies or even on their strengths, it can become problematic or counterproductive. Some high-achieving students are vulnerable to perfection-driven underachievement (for example, not completing or turning in assignments unless perfect) or emotional turmoil (such as feelings of worthlessness when they cannot meet unrealistic expectations). When people think that journeys and outcomes must be perfect, it can interfere with their pleasure, and ultimately with their achievement.

Perfectionism can lead to task avoidance, over-commitment, underachievement, unhappiness, anxiety, and other performance-related issues. There are many possible reasons for perfectionism. It can stem from an overriding focus on what ought to be done—sometimes with an "all-or-nothing" perspective—or from standards that are extremely high or rigid. Some children find it problematic living up to a gifted label. Others have difficulties with time management, work habits, or decision-making, any of which can make perfectionism even more draining. It's good that children want to excel, provided they don't take it to a point where it becomes incapacitating.

Perfectionists tend to overwork, invent excuses if they can't accomplish what they set out to do, and feel tremendous pressure to succeed. To address these tendencies, parents and teachers can help children understand that their worth doesn't depend on their achievement, and that criticism can be productive.

If your child is perfectionistic, you can assure them it's okay if something is late sometimes, or messy, or unfinished. You can assist them with setting goals, thinking about priorities, and matching timeframes to the scope of tasks. Encourage your child to aim for improvement rather than perfection, to keep evaluations and grades in perspective, and to value learning for its own sake. Examine together the lives of eminent people, looking at the obstacles, setbacks, risk-taking strategies, management behaviors, and accomplishments of others, and recognizing that achieving at an advanced level is not easy, even for individuals who are held in very high regard.

For the most part, gifted learners exhibit healthy levels of perfectionism, marked by high personal standards and organization. "There is no empirical evidence that the incidence of perfectionism is greater among gifted individuals. To be precise, there is no evidence supporting the psychological construct of perfectionism as currently conceptualized as characteristic of gifted individuals."[20] Sometimes highly able students who exhibit signs of perfectionism simply need extra reassurance and encouragement, including friendly, clear delineations of realistic expectations, in addition to consistent and supportive modeling about when to say, "This is good enough for now; it's time to stop and let it go."[21] And, sometimes the most sensible course of action is to try and step away from a task.

Other times, however, perfectionism can be a sign of deeper problems requiring professional attention. When the suggestions we provide here (both in connection with perfectionism, and throughout the book) are not enough, it's wise to seek professional help.

Arrogance

> *"That question was too hard. Nobody could get it. Or maybe you didn't ask it right."*

One of the stereotypes about gifted learners is that they're intellectually arrogant, and think they're smarter (and, by implication, better) than others. In fact, it's often the reverse; children who are annoyingly superior in their manner often have serious self-doubts.

Rather than thinking they're better than others, some exceptionally capable learners are actually afraid they're not as smart as others might think, or feel they're valued only when they're clever, and therefore, they need to constantly prove how smart they are. Such children usually have trouble admitting they're wrong, and are embarrassed when they can't understand something quickly. Arrogance can be a way for them to conceal their insecurity. They might mask their embarrassment by blaming someone or something else, or by anger, impatience, or annoyance, all of which look and feel like arrogance to the recipient.

There's another reason for apparent arrogance among gifted learners. Children who are passionate about learning and want to know everything sometimes assume that other people (including classmates, siblings, parents, and teachers) also want to know things, and be made aware of their errors. Such children are likely to get into trouble with peers who are not receptive to having their mistakes pointed out to them, and with teachers who have control or self-esteem issues of their own. Arrogance here lies in the other person's perception. The child does not perceive themselves as superior, but rather is making the possibly erroneous assumption that the other person is as keen to learn as they are.

Help your child understand that people do not always appreciate being corrected, and that it's usually better to wait to be asked before giving someone advice or telling them where they've gone wrong. If an arrogant manner is their way of masking embarrassment about mistakes or ignorance, demonstrate how to welcome failures and mistakes as opportunities for learning. Similarly, chat with them about their impatience, and help them realize that sometimes people take longer to complete tasks they find easy. This impatience can appear to be arrogance, and, regardless, they'll do better in life if they learn to respect and accommodate others. Eventually, most kids do learn these strategies, and manage to get along better as a result.

Anxiety

> *"Anxiety disorders are the most common of all child and adolescent mental health disorders, both in the United States and around the world."*[22]

> *"Adverse childhood experiences (ACEs) and toxic stress contribute to the rise in anxiety and occur on average in 11% of children and youth."*[23]

> *"Alexis used to be incredibly shy. She's still shy, but now she also seems to fume about absolutely everything and overreacts to even the smallest challenge. I can't get through to her at all, and her emotional outbursts are becoming more frequent."*

Symptoms of anxiety include sleeplessness, lack of appetite, poor academic performance in school, withdrawal from peers or interests, disciplinary issues, substance abuse, muscle tension, stomachaches or headaches, excessive fidgeting, anger, and irritability. Left unaddressed, these symptoms can worsen, leading to more serious problems, including exhaustion, depression, disillusionment, school avoidance, isolation, and even suicide.

During the COVID-19 pandemic, children's anxiety and mental health problems intensified. Sickness, vulnerability, school closures, economic ramifications, unemployment, and unparalleled mortality rates led to anger, frustration, despair, fear, and anxiety in adults, and children are of course sensitive to the feelings of the adults in their lives. The pandemic changed the nature of social interactions, educational landscapes, and individuals' sense of "normalcy," and nobody knows how quickly we'll rebound as we move into the post-pandemic period.

Pediatrician and gifted advocate Marianne Kuzujanakis writes about anxiety in children and young adults.[24] Troubled by grave and unsettling events (including COVID-19), Kuzujanakis advises that, "Parents and adults caring for children and youth should provide first and foremost reassurances and positive mindsets, and not dwell themselves in hopelessness and worry."[25] *Internal* factors exacerbating a child's anxiety might include asynchronous development, multipotentiality, intense idealism, or self-criticism when their performance doesn't align with expectations. *External* factors increasing anxiety might include undue pressure to achieve, excessive or disturbing social media, issues with study skills, or trouble with sibling or peer relationships possibly leading to difficulties "fitting in" or to experiences of isolation or bullying. Kuzujanakis notes that although anxiety can affect children of any race, gender, ethnicity or socio-economic status, gifted children and youth, as a whole, are both more prone to anxiety, and experience anxiety at higher rates than the general public.

Kuzujanakis offers several strategies to help children who are struggling with anxiety. "Using a variety of meditative and mindful techniques can empower the individual to follow through on actualizing what is important. Finding purpose. Developing resilience. Planting hope. Connecting with others and self through empathy. Awakening our common humanity." Other recommendations include engaging in physical activity and creative expression.

Social worker Katie Hurley's suggestions for children experiencing symptoms of anxiety also emphasize mindfulness. They include deep breathing, coloring with friends or family, playing outdoors, creating a relaxation zone or cozy spot, reading old favorites, taking a bubble bath, hugging, or going for a mindful walk. She writes, "Childhood should be full of bike rides, laughter, love, and silliness. It should be full of wonder, curiosity, courage, and support. Childhood should be happy. Every child has the right to be a child. And every child has the right to play." Hurley cautions that "the race to the finish can overshadow the moments of messy play and boundless curiosity that *should* define childhood."[26]

If your child is experiencing a worrying degree of anxiety, it's time to consider consulting a professional. You can also consult one of the many good online resources that provide support to parents looking for ways to support their child's resilience. As with all other concerns, it's essential to maintain your own mental health and positive attitude.[27] "Anxiety is highly treatable, and early intervention is particularly effective. We have gotten very good at helping individual children and adolescents in need; now we need to get better at identifying the vast majority who don't get help."[28]

Suicide

"There is no compelling evidence that being gifted places a student at risk for suicidal ideation, gestures, attempts or completions... Claims in the literature are speculative at best."[29]

Suicide rates in young people have been climbing alarmingly. As of 2018, suicide was the second leading cause of death in the United States for those between fifteen and twenty-four.[30] While giftedness can bring emotional risk factors, and we should be concerned about the social and emotional health of all children, including those with exceptionally advanced cognitive abilities, there's no reason to expect suicide more frequently among gifted learners.[31] There's some controversy in the field about this, but at this time, there's no evidence that giftedness is itself a risk factor for suicide.

Parents and teachers can lower the risk of suicide for young people by nurturing positive social relationships; providing opportunities for the development of their strengths, interests and abilities; and creating environments where children and adolescents feel safe talking about their problems as well as their hopes and dreams. Katie Hurley writes that kids need empathy, emotional comfort, and strategies for coping. Families do better themselves and provide important support for others when they connect with one another, extending helpful hands to provide anchors or assistance. Resilience builds over time and does not just materialize during times of adversity or hopelessness. "It's like a muscle, you work on it little by little, as you learn and grow and practice new coping strategies. It's a very long-term goal."[32]

A welcoming and inclusive school, where people truly care about one another, and where there are safe spaces, can make a difference to a young person's coping. It can be literally life-saving when children and teens feel they can seek help from teachers, counsellors, or peers.

On a broader scale, it's vitally important to pay attention to the stigma surrounding mental health issues among youth, and to help them feel more comfortable discussing their concerns and feelings, including any possible suicidal thoughts.

Psychologist James Webb offered suggestions to help gifted learners manage their emotions, nurture their idealism, and find empowerment.[33] He wrote about loneliness, sources of depression, disillusionment, coping styles, and more, offering insights, understandings, and guiding principles to consider. He also focused on hope and contentment. Webb wrote, "Each person has to make a choice about being hopeful, and each has to find his or her own meaning and path in life."[34]

Psychologist Tracy Cross has studied suicide and gifted students extensively.[35] He emphasizes the need for more research, noting that suicide is far too pervasive. Cross discusses the lived experiences and suicidal behavior of children and teens with gifts and talents, and he considers preventive measures and ways to foster well-being, including provisions such as mental health supports and counseling strategies. For families grappling with suicide concerns, the most potent resiliency factor is a network of social support. Communication, care, and intervention by parents, teachers, and friends can be instrumental in preventing loss of life, and there are hotlines for immediate access as well.[36]

Strategies for Supporting Emotional Well-Being

Self-control is "the ability to manage or regulate impulses and desires in a socially appropriate way, rather than be managed or regulated by them."[37] Poor self-control can result in problems with restlessness, impulsivity, aggression, distractibility, and lack of persistence and tolerating frustration. It affects relationships, academic achievement, and other endeavors. Clinical psychologist Liliana Lengua has demonstrated that children who experience adversity can experience challenges in achieving self-control and well-being.[38] Difficulties with self-control in childhood predict behavior problems in adolescence, as well as health concerns, poverty, and criminal activity in adulthood.[39]

Thankfully, teaching self-regulation skills can make a long-term difference to a child's development, whether they're implemented in early childhood or later.[40] Research scientist Stuart Shanker has developed a self-regulation teaching program that enables adults to help children and teens reduce stress, become "calm, alert, and ready to learn," and develop healthy habits and routines for sleeping, eating, exercise, and daily behaviors.[41] Action steps involve reframing behavior, recognizing stressors, reducing the stress, reflecting, and responding with personalized strategies that will foster resilience and restoration. By learning to assess, monitor, and address their own physical needs, kids can acquire self-regulation tools that will ease tension, and serve them well over time. On the basis of extensive research, Shanker states that patient soothing works to reassure kids who are having issues controlling their feelings or behaviors.

Psychologist Sarah Chana Radcliffe writes about the importance of naming and accepting children's feelings, listening carefully, reflecting their feelings back to them, and thereby validating them and encouraging their release. Radcliffe suggests various strategies for emotional healing including breathing exercises, journaling, and other techniques for focusing. She also offers daily parenting posts delivered to parents' inboxes.

You can explore options for strengthening your child's emotional well-being while keeping in mind that life is a balancing act, and each child has different needs at different times. There are counsellors, psychologists, medical practitioners, social workers, and other professionals you can consult. However, by providing a dependable environment, and modeling effective coping skills and good problem-solving attitudes, you can go a long way toward helping your child respond effectively to adversity and acquire the emotional resilience they'll need for making the most of their abilities.

If you're concerned that your child may be experiencing serious mental health concerns, it's time to consult a professional.[42]

Behavioral Concerns

> *"I'm fed up with all of the disciplinary problems in my daughter's class. Some of the kids are off the wall!"*

> *"Rafe has been the class clown since he started school. He gets bored quickly and loves to make things happen."*

As with social and emotional problems, giftedness neither increases nor reduces the likelihood of behavior problems. Exceptional cognitive ability can complicate things, though, so in this section, we consider how best to respond to issues with a gifted learner's behavior.

Classroom Behavior Problems

Adults who encounter badly behaving children and adolescents often begin by wondering what's wrong with the young person, sometimes going so far as to look for some kind of pathology. However, when thinking about behavior issues and giftedness, it's important to distinguish real problem behaviors or conduct disorders from a child's ill-advised or high-spirited attempts to make school more interesting and relevant. Many creative, well-adjusted, and capable students are seen as badly behaved, when all they're trying to do is make their school experience more stimulating and meaningful, as seen most stereotypically in the class clown.[43]

In cases like that, it's sometimes the teacher who needs assistance, rather than the child. It may be a matter of providing support with classroom management strategies, as well as more suitable programming options for highly capable learners. The child may also need to learn to regulate their own behavior, as well as to appreciate the teacher's point of view, and to respect other students' rights and spaces. When learning opportunities don't match a child's developmental level, then boredom, frustration, unhappiness, or misbehavior can be expected. (In some cases, this can lead to a misdiagnosis of attention or conduct disorder problems.[44])

Some children have problems with attention and executive function, which can also show up in problems with planning, problem-solving, organization, and time management, all of which can look like bad behavior. And some children are born with a difficult temperament, something we address in Chapter 10.

Before having your child assessed for a behavior problem or conduct disorder, make sure your child has a physical evaluation, including screening for vision, hearing, allergies, and other disorders. Arrange also for a psychoeducational evaluation, including an assessment of intelligence, achievement, and social/emotional factors such as self-concept. Consider, too, the situations in which the problem behaviors occur, recognizing that a child's inability to stay on task (particularly in school), may be caused by a combination of high ability and personality characteristics. Some problems are rooted in the environment, and not in the child.

A child having difficulty adjusting to school change, a new peer group, or increased academic demands may exhibit inappropriate behavior in class. This might involve task avoidance, attention-seeking, or rule-breaking. An additional complication is that kids with behavioral problems are not usually tolerated by their peers for long, especially if they repeatedly disrupt classroom activities or compromise their classmates' learning. When badly behaved children are ostracized, it tends to increase both their emotional and their behavioral problems.

If not addressed, behavior problems can become more serious, such as when a child hurts or intimidates peers, or causes property loss or damage. Conduct that is persistently disruptive and aggressive can indicate serious underlying problems, and needs attention. When a child hurts other children, violates their property, breaks fundamental rules, or ignores age-appropriate norms, it's time to seek professional help.

Computer Use and Digital Behaviors

> *"I've been called a 'geek' and a 'brainer.' I enjoy working on the computer, but I like doing other stuff, too, you know."*

> *"Just how did our children become slaves to the devices that were supposed to free us, to connect us, to give us more time to experience life and the people we love?... Your kids' devices are stealing their time, devouring years of their lives in little parcels....It's important to consider: are they using technology or is technology using them?"*[45]

Technology can be an enormously positive force, provided it's used responsibly and intelligently. It can fuel children's and teens' curiosity, creativity, entertainment, and be a portal to global possibilities for exploration, discovery, and connection, which are especially meaningful for gifted learners. At the same time, there are real reasons for concern when young people spend too much time with screens. Two key questions parents might ask are, "Is the time well spent?" and, "What else is going on in my child's life?"

Media expert Devorah Heitner consults on matters relating to "digital citizenship" and "digital fluency." She advises that—contrary to many parents' fears—learning to relate to people and strong digital skills go hand in hand. She writes, "Anyone can learn the technical aspects of using apps and devices, with enough practice. True screen wisdom is about relationships. It's about the kinds of connections we can have with one another. It's about trust. And balance."[46]

Children may need mentoring (as well as monitoring), including assistance with managing their time and choices online, as well as avoiding inappropriate online distractions and autopilot surfing. Neuroscientist Nicole Tetreault cautions, "There is now a wide body of evidence that points to the fact that heavy use of smartphones, Internet, and many social media platforms can have debilitating effects on our neural processing, cognitive performance, and behavior."[47]

Psychiatrist Shimi Kang specializes in youth addictions, and she writes that teenagers check their phones on average up to 150 times daily—approximately every six minutes, or a total of seven hours each day.[48] She discusses "phubbing (phone + snubbing)," and "technoference (technology + interference)," and "smombies (smartphone zombies)" as well as "mindless scrolling through bottomless feeds"—and how these behaviors negatively affect relationships and developing minds. Aside from possibly "changing the structure and function of children's brains," Kang's concerns include "cyberbullying, sleep deprivation, poor posture, back and neck pain, sedentary behaviors, loneliness, diminished eyesight, anxiety, depression, body image disturbance, and addictions.[49]" Staring into screens can become habitual, interfere with learning, alter behavior, and compromise performance outcomes on other tasks.

In some situations, children retreat farther into a virtual world, and their social connections and personal validation become shaped or engulfed by their involvement with media platforms and technology. By consistently choosing electronically mediated interactions or gaming over real-world social interactions, children can become increasingly dependent on these activities or become isolated, and either way become less comfortable spending time with real people. If you're concerned that screen time may be compromising your child's ability to engage with the real world, or interfering with their healthy physical and social development, or if they seem to be stressed out, addicted to, or overwhelmed by electronic devices, it may be time to reconsider the screen rules and practices in your home.

Gadgets can be powered down, and habits and neural pathways can be changed. If you have concerns about your child's or adolescent's use of digital devices, you could start by identifying an activity that taps their interests and strengths, provides opportunities for success, and requires an element of human interaction. They might be interested in joining a computer club, working collaboratively on a software project, or becoming a computer trouble-shooter or mentor. Such activities can open them to positive social experiences that lead over time to increased real-world social engagement. Technology use can also be harnessed to benefit their mental, spiritual, or physical health (thinking about calming apps, music playlists, fitness trackers, and online creativity and wellness programs), as other avenues to explore.

Technology expert Joanne Orlando provides additional suggestions for balancing computer-based opportunities and challenges. Like Heitner, she perceives digital literacy to be grounded in a relationship between the individual and technology, and recommends that you help your child develop healthy tech habits, use quality and safe apps, and navigate online venues with care and confidence. Orlando discusses positive behaviors supporting children in using devices in healthy ways, and provides parents with many resources and options to explore.[50]

As with other behavior concerns, it's important to consider computer-related activities in the context of what else is occurring in your child's life. Discuss how to become content creators, not just consumers. Encourage each family member to think about their computer habits, online relationships, and time management, and to be "screenwise." Heitner says, "The landscape is different now, and the rules are changing rapidly. Our kids need help, even if they think they don't."[51]

It's all about connections and balance but parental guidance is paramount because apps, devices, platforms, and digital frameworks continue to evolve, and there's increased emphasis on homeschooling, remote learning, and academic and extracurricular programming. Portals for kids, from primary levels through high school and beyond, offer potential benefits for technological engagement. Those who are online with others put themselves into social situations which, with patience and appropriate support, *can* be channeled productively.

As with other social, emotional, and behavioral concerns, excessive or problematic computer use can signal more serious issues that require professional help.

Bullying

> "*Lateesha loves learning but she's reluctant to go to school. She says there are bullies.*"

> "*They make fun of me because I know the answers. I'm not answering anymore.*"

> "*Ryan was suspended yesterday for kicking a classmate. The other kid had been ridiculing him all year, and the teacher refused to do anything about it, and so he had to do something to put an end to it.*"

Bullied children are at much greater risk than others of experiencing emotional, social, academic, and behavioral problems, sometimes lasting well into adulthood: "Bullying can be part of a downward spiral of developmental functioning, cascading to influence many aspects of development."[52]

There are many forms of bullying, including racism and sexism. Definitions of bullying vary, but there's a general consensus that it involves harassing, humiliating, or harming someone smaller, younger, weaker, or lower in status. It happens on a spectrum from deniable actions like ignoring or being dismissive of someone, to more overt behaviors such as ganging together with others to mock or damage a person to the point of serious psychological or physical harm. Children who are different than others—including those who are academically advanced—are more likely to be the targets of bullying than others.[53]

There's a complex connection between bullying and victimhood. What appears to be bullying behavior is often the so-called bully's response to real or perceived earlier victimization, reflecting a choice to become the winner instead of the whiner. There are variations of this. For example, a child might misinterpret someone's words or actions, or take them too personally and perceive them as being aggressive or hurtful, and rather than being victimized, choose to be aggressive right back. Threats, blame, bossiness, antagonism or aggression can be used defensively, even though such behavior is a form of bullying, too.

Getting past the destructive and downward-spiraling aspects of situations like this—on both the giving and receiving end of aggressive behavior—requires that a child feels safe. Children require a secure environment and the necessary resources to feel protected without having to resort to being aggressive or submissive.

A child who has been involved as a bully or a victim (or both) needs help learning if or how their own actions and reactions might be contributing to their problems. In order to encourage bullies and victims to take a positive look at others' words and actions (a crucial first step in moving forward), it's imperative they feel they're being listened to.

What can parents do to increase their child's resistance to bullying effects? [54]

1. Create a safe and loving home environment where children feel free to share their concerns, and know they can trust others to guide and assist them.

2. Reinforce your child's strengths, abilities, resilience, and confidence.

3. Encourage positive sibling connections.

4. Welcome your friends, extended family, and your child's friends into your home.

5. Maintain open lines of communication with your child.

6. Be aware of your child's social and emotional well-being. Be particularly attentive to any changes in their moods or behavior.

7. Help your child find common ground with others and develop good social skills.

8. Monitor the places where your child likes to spend time, ensuring they're safe.

9. Keep on hand age-appropriate resources on friendship-building, conflict resolution, and other related topics so your child can refer to them in times of need.

10. Get help when needed.

What can a child do to avoid being bullied? Here are ten suggestions:

1. Build friendships.[55]

2. Buddy up.

3. Become aware of signals such as raised voices or angry tones or expressions when things first start going awry.

4. Don't over-react.

5. Be assertive not aggressive.

6. Keep a sense of humor.

7. Respect others' viewpoints.

8. Don't be critical.

9. Know when to walk away from a stressful situation.

10. Tell an adult, or call a hotline. [56]

Cyberbullying

"Our daughter is being harrassed online just because she's smart. How can we track and deter the aggressive behavior?

Cyberbullying is an increasingly prevalent form of harassment. It involves the use of information and communication technologies including cell phones, instant messaging devices, websites, e-mail, blogs, and social media networks to engage in hostile online action with words and images. Bullies often cannot be traced, and because their identity is protected by anonymity there may be no consequences for their behavior. Feelings of disdain, intolerance, or even hatred can inflict serious harm when expressed in this disconnected way.

TIME Magazine's 2020 "Kid of the Year," Gitanjali Rao, is a highly accomplished fifteen-year-old. Among her achievements is the creation of an app, appropriately called Kindly, to help students feel safer. She developed a "one-of-kind service that can detect and prevent cyberbullying based on Natural Language Understanding/Processing Artificial Intelligence algorithms."[57] It can be invoked on a variety of different platforms. As the app expands, Rao challenges users to come up with their own approaches to preventing bullying, thereby encouraging everyone to take some responsibility and to share ideas for eliminating this kind of behavior.

Cyberbullying continues to be an area of complex and evolving knowledge, and so it's imperative that parents and teachers know what children are doing online.[58] To do that, adults need savvy Internet skills themselves, including learning about cyberbullying and its potentially devastating effects.[59]

A Path Back from Bullying

Bullying, whether online or face-to-face can be demoralizing. Whether a child's problems have been as victim, bully or both, parents and teachers can help the child maintain dignity, keep an open mind, be respectful of diversity, and build positive relationships. Learning processes are even more effective if conflict resolution skills are developed and practiced on a wider scale, as the following account illustrates.

A Justice League for Children

Jack felt things very deeply when he perceived an injustice, either against himself or against others who might have trouble defending themselves. Partway through fourth grade, Jack was given a three-day suspension from school because he used physical means to defend himself against a teacher he thought had intervened unfairly and aggressively in a dispute between two other children. Jack felt that the teacher had not listened to his point of view and had used undue force against him.

Jack decided to take advantage of his suspension by creating what he called a Justice League for Children. He designed this as a school Grievance Court to ensure that children got a fair hearing from a panel of their peers and a teacher, should there be similar cases in the future in which a teacher and student disagreed about something, or in which two students had a serious disagreement and wanted to be heard. His mother helped him write a manifesto for the Justice League for Children, and when he got back to school, he set up a meeting with his classroom teacher to discuss it.

Jack's teacher was impressed with Jack's preparation and idea. After the meeting, she announced in class that there would be a lunchtime meeting to discuss forming a Justice League for Children. She said that Jack had a very good idea and that it was an opportunity for the fourth-grade class to take some leadership in the K-6 school. Over the next few days, Jack's teacher made time in class for Jack and a few of his classmates to work together to figure out the details, and write a serious proposal to present to the principal.

The group of five fourth-graders who worked on the proposal met with the principal, who loved the idea, and before long, Jack and his team were going into each of the classrooms in the school to discuss their concept.

Simultaneously, Jack's parents were working with him (along with a counselor) to help him learn some better anger management and conflict resolution skills. By the end of the school year, Jack was feeling much happier about himself. The teacher reported that the school had benefited in all kinds of unexpected ways by Jack's proposal, and that other parents had observed some subtle and not-so-subtle changes in school culture, as people (including the primary children) were talking more openly about how to solve problems together. By the end of fifth grade, Jack was perceived as a school leader, and was looked up to by other students. Children across all grades often went to him when they had problems that needed solving, and he willingly shared ideas to help them learn how to resolve matters themselves.

With some help from his parents, teacher, a counselor, classmates, and principal, Jack had converted what started out as a terrible situation into an opportunity for learning and growth.

Jack learned to reinterpret the actions and words of others, including showing the benefit of the doubt by looking for what's helpful, positive, or useful in what others say and do; considering if there night be reasonable motivation or good behavior underlying the person's behavior; and not taking offense too quickly. He learned to pause whenever he assumed another child was being mean, before making a negative attribution of another's actions or words, and before responding to a perceived threat. He was given coping techniques like taking a deep breath or counting to three before saying anything, and then moving that up to two deep breaths or counting to ten, and so on. It calmed him down, and gave him a window of opportunity to think about how to respond as if the other child's intentions were not meant to be aggressive. All of this not only helped Jack in his relationships at school, it allowed him to become a school leader in a critically important dimension of establishing a positive school culture.

We've seen other circumstances in which a school climate became friendlier and fairer because one family responded creatively and thoughtfully to ensure a healthy, school-wide approach to conflict resolution. Interestingly, when these kinds of situations are addressed constructively, with reconciliatory justice at the core, students like Jack who have had problems with aggression often become much better than others at resolving situations collaboratively and productively.

Leadership activities can be particularly important for children and adolescents who have advanced social understandings, and want to do something about injustices like racism, sexism, and other forms of bullying, as Gitanjali Rao did with her cyberbullying app. It can be transformative both for the individual and for others when a young person finds a good fit for their intelligence, creativity, and initiative. Leadership activities like the one that Jack helped create can provide authentic outlets for kids to apply their knowledge and skills; affirm their competence; develop a sense of responsibility; enjoy contributing to the greater good; and shine in socially acceptable ways. (We discuss leadership activities in the context of differentiated classroom experiences in Chapter 6, and in school settings in Chapter 12.)

Strategies for Dealing with Behavioral Concerns

> *"When I came to view problematic behaviors as adaptive responses and not purposeful misbehaviors, I shifted nearly all of my beliefs about how to help children and families."*[60]

Sometimes children's problems are too big or too complicated to solve without help. If you have a child who is engaging in physical aggression (like biting, kicking, punching, or spitting), or behaving in defiant or oppositional ways that feel like they're beyond control, it's time to consider professional help.[61]

For less serious (but still troublesome) behavior problems, however, a parent who is sensitive and responsive can increase the likelihood those problems will be successfully resolved. Here are three useful strategies:

Mind/Body Approach: Understanding what underlies children's behaviors is a logical starting point for addressing them. Psychologist Mona Delahooke incorporates findings from neuroscience and psychology into her clinical work with troubled kids, and writes about behavioral problems and what to do about them.[62] She proposes taking a mind/body approach, and discusses the "iceberg of causality," whereby a child's visible behaviors are the "tip," reflecting only a small portion of what might be going on within the child who is struggling with challenges. Delahooke provides practical strategies for parents, teachers, and kids. She suggests paying attention to sensory systems, relationship-building, physiological stress, and learning "how to deconstruct behavior challenges to discover their causes and triggers." She also discusses how family members can build positive experiences for one another.

Psychosocial Skills: If your child is behaving badly, and specific supports or an intervention is required, success will depend on collaborative efforts, and of course, time, patience, and commitment. There are several important psychosocial skills that adults can reinforce.[63] Gifted education expert Paula Olszewski-Kubilius offers the following suggestions:

○ the importance of finding one's passions, and committing to them over time

○ self-control, day-to-day focus, and effort

○ an understanding of the value of learning

○ a strong work ethic, motivation, and a desire to develop abilities and talents

○ contentment spending time alone, engaging in reflection and independent pursuits

○ resilience; understanding that success is neither instant nor consistent, and that "success and failure often go hand in hand"[64]

○ optimism

○ autonomous learning, inside and outside of school

○ coping skills for dealing with stress and anxiety

○ willingness to take on challenge, reasonable risks, and opportunities to grow—within levels of comfort.

Children and adolescents may need assistance cultivating and then honing these psychosocial skills. Parents can provide that assistance, and also be a role models through their own use of these strategies.

Bibliotherapy: Reading can lead to greater knowledge, deeper empathy and understanding, changed attitudes, increased motivation, and altered behavior. Some books are particularly useful for helping children come to terms with problems, such as behavioral or friendship issues, or feelings of differentness.

Bibliotherapy refers to a specific therapeutic process whereby selected reading material is used to help a person deal with personal problems. A modified version of the same concept can be used to encourage children's awareness, empathy, and emotional development more generally, whether or not they have an immediate problem to solve.[65] When the reader interacts with a literary character, it can enable self-knowledge and insight into their own difficulties, if only to show them they're not alone. As children come to identify with a character in a story, they may imagine themselves acting or resolving problems in similar ways, or forging a different path.

Educators and parents can use books as a foundation for shared exploration, helping children address giftedness and other aspects of their lives such as adjustment to changes and challenges, personal growth, values, identity, social and cultural concerns, and family issues. Reading can also be used to help anticipate and solve problems before they occur.

You can enhance the value of this process by becoming familiar with the books your child is reading, and being prepared to engage in discussions about their observations, and to answer their questions. Like any therapeutic technique, however, bibliotherapy should be approached with care, remembering that children's problems can sometimes be exacerbated rather than solved by reading about someone going through something troubling they are experiencing themselves. If you have serious concerns, it's time to consider professional advice.

Supporting Children's Social, Emotional, and Behavioral Competence

At this time in history, more children, teens, and families are experiencing stress than ever before, stress that translates into increased likelihood of social, emotional, and behavioral problems. That is at least as true for families with one or more exceptionally capable learners, if only because of the necessity of finding appropriate accommodations for the exceptionality, and the feelings of not fitting in. We've discussed in this chapter some of the issues of particular interest when it comes to giftedness, including some recommendations pertaining to each of those. Here are some general suggestions for parents who want to prevent or address issues of concern, and to support their children in thriving:

1. *Ensure a loving home environment.* Help your child experience home and family as a welcoming haven, where they feel safe and supported. Be tolerant, patient, and flexible, remembering that your child (like the rest of us) is striving to succeed.

2. *Prioritize your relationship with your child.* Be available. Be a good listener. Work toward positive, open, and engaged communication so that your child feels respected and secure, and knows they can trust and confide in you.

3. *Encourage your child's curiosity and creativity.* Support them in following their interests, and possibly developing them into passions.

4. *Be positive.* Affirm your child's ability to learn and thrive. Tell your child often what you appreciate about them.

5. *Keep calm.* Try to reduce sources of anxiety in the family, and in daily life. Consider the causes, nature, intensity, and duration of any current stressors. Work together to minimize or eliminate those that impede health and well-being.

6. *Encourage resilience.* Welcome failures and setbacks as positive learning opportunities. Remind your child and yourself that all learning and growth happens one step at a time, with effort and persistence.

7. *Consider the whole person.* If you run into trouble (and every parent does, from time to time), remember that each child or adolescent is a unique individual whose sense of self is affected by complex interacting factors. Consider your child's temperament, and get help with that if necessary.[66] Think about your child's physical needs for sleep, nutrition, outdoor exercise, and the possibility of problems with vision, hearing, allergies, or something else; emotional needs for love and security; social needs for connections with other children and adults; and the balance in their life of stimulation and downtime.

8. *Create a network of social support.* Every member of the family benefits from feeling connected not only to each other, but also to the extended family, the community, and globally. This is true always, but especially during times of change and challenge.

9. *Encourage positive interaction between home and school.* Work together with teachers, administrators, consultants and others toward an Optimal Match approach that aligns what's being provided for your child's education with their learning needs, across subject areas, and over time.

10. *Seek help if necessary.* Remember that some situations require professional help, and that there are people with the necessary expertise to assist with more serious problems.

CHAPTER 10

How Does Giftedness Develop? (And What Role Do Parents Play?)

Nature or Nurture? Back to Origins

"Even highly gifted children have to learn the hard way. Mozart still had to learn and work very hard for an extended time (more than 10 years) before he was able to produce his first masterpiece."[1]

"For developmental scientists, the nature versus nurture debate has been settled for some time. Neither nature nor nurture alone provides the answer. It is nature and nurture in concert that shape developmental pathways and outcomes, from health to behavior to competence."[2]

"Where does intelligence come from?" This is a question that researchers, the popular media, and the rest of us have been debating for at least a century. Current findings in the neurosciences, as well as in developmental and cognitive psychology, show that we cannot effectively separate inherited from environmental influences, and that it's the dynamic interaction between nature and nurture that leads to intelligence.[3] It makes little sense to assign percentages to the relative influences of innate inheritance (nature) and environment (nurture) on an individual's intelligence. Who we are and what we eventually become, including our intelligence, is a result of all that we experience, shaped by how we experience it, and influenced by myriad genetic predispositions. A person's intelligence is a result of early nurturing experiences, the various environments experienced, the surrounding cultural milieu, educational paths and circumstances, life events, and other factors, all interwoven with inherited genetic patterns, and organized by the individual as an active agent in creating their own intelligence.[4]

Because one's intelligence is a result of dynamic interactions over time, it's considerably more mutable than it was once thought to be. Several noted researchers have conducted and analyzed comprehensive studies of high-level linguistic development, for example[5]. Based on their work, it appears that linguistic giftedness develops where it is systematically encouraged, nourished, and nurtured. Environmental differences in children's opportunities to learn from their earliest days can be critical. Where language use is valued in the child's home, community, and/or scholastic experience, *and* where time, attention, and opportunities are provided for its ongoing development, then, barring major biological or psychological constraints, a high level of linguistic competence (or even, perhaps, linguistic giftedness) can be seen as a logical, predictable, developmental outcome.[6] This is not to say that genetic predispositions for certain kinds of intelligence are trivial or nonexistent, but rather that the human brain's capacity for learning is much greater, and more amenable to learning and growing, than most of us realize.

Developmental Pathways

> *"Inherited influences on people's achievements are not direct, not reversible or immutable, not inevitable, and not inescapable."*[7]

> *"It may be that genes and environment work together to create not simply the ability itself but also the psychological factors that are prominent in geniuses and that foster the development of talent over time, such as specific fascinations, sustained attention, the love of challenges, the enjoyment of effort, and resilience in the face of setbacks."*[8]

Simply put, each child's developmental pathway is unique, and it may or may not be smoothly paved. All children have strengths and weaknesses that vary from a lesser to a more profound degree in one or more areas at any given point in time. Whether or not the strengths manifest themselves at the highest levels depends on a great many factors, including culture, family values, supports, and suitably targeted opportunities to learn and explore, as well as extracognitive factors like effort, resilience, persistence, and motivation.

The developmental pathways that lead to the individual differences that characterize giftedness remain complex and fascinating scientific puzzles. The more exceptional a person is in one domain, the more likely it is that there are wide discrepancies across domains and over time.[9] For example, picture an 11-year-old boy with advanced physics and biology texts peeking out of his knapsack, but giggling at a silly prank. Imagine the nine-year-old girl who can sing intricate musical passages, but whose fine-motor skills are impaired. Or think about a first grader who can solve complicated math equations, but has trouble memorizing multiplication tables. Differences across areas of ability—also called developmental asynchrony—are far more frequent than most people realize.

Now consider children's development over time. What are we to make of a 10-year-old girl who appreciates the complexities of Shakespeare, yet fails to do well in high school, or the boy who barely passes middle school, but goes on to become an extraordinary graduate student? How do we account for such disparate patterns of development?

Two of the most vulnerable periods in human development are early childhood and early adolescence, and what happens during these periods can influence whether individual differences will develop into gifted-level achievement, or not.

Gifted Development in Childhood

"Steve is only in Grade 1 and has a lot of trouble sitting still and doing his work."

"Mae-Lin came home from her first day in kindergarten in tears. She said that all they did at school was play. She's

ready to work hard, and she feels insulted when the teacher treats her and the others as if they're little children."

"The problems pertaining to early identification arise because of questions about whether giftedness can be reliably identified during infancy and early childhood."[10]

Up to and through the primary years (from birth to about age seven), most of a child's learning is about the pleasures to be found in exploring and understanding their world in their family, playgroups, classrooms, and community. Whether or not a young child is formally identified as gifted is not usually relevant to the child or their developmental outcomes. What does matter is that the adults in their life respond to their individual interests, respecting the child, listening to them, playing with them, and providing opportunities for them to learn what they can do and want to do next, all in a context of predictable stability and support. The most important achievements of the early years are the construction of a foundation of secure self-confidence, enthusiasm for learning, and resilience, all of which can usually be accomplished without a formal gifted identification or assessment process.

Parents may wonder if their children will grow up to be proficient, high-achieving, or even eminent in one way or another. If a young child is advanced for their age or seems to be exceptionally creative, does that signify great things to come? Increasingly, experts are saying, "No, not necessarily."[11] One's destiny depends on many factors, not the least of which are environmental influences, learning opportunities, temperament, motivation, and good old-fashioned hard work mixed in with a little bit of luck.

Early Childhood: A Sensitive Period

"Early novel experiences play an important role in shaping the healthy development of brain systems that are important for effective learning and self-regulation, in childhood and beyond."[12]

"Parenting a child like mine is like attempting a jigsaw puzzle when someone keeps throwing in extra pieces and you've never seen the finished product!"

"To parent right from the start means knowing and accepting
that children must struggle in order for their brains to grow.
A smooth ride with no upset, no invitation for strife, no need
to accept that which cannot be does not produce growth. It
produces stagnation....No challenge. No growth.[13]*"*

Every single day, life unfolds and presents children with different challenges and learning experiences. What transpires before a child enters the educational system is not just a prelude to real learning; in fact, there are good reasons to think that the most important learning in a person's life occurs before they start their formal education. Language acquisition, motor development, social interaction, and play are just a few of the early learning activities that shape a child's future. However, whereas all infants have potential to learn, not all young children receive the kind of nurturing and learning opportunities that are likely to optimize their healthy overall development across the years.

Although there's considerable debate about developmental timing constraints (also referred to as critical or sensitive periods, or optimal windows of opportunity for certain kinds of learning), the scientific community generally agrees that the early years are tremendously important in an individual's development. At least for some competencies, like learning a language, there are periods when a child may be more sensitive to certain influences—times when neurological development best supports specific kinds of learning.[14]

One of the ways that exceptional learners can be exceptional is in their maturational timing—they experience the sensitive learning periods earlier, later, or differently than other children. In the case of gifted learners, they tend to be advanced relative to average timelines, with some (but not all) aspects of their development occurring earlier than normal. Because learning happens according to complex, highly individual schedules, parents should recognize that from infancy on, and regardless of age-normal sensitive periods, it's important to respond to children's curiosity and encourage their engagement in learning.[15]

Children thrive when they feel loved and secure, when they have access to a variety of learning possibilities, and when they're encouraged and empowered to gain competence in various domains. Self-confidence, a positive attitude toward learning, and the drive to achieve are all strengthened when parents encourage their children's curiosity, creativity, and emerging needs to know and experience more about themselves and the world.

The Importance of Play

"The truly great advances of this generation will be made by those who can make outrageous connections, and only a mind which knows how to play can do that."[16]

"Schoolwork, most notably test preparation, has now eclipsed play from preschool onward. The growth of structured work times for American children has been accompanied by a drop in the hours apportioned to play."[17]

"When play and safe, stable, nurturing relationships are missing in a child's life, toxic stress can disrupt the development of executive function and the learning of prosocial behavior."[18]

Child development experts have become increasingly worried about the erosion of children's playtime, to the extent that the American Academy of Pediatrics recently issued a revised policy statement requesting all its members to inform their patients of the importance of play in children's lives.[19]

Think about the times in your life when there's been too much work and too little play for too long. Not good. As unhappy and unhealthy a situation as that is for an adult, it's even more troubling when it becomes a chronic reality for children. In many of the families we work with, children's schedules are so full that they have little or no time for unstructured invent-it-yourself imaginative play. In addition to school, which can sometimes involve long commutes, children may participate in various organized activities that require practicing, performances, and homework. This leaves little discretionary time for play—very few hours when kids have the time and energy to think about what it is they want to do. Then, in those moments when play might be possible, they may find it easier to turn on a television, computer, or electronic game than to invent their own play activities or engage in play with others.

In addition to meaningful opportunities for engagement with learning, giftedness develops with ample unstructured time. Time is a basic requirement for the kind of play that leads to self-discovery and skill development. Although parents and educators of high-ability learners often feel a sense of responsibility for keeping their children entertained, occupied, and stimulated, it's sometimes better to let children be bored so that they're motivated to create their own fun, and discover what they want to learn next.

Play is not only a pleasurable activity, engaged in for its own sake, but it's also an essential part of children's development. It serves many purposes in people's lives,[20] including friendship-building, tension release, cognitive stimulation, sensorimotor development, and the exploration of possibilities. Children learn the mechanics and specifics of social interaction through play. They learn about possible ways of being, and the consequences of different ways of behaving. Through play, they practice the various roles that they'll assume later in life, and they have opportunities to imagine and try out possible roles. In play, children practice and exercise their social, cognitive, and physical competencies and skills, and they test their limits with less anxiety than is associated with many other pursuits. Imaginary play encourages the development of creative habits of mind. Too much emphasis on academic drilling and intensive attempts to hasten children's education are detrimental when they erode play opportunities or compromise the important aspects of social, emotional, and cognitive development that play affords.

Children who use their imagination are free to explore and consider alternate realities, and roam through the regions of their minds, figuring out who they are, what they care about, and how they might like to spend their time. However, although we're emphasizing here the importance of play and plenty of do-nothing times and inventiveness, we don't want to encourage a tyranny of playtime in which children are forced to play games or participate in activities that adults think are fun and playful. Each child and each developmental pathway is unique, and one child's play can be another's misery. Some children so love to acquire academic skills that school-learning really is play to them. We know children who spend countless hours inventing play-school games in their free time; it would be counterproductive to take away their books and whiteboards, and insist that they play with stuffed toys and building blocks instead. What's important is to strike a respectful balance with the type and amount of play in children's lives, and make sure they have enough time to figure out what it is they enjoy doing.

Play is particularly important in the early stages of the development of any talent, whether it's mathematical, linguistic, athletic, artistic, musical, spatial, or something else. Gifted-level outcomes in all areas start with playful exploration, and proceed through skill acquisition, then through increasing mastery and expertise, to creative performance or outstanding productivity.[21]

Curiosity

"I have no special talents. I am only passionately curious."[22]

"There is no better time than now to open up to all your wonder and possibility."[23]

One of the best ways to encourage your child's love of learning and subsequent giftedness is to foster their curiosity. Curiosity changes the brain, enhancing a child's attention, exploration, information-seeking, retention, and learning.[24] It also motivates problem-finding and problem-solving, and fosters highly effective pathways to learning, understanding, and the development of higher-level reasoning skills.

Curiosity helps children become self-directed learners. They learn to listen, observe, and reflect. They become more discerning. They learn about patience and resilience; how to be nonjudgmental; and how to take a chance and welcome opportunities.[25] In order to support your child's curiosity, listen to their questions, follow their interests, and help them explore their enthusiasms and discover their strengths.

Expose your child to experiences that are as varied as possible. This includes "reading, drawing, and activities in a range of areas—scientific, mathematical, linguistic, athletic, musical, and technological.

It's never too soon to encourage fresh perspectives, a positive outlook, and original ideas. Enable multisensory explorations and discoveries, outside in nature, inside the kitchen, and all around the town."[26]

Pay attention to your own curiosities. Draw your child's attention to questions that cross your mind, like "What makes sugar sweet?" "If you had wings, where would you fly?" Pay attention to your child's questions, whether they're whimsical or serious. Listen, and help them find the answers. We recently overheard a five-year-old we know ask Siri who was going to win an upcoming election. This is a child who feels confident in her curiosity, and equally confident that an answer can always be found.

Support your child's inquisitiveness, while offering ample time for free play and opportunities for them to follow their passions. This will help to nourish their curiosity and imagination, and enhance their decision-making and friendship skills.

Recommendations for Supporting Gifted Learning

Here's an overview of some of the ways to support gifted development in children from toddlerhood through to early adolescence:

- ○ Create an environment of predictable stability and support.

- ○ Provide a variety of age-appropriate play materials, thinking about as many domains of development as possible (including physical, musical, social, mathematical, linguistic, and visual/spatial).

- ○ Play with your child.

- ○ Encourage them to have an attitude of playful exploration. Model that attitude yourself.

- ○ Listen to your child.

- ○ Respond enthusiastically to your child's interests.

- ○ Respect your child's personhood, including their feelings and opinions.

- ○ Provide opportunities for them to learn what they can do, letting them stumble and fail, within reason.

○ Help them think about what they want to do next.

○ Offer guidance, support, and encouragement as needed.

○ Help your child set reachable goals.

○ Help them learn to take setbacks in stride, asking what they can do differently next time.

Early Adolescence

"I got through my own adolescence, but I'm not sure I can make it through my daughter's."

"How do we manage to survive the anxieties, the heartache, the worry, the exasperation? Well, I've repeatedly asked my husband to knock me out with a blunt, heavy object and then wake me when it's all over, but he refuses."[27]

"Adolescents may not want to practice as much as before, their peers may disapprove of academic effort, or students who had coasted along before may be afraid of the new challenges and turn away from school."[28]

People are more vulnerable to environmental influences and experiences at some developmental stages than at others. Early adolescence is second only to early childhood in its volatility and sensitivity, in its possibilities both for developing and for suppressing giftedness and talent.[29] Eleven- to 14-year-olds are engaged in the complex and sometimes overwhelming experience of dealing with puberty. Everything in their lives is changing all at once: their body shapes, voices, hormones, sexuality, emotions, and cognition, to say nothing of their changing relationships with parents, siblings, friends, and others. Some children experience this period in their lives more easily than others. This might be because they're maturing at the same time as their peers, because they have strong social support networks and resources, or because they have few other stressors operating in their day-to-day existence.

An early adolescent is also moving from predominantly concrete to more fluid, abstract thinking. This shift might have started earlier, but it becomes more solid at this time. With the development of stronger abstract reasoning abilities, early adolescents become more cognitively flexible, more capable of simultaneously considering several dimensions of a problem.[30] That sounds like a good thing, and in the end, it usually is, but in the process of giving up the naïve but comforting certainty of childhood, with its clearly defined notions of right and wrong, good and bad, early adolescents tend to undergo a period of doubting almost everything. They frequently come to believe that reliable conclusions cannot be drawn about anything, and nothing seems trustworthy or dependable, including, and perhaps especially, their parents' statements and ideas.

Complex changes in identity are also occurring during this period, including sex-role orientation, gender identity, and growing interest in cultural, political, and other affiliations.[31] Identity formation is a lengthy process which involves moving toward an eventual separation from one's parents. To facilitate the separation, teens may initiate stronger peer connections, experiencing a need to be like their peers and to be liked by them to fit in with what is considered typical for their age at that time and place. This is when being cool, or conversely, being a *dork*, can mean everything. Peer relationships are very important to the developing self-concept of an early adolescent. Often, school is significantly less salient than peer relationships or than it previously was.

Given the complex and interacting changes occurring at early adolescence, one might expect a variety of problems to become more prevalent at this time, and that is, indeed, the case.[32] Life stress increases steadily through childhood and into early adolescence, which is a time of heightened risk for a number of social and psychological problems. For example, heightened self-consciousness; greater instability of self-image; lower self-esteem; reduced conviction that parents, teachers, and same-sex peers hold favorable opinions of them; and greater likelihood of depression. Parents who have navigated their children's adolescence are usually not surprised to hear that this is a time when parents, too, are at increased risk of stress, insecurity, feelings of inadequacy, and diminished marital satisfaction. And, as if all that wasn't hard enough, all too often, children's early adolescence happens to coincide with their parents' midlife reappraisals.[33]

Early adolescence tends to be a difficult phase in a young person's life, and in their parents' lives, because so much is changing. It's a period of social and emotional vulnerability. Somewhat surprisingly, however, most children do not experience serious problems at this juncture, and many young people enjoy this time in their lives.

Nevertheless, identity formation continues to be a major challenge during the adolescence years.[34] At early adolescence, there's a strong need to be just like one's age-peers. Yet there's an equally powerful need to be unique, a desire to be completely and unmistakably oneself. These conflicting pressures are demonstrated in the conformist nonconformity of young people who see themselves as expressing their individuality through their clothes and music, but who dress just like their chosen peer group and who listen to the same songs. Students who've been identified as being academically exceptional (such as gifted) can experience more anguish than others in their attempts to identify with their age-peers.[35] Some of them experience more pressure to be just like everybody else because there's an official designation—gifted— that indicates otherwise.

A young person who really *is* different from their peers in such a basic way as how they learn and understand might be expected to see themselves as truly different than others and therefore as the subject of uncomfortably intense scrutiny. An added burden of loneliness and ostracism can ensue from the self-consciousness that results from that kind of real differentness from one's peers.

Early adolescence is when developmental asynchrony can become particularly difficult for some children. Strengths are sufficiently well-developed at this stage that gaps between areas of ability are getting noticeably wide. The twelve-year-old who expresses themself like an eighteen-year-old is usually closer in emotional maturity to their chronological age than to their intellectual age, but that doesn't stop them from making an excellent eighteen-year-old argument for privileges that their twelve-year-old emotional maturity can't handle: "Often gifted children will have critical and analytical skills that exceed their judgment and restraint."[36]

Although early adolescence is a critical developmental juncture, it's certainly not the case that every exceptional learner has serious issues during this time period. However, when the risk factors of early adolescence and educational exceptionality interact with other risk factors, such as gender identity issues, cultural conflicts, or family disruptions, they create a situation of greater potential for problems. In such cases, it is more important than ever that the principles we discuss here of active listening and support be solidly in place. And if problems become too difficult to manage, it's wise to seek professional guidance.

Differences Between Boys and Girls

"Adolescent boys and girls differ dramatically. It is important to remember, though, that gender differences in characteristics and behavior do not mean that all males are one way and all females are another."[37]

Developmental pathways are highly individual and diverse. Broad categories such as *gifted* and *female* and *Black* can sometimes assist parents and educators in thinking about how to proceed with a child's education and development, but it's critically important not to lose sight of the unique person behind any label or grouping. In this section of the chapter, we discuss diversity within giftedness, and ways in which combinations of attributes and abilities can influence individuals' lives.

Current evidence shows that when children are learning mathematics, girls' and boys' brains are using the same neural processes.[38] Despite this fact, sex differences persist in the pursuit of Science, Technology, Engineering, and Math (STEM) careers, differences which are sometimes explained as the masculinization of mathematics education.[39]

Although the gap is narrowing in many dimensions of academic and career success, the research continues to show males ahead of females in some aspects of mathematical reasoning ability, particularly spatial reasoning.[40] On certain mathematics and science tests, at least in the U.S., boys tend to score higher than girls, and the more competitive the test in its construction and administration, the truer this is, and the higher the ability level, the greater the difference.[41]

Research using Problem-Based Learning shows females achieving as well as male students, and increased engagement and retention in mathematics for both females and males.[42] Similarly, changing the test to better match girls' interests erases the gap with spatial perception tests.[43] It appears, then, that there's a bias favoring boys built into the most frequently used measures of STEM abilities, a bias that accounts for most of the sex differences found in analyses of STEM achievement and interest.

Girls tend to do better than boys at school, particularly in verbally oriented tasks and tests, right through to the end of high school. In general, girls begin to read at an earlier age, and tend to be smarter in areas of social and emotional intelligence. Exceptionally capable children (both boys and girls) are inclined to be more androgynous in their interests, incorporating elements both of the feminine and the masculine stereotype into their preferences and activities,[44] and are more likely to choose interests without regard for traditional gender stereotypes. One caveat when considering sex differences in giftedness: most of the research findings apply to mainstream rather than to minority populations. There's considerable evidence that the findings vary across cultures, and depend on cultural values.[45]

Girls and Giftedness

> *"Historically, it is only relatively recently that females were seen as deserving of the same opportunities in learning as males, at least in Western society."*[46]

> *"Here's to strong women. May we know them. May we be them. May we raise them."*[47]

> *"Become the change-makers. The world needs you."*[48]

Typically, girls start off their school careers doing better than their male peers. They mature at a younger age, and are better able to sit still and do what teachers want them to do. When they're young, they tend to be more interested than boys in typical school tasks like reading and writing. Girls' academic advantage over boys disappears, however, as they enter adolescence and gender identity becomes an important mitigating factor, especially for girls.

Although some girls go through adolescence apparently oblivious to the feminine stereotype that excludes high intelligence and ambition, others "dumb down" their academic performance or behavior for the sake of social acceptance or popularity, or because they see themselves as less capable than they really are.[49] This has serious consequences because choices made early on can influence the availability of subsequent choices. If a girl decides not to take trigonometry, calculus, or physics, she cuts off many future careers, such as medicine, engineering, architecture, and the sciences. Alternatively, for some girls, participation in gifted learning opportunities and commitment to authentic self-discovery gets them through an otherwise painful adolescence.

One explanation for sex differences at the highest levels of math achievement is that there are sex differences in coping with setbacks and confusion, many of which disappear when the environment supports students in acquiring a growth mindset.[50]Another explanation for differences across the highest levels of all STEM subjects concerns cultural attitudes. In many countries outside the United States, there are no differences in math and science test scores, or the differences favor girls. In the United Kingdom, for example, the gender shift, with girls now outperforming boys even in the hard sciences, has been attributed to gender equity policies and practices.[51]

For Black girls with gifted learning needs, there can be a double stigma. They're often overlooked when researchers and educators are considering problems experienced by girls in general, or problems experienced by Black students, where much of the focus is on Black boys.[52]

Although changes have been slow in coming, there are many reasons for optimism, as educators discover girl-friendly assessment and programming approaches, which erase sex differences in STEM subjects.[53] It's also encouraging to learn that Nobel Prize winner Malala Yousafzai has recently signed a multiyear programming partnership with Apple TV+ to develop programs that enhance learning opportunities and equality for girls around the world.

Boys and Giftedness

> *"Gifted boys are often held to rigid stereotypes of masculinity."*[54]

> *"Jared is busy with chemistry, photography, and computer graphics. He doesn't want to socialize or participate in sports, and he has no close friends. I worry because he seems to be more interested in products than people."*

As with girls, boys can experience several varieties of giftedness-related problems. Active, curious boys who are enthusiastic hands-on learners often have trouble in the first several years of their schooling. They need to get up and get moving rather than sitting still for long stretches, and some decide that they hate school when they're very young. Another problem stems from the cultural pressure placed on boys to develop their independence, self-reliance, and responsibility, all of which help to facilitate high-level academic and career achievement. But for some boys, this can be too much of a good thing. The challenge of learning can be more rewarding than the rigors of socializing, and so they opt out of their social and emotional development, which causes problems in relationships and career development. Alternatively, the pressure to conform to cultural stereotypes of masculinity can be overwhelming. Exceptionally capable boys are more likely than their female peers to have problems with low academic achievement and dropping out of school.[55] Interestingly, those who go on to succeed at very high levels make considerably more money than similarly capable women, but often report lower happiness and life satisfaction ratings.[56]

Although because of men's domination in high-paying and high-status occupations, a lot more research has been done investigating problems with female achievement, there's also reason for serious concern about minority males: "It is evident that some minority males (i.e., African American and Latino) are faring more poorly than are females."[57] This has been shown in high school graduation rates, as well as enrollment in and completion of college.

And, although stereotypes for women have relaxed considerably over the past 30 or 40 years, stereotypes of masculinity regarding acceptable interests and behaviors for boys and men remain troublingly rigid. There are still people who believe that boys should not consider professions that are associated with stereotypically feminine attributes of artistic sensitivity and caring about others. Gender stereotypical views like these can undermine boys' motivation to explore and develop their gifted abilities. In many situations, for a variety of reasons, it may be tougher for boys than for girls to be true to themselves.

Gender Stereotypes and Encouraging Gifted Development

> *"I'm not sure what to do about Zack. I know I should let him play with dolls if that's what he wants to do, but really… That's his favorite activity, and it worries me."*

A home or classroom climate that's conducive to optimal development for children of both sexes is one in which parents and educators are aware of the nature of differences between boys and girls, but are also unbiased in their expectations and values. Adults who realize that it's normal for boys to be delayed relative to girls in their ability to sit still, for example, will be patient with primary school children (both boys and girls) who are restless, and they'll offer plenty of opportunities for them to exercise and explore. They'll provide all children with opportunities to choose stereotypically girl-friendly activities and resources (such as books and dolls), as well as stereotypically boy-friendly activities (such as trucks and building toys). All of this becomes more interesting and difficult at early adolescence, when gender stereotypes are at their strongest, and when a stereotypically feminine interest in dolls might have shifted to make-up, and a stereotypical masculine interest in toy trucks might have shifted to real trucks.

Here are some suggestions for supporting gifted development that can help young people excel, avoiding the damaging effects of stereotyping:

○ Encourage young people to be themselves, and to explore who they really are, rather than who others think they should be. Support girls in their achievement-oriented behaviors and activities. Help them see that it's possible to be feminine, attractive, and popular (top priorities during this stage), and also intellectually curious and competent in all subject areas. Help boys discover that it's possible to be masculine, respected, and tough, and also sensitive and aesthetically engaged.

○ Bolster a child's or adolescent's learning in subject areas they perceive as weaker.

○ Provide opportunities for competitive as well as collaborative learning.

○ Engage children with authentic learning and hands-on activities with a real-world focus.

○ With all students, but especially girls, discuss and illustrate the importance of math and science to subsequent career choices.

○ With all students, but especially boys, emphasize the importance of social intelligence and relationships in all areas of achievement, as well as personal happiness.

○ Create academic and career development workshops and speaker forums, ensuring that kids can explore nontraditional and non-stereotypical choices.

○ Provide job shadowing and mentoring opportunities with accomplished people who enjoy their work, from a wide range of demographic backgrounds.[58] (We discuss mentorships in Chapter 7.)

○ Provide access to counseling when needed.

Adolescence

Parent: "I quit! We used to discuss things, and I was able to reason with her. Now we barely communicate."

Adolescent: "They won't quit! We used to discuss things, and I was able to reason with them. Now we barely communicate."

The same parenting skills that foster gifted level development in early childhood can become problematic in certain situations and at other times. Parents who are very involved in their young child's life—parents who are aware, caring, stimulating, and responsive, and who provide lots of opportunities for learning—may experience developmental challenges of their own as their child becomes an adolescent. Parents of pre-teens and teens have to learn to back off, to become reactive instead of proactive.[59] They have to trust that their child has the necessary resources, including parental support and guidance, to deal with the consequences of wrong decisions. They have to find ways to understand that their child's decision-making skills, like their own, must be acquired like all others, through practice, including some trials that result in errors. Parents who are raising a child or adolescent will inevitably face challenges and have concerns about their child's development and well-being. Although mothers tend to have more trouble letting go of their children than do fathers, we've certainly seen fathers challenged in this way, too.

One way to put this in perspective is to think about adolescence as an opportunity for young people across the learning spectrum to acquire and practice the skills and habits conducive to a successful and independent adult life. By the time a teenager is ready to leave home at age eighteen or so, you want them to be able to take care of their laundry and cooking; be able to get up on time; complete their work without being nagged; and make other decisions about what to do and with whom. In order to get to that point, puberty is an opportune time to start practicing how to be an adult. If your teenager is lucky, they'll be able to do this in the context of a safe, supportive, and caring environment, in a home with adults who love them and are able to provide respectful and helpful guidance as they need it.

With all this in mind, we offer a few pointers for the parents of gifted adolescents.

1. *Decision-Making.* An adolescent's ability to handle sexual intimacy, decisions about drugs, and other potentially dangerous peer pressures is not improved because of their intellectual or reasoning ability, no matter how persuasive they are.

2. *Power/Conflict Issues.* These cannot always be avoided, and that's all right. In fact, the best long-term developmental

outcomes occur in families characterized by lots of warmth, as well as plenty of intergenerational discussion, much of it heated and conflictual in nature.[60]

3. *Parent Development Issues.* Learn to relax and let go, while providing backup support. Let your teen make mistakes. You holding firmly onto the reins can prevent them from learning from setbacks, or achieving the independence that's an important developmental task at this stage.

4. *Rules.* Make rules only about those things that really matter. You'll likely be spending a lot of time defending the rules you establish, and that's easier to do if you really believe they're necessary.

5. *Identity Issues.* Work on relating to the person they are underneath the style choices and mannerisms, no matter how annoying or surprising you may find them. Trust they'll be their true self even if that requires time and effort as they work their way through any identity issues.

6. *Gender Identity.* Continue to support your adolescent in their intellectual endeavors while accepting their gender identity explorations (for example, your daughter's yearnings to be attractive and to develop her own sense of style, or her decision that she has no interest in her grooming; your son's realization he's gay or his decision to put all his energy into sports and become the school jock).

7. *Cultural Issues.* When the family background is different than the surrounding culture, recognize that your teen is growing up in that culture, and that their healthy identity development depends on peer identification and acceptance. Try to minimize their problems with conflicting cultural values.

8. *Academic Engagement (or lack thereof).* Encourage your adolescent to find something they really want to learn about, and to keep as many educational and career options open as possible. Understand that school may not be at the top of

their list of what matters for a few years, and that's okay. It's more important they figure out who they are and feel good about it—everything else builds on that.

9. *Unpredictability.* What a gifted adolescent needs is predictably unpredictable and changing all the time. This means that a parent's job is a challenging balancing act, requiring constant vigilance and flexibility.

10. *Cultivation of interests.* The teenage years are an ideal time to continue to explore interests and abilities, and to discover new ones. Adolescents benefit from wide exposure to various subjects, activities, circumstances, and people.

Being Smart and Being Funny

"While students with musical aptitude may be shown to the music room, students with humor ability are often sent to the principal's office."[61]

"The quick and cutting remark is a special skill (of dubious value) that often accompanies verbal giftedness and, if not controlled, may imperil relationships with peers and adults."

As with play, humor can be critically important to children's healthy development. Humor can provide an essential outlet for difficult feelings, a way to cope with stress, or a means to connect with others. It can also be a way of masking or handling anger, unhappiness, bitterness, or loneliness, or of taking charge of a difficult situation.[62]

A recent study shows that intelligence is a critical dimension of humor, and that smarter people are funnier.[63] A large study of class clowns illustrates that there are many types of class clown, and that they're generally high in leadership skills as well as humor, but low in self-regulation, modesty, honesty, and perseverance.[64] They have more friends than other kids, but are also more likely to be disruptive or aggressive.[65]

Being funny helps initiate social interactions and establish friendships.[66] In a study of sixth to eighth grade students in a gifted program,[67] one sixth-grade boy explained, "When you're funny, people like being around you." Some interviewees discussed how their talent for humor had facilitated the move from their neighborhood school to the special gifted class at a new school. Humor had helped ease them into a new social group, as well as deal with the sense of loss experienced by leaving old friends. According to one girl, "Being funny breaks the ice since people can't hate you if they're laughing with you." A funny child is less likely to be classified as boring, which is a dreaded designation. Once a friendship is formed, that same humor serves to solidify and enhance intimacy, particularly when private jokes are shared.

Some of the gifted humorists in this study admitted to deliberately using humor for manipulative purposes to achieve social control or power. Making a joke can help extricate a young comedian from a difficult situation, especially with peers, but also with parents. Several interviewees complained that these techniques weren't usually so effective with teachers. "Teachers don't want you to be funny. They think you're making fun of them or trying to disturb the class." Many of the children saw humor as a potent force that can be used to change both circumstances and people. They knew that they could change the atmosphere in a classroom by employing humor.

These children recognized humor as a way to irritate, cajole, empower, change, help, or control others. Students who are gifted humorists need opportunities to exercise and develop their special talent. Teachers can recognize the contributions class comics make by encouraging their leadership and creativity. When parents appreciate children's humor, and comprehend its possible meanings and functions instead of punishing the child for their distracting behaviors, they simultaneously take advantage of an enlivening resource, and they support the optimal development of those who bring smiles to others. Charles M. Schulz (creator of the cartoon strip Peanuts) sums it up nicely with these words, "If I were given the opportunity to present a gift to the next generation, it would be the ability for each individual to learn to laugh at himself." And, just as importantly, to laugh along with others.

Passion, Zeal, and the "Rage to Master"

"Neither a lofty degree of intelligence nor imagination nor both together go to the making of genius. Love, love, love, that is the soul of genius."[68]

"Zeal seems to be a characteristic common to all the prodigies described here. They are obsessed with numbers, treat them as familiar friends, and actively seek closer acquaintanceship with them."[69]

People are at their most productive when they're doing what they love to do. Psychologist Ellen Winner identified one common characteristic across the otherwise highly disparate prodigies she studied. She called this characteristic a "rage to master," an intense desire to take learning as far as possible. She argued that a passionate drive to learn was an essential component of all extraordinary accomplishment.[70] This same quality has been called other things by researchers—for example, the zeal that Butterworth describes when studying mathematical prodigies,[71] or the intellectual overexcitability that Dabrowski discussed.[72] No matter what it's called, it appears that an intense motivation to understand and learn more and more is an important driving force in all gifted-level achievement.

Parents and educators who want to support their children in attaining gifted-level outcomes can help them find what they love to do, and give them the opportunities and the support that they need to pursue their passions and continue to learn.[73] Over time, it's the love of one's work that drives the effort, discipline, and perseverance that's required for productive achievement.

Effort, Persistence, Perseverance, and Practice

"Students must learn to view setbacks as normal."[74]

"Extraordinary scientific accomplishments require extraordinary commitment both in and outside of school."[75]

Although playful exploration opens up possibilities for talent development, what's needed next is more like work than play:

persistence, perseverance, and plenty of practice. In every domain, gifted level outcomes are built on many, many hours of practice, in a context of scaffolded support for learning.[76]

Mindset influences attitudes toward failures and setbacks. A child's mindset is one of the most potent predictors of whether they're likely to persist and to invest the necessary effort in gifted-level achievement. The way a child approaches challenges, obstacles, and errors has a powerful influence on how successful they'll become. Those with a growth mindset think of ability as developing incrementally, one step at a time, with effort and practice and engagement, and they're not fazed by setbacks. In fact, they see failures as a predictable part of the learning process, as opportunities to figure out where they need to concentrate.

Children with a growth mindset are much more inclined to persevere through tough times, and are measurably more successful in the academic, career, and psychological dimensions of their lives.[77] However, those with fixed mindset beliefs—that is, those who think that intelligence is fixed and innate, and that smart people don't have to work hard—tend to interpret failures as shameful indicators of intellectual shortcomings. No wonder those with a fixed mindset have a harder time persisting through difficulties, and are far more likely to avoid risk-taking and tough challenges.

You can encourage your child to develop persistence, practice, and perseverance by fostering a growth mindset (which we discuss in Chapter 1, and elsewhere in this book), and by looking for opportunities to enthusiastically support their hard work and help them gain confidence in areas of interest.[78]

Cultural, Linguistic, and Economic Diversity

"Fostering advanced achievement and equity need not be mutually exclusive."[79]

"Gifted and talented students come from all cultural, linguistic, and economic backgrounds."[80]

"Racial inequalities in the identification of gifted students have been a constant throughout our history, and they persist today."

Those who are culturally, linguistically, and economically diverse (CLED) continue to be underrepresented in gifted education.[81] Donna Ford, an expert on diversity and giftedness, has described American schools as "places of inequity and barriers to talent development,"[82] and she writes extensively about systemic change. Ford has suggested there's a "pervasive deficit orientation"[83] in which group differences are interpreted as shortcomings of minority group members, rather than as opportunities to enrich society through embracing diverse ways of being. Ford and others have made recommendations for addressing these concerns. We review some of their recommendations, and additional ways of supporting gifted development more broadly here.

Unfortunately, the underrepresentation in gifted programs of certain groups has proven highly resistant to change. Many solutions have been proposed, tested, and discarded through the decades. The Jacob J. Javits Gifted and Talented Students Act, passed by the United States federal legislature in 1988, has provided funds to promote research and demonstration grants to increase the inclusion in gifted programming of students in underrepresented populations.[84] Since the passage of this Act, tens of millions of dollars have been spent addressing issues such as access to gifted programs, support for minority learners, and appropriate opportunities to learn.

Many of those who work with students in minority populations recommend comprehensive, multi-factored assessment approaches that attempt to discover minority students' strengths, especially when these diverge from mainstream notions of intelligence.[85] Those students who show promise of being exceptional (in the absence of meeting gifted cut-off criteria) can also benefit from "pre-gifted" programs designed to foster their talents and enable successful transitions to gifted programs.[86]

A "Bill of Rights for Gifted Students of Color"[87] provides an eight -point structural framework to guide educators in developing understandings about equity and cultural responsiveness. The material is informative for parents as well as educators, and deals with what students have the right to expect with respect to acquiring appropriate learning provisions. "This Bill of Rights addresses advocacy; access; program evaluation; testing and assessment; educator training;

curriculum, social, and emotional development; and family and community empowerment." Educator Joy Davis discusses those issues and more in her book *Bright, Talented, and Black*.[88] Davis' work centers on helping families navigate the challenges that are often confronted by Black students within current educational systems.

An innovative way to address cultural, racial, and linguistic equity concerns is to spend less time looking for ways to label more minority students as gifted, and work instead to ensure that every child has the kind of opportunities to learn that research shows lead to gifted developmental outcomes.[89] Although underrepresentation of minority students in gifted programs continues to be problematic, many of the experts working in this field are advocating that the most productive way forward is to put more effort into ensuring high-level outcomes in all learners. Other recommendations that are consistent with the Optimal Match approach to understanding giftedness focus on providing flexible grouping and choice within a wide range of programming options.[90]

We're also encouraged by a new book for educators that addresses why children's advanced learning needs are sometimes not met due to race, socioeconomic status, ethnicity, sexual orientation, gender identity or other realities. *Empowering Underrepresented Gifted Students: Perspectives from the Field*[91] reflects the voices and views of experts and students, and provides strategies to help educators remove barriers, rectify injustices, and better serve underserved populations.

Yet another path to consider in moving gifted education out of the categorical exclusivity it has too often inhabited is the lived perspective on exceptional ability of Indigenous people in Canada, whose approach is an exact fit with the Optimal Match approach that we advocate. We discuss this further in Chapter 12.

A final but important recommendation is to ensure that all teachers receive the professional development and ongoing support they need.[92] By learning how to implement inclusive and flexible giftedness policies and practices, and by opening up a wide a range of options to as many students as possible, educators can support high-level development and work to rectify some of the historic inequities in education.

Prodigies and Extreme Giftedness

> *"Even in prodigies, talent is accompanied by a tremendous zest for the skill domain and by sustained engagement in it."*[93]

> *"Most prodigies do not become major creative contributors to their fields; their distinctive characteristics are very rapid mastery of existing knowledge and skill, but relatively rarely does a prodigy transform a domain in a significant way."*[94]

> *"The further students deviate from the norms for their age, the greater is the differentiation in curriculum and learning environment they require in order to learn optimally."*[95]

Child prodigies provide the most extreme example of developmental asynchrony. They have extraordinarily highly developed skills, exhibiting professional adult-level ability in one area, and are closer to average in others. The domains that tend to produce prodigies are music, chess, and mathematics, in that order. These domains share several characteristics, including that they're highly rule-bound, have relatively transparent knowledge structures, have developed technologies for transmission of their knowledge, have accessible criteria for excellence, and can be adapted to the capabilities of very young children.

While most prodigies don't achieve renown as adults, some continue to learn and grow extraordinarily, finding ways to become adult innovators in their areas of passion. A good current example is Taylor Wilson, a physics prodigy who holds several patents on important inventions, including a specialized particle accelerator that could revolutionize the production of diagnostic pharmaceuticals, at one-thirtieth the cost and one-tenth the floor space of conventional methods; and a portable neutron detector that promises to counter terrorism.[96]

Taylor's life up to the age of twenty-one was chronicled by journalist Tom Clynes, who raised important questions about the nature of genius, concluding that parents have an enormous role in nurturing its development. Clynes wrote, "The challenge is to find the outlet that best fits a person's unique set of interests and characteristics." He added, "As a start, give kids lots of exposure to different experiences in their younger years, and pay attention to what they pick up on." Clynes recommended pulling kids out of school if that's the best way to give them authentic learning experiences in areas of deep curiosity. He observed that attendance and grades are a lot less important than actual learning, especially in the early years.

When people talk about extreme or high levels of giftedness, they're generally basing this characterization on intelligence test scores, rather than adult levels of competence in a particular domain. Traditionally, the gifted designation has referred to those who score two or more standard deviations from the mean—that is, above 130 IQ, or above the 98th percentile. Using the same traditional designator, those who are even more exceptional, or who might be called "extremely" or "profoundly" gifted ("PG"), score above 145, or the 99.9th percentile.

A score above 99.9% indicates that the child has scored higher than 999 people out of 1000. They're exceptional even within the gifted exceptionality. In terms of their intellectual ability (at least as measured by IQ), they're as much out of step with other gifted learners as gifted learners are from the norm. In a gifted program, these extremely or profoundly gifted children can feel even more alone and different than they did before, finding that they *still* have to restrain their minds and communication, that the so-called gifted learning opportunities are nowhere close to meeting their needs, and that neither the other kids nor the teacher understand their thinking unless they "dumb down" their communication. Since adults and other children have no prior experience upon which to draw, they may in fact be intimidated or confused by these exceptional learners, and respond with alarm or rejection.

As with prodigies, extreme giftedness is almost always accompanied by a high level of developmental asynchrony. More than 95% of extremely gifted learners show a strong disparity between mathematical and verbal competencies, and extraordinarily strong mathematical and spatial capability often accompany average or even deficient verbal abilities.[97] Because they are so asynchronous in their development, if they receive "globally gifted" instruction, such children can experience frustration both in their weaker and in their stronger subject areas.

It's especially important that such children receive domain-specific learning opportunities adapted to their particular strengths as well as any possible areas of weaknesses.

Extreme giftedness brings with it a risk of social isolation. There's also the potential for problems with anxiety due to heightened self-expectations in combination with the extreme asynchrony, and a sense of alienation and differentness which they sometimes interpret as something being wrong with them. Just as those who work with profoundly developmentally disabled learners must tailor their expectations and attitudes so, too, must parents and educators of extremely gifted learners strive to be sensitive to their extreme exceptionality and attendant learning needs. This means supporting children's content mastery, higher order thinking skills, and productive use of abilities. Some strategies to consider:

○ radical acceleration, either subject-specific in the area of extreme advancement, or globally across grades

○ mentorships in areas of special interest and ability

○ project-based learning that involves independent guided study on topics of interest

○ self-directed learning

○ diverse and flexible learning possibilities, including different forms of acceleration; in-school, cross-subject, or cross-grade learning; and extra-curricular enrichment activities, such as university-affiliated, community-based, or business-sponsored programs

○ opportunities to develop other skills, such as athletic, artistic, or leadership abilities

○ involvement in community, regional, national, and international competitions and programs

○ the luxury of time and space to explore their curiosities and passions, in areas of extreme giftedness, and other domains

Exceptionally gifted learners have highly individualistic schooling needs.[98] In some circumstances, home schooling is the best possible option for a certain time in their lives. In other cases, a child may go through more conventional school pathways until college, and then diverge widely from the norm. In yet other situations, there may be a variety of approaches tried through the years, some deemed successful and some less so. It's important to provide a wide range of learning options, helping profoundly gifted learners balance their needs for both autonomy and support, and staying responsive to their changing needs over time. "The body of academic knowledge on the profoundly gifted…is imperfect—it is certainly limited—and endemic with particular research challenges unique to this smaller subgroup of the larger gifted populace."[99] Resources for parents are available online through the Davidson Institute.[100]

Twice- or Multiple- Exceptional: Learning Problems and Gifted Development

> *"The complexities of dual diagnosis…are best served through a strength-based, talent-focused approach."[101]*

> *"As important as it is to help twice exceptional students overcome their weaknesses, it's even more important to maintain the primary focus of their education on their strengths."[102]*

Many experts on learning problems are as tentative about the use of the label "learning disabled" as we are about the label "gifted."[103] The position we take on the subject of learning disabilities is consistent with our approach to giftedness. It's that there are naturally occurring variations in all aspects of all children's development, and that to be successful learners, different children need different teaching strategies and learning experiences at different times in their schooling. Just as with the gifted exceptionality, for a variety of reasons, some children have serious learning difficulties if instruction is not adapted to meet their needs, and we prefer to avoid using the labels unless they're necessary in order for the child to receive the appropriate modifications to their educational programming.

The fact that we prefer to avoid labels whenever possible does not mean we don't recognize the prevalence of children with two or more exceptionalities, which has been estimated at more than 20% of the population.[104] Although it was once considered impossible to have gifted abilities and also learning problems—in many jurisdictions, only one exceptionality could be identified and addressed, and any others would be ignored—there's a rapidly growing body of research on this topic, with resources, strategies, conferences, and supports increasingly available to teachers and parents.[105]

As we note throughout this book, children vary tremendously in the maturational timing of their development, their degrees and domains of advancement, their interests, their study skills, their test-taking skills, their environments, and their social/emotional development. These variations are both interpersonal (between children), and intrapersonal (within a given child). It's the intrapersonal variations, or developmental asynchrony, that we address in this section, noting that it's not unusual to find children who have gifted learning needs, and yet also have trouble (whether diagnosed or not) with one or more aspects of their schooling.

The most prevalent learning problems that co-occur with gifted learning needs concern attention, sometimes diagnosed as Gifted/ADHD (Attention Deficit/Hyperactivity Disorder); cognitive processing, sometimes labeled as Gifted/Learning Disabled (LD); and social processing, sometimes labeled as Asperger's Syndrome or Nonverbal Learning Disability (NVLD).[106]

Some children have highly developed reading and verbal reasoning skills but closer-to-average or lower fine-motor skills. They find that their thoughts come a lot faster than they're able to write them down, and they're unhappy with how their ideas look on paper. Not surprisingly, children with this profile of exceptional strength in their reading and reasoning abilities but considerably weaker fine-motor skills tend to hate writing and find ways to avoid tasks that require it. Over time, this can undermine their learning motivation and achievement. With this, as with all other patterns of dual or multiple exceptionality, parents and teachers should address the learning problems early and compassionately, while simultaneously encouraging the child's abilities, enthusiasms, and curiosity.

The twice-or-thrice-exceptional pattern is almost always characterized by a high level of frustration and unhappiness on the part of the child.[107] It can lead to serious problems with self-esteem, depression, and behavior, often spilling over into other aspects of the child's life and later into adulthood. It can also be difficult for parents who seek ways to encourage their child's learning and well-being.

It's best if dual or multiple exceptionalities are addressed sooner in a child's academic career rather than later, starting with helping the child realize that everyone has areas of strength and weakness, and that the more exceptional a person is in one area, the more likely they are to experience a wide gap across areas of competency. Learning to enjoy developing their strengths while mastering their challenges is an important achievement, and essential to high-level accomplishment over time.

Identification Issues with Twice- or Multiple- Exceptional Learners

"I am different, not less."[108]

"One common scenario is the 2E student who remains unidentified for gifted services because his disability masks his giftedness. Another frequent example is the 2E student who struggles all year in an advanced class because special education services are not believed to be appropriate for gifted students."[109]

Those words are particularly ironic, given that gifted education *is* a form of special education. Identifying gifted learning needs becomes complicated when a child has learning problems, because the different exceptionalities can mask one another. A child might exhibit their strengths in oral contributions to class and in conversation, but not achieve very well in their schoolwork. Their teachers might describe them as lazy, tuned-out, or as a disturbance in class, rather than as keenly and effectively engaged in learning. All too often, parents or teachers will assume that a child is not working hard enough, and insist they try harder, when in fact, they're already trying as hard as they can. Quite predictably, the child may begin to have emotional or behavioral problems. Not infrequently, the reason for children with dual exceptionalities coming to the attention of school psychological services is because of emotional or behavioral problems, with neither giftedness nor learning disabilities suspected.[110]

Depending on the nature, severity, and extent of the problems that a child is experiencing, as well as how entrenched their sense of frustration or despair, they may not achieve the necessary test cut-off scores to qualify for gifted identification even if they come to attention for possible giftedness. This can be a problem of psychometrics and test interpretation practices when scores are averaged across several ability areas. When someone scores exceptionally high in one area and very low in another, their scores can put them in the overall "average" IQ category. Although all too widely employed when it comes to gifted identification, this tactic is clearly ludicrous. Would we say that Kawhi Leonard is an average athlete because although he's an exceptional basketball player, he doesn't swim or play hockey very well? Yet this is exactly what's done when IQ (or some other score that represents a combination of several abilities) is used to identify giftedness. Thankfully, there are indications that increasingly, psychologists and educators are paying attention to a breakdown of separate scores, particularly when scores are widely discrepant.

There are three common patterns of giftedness as it combines with learning problems:

1. *Learning problems are masked by giftedness*: the child's gifted level abilities are evident and they're able to use the skills related to their giftedness to compensate for their problems.

2. *Giftedness and learning problems mask each other*: neither giftedness nor learning problems are evident.

3. *Giftedness is masked by learning problems*: the child appears to have one or more learning problems while giftedness is not evident.

Which of these patterns applies to any given child will depend on personality and coping skills, as well as on the nature and degree both of the giftedness and the learning problems, and the acuity of the child's parents, teachers, or school counselors. Sometimes children move across these patterns, with the problems becoming more apparent with age, and interfering increasingly with gifted-level functioning.

Parents can be proactive. "Do not hesitate to express your concerns to your child's teacher, principal, or counselor, or to make an appointment to discuss your child's behavior with the gifted education coordinator or special education director."[111] These sensible words, written by gifted expert Sidney Moon, are informed by her experiences with families in her counseling practice, and with her own son, a 2E learner. The way forward involves collaborative effort and resolve.

Recommendations for Addressing Twice- or Multiple-Exceptionality: Reading Issues

> "Use…materials rich in ideas and imagination coupled with a focus on higher level skills…. Both self-concept and motivation are in jeopardy if prolonged use of compensatory strategies and basic level materials are used in the educational process of these learners. Challenging content with a focus on ideas and creative opportunities are essential to combat further discrepant performance."[112]

As with all children, but particularly those with extreme patterns of strengths and weaknesses, it's essential that parents and educators emphasize creative possibilities, and that they encourage the development of individual strengths. This helps to create a strong foundation of learning, confidence, and self-esteem.[113]

When children's weaknesses are addressed in the context of their strengths, learning is more pleasurable, motivating, and successful. For example, if a child has difficulties with reading but enjoys art, that interest can be used toward developing reading skills. The child can create books, illustrating others' words or their own, enlisting when necessary the aid of someone else to write the words or the captions for the pictures, which are then collected and assembled in story format. They can dictate the story to a parent or older child and read it back. They can look at beautifully illustrated books on topics they find interesting. They can draw, trace, copy, and/or design letters, words, names, and signs. Dramatic enactments of plays and stories are another way to encourage a child's development of more fluent reading skills. Trips to bookstores and libraries can be planned as enjoyable excursions.

Becoming a Reader: A Library Expedition

For a long time, nine-year-old Stacey tended to steer clear of reading independently because she found the words were often jumbled on the page. Nevertheless, Stacey's favorite time of the week was Thursdays after school. Her Aunt Lena would come over and they'd go to the library. Stacey used to feel that the library was a stuffy kind of place. "There are too many fat books, and I'll never be able to read them in a million years!" she told us. However, she soon learned that reading could be a wonderful adventure. Each week, on the way to the library, Lena would ask Stacey what topic she wanted to explore. One time it was sea turtles, another day it was clowns, and on one particularly cold afternoon it was hot chocolate. Lena and Stacey enjoyed the time they spent together researching the chosen topic, reading about it, and making a shared journal entry. Stacey would select a book to take home. It was always her choice, even though Lena would make suggestions.

Stacey's teacher, who was helping her with reading problems, encouraged Stacey to bring her library books into class. Stacey would read a book (or parts of it) over the weekend. Then, on Mondays, she would share ideas from it with her teacher, creating a link between reading activities happening inside and outside of school. Stacey was enthusiastic about the learning experiences, felt pleased with herself and her reading progress, and told us, "I might get through those fat books after all!"

Pleasurable reading activities for children who are keen to learn but who find books daunting might involve the child spending some time with another reader, usually an adult, who is willing to encourage their selections and share reading-related pleasures. Seeing others enjoying books and hearing them talk about their reading with one another also encourages a child to further develop a love of reading, which is so important to learning. Another approach is to encourage a child to help someone who is younger and whose reading skills are not as well-developed. By helping a younger child with reading, a child can consolidate their own skills and learn where some of their own reading problems might lie. Reading with a grandparent or trusted friend or family member can also be enjoyable.

Additional Strategies for Addressing Twice-Exceptionality

The following strategies for parents and teachers can benefit all children but are particularly useful for those with dual or multiple exceptionalities and accompanying learning challenges.

Emotional and motivational ideas

○ Accept your child just the way they are.

○ Focus on what your child can do, not on what they can't do. Help them find purpose, and steer clear of self-doubt. Positive statements or self-talk ("I know what to do next!" or "I can do this!") help to build confidence, prolong persistence, and improve performance. Professional athletes often use this technique,[114] and it can work in other applications, too, including academics.

○ Provide as much choice as possible in every dimension of learning, including a range of topics and formats (such as discussion, hands-on activities, individual or group learning).

○ Encourage different products (such as videos, Minecraft, musical performances, role-playing, art projects).

○ Invite and celebrate success. A sense of competence and feelings of accomplishment lead to more of the same.

○ Incorporate the arts as an outlet for furthering learning, and self-expression, and as a way of integrating experiences.[115]

○ Welcome creative self-expression in all areas. This might be in the form of music (as we note in Chapter 12), dance, drawing, drama, improvisation, or writing.

○ Teach mindfulness techniques like deep breathing.

○ Help your child learn to expect the unexpected.

○ Acknowledge cognitive dissonance, discomfort, stress, confusion, or other emotions.

○ If your child experiences intense sensory reactions (whether olfactory, visual, auditory, or tactile) that interfere with their functioning, help them learn to survey their environment to identify what might be causing them problems, and to determine how to make themselves more comfortable. Examples might include softening lights to address photosensitivity; wearing colored lenses to decrease visual distortions; using noise-canceling headphones; seeking odor-free spaces; practicing mindfulness; and connecting with others with similar sensory receptivity issues so they know they're not alone.[116]

○ Help your child design "escape valves" by fostering self-awareness and self-regulation.

○ Demonstrate how to handle stress, to vent in healthy ways, and to make time to unwind.

○ Help your child create self-reminders, and develop "inner coaching" strategies.

○ Maintain reasonable expectations so your child does not feel overwhelmed.

○ Model resilience and positive ways of dealing with difficult situations. Help your child embrace the idea that they can overcome setbacks, and that doing so will help illuminate how they can move forward.

○ Build a community of support. This might include family members, professionals across disciplines, and online groups comprised of individuals who are dealing with twice- or thrice- exceptionality challenges and who may have helpful resources and strategies to share.

Details for instruction and learning

○ Focus on your child's strengths and use these as motivators to help overcome challenges.

○ Eliminate rote and repetitive work where possible.

○ Emphasize quality rather than quantity of work. Reduce the volume of work.

○ Use visual aids such as colorful charts, diagrams, and graphs.

○ Break large tasks into smaller, more manageable ones. Help children appreciate that small steps or changes can lead to bigger ones with time, patience, and effort.

○ Be aware of when (and how) to praise, reinforce, scaffold, step aside, or join in.

○ Provide opportunities for authentic problem-based learning activities.

○ Teach critical and creative thinking skills in the context of content learning.

○ Repeat directions in different modalities (spoken, written, notes).

○ Monitor your child's progress and give frequent constructive and affirming feedback.

○ Teach organizational strategies such as prioritizing, outlining, underlining, simplifying, color coding.

○ Work with suggestions offered by your child's team of professionals at school.

○ Structure learning activities so they include previews, reviews, limits, and reminders.

○ Take advantage of technological advances. This might include dictation software, visual or auditory aids, or other specialized apps.

○ Teach memory aid strategies (such as mnemonics).

○ Reduce or eliminate timed tests to accommodate differences in children's desire or ability to work quickly, but also teach test-taking skills.

○ Create a calming space for independent work time.

○ Promote and model collaborative activities and the sharing of ideas.

○ Teach social cues such as vocal tones, facial expressions, and body language.

○ Make rules and expectations as explicit as possible. Post them in clear view.

○ Set boundaries. Maintain a predictable schedule, minimize variance, and encourage structure, but also demonstrate how to restructure when things go off track.

○ Introduce novel concepts and approaches, but don't over-stimulate.

○ Look for ways to encourage peer support.[117]

These strategies take into account a young person's affective and social development, as well as cognitive concerns. The best interventions capitalize on all available strengths and resources, including those within the home, school, and community, as well as the child's own capacities. In other words, explore multiple perspectives when acquiring information or strategies, and encourage your child to have faith in their own abilities. When parents and educators work together to find and implement the appropriate and necessary supports, it increases the likelihood that children with diverse learning needs, including those with dual or multiple exceptionalities, will thrive.

Late Adolescence: Considering Career Choices

"Career education is on nearly every list of program advice in gifted education."[118]

We began the discussion of career exploration in Chapter 6 in reference to differentiated curriculum options for gifted learners. We come back to this topic once again as an important issue in gifted development. Gifted learning ability often prompts those giving career guidance to simply suggest jobs that require a longer time in school, such as engineering, medicine, or law. While this can be excellent advice for some exceptionally capable learners, it's not appropriate for others. As is true in so many other areas, academic and career guidance for exceptional students is complicated, and must be tailored to the individual's unique interests, strengths, possibilities, aspirations, and constraints.[119]

Another reason for parents to pay close attention to career education and counseling is that few school guidance counselors have the training or experience required to consider the ways that giftedness can have an impact on career development. Published materials (such as career interest inventories and decision-making guidelines) don't have a wide enough range to encompass the needs, interests, and possibilities of those who are exceptional in their abilities, on both ends of the ability spectrum. Because of this, adults who live or work with such children and adolescents have an extra burden of responsibility to pay special attention to career education.

Multipotentiality

"We deserve to be more than one thing."[120]

"Two roads diverged in a wood and I—I took the one less travelled by and that has made all the difference."[121]

Multipotentiality is the term used to refer to someone who has many areas of high-level ability and interest that, with development, might lead to gratifying explorations, discoveries, and eventually, possible careers. Gifted education experts Thomas Hébert and Kevin Kelly discuss conflicting findings on multipotentiality, concluding that it's "not a defining characteristic of gifted students." Others however, such as gifted education experts Anne Robinson, Bruce Shore, and Donna Enersen conclude that multipotentiality is a reality for many gifted learners.[122] Benefits of multipotentiality can sometimes include adaptability switching between areas of strength; exposure to a broader spectrum of people and activities of targeted interest; development of skillsets in multiple subject areas and the ability to synthesize ideas and make connections across them; and wide-ranging knowledge upon which to build creative ideas and solutions to problems. Some famous people who have demonstrated high-level abilities across many areas, include Maya Angelou, David Bowie, Benjamin Franklin, Galileo Galilei, Steve Jobs, and Beatrix Potter. Perhaps you can think of other people who have demonstrated multipotentiality.

It sounds like a wonderful bonus to have many areas of exceptional strength, but there are also some challenges. The aphorism "jack of all trades, master of none" is one that some guidance counselors (and parents) use when trying to caution kids who have more than one calling, or when attempting to channel them into a particular career path. This may be well-intentioned, but it can be premature. A multi-talented adolescent or young adult is fortunate to be able to select from several possible areas of high-level achievement, but multipotentiality can also cause confusion and unhappiness as they contemplate which of their favorite pursuits they'll continue to focus their energies on, and which they'll have to let go or develop only to a mediocre level.

Some gifted learners are keen to be involved in numerous activities. They may opt to participate in band, choir, chess club, writing, and competitive sports, while at the same time taking a few Advanced Placement classes. Sometimes multipotentiality results in "burn-out" from trying to do everything well, and other times it results in "rust-out" from doing nothing very well. And often it works out just fine. An individual's temperament, resilience, and support systems, in combination with external influences, will factor into that.

Mentorships can be helpful for young people with many abilities, as can opportunities to try different areas of specialization without pressure to perform.[123] With a little creative thinking, energy, and networking, two or more disparate areas can be combined. For example, a student who is athletically gifted and loves science might become involved in sports medicine, or someone who's advanced in mathematics and has heightened social awareness might choose to study psychology, sociology, or urban studies, In other situations, one interest can be developed into a vocation, while another continues to be developed as an avocation, as in the lives of many doctors who play instruments in community orchestras, or professors who write fiction or poetry in their spare time. Young adults can combine financially rewarding careers with hobbies that are meaningful or, alternatively, choose authentically gratifying careers and stay open to extending other options along the way.

When it comes to multipotentiality, an Optimal Match approach is most fitting. Finding a match between a person's abilities, interests, and preferences, and their learning environments and opportunities, can lead to positive outcomes for the present and well into the future.

Certainty, Uncertainty, and Time Out

> *"I'm going to be an astronaut. For sure."*

> *"I wish I had a better idea of what to study. Everyone else in my class seems to know what they want to be when they get older, but I really have no clue yet."*

> *"Given the fast pace of changing technology, the careers our children might eventually enter might not even be invented yet, much less have majors to lead them there."*

Some children decide on a future career when they are young and never deviate from that, ending up making that childhood dream come true, and enjoying the journey. For others, this kind of early commitment forecloses other possibilities and leads to an unhappy sense of being trapped in a career without ever having fully explored options. Early commitment reduces uncertainty and anxiety, both for the child and their family, and enables them to move smoothly through their schooling. However, it can also carry a heavy price later.

Uncertainty about career choice can last into early adulthood, and although it can feel uncomfortable and worrying, it's not necessarily detrimental to a young person's development. Rather than going through uninterrupted schooling from kindergarten to graduate studies, it's sometimes healthier to take some time off somewhere between 17 and 25 years of age to engage in search-and-discovery initiatives.[124] The "time out" can be spent working or traveling, and simultaneously engaging in active self-exploration, reading, thinking about society, observing oneself in interaction with others, and figuring out how to be independent, interdependent, and happily productive. Ideally, this career and self-exploration interlude should be a time of learning about various kinds of responsibility, including financial, emotional, motivational, and social. Once a young adult has worked out some of these issues of self and how they perceive of their place in society, choosing a career usually becomes a little easier.

Additional Career-Oriented Recommendations

Adults involved in supporting exceptionally capable students through academic and career decision-making processes should recognize not only their exceptional thinking ability, but also other potentially complicating factors such as interests, values, habits of mind, and temperament. Parents and educators can encourage understanding and thoughtful reflection by inviting people who work in different fields to speak to kids about their work. Other parents, as well as friends, neighbors, acquaintances, and relatives, can be asked to discuss the fulfilment as well as the issues that they've experienced in making and settling upon career and life decisions.

On a larger scale, teachers and parent volunteers can work together to plan a "Career Day" where various speakers talk to students about their careers. Considerations in planning such events include making sure that a range of representative possibilities is explored, including both conventional and unconventional occupations. This can be done virtually or in person. Speakers (both men and women, as racially and culturally diverse as possible), can discuss their own career paths—how these may have diverged; how they became interested in what they're doing; and what kinds of complementary routes they plan to pursue in the years ahead. When students hear about the educational prerequisites and other qualifications required for various vocations, they learn that their own career interests can be supported or damaged by the choices they make. For example, choosing not to take advanced level high school mathematics courses can compromise a student's ability to pursue careers in technology, sciences, medicine, and architecture.

Other methods for facilitating career exploration include job shadowing that starts by asking students to investigate occupations that interest them. They can conduct interviews with practitioners and share information with classmates. Activities like these make good topics for social studies and other subject-specific assignments, and can stimulate meaningful classroom discourse that benefits all students, while supporting exceptional learners in thinking about a wider range of possible futures than they might otherwise have done.

Further activities that can help diversely gifted learners consider alternate career paths include mentorships, extracurricular camps and clubs, and contests or fairs at local, regional, national, and international levels that enable students to engage intensely for a short period of time in areas of strength and possible future interest.

Here are some ideas for parents of those who may be struggling with academic and career decision-making:

○ Think about what you're good at and what you enjoy doing, and why. Passion and purpose can drive decision making processes. Sharing your experience can help your child think about what they're good at and enjoy doing, too, and empower them to forge their own way forward.

○ Think about what you're good at and what you enjoy doing that might also be useful to others. Conveying that information to your child can enable them to better appreciate how they, too, might become a contributor to the greater good.

○ Encourage your child to look beyond established professions, careers, or jobs. Many of the most interesting ones are created by the person doing them, frequently custom-made patchworks of activities rather than easily defined occupations. Investigate pathways that have next-level possibilities or interesting off-ramps.

○ Remember that loving your work is an enormous bonus for anyone who wants to be happy and successful in their career. However, children may need assistance as they seek and discover what they enjoy learning for the short haul, and possibly even longer.

○ People are changing jobs more frequently today than used to be the case. Children who appreciate this will understand that flexibility is important. Early decisions are starting points for future career options, and getting to final destinations requires time, patience, and ongoing support.

In the next section we discuss how parents and teachers can support children and adolescents as they make decisions, grow, and develop in their own unique ways.

Section V
Being Smart About Changing Realities In Gifted Education

CHAPTER 11

Parents And Teachers: Supporting Children's Gifted Learning Together

"More than 80 years of research and experience demonstrate that the education of any child is made more effective by sustaining and increasing the role of parents at home and in partnership with the schools....parents and teachers must work together each year of the child's school life."[1]

Parents play a bigger role in their children's education than many people realize. In fact, a child's learning outcomes and eventual academic achievement is more influenced by what happens at home than by the school they attend.[2] While you want your child's school experience to be a positive one, it matters more that their relationships at home are positive, that there are open lines of communication in the family, and that you're actively engaged in their academic life.[3]

Parents: Thinking about Change and Making Decisions

"My son's teacher just doesn't know what to do with him. She says she's never had a student like him before."

It's an unfortunate but predictable reality that education systems designed to meet the learning needs of most children are less effective in meeting the needs of those who are exceptional. Even the most competent educators don't always have the freedom, knowledge, or support they need to work effectively with gifted learners. This means that parents have an important role as advocates to ensure their child gets the accommodations they need. There's been very little research done on parents' roles in gifted development specifically,[4] although there's ample research on parents' roles in furthering their children's educational and intellectual development.[5]

Children thrive with security and stability, and change is disruptive for everyone in the family, so understandably, parents generally prefer to make schooling decisions they think will stay in effect for several years, rather than having to revisit those decisions more frequently. With exceptional learners, however, that isn't always realistic. Because their learning needs are different than other children's needs, what works today might not be an optimal match next year or the year after that. With planning, flexibility, and good luck, it sometimes happens that one schooling approach works well for several years. In general, however, it's wise for parents to approach decision-making for exceptional learners as an ongoing work-in-progress, and to expect they'll need to consider changes as time goes by.

An Individual Education Plan

An Individual Education Plan (IEP) can pave the way for thinking about making a change. An IEP is a written document outlining assessment results, along with a special education program or set of accommodations for addressing the exceptional learning needs of an individual student. It provides a framework for making changes, and is typically updated yearly. The updates are a good way to monitor the student's progress, and for communicating updated information across various subject areas over time.

An IEP typically consists of

○ a description of the child's learning challenges and areas of strength, based on current assessment data, including classroom performance and grades

○ an individual program description, including recommended annual goals and specific skills or learning expectations

○ special strategies and required accommodations

○ recommendations for evaluating student progress

○ additional material such as transition plans, timelines, and information sources.

Most districts have established standards and documentation protocols for IEPs, and schools are required to comply with these. An IEP identifies learning expectations that differ from normal grade expectations. It isn't a daily lesson plan detailing every aspect of a students' education, but rather a summary of a students' special learning needs and accommodations, as well as their achievements over time.

Considering a Change

"We want her to stay with her age group, but she's far ahead of her classmates in most subjects, and her mind never seems to take a break. She told us she feels different from other kids. How do we strike a balance?"

If you're concerned about your child's gifted learning needs not being met, and wondering whether a change in programs or schools might be advisable, consider the following questions:

○ Why is change needed?

○ What are the advantages and disadvantages of each of the educational options under consideration (including staying in the current circumstance)?

○ How does your child feel about a possible change?

○ If changes are made, how will the process be enabled by you, your child's teachers, and the school administration?

Some factors to consider when analyzing the options are whether or not your child will need an assessment, and what that might entail; social-emotional considerations, including leaving neighborhood friends; and whether or not your child will be able to continue with their extracurricular interests. Consider also your family's circumstances, including siblings' schedules; any issues with health, finances, and travel schedules; and parents' work schedules.

Another important consideration if you're contemplating switching schools is commuting time. Transferring your child from a neighborhood school where there are no gifted programming provisions to another school where a better learning opportunity exists may mean extra travel time to and from school. This could curtail your child's ability to participate in sports and other activities that are a healthy part of balance in their lives, and that they enjoy. It may mean moving from an environment where they have good friends, but no targeted gifted programming, to a situation where they worry about not knowing anyone. It may involve a switch from a good-enough learning situation to one that appears better but has financial ramifications. Homeschooling is another option and it, too, is not without challenges. (We discuss homeschooling in Chapter 7.)

Being smart about educational change means staying attuned to your child's learning needs and also to their well-being, providing the necessary supports, and helping them adapt to the change. When considering the available resources, remember that although parents are the first line of support, there are others who may be happy to be part of the network, including grandparents, extended family members, teachers, neighbors, community members, faith-based contacts, classmates, and friends.

Children's attitudes and adjustments to change, whether at school or at home, with peers or with siblings, are as diverse as the children themselves. In order to increase the likelihood of a successful transition, be available to respond to your child's questions, and reassure them of their resources and supports for coping. Listen carefully, with your full attention, and be as available as your child wants you to be to discuss decisions that may feel uncomfortable or enormous for them.

You can help demystify giftedness for your child by discussing how everyone has strengths and challenges, and that the new environment provides a better chance of experiencing a good match for their ability. Explain the Optimal Match perspective to them; it can help your child understand the nature of their exceptionality, and accept the need for changes it may bring with it.

Finding Reliable Information

> *"I found this great website... I just kept wandering through it. I found an article written by a mother who was feeling confused, and I was sitting there crying, going 'I know! I know!'"*

Although there are plentiful sources of information about gifted development and education, it's not always easy to distinguish thoughtful evidence-based material from that which is inaccurate, overly simplified, or even misleading. A library or bookstore with an education or child development section is often a good place for parents to find useful resources, and school librarians, counselors, and teachers may also have helpful and relevant suggestions.

In addition, there are advocacy organizations that post online lists of recommended reading material where you can find announcements about regional or national conferences, contests for kids, updated booklists for avid readers, and so on. Some publishing companies specialize in giftedness, child-development matters, or up-and-coming educational trends. Technology enables opportunities to connect with "texperts" in any field—individuals or groups who can be sources of technical information and support.

University-based gifted education centers (which we discuss in Chapter 12) are excellent portals for reliable information-gathering by parents, and they're accessible online.[6] Articles in online periodicals and special-topic journals can also provide valuable and current information. There are pieces on gifted-related topics such as homeschooling, equity and diversity, assessment concerns, gender issues, developmental stages, at-risk students, talent development, and more.

Choosing a School

> *"In a large city like New York where there's an abundance of options, how does one determine which are the best ones?"*

> *"We live in a rural setting, and the only school nearby is not working out for our son."*

Mapping out a child's education means more than selecting a program you think should work well for your child. It's also necessary to think about the school itself, including both advantages and disadvantages. Some families live in communities where there are many choices for responding to giftedness; others live in areas where the options are limited. Either way, there are schooling decisions to make.

Generally, a good choice to consider is the regular classroom in a local publicly funded school. Such a placement facilitates finding nearby friends to play with informally on their own initiative. Going to the local school encourages a sense of belonging to a neighborhood, and it assists in a feeling of autonomy and mastery to know how to get to school on one's own. These factors continue to be important as a child matures. At the secondary level, extracurricular sports, drama, music, student government, and other school-based activities make proximity important as well.

When determining how to create a suitable fit, the child should feel a part of the decision-making process, within reason, and as appropriate to their age and maturity. A child may prefer a certain school simply because the playground or computer lab looks better, or they have a friend who goes there. Not trivial reasons, but probably not the highest priorities in making the decision. The older the child, the more their input and preferences should be considered, including areas of strength and weakness, interests, and personal preferences.

Public school classrooms tend to provide a wider experience of children from diverse cultures and circumstances than most private schools. These settings encourage a child to consider and develop their own way of being, in the context of lots of possibilities, with wider opportunities for experience, exploration, and discovery than may be experienced in more exclusive circumstances. On the other hand, sometimes a student who is extremely advanced needs more challenge or a differentiated curriculum that's not available in a particular neighborhood public school.

If a family is lucky enough to have a choice between two or more possible schools, they have multiple factors to consider, including proximity, affordability, after-school options, stability, and the needs of others in the family, to say nothing of the often unpredictable future needs of the learner. This is complicated by the fact that it's difficult to know what kind of education a school really provides, and how that might change over time.

Decision-making can sometimes feel like a nightmare. Some parents become immobilized with worry in their deliberations over selecting schools. If that describes you, keep reading; we'll attempt to take some of the confusion out of the process.

Questions to Ponder

> *"What can I expect my child's teacher to know about address-ing Kai's specific needs, including his incessant curiosity, and his remarkable breadth of knowledge?"*

When parents ask us for help with school-choice decision-making, we suggest they think about the following questions—and to keep in mind that where issues are not being addressed, there's the option of advocacy efforts (which we discuss further along in this chapter).

#1 Teacher Considerations

○ Is there support within the school for teachers' ongoing professional development in differentiation, including for gifted learning needs?

○ For middle school and high school, do teachers hold graduate degrees in their subject areas?

○ Do teachers display intellectual curiosity? Do they welcome and implement innovative approaches?

○ Do teachers understand the importance of "mismatch diagnostics"—that is, identifying and addressing children's advanced abilities and strengths, as well as learning problems?

○ Do teachers display and encourage a sense of humor?

○ Do they listen to parents? To children? To each other?

○ Do they respond promptly to children's questions and behav-ioral issues, with patience and understanding?

#2 Programs and Classroom Settings

- ○ Do the school and classroom have a welcoming, supportive, and inclusive atmosphere?
- ○ Are academic standards high, as well as realistic?
- ○ Are expectations clear?
- ○ Is programming both flexible and challenging?
- ○ Are students given ample opportunities to interact with their intellectual peers, as well as their age peers?
- ○ Do classroom activities encourage creative expression?
- ○ Do problem-solving activities allow for many possible answers and lots of exploration?
- ○ Do children have sufficient time and opportunity to muddle through problems and work them out by themselves or with others?
- ○ Do teachers and students appear to be engaged and stimulated by what they are doing?
- ○ What extracurricular activities are available?
- ○ Do teachers and students display mutual respect?
- ○ Are there channels of communication across grade levels and subject areas?

#3 Administration

- ○ Are the administrators' priorities consistent with your child's needs and your concerns?
- ○ Do the administrators exhibit accepting and respectful attitudes and flexibility toward gifted and other special needs learners?
- ○ Does the administration encourage teachers to take advantage of professional development opportunities, including on differentiation and gifted education?
- ○ Does the administration encourage parental involvement in the school?

There are always unknown elements when choosing a school, and no teacher, program, or school can meet all the criteria we discuss here. However, the more informed you are about possible learning environments, the smoother your decision-making and change processes will be.

Making the Decision

"When does school choice become more the child's decision? I know some families who seem to give far too much weight to their kids' opinions at a very young age."

"I'm not sure if the decisions we make are binding or if there's a grace period. What if Emma hates the new school or the gifted program?"

We've identified a lot of questions to consider, but overall, what you want for your child are learning opportunities appropriate to their mastery level and pace in a context that fosters their optimal development. The objective should be to find the best-fit program on an ongoing, year-by-year basis, taking into account both the available options at that level and the child's educational, social, and emotional needs at the time.

Each programming approach and situation has its own goals, content, problems, and advantages, and academic fit is not always the most important factor. Consequently, choosing an appropriate plan at any given time can be a complex process that involves research, advocacy, and collaboration between home and school. Finding the right program requires flexibility from parents and teachers, often involving deciding on a combination of options and/or changing programs from time to time as circumstances dictate.

School-based team meetings, whether formal or informal, can be useful for monitoring your child's learning process and for working through decisions. In most jurisdictions, there are official processes in place for such purposes. In school-based team meetings, parents have an opportunity to consider their child's needs with the help of teachers, the principal, a school psychologist, or other consultants as needed. In some cases, the child is also included. Everyone gives input during a discussion that's structured and led by the team leader, usually the principal.

A meeting might involve reviewing samples of the child's work, the psychologist presenting test results, educators describing their views, and parents (and possibly the child) expressing their concerns and suggestions. Such a meeting can help to identify and clarify issues, and provide a multidimensional consideration of a child's exceptionality and educational programming needs. A good technique for keeping the discussion focused and productive is to keep in mind that the real question is not, "Is this child gifted?" or "Is the child eligible for the program?" but rather, "How do we create the best possible learning fit for this particular child?"

Helping Your Child Adapt to Change

> *"We're thinking about changing schools. But I know Jenna will have a really hard time making that adjustment. What should we do?"*

Once you and your child have decided to make a school-related change, how can you support your child in feeling as self-confident, motivated, engaged, and content as possible? Begin by paying attention to the way they experience the situation as it unfolds, remembering that every child and every situation is unique. A child starting a full-time gifted program might worry about being viewed differently by their old friends, making friends in the new environment, being burdened with an increased workload, or navigating their way around a new school.

Parents can help their child learn about the specific circumstances involved in the change process, familiarize themselves with the new teacher's expectations for learning, and in general become as knowledgeable as possible. You can offer reassurance that change is part of everyone's life, and remind your child of the competence they demonstrated to qualify for the new program. Remind them, too, of changes they've already successfully navigated, such as when they first entered school, or tackled a new activity, or conquered a personal challenge. Talk to them about friends they've made in previous situations, and other social and academic successes they've had. Stay patiently attentive through the change process, emphasizing that there's more in their life that is *not* changing than *is* changing.

Because change, by definition, alters the status quo, it can be controversial for one or more of those people who are affected, if only peripherally. It helps if everyone involved (teachers, administrators, parents, other family members, and the child themself) feels part of the change. Those likely to be affected are usually more accepting if they're kept informed and given a chance for input. Effective change processes include collaboration, clarifying expectations, regular monitoring, reflection, and dialogue.

Talking to others who are going through the same kind of experience can help. See if you can find others somewhere in your network of friends, family, and neighbors. There are also social media groups, online resources, and parent associations that can connect you to support groups, information, and opportunities to network. Other information sources include books, journals, websites, and professionals experienced in working with gifted-related issues.

Making the Choice Work

"We've chosen a new school. Selena starts next week. I hope she'll be happy."

Once you've made a choice about a new school or program, how can you help your child stay challenged, engaged, happy, learning, and secure? We present a six point "A" list of strategies for parents, each with a few examples for getting started. All of them can be used at home to complement schooling situations.

Activities for Rainy (and Not So Rainy) Days

○ Collect a "bag of tricks." Replenish it frequently so that it always contains fresh surprises such as books, games, discussion starters, puzzles, art supplies, a writing journal, costumes, props, paints, crafts supplies, ideas for outings, experiments, and so forth, for use when your child feels bored, anxious, discouraged, or needs time alone.

○ Go outside with your child. Stomp in mud puddles. Taste snowflakes. Skip rocks. Harmonize with birds. Follow animal tracks.

○ Suggest that your child compose a poem, song, or story or make pictures about what they're experiencing. Offer to help with that.

○ Read for your own pleasure and learning. Read with your child. Read to your child.

○ Bring into your child's life activities and people that are as diverse as possible. This may involve visiting art galleries, libraries, bookstores, museums, concerts, and/or participating in other cultural activities.

○ Take virtual vacations together. Enjoy the spirit of adventure, and the possibilities for learning.

Augmented Learning

○ Cultivate your child's interests and areas of strength. Be creative in finding ways to use these as springboards to other learning.

○ Provide guidance appropriate to your child's questions and interests. When you don't have an answer to a question, try to find it, searching together with your child, following their suggestions, and using various resources.

○ Demonstrate the value of learning in your own life. Discuss ideas that you have or hear about, and take note of current events. Include children in discussions.

Accounting

○ Keep track of learning activities that your child enjoys. Share that information with others who might benefit from knowing it.

○ Keep a log, scrapbook, video, or written journal relating to family activities.

○ Encourage your child to keep a record of positive learning experiences and personal accomplishments, and/or create a record together. This kind of portfolio encourages reflective habits of mind, and can boost their self-confidence.

○ Maintain a record of any certificates, accolades, or awards that might prove useful for consideration for advanced standing or career opportunities. For example, a young person's musical, artistic, or athletic accomplishments and other lived experiences can be evidence of a strong work ethic, self-confidence, and capability when interviewing for an internship, mentorship, or placement.

Achievement

○ Set realistic expectations of success.

○ Reinforce feelings of accomplishment. Look for opportunities to praise and honor authentic achievements. (We discuss praise in Chapter 8.)

○ Show faith in your child's ability to do well. Children who sense that their parents have confidence in them are more likely to be self-assured, and will be more motivated to take on challenges.

○ Think about how to piggy-back achievement so that one success might lead to another. Get creative and brainstorm. If your child enjoys writing poetry, could it lead to songwriting? If they exhibit strength in art design or drawing, how might that translate into community service of some sort? Perhaps they can get involved with seniors' homes or daycare settings.

Autonomy

○ Respect your child's need for autonomy. Kids thrive in relaxed settings where they have the freedom to explore, play, and create on their own terms, independently as well as with others.

○ As much as safely possible, respect your child's desires for independence and privacy. Don't hover or micromanage their activities.

○ Let your child figure out what they're interested in.

Attitude

○ Ask questions that matter. Always listen to the answer.

○ Work together to find ways to overcome problems and concerns.

○ Lighten up. Maintain a sense of humor. Don't be overly serious, demanding, or critical.

○ Be enthusiastic about the things that you do.

○ Welcome challenges and setbacks as opportunities to learn.

○ Demonstrate perseverance.

○ Model sensible risk-taking.

Advocacy: Helping Schools Meet Children's Needs

"Five ingredients for success…passion, preparation, inspiration, perseverance, and the ability to take advantage of serendipity."[7]

"Gifted programs are easy targets for spending cutbacks."

An advocate is a person who notices a problem and works to solve it, often on behalf of someone unable to advocate for themselves. Because schools are not typically designed for children whose learning needs are different than average, advocacy is particularly important in the lives and education of exceptional learners. Concerned parents, teachers, psychologists, and students are often required to take on advocacy roles, especially in the face of changing educational policies or legislation, and funding cutbacks.[8]

The Advocacy Process

Gifted advocacy occurs on various levels, from individual parents working toward more appropriate educational programming for their own child, to a concerned group improving the way an entire district or jurisdiction deals with gifted education. In order to be effective, advocacy requires patience, attention, and respect for all participants, including the realization that no-one needs to function alone, and that advocates can often learn a lot from those who seem to be oppositional. Successful advocacy can be thought of as a problem-finding and problem-solving process, characterized by a commitment to actively listening to all stakeholders.

Informed parents can be strong advocates for their children, and the first step is to gather information about what might be a problem, including relevant processes, players, relationships, goals, and commitments. There will be questions to ask and answer. For example, what are the governing rules, principles, and politics within a particular school? What are the costs of current programs? What are the costs of proposed changes, and how will they be funded? How and when will changes be implemented? Who will be in charge? Who will monitor the changes to see if they're working? What's the timeline? What are some possible unplanned implications of the change?

We've been involved in advocacy situations where we worked with parents to ensure that an individual child's learning needs were well met; with principals to help a school move toward better learning provisions for all students; with gifted consultants to help a board of education move toward more inclusive giftedness policies and practices; and with parent groups to address needs for system-wide changes. In all successful cases, there was at least one keen, patient, and persistent advocate who had a flexible vision of the way things could be, and who was willing and able to become informed, to actively listen to all stakeholders, and to see the advocacy process as a long-term collaborative endeavor.

Unsuccessful or counterproductive advocacy attempts often involve an adversarial or self-righteous attitude on the part of the would-be advocate. We've observed that one of the biggest challenges experienced by passionate advocates is respecting other points of view. It's only by understanding others' opinions that one can develop an argument for change in a meaningful, targeted, and sophisticated way, and communicate this persuasively.

When an advocacy effort is successful, it's often those who initially appear to be adversaries who will be in charge of implementing the changes. And it's those same adversaries who will be in the best position to sabotage the changes if they haven't been convinced of the value of them. When advocacy is handled well, those who appear to be an advocate's opponents turn out to be important friends. Nevertheless, we recognize that there are some situations that cannot be rectified by advocacy, and it may be necessary for parents to advocate in a different way, namely by finding a different situation for their child.

Advocating for Your Child

"I think teachers should use different ways to assess kids' learning. But how can I actually make this happen in my son's school?"

If you conclude that action is necessary, you'll want to do some forward planning. A comprehensive plan is critical if a change is not going to be a jump-start to a dead-end. The following basic advocacy guidelines can help:

- ○ Before setting out to advocate for any changes, define specific needs to be met.

- ○ Be practical and realistic about what can be altered.

- ○ Prioritize. You cannot change everything at once.

- ○ Try to define a sensible timeline, fair tasks and responsibilities, and workable parameters. Then show flexibility.

- ○ Because a school community is a complex and interdependent workplace, strive for collaboration and mutual respect. Work to maintain open communication channels among children, parents, and teachers. Aim for free-flowing dialogue.

- ○ Remember that change is an emotion-laden process. Optimism, pessimism, anxiety, and confusion are some of the feelings that can be experienced by those involved, all feelings that can interfere with people's ability to be reasonable. Try to be calm, patient, and level-headed, and to monitor and regulate your own emotions.

○ Maintain your resolve.

Successful change depends on the interaction of many complex and dynamic variables, including the educational setting, teacher commitment, administrative support, parent-teacher collaboration, other parents and teachers in the setting, and children's ability to cope.

Find others with similar concerns and work together. Members of an advocacy group can broaden the circle of awareness, and fine-tune their perspectives and plans. As concern widens and builds, it can generate a growing momentum toward change through recognition, commitment, and compromise. By publicizing the positive aspects of the process, expressing appreciation where it's due, and developing sound policies, parents and other advocates can sustain the momentum. Ultimately, action can be taken to rectify the problem or concern.

Advocacy can take a tremendous amount of time and energy. Here are four additional points to think about before embarking on advocating for change to gifted education policies or program offerings:

1. *Become informed about gifted assessment and programming.* How are students selected for special programming? What do your child's assessments show? Parents need to be well informed in order to understand the implications, to explain things to their child, and to participate intelligently in decision-making and advocacy processes.

2. *Learn all you can about available educational opportunities.* Inquire about core and supplementary programs being offered locally. What are the administrative policies, programs, and provisions for gifted learners? Is there a special education coordinator with whom you could speak, or a gifted resource specialist who can provide information about the various services available? Is there a parent advocacy group? If not, consider starting one.

3. *Arrange onsite visits.* When thinking about viable options, you can make appointments to visit promising schools or possible programs. Ask for a tour. Talk to the principal. Listen. Observe. Be respectfully inquisitive. Do academic programs appear to be responsive to students' individual profiles of subject-specific abilities, learning styles, and interests? Do children seem happily engaged and motivated? Does the learning environment seem like a positive place that encourages children's emotional and social growth? Are children receiving individualized attention as needed? Do staff members look like they're enjoying their work with students?

4. *Investigate alternatives.* Sometimes the perfect educational match for your child is the regular program at your neighborhood public school, albeit with a bit of revising. A greater emphasis on differentiation might resolve matters (see Chapter 6), so you may decide to become an advocate of extended learning opportunities in your child's current educational setting. You can also help to promote a wider conception of talent development by tapping into community resources in order to build richer, multi-dimensional, and collaborative learning environments. Different sectors of society, including business, industry, media, professionals, and seniors, can help extend the range of learning options for children.

Advocates should think carefully about focus and relevance, making sure their driving principle is to find or create a better fit between children and their schooling. Remember that advocacy processes and subsequent changes almost always take longer than anticipated. Be patient.

Advocating for All Kids

> "Parents have a great deal of power. They can advocate for students and the program in ways that a teacher cannot, such as talking with administrators about specific needs and concerns."[9]

Parents have considerably more power to make change than many people realize. When parents get together with others who share their concerns, they can be a powerful force for change. Out of necessity, parents of children with special needs have long realized the importance of being effective advocates. One of the unexpected benefits of thoughtful advocacy is that school can change for the better for a lot more children than those in the initial target group, in some cases having an impact on all students as well as teachers.

We've seen many circumstances where a parent advocating for one child makes a far bigger difference than they had anticipated, with the teacher and principal learning more about matching learning provisions to each child's educational needs. If that one teacher is an enthusiastic practitioner who happens to be a leader in their school environment, and if the school culture is ready for change, there can be a dramatic shift in the way student learning needs are met throughout the school. Sometimes advocacy efforts can have strong ripple effects across an even wider region.

Luc Kumps is the father of Felix, who we introduced in our discussions about above-level testing [Chapter 4] and early entrance to college [Chapter 7]. Luc had a remarkably effective advocacy experience, which we recount here.

A Father's Advocacy

In the process of addressing their own concerns, Luc, another parent Elke, and a teacher friend, Magda Vandoninck, formed a support group for parents and teachers. Over time, they became much more than that, for they design and deliver sold-out workshop series to parents and teachers, have an active website, have dramatically changed educational provisions for mathematically advanced students in Belgium, and are involved in effective political advocacy.

Luc and his colleagues realized that a major problem in the administration of above-level tests was screening; that is, deciding who to select for above-level testing and possible programming adaptations. Selecting too many children for screening results in a lot of work for the test administrators, as well as risking demoralizing kids who don't do well. Selecting too few students excludes some children with gifted learning needs. Luc and his fellow advocates conducted some research to measure the effectiveness and efficiency of a simple screening method they devised, the Ten-Question Extension (TQE).

Based upon their research, the TQE was made available free of charge to all primary schools in Flanders, and 700 (out of 2000) schools are now using this system. The TQE is never used to exclude a child from above-level testing. If a parent, teacher, or child thinks it would be useful to administer an above-level test, schools are instructed to do so, no matter the score on the TQE. The results of the full testing yield important insight in the areas in which the children are proficient and the areas in which they still have something to learn. This helps teachers better understand when to differentiate (and when not).

When working together in a spirit of collaborative advocacy, parents, teachers, students, and administrators can create a school culture that supports high-level learning in more children, as Luc and his colleagues did. Not only was Luc's son the beneficiary of this advocacy effort, so are thousands of other students who are getting the advanced programming they need.

Parents who are involved with their child's schooling enhance the likelihood of their academic engagement and success. Teachers who listen to and respect parents' views can find their teaching enriched and their professional satisfaction greatly increased. Children who are involved in self-advocacy learn important skills of reflection, co-operation, negotiation, self-respect, and independence, as well as feeling empowered to make other changes as needed. Administrators who support positive change find their school is better attuned to children's individual learning needs, as well as parents' concerns.

Parents can also advocate for enhanced professional development opportunities for teachers, enabling them to better recognize and address their own diverse needs as well as those of their students.

Teachers: Important Considerations

"Perhaps there is no intervention more completely researched and confirmed in the field of education than the efficacy of teacher preparation and professional development."[10]

"I've come to a frightening conclusion that I am the decisive element in the classroom. It's my personal approach that creates the climate. It's my daily mood that makes the weather...I can humiliate or humor, hurt or heal. In all situations, it is my response that decides whether a crisis will be escalated or de-escalated and a child humanized, or dehumanized."[11]

Because gifted learners are diverse in their talents and abilities, teachers need access to a wide range of educational options. No one option can do a good job for all children within a particular classroom. And if teachers are to meet diversely gifted learning needs, they need to acquire support for themselves, as well as access to readily available learning options and resources for their students. Unfortunately, most teachers—even those working in gifted programs—don't receive the training, resources, and support they need in gifted education.[12]

Gaps: What's Missing?

Addressing the diversity of learners in a classroom requires considerable know-how even for experienced educators. Although the needs of students with learning difficulties usually become obvious, teachers can be unaware they have students with gifted learning requirements. Generally speaking, in the process of teachers' professional development there may be some focus on exceptional learners, but it's rarely substantial.

Regrettably, the situation is usually not much different in designated gifted programs. In most jurisdictions, teachers of gifted learners have little or no special training—perhaps only one or two introductory courses on giftedness. They have limited theoretical understanding of exceptional development, and little experience in adapting curriculum to meet exceptional learning needs. Teachers in gifted programs can find themselves working alone or perhaps with one or two colleagues to invent a curriculum. As a result, what's offered to students in gifted programs can vary tremendously. Although programming could be (and sometimes is) reflective of a more progressive Optimal Match approach, it's far from the norm. Gifted programming sometimes means giving exceptionally capable students extra work, with insufficient attention paid to the nature or extent of their abilities and interests. Other times, it can be an emphasis on "creative activities," with minimal focus on content mastery or higher-order thinking.

What Teachers Need (And What Parents Need to Know)

"Children are languishing in programs that just don't work for them because there's nothing else available."

Ideally, every teacher would have the tools, resources, and support necessary to provide appropriately differentiated education for exceptionally capable learners. Although professional development in gifted education is often provided piecemeal when it's provided at all, it should be coherent, well-targeted, and strategic, focused on giving teachers the knowledge and skills they require to encourage the best possible learning outcomes for their students.

The National Association for Gifted Children offers recommendations for comprehensive professional development programs that address the needs of gifted learners. NAGC offers resources, conferences, programming models, and hands-on sessions for educators at all grade levels.[13] Their recommendations include that teachers frequently assess their own professional learning needs, engage in coaching and learning in accordance with these needs, develop and monitor their plans, and align their outcomes with performance and curriculum standards. NAGC notes, "The effectiveness of professional learning is assessed through relevant student outcomes." NAGC also provides resource information for parents who have gifted-related concerns, or who want to learn more about provisions for gifted education.

Teachers usually have good ideas about what they need to know, particularly as it reflects their changing classroom circumstances and demands. The most effective learning happens when teachers feel they're an integral part of the consultation and planning process, and when their learning experiences are personally relevant. As with students, when teachers are directly involved in needs assessments and development planning, they're more likely to be engaged in their learning. An enormous benefit of teachers' involvement in this process is that it provides them with an excellent model for facilitating the same process with their students.

We've spoken with many teachers about what further learning they want in order to be better prepared to work with gifted learners. We've organized their ideas into three general areas. Parents who are aware of this "wish list" are better positioned to advocate for what's on it, and thereby increase the likelihood their child will experience an optimal match.

Assessment Information and Ongoing Support

- ○ discerning the practical implications of children's assessments and individual learning profiles, in terms of specific learning processes, achievement goals, and evaluation methods

- ○ acquiring opportunities for working collaboratively with the parents of special needs learners, other educators, and other professionals

Curriculum Information and Support

- ○ better understanding of how official curriculum guidelines apply to gifted learners, including how much leeway teachers have to deviate from mandated content and expectations

- ○ information about the range of possible placement options

- ○ practical strategies for modifying lesson planning in order to differentiate for individual differences

- ○ information on flexible instructional strategies, targeted curriculum adaptation, and appropriate evaluation models

○ materials to foster gifted learning needs, including access to a gifted resource facility or university-based education center for information, connections, and support

○ support for learners with dual exceptionalities

○ strategies to help students connect learning to their own life experiences, family situations, languages, and spiritual and cultural understandings

○ ways to enable students to demonstrate aptitudes, abilities, and learning

○ information about and access to community-based learning options

○ access to advocacy networks

○ opportunities to attend conferences and workshops

○ regular and frequent opportunities for collaboration with colleagues, including leadership and networking opportunities within the district and beyond

○ opportunities to suggest and choose areas of focus for staff development

○ administrative support for trying out different programming applications

○ encouragement to engage in action research (that is, teacher-directed research embedded in their classroom practice)

Information and Support on Specific Topics

○ motivation and engagement

○ self-confidence

○ identity development

○ creativity

○ higher-order thinking skills

○ differentiation

○ neuroplasticity and other relevant aspects of brain development

○ flexible grouping practices

○ twice-exceptional learners

○ gender issues

○ underrepresentation of minority students

○ equity and diversity

○ emotional, social, academic, and cultural dimensions of giftedness

○ study skills and work habits

○ classroom management techniques

○ technological advances (portals, data collection, tele-mentoring, simulations, etc.)

○ mentorships

○ addressing misconceptions about giftedness in the school and parent communities

○ leadership and community service opportunities

○ cooperative learning

○ and more topics, depending on the context, age of students, and teachers' interests

Despite the large number of points on this list, it can't be comprehensive, because meaningful professional development is flexible and fluid, taking its shape from the questions, concerns, and needs of participants. Teachers can create their own professional development experiences, working collaboratively to decide on an agenda that includes themes or topics they'd like to have addressed. They can speak to administrators about regular workshops, lunch-and-learn seminars, Zoom meetings, question-and-answer forums, or sessions for reading and sharing resources. There are, of course, logistics to consider (dates, times, location, goals, format, presenters, materials, assessment and follow-up aspects, and so forth). However, these can be readily addressed if everyone contributes to the effort, and if administrative support is in place.

Administrative Support

"Professional learning is at the heart of teacher professionalism."[14]

Meaningful professional development does not occur in a vacuum. It often comes about as a result of advocacy efforts, and requires the involvement, collaboration, and support of principals and other members of a school's administrative team. By becoming familiar with the issues in gifted education alongside teachers, and by listening carefully to parents and community advocates, principals are better equipped to enable educators to plan and implement well-designed programs.

Teachers who feel that school principals and other administrators are encouraging their efforts feel more comfortable about examining their own practice in serving high-ability students, and trying out suggested or newly acquired strategies for differentiating their instruction. NAGC recommends that administrators ensure that teachers have access to "sustained, intensive, collaborative, job-embedded, and data-driven learning." In addition, administrators can arrange for resources, release time, and funding for continuing education efforts.

Administrators who understand gifted learning needs and who think creatively can find context-sensitive ways to support teachers in enhancing learning options for the high-ability students in their schools. In order for this level of proficiency to become a reality, administrators have to be accessible, listen to teachers' aspirations and concerns, and help to identify, understand, and plan for individual learning differences. Administrators should also connect regularly with one another to build better instructional and evaluative processes across schools and districts. Staying in touch with parents and advocacy groups is vital, and facilitates attunement to ongoing initiatives, and the priorities and pulse of the community. Administrators can take an effective leadership role by strengthening staff cohesion and best practice, and by participating in professional development themselves.

Nancy Steinhauer is the principal of The Mabin School, Canada's first independent Ashoka Changemaker School, recognized for instilling the qualities of leadership, teamwork, problem-solving, and empathy. She told us recently that her school is going through a period of construction now, as they build "a beautiful community wing where we can host multiple classes collaborating in our learning commons, a new Kindergarten set-up, an art studio, intergenerational programming, educator institutes, parent conferences, and our Saturday morning parenting center."

Steinhauer shared the following inspiring story about the early stages of planning for the school expansion.

Empowering Children and Building Community Through Authentic Problem-Solving

The Grade 6's had just done an incredible project, designing a community space based on the nine principles of sustainable architecture, and building models of their ideas. They then decided to create a scale model of the inside of the new addition to the school so they could take part in designing it.

In the original plan, the proposed art room was smaller than our current one. The students figured this out, and advocated for a better, bigger space. We contacted the architect, and now the Art Studio will be larger and in prime real estate (the northwest corner of the Community Learning Lab).

We love to give students the opportunity to make a real difference through authentic problem-solving.

Nancy Steinhauer and her colleagues—the parents, kids, and teachers at The Mabin School—are creating the kind of environment where everyone can thrive, and where giftedness, creativity, and a collaborative spirit will continue to flourish. When a school community is provided with opportunities to think constructively about learning possibilities, and implements sound strategies for working with high-level learners, the school and all children in the system benefit tremendously.

How Can Parents of Gifted Learners Support Teachers?

> *"Gifted learners are entitled to be served by professionals who have specialized preparation in gifted education, expertise in appropriate differentiated content and instructional methods, involvement in ongoing professional development, and who possess exemplary personal and professional traits."*[15]

Every parent has the right to expect that their child will be able to learn in an environment in which they'll feel challenged, safe, and welcome to explore creative ideas and express their uniqueness. To that end, parents may want guidelines for supporting teachers' professionalism.

Parents of gifted learners can consider advocating for teachers' *equitable and respectful treatment of learners* (including being sensitive to the various factors that influence students' learning); *professional development and knowledge of teaching practice* (including being current about learning theory, pedagogy, gifted development, curriculum, and educational research); and *planning for instruction* (including recognizing children's domain-specific areas of strength and weakness, and adapting teaching strategies).[16] These standards are predicated on learning developed through collegial and professional interactions.

Although different school boards and institutions have different mission statements, when parents are aware of standards like these it helps to inspire a shared vision for both teaching and learning processes. Moreover, it provides greater awareness and support of the values, skills, and knowledge involved in teaching.

Preservice training (teachers' college) provides the fuel and thrust needed to become an effective teacher. In a perfect world, the principles of special education, including the range of gifted learning opportunities, would be a mandatory part of preservice teacher education, but that's not usually the case. However, new teachers and teacher candidates (student teachers) often ask important questions, and they have fresh and valuable perspectives, insights, and action research ideas to share. It's vital for the teaching profession, and for students, that these novice and future educators sustain their spirit of inquiry and concern, and that other teachers, school administrators, and parents encourage them to do so. Appreciating and encouraging new teachers' curious and engaged attitudes toward the learning process can enrich gifted education and foster dynamic professional development for all educators and the communities in which they work.

Inservice training (professional development of teachers already engaged in practice) replenishes the source and sustains the momentum. Most of the gifted-related training that teachers receive comes in the form of inservice or professional development learning experiences. Unfortunately, that approach is typically insufficient and sporadic.

Whether they're teaching exceptional students in regular or ability-grouped classrooms, teachers need both the training and the support that's necessary if they're going to be able to provide their students with an education that matches their abilities. This involves knowing how to create a classroom environment that addresses domain-specific giftedness, facilitates engagement and participation, incorporates an emphasis on higher-order thinking, and provides opportunities to acquire solid work habits and study skills. Teachers thrive both personally and professionally when they're given the opportunities they need to stay on top of their subject areas, and to keep learning about what they need and want to know.

Being Smart about Professional Development Opportunities

Teachers can find and create good learning opportunities for themselves, outside what might otherwise be provided for them. For example, they can

- ○ participate in conferences and workshops that focus on specific areas of interest such as giftedness

- ○ form study groups or book clubs with others with shared interests

- ○ network with colleagues, parents' associations, and community organizations

○ arrange opportunities to observe and share exemplary practice

○ enroll in academic courses offered at universities or colleges or through distance education programs

○ work with colleagues to develop innovative curriculum materials or to engage in action research initiatives

○ read and contribute to journals and educational publications

○ increase levels of competence in technology

○ collaborate with specialists in areas in which they wish to learn more

Learning how to meet the educational needs of exceptional students gives teachers skills and understandings that help them create a more dynamic classroom climate for all of their students, and that can have a spillover effect for their colleagues, too. When educators work together to consider the nature of high-level learning and the specifics of appropriately responsive teaching, they also become part of a network offering peer support and a rich sharing of resources over time.

As another component of professional development, teachers also need access to consultants with expertise in gifted development and education. This can help them apply their knowledge in action, as they encounter challenges and situations, as well as learn about emerging options and about how to implement appropriate strategies for the students in their classrooms.

The Dynamic Scaffolding Model (DSM) of Teacher Development

"I need some practical ideas for differentiating my students' learning. But I also need help figuring out how to put those ideas in place for individual kids."

Emerging out of our experiences supporting teacher development, we designed an approach we call the Dynamic Scaffolding Model. It involves teachers working with a gifted education consultant who scaffolds their professional development, starting where they're at, and building incrementally from there. A consultant can help teachers learn about gifted education in practice, including how to address diverse learners' special learning needs, with an emphasis on the importance of ongoing teacher collaboration, access to professional expertise, and ways to consolidate and build on their own prior knowledge.

Based on research about how learning happens (which applies to teachers as well as to their students), we created a three-tiered model of teacher support:

1. appropriate professional development in collegial settings

2. ongoing individual consultation opportunities targeted to teachers' immediate questions and concerns

3. diverse liaisons and networking opportunities

A readily accessible gifted education consultant can provide teachers with increased know-how, timely resources, and ongoing encouragement. The consultant can help teachers provide flexible, lively, and challenging learning environments designed to meet individual students' interests, needs, and domain-specific strengths. The teachers can oversee, steer, and champion a range of learning options that can be individually tailored.

Parents have a role in making this happen; they can advocate for access to consultants where appropriate.

In some jurisdictions, there are special education consultants who circulate among schools, offering support and addressing programming needs across the spectrum of special education, from those students experiencing behavioural, sensory, or learning problems, to those who are gifted learners. These specialists are often spread thinly, and their focus on advanced learners is limited by constraints of time, available resources, and the extent of their own expertise. Some school boards offer self-contained gifted classes for students, but teachers may lack credentials or expertise in gifted education, and be given inadequate support for their work with diversely exceptional students. In such systems, not only is the gifted programming problematic, but also little or no attention is paid to high-ability learners who don't participate in such programs.

Where there's a designated gifted program coordinator, they typically handle administrative functions (such as organizing and chairing identification and placement meetings), respond to parents' queries, check curricular issues, and review student progress. However, they rarely have the time to offer teachers extensive professional development, or to consult with regular classroom teachers. We're always pleased when district coordinators recognize the value of offering extended consultation opportunities to teachers, including planning mini-courses and conferences, and inviting gifted education experts to present relevant material. Sadly though, massive funding cuts and the reallocation of funds in some places are having a detrimental effect on such proactive initiatives. (We discuss this in Chapter 12.)

Some schools and districts already provide students with excellent learning opportunities that are well-targeted to their special educational needs. This occurs most frequently where there's an explicit commitment to adaptive instruction, and to respecting and attending to individual differences generally. It also occurs in some schools and programs that are especially designed for high-ability learners and that provide their teachers with the resources necessary for matching their students' individual learning needs.

Most importantly, parents can support their child's education by considering what teachers might need in order to provide an optimal learning match for their students. In some situations, there are consultants who are hired by the board of education, the district, or the school, who can help in that process. They can address the concerns of parents, recommend resources, and coordinate open panel discussions or forums on specific issues, educational practices, and other relevant concerns. These discussions give parents an outlet for their ideas, suggestions, and questions. A consultant can encourage ongoing networking and liaison activities by creating an interactive website where participants (parents, teachers, principals) can discuss matters, provide mutual support in problem-solving, and share resources and effective techniques.

Ideally, the consultant in a Dynamic Scaffolding Model implementation will have a rich background of understanding and expertise in gifted development and education; be able to provide meaningful advice and learning experiences; enjoy working collaboratively; demonstrate leadership skills; promote outreach opportunities; and be approachable and encouraging. The consultant should be enthusiastic about building a strong conceptual foundation for learning, as well as building bridges among stakeholders in the learning process—parents, administrators, policy makers, educators, and students.[17] Realistically, a consultant may not have all these skills, but what they do bring to the table can contribute to the provision of an Optimal Match approach in schools.

Because of the highly political nature of education in general, and gifted education in particular, being responsive to individual differences and to changing circumstances and contexts (the *dynamic* part of the scaffolding model's name) is essential for enacting any kind of change in gifted education. Opening up a wide range of dynamically responsive and scaffolded support mechanisms to teachers, schools, districts, and boards can enhance their commitment to the learning needs of all students, and increase their opportunities for gifted development.

Putting it All Together: Our Recommendations

Based on our experience working with teachers across grade levels and subject areas, and having provided workshops and professional development sessions to many groups of new and experienced educators, we've devised a list of recommendations for gifted-oriented professional development. We suggest school districts provide opportunities for teachers to learn more about

- ○ individualized instruction, differentiated programming, and pacing

- ○ changing technology

- ○ selection and development of materials that address diverse exceptional learning needs

- ○ meaningful interaction with parents, and determining how they can be effectively involved in their child's education

○ promoting healthy social-emotional development of gifted learners

○ assessing, managing, and preventing problem behaviors

○ information on gifted assessment, identification procedures, and placement options

○ fostering children's motivation and self-regulatory abilities

○ knowledge and value of the origins and nature of high-level intelligence, including the developmental needs and potential challenges experienced by gifted and talented learners

○ access to advanced subject-specific content

○ helping students perceive the relevance of learning (as it relates to family, personal and cultural beliefs, spoken languages, and other aspects of daily life)

○ providing a range of ways for students to demonstrate aptitudes, heightened abilities, and learning

Last Words about Parents' Influence and Engagement in Teaching and Learning

"Teaching is wonderful, but it's draining!

"My daughter has a teacher who is new to the profession. I'm worried he won't know what to do to help her excel."

Parents are the single most important factor influencing children's and adolescents' engagement in learning and academic success. [18] Teachers are free to do their jobs better when their students experience strength-based parenting, and their parents encourage their individual interests, personality, and talents.

Here are two guiding principles for parents who want to support both new and experienced teachers.

Principle #1: Support Reflective and Collaborative Efforts

Help teachers feel empowered and engage in learning about gifted education by facilitating their involvement in collaborative endeavors. Support administrators and gifted education consultants who can coordinate professional development sessions and interactive learning processes among educators of varying experience.

Principle #2: Embed Teachers' Learning Within a Supportive Milieu

Too often good teachers are overworked and underpaid. They'll persist with focused engagement in teaching and learning when they feel supported in a community of lifelong learners and caring parents, and when they see a solid return on their investment of time and energy. By nurturing their development and advocating for opportunities for them to participate in co-creating their own professional growth, parents can help increase the likelihood of teachers sustaining or even strengthening their engagement in education.

We've observed firsthand the motivating effect of learning experiences that act as springboards to better gifted education. We've also observed the power of parents' advocacy efforts that encourage teachers' work and professional development. Collaborative efforts help teachers feel respected, energized, resourceful, and informed, leading to enormous benefits for their students, for the communities they live in, and for tomorrow's world.

CHAPTER 12
Optimal Learning
For All Children

Our Changing World: Solving Problems Together

"Change is the law of life. And those who only look to the past or present are certain to miss the future."[1]

We're living through a time of accelerating change, creating unimagined possibilities as well as uncertainty and stress for people, and for the communities in which they live. As we experience the unpredictability of daily life (including, as we write this, contending with a global pandemic), our health and prosperity depend on effective coping, communication, and decision-making skills.[2] We're reaching a crisis in education—one of the milieux in which individuals learn these skills—with too many children and adolescents having more needs than teachers have resources to meet.

This predicament poses some particular problems for exceptionally advanced learners and their parents. Although giftedness is generally perceived as a strength, it can also be a liability. In a context of urgent and competing needs, gifted learning needs can be assigned a low priority and be ignored. When exceptionality is not addressed appropriately, it can lead to feelings of differentness, loneliness, boredom, frustration, and disengagement from learning. Children and adolescents who perceive more of what's happening around them and throughout the world don't necessarily have the psychological maturity to manage their increased knowledge. They need adults who can answer their questions, respect their feelings, understand their concerns, and help them cope with difficult and troubling circumstances.

In spite of political forces working toward educational standardization, many educators realize they must target instruction to individual patterns of interest and ability in order to be effective. This is the very essence of the Optimal Match perspective. Putting it into practice requires vision and courage.

Home-Based Experiences

One solution to the problem of educational resources that are stretched to (and sometimes past) the breaking point is to look beyond the school walls. Home is a good place to start.

Author Jessica Lahey surveyed parents online about their kids' learning experiences at home in the midst of the COVID-related challenges families were facing at that time. Here's a sampling of the parents' views on how their children and teens viewed their home-based development over the course of a difficult year:

○ made friends online from around the world

○ had more time for passion-inspired projects and creative pursuits

○ developed an entrepreneurial spirit

○ spent quality time with family

○ got more sleep

○ had a better balance of work, relaxation, and play outside

○ explored a greater range of online extracurricular programs

○ found joy and gratitude in the small things in life

In addition, parents said their families went on nature walks, hugged, danced, read more books, did giant sized puzzles, laughed, watched old movies, and took virtual trips together. Striving for health and happiness took precedence over academic and professional achievement.

Authors Daniel Siegel and Tina Payne Bryson[3] emphasize that every single day offers a wealth of shareable interactions for enabling children's growth, and that parents can use those daily moments, "the stressful angry ones as well as the miraculous adorable ones—as opportunities to help them become the responsible, caring, capable people you want them to be." The authors discuss a "whole-brain" approach to helping kids thrive, encouraging children's understandings of how the brain works, so they can "in turn understand themselves, and their behavior and their feelings in new and more insightful ways." Parents can use whole-brain strategies to help their child find joy and fulfillment. Connections, engagement, reflection, and self-awareness are especially important.

Collaborative Efforts: Sharing Ideas and Resources

"The better networks we build, the more likely it will be that we stumble across the random bit of information or insight that can help us solve an important problem."[4]

Wonderful things can happen when parents, educators, and students work cohesively, reaching out to the community and even further for relevant and authentic learning opportunities. It's possible to solve many of the most intractable problems in gifted education when people share their perspectives in collaborative problem-solving forums. This is what Deborah Meier and her colleagues did, as described in the book, *The Power of Their Ideas: Lessons for America from a Small School in Harlem,*[5] as educators worked together with students and parents to ensure that there were learning opportunities across the ability spectrum.

In order for school-community partnerships to succeed, everyone has to be involved:

It's important that the *student* feels engaged in and responsible for co-creating their own learning. And, in the process of contributing meaningfully to their education, they're also reducing the burden on the teacher to find ways to differentiate effectively.

The *teacher's* role can become that of a flexible expert—someone who can facilitate productive problem-finding and problem-solving;

be knowledgeable about and responsive to individual, developmental, and cultural differences in learning needs; and guide students intelligently through the learning process.

The *parent's* role varies across situations. Parents can provide the necessary supports, including day-to-day nurturing, as well as investigating learning opportunities in the community and beyond.

The *school administrator's* role is one of facilitation, network-building, and coordination. This can be on an individual or systemic basis, and it requires skills in negotiation and leadership.[6]

All this may sound like an intensive investment of time and effort directed at each student in situations where there's a limited cadre of professionals working to educate students in large, growing, and increasingly diverse classrooms—and it is. However, this collaborative approach to solving gifted-related learning problems is almost always worthwhile. It prevents further problems, helping each student realize their capabilities.

We've seen this kind of cohesive effort in action. As positive outcomes happen for one student, teacher attitudes begin to change—and through a spirit of shared learning, the school climate improves. Teachers begin to realize that they have excellent curriculum development allies and resources in their students, parents, and administrators, and that there are opportunities available outside the school that can supplement the resources within its confines. Parents are relieved that their child can be academically challenged and successful. In our experience, even the busiest parents are glad to help make that happen. They discover that a relatively small investment of their time has big payoffs in their child's engagement in the learning process. This, in turn, enhances academic achievement, and makes an important contribution to school attitudes and practices that can benefit all students.

The three basic tenets of the collaborative approach involve facilitating:

○ each student's engagement in their own learning
○ partnerships between the school and the family, and
○ community involvement in students' learning.[7]

Collaborations across individuals, families, schools, and communities generate the best educational responses to a rapidly changing world by accelerating resource access, and reducing burdens. Educators find themselves professionally reenergized when they realize that they don't have to do it alone anymore, and in fact, it's better if they don't.

Teacher development is an excellent catalyst for bringing together all the pieces of a collaborative approach to gifted education. Robust teacher education programs can be transformative. When these occur in the context of a vibrant university-based gifted center that acts as a central information clearing house, it provides a range of support for students, parents, administrators, and others, so that change can begin to happen rapidly.

University-Based Gifted Education Resource Centers

"With renewed attention to equity and students' individual needs, gifted education can serve as one pathway through which students of all backgrounds can have their needs met."[8]

"I read with interest about the proposed center for gifted education. What I wouldn't give to have a place where I could learn more about my daughter's special needs!"

Some universities have developed gifted education resource centers that are active, inclusive, vibrant places of learning, support, and interaction for educators, parents, and children.[9] Most such centers are involved in developing curriculum, providing and evaluating programs for high-ability students, conducting research on gifted development, disseminating information, reaching out to diverse communities, and supporting teacher development. However, each one has its own focus and areas of specialization. We've been involved in initiatives to create such centers, and we've consulted with people at other centers. Here's a synthesis of our experiences, and some specific suggestions.

Objectives of a Gifted Center

Gifted centers can

○ provide information and support for parents, educators, and academics interested in understanding and meeting the needs of exceptionally capable learners

○ act as a catalyst for gifted program development, evaluation, and improvement

○ foster gifted-level outcomes among diverse learners

○ forge local, national, and international connections

○ stimulate professional networking opportunities

○ create libraries for information, resources, and expertise

○ generate interest in and knowledge about gifted education

○ act as a clearinghouse for information about professional services

○ promote educational liaisons and collaborative networks at all levels

○ stimulate research on high-level development and education.

Activities of a Gifted Center

A well-planned, well-funded, and well-run gifted center can work to bring together teacher development and support; student and family support; research and dissemination activities; and provide access to a wide range of local, regional, national, and international learning opportunities. It can create the invigorating confluence of activities, energies, and expertise that underlie pathbreaking exploration and discovery. A university-based center can provide a link among existing activities and programs related to higher education, including coordinating resources for students, families, and teachers, stimulating real understanding of the nature of giftedness, and optimizing learning and life experiences for many people.

Support and Networking for Parents and Teachers

A university-based gifted center can provide

- ○ expertise and resources including current information, workshops, and activities on a variety of gifted-related topics

- ○ teacher training for new educators, professional development for experienced teachers, and graduate courses, programs, and degrees

- ○ access to a network of resources and opportunities for best practice and for gaining knowledge about differentiation and high-level learning

- ○ connections with others interested in research, seminars, workshops, and conferences on giftedness issues, and forums for building relationships and sharing ideas

- ○ access to experts in the field of gifted education

- ○ clarification of identification and assessment issues

- ○ suggestions for different instructional models and approaches

- ○ support for those interested in fostering school cultures where gifted learners are challenged, and high-level ability is nurtured

- ○ resource banks of material at different grade levels and in various subject areas for use by those who work at home or school with children who are advanced in particular domains, or have multiple exceptionalities

- ○ support for interschool collaboration locally and across districts

- ○ information about proactive inclusion of at-risk students in high-risk neighborhoods

- ○ support for those interested in fostering school cultures where gifted learners are challenged, and high-level ability is nurtured

Support and Networking for Children, Adolescents, and Families

○ support for learning and other gifted-related needs

○ access to diverse extracurricular programs

○ information on counseling and mentorships, including access to university mentorships

○ connections to other children and adolescents with similar interests and concerns

○ opportunities to connect with other parents with giftedness concerns and ideas to share

○ access to reliable information about programs and professional services

○ opportunities to network with educators

○ help for siblings of gifted learners who may have issues or special learning needs

○ place to acquire a stronger sense of community

Support and Networking Further Afield

○ connections to local museums, dance companies, galleries, music schools, and other cultural institutions that support talent development

○ coordination of resources within the university, across programs, and departments, including collaborative explorations of high-level development in different disciplines

○ collaborations with parent groups, business partners, government connections, and educational relationships that are local to international in scope

○ interschool mentorships

○ advanced technological services for networking purposes

○ connections to other gifted centers around the world

Networking for Purposes of Research, Publication, and Dissemination

○ support for collaborative investigations

○ symposia for shared learning

○ research on gifted development and education

○ a nexus for information for the community, including media and policy makers

○ active and dynamic learning and sharing of material

A gifted center can be virtual, but ideally, it's also a real place, where people can find someone to talk with about their concerns, and put their hands on actual books and journals. Its virtual dimension should include a comprehensive website where people can find current information on gifted development, educational options, and the latest research findings. A gifted center can make a significant and lasting difference for children, parents, and teachers as well as for the community as a whole. In our opinion, anywhere that teacher training is happening, there should be a gifted center.

Different communities have different priorities and resources (financial and otherwise), and a gifted resource center has to be designed within that context to meet local needs. If you live in a place that has such a center, use it and work with it to help make it better able to meet your family's needs. If you don't have a facility like this available in your area, think about linking to one online, or getting involved in advocacy efforts to support the establishment of such a resource in your community.

Time-Honored Wisdom for Meeting Today's Challenges

"Sooner or later, everything old is new again."[10]

"Much in education—especially higher education—is cyclical. New ideas, resources and tools, come and go. Some will stay. But through it all, it is only the timeless lessons that can become foundational to the ways we lead and learn."[11]

As much as the world changes, some aspects of life remain constant. Being a parent means loving your child with a deep, protective passion; being a child means exploring, discovering, and learning through play.

What follows are some approaches to teaching and learning that have transcended time and can support the development of giftedness broadly across the population.

Leadership

"I've learned that you shouldn't go through life with a catcher's mitt on both hands; you need to be able to throw something back."[12]

"If your actions inspire others to dream more, learn more, do more, and become more, you are a leader."[13]

Young people can use their strengths to become change-makers in a challenging world. Increasingly, students are using their voices and their enthusiasms to make a difference.[14] As with any change-oriented initiative, patience, resolve, adaptability, and resilience are essential. Jaime Malic is the Leadership Program Coordinator at a large independent school for girls from Grades 1 through 12. She shared some thoughts with us:

Nurturing Leadership: Values, Service, Reflection, and Support

"As education continues to evolve, leadership development is moving from the periphery to the core. Young people are witnessing powerful movements for social change, keen to have their voices heard and lead the way forward. Just as they require academic training so, too, do they need learning about leadership—perhaps now, more than ever before. Having had the honor and joy of working with hundreds of young leaders over the years, I see leadership development as an incremental and ongoing process, driven by values, defined by service, and anchored by continuous reflection and support.

Before young people can lead others, they must be able to lead themselves, which means knowing who they are and the values for which they stand. They discover those values through the recursive process of experience and reflection, so it's important that, throughout their education, they learn and talk about character traits, take stock of their own principles, face ethical dilemmas, and debrief those learning experiences with their teachers, advisors, coaches, parents, and peers.

As they connect with one another to pursue common goals within their school communities, it's vital for young people to have multiple opportunities to serve in different capacities. Whether contributing to a team effort or starting a new initiative to meet a community need, they'll learn from experience that it's not the title that makes the leader, but rather the actions and words of the individual who cares about, inspires, and amplifies the voices of others. Collaboration within any community requires risk-taking and will inevitably result in both success and failure. As young leaders encounter those realities, the guidance of trusted adults can help them see and apply important lessons, as well as acknowledge and celebrate the strength that comes from diversity in its many different forms.

When young leaders take steps beyond their schools to lead within their local, national and global communities, they have a lasting impact. Former students with whom I've worked are now inspiring and serving others in many ways, including as activists and advocates, educators, entrepreneurs, journalists, medical professionals, and researchers. With educators and parents working together to nurture the development of young people's leadership knowledge and skills, today's learners will become tomorrow's change-makers, confident in who they are as individuals, collaborative within the communities of which they are a part, and capable of making a positive difference in the lives of others."

It's vital to children's leadership development that adults support and reinforce their character strengths, emotional intelligence, and well-being. There's much at stake, including children's abilities to relate to others; to cope with uncertainties, challenges, and vulnerability; and to make wise decisions in their lives. There's increasing focus in the field of gifted education, and in schools generally, on the importance of leadership development. It's taking many forms, including an emphasis on wisdom; community involvement, connection, outreach, and service; social context; psychosocial strength training; and social/emotional development.

Opportunities abound for children and teens to become involved in personally rewarding and socially beneficial activities and community service that support the development of leadership skills. Such activities can

○ allow kids to test and further develop their leadership skills

○ offer a chance for them to acquire experience in leadership roles

○ foster a sense of responsibility and fulfillment

○ lead to productive and fulfilling interactions with others

○ provide preparation for future work endeavors

○ help with career selection

○ lead to references and networks that may prove important later on

Malcolm Gladwell, author of *Outliers: The Story of Success*, wrote: "If you work hard enough and assert yourself, and use your mind and imagination, you can shape the world to your desires."[15] Parents and educators who work together can help children become more emotionally knowledgeable and secure, ready to become leaders as well as becoming more socially responsible, competent, and caring.

Science journalist Daniel Goleman describes how emotional competencies required for effective leadership (such as self-motivation, mood regulation, and hope) can be learned.[16] Adults can use resources like his books and articles to help children gain self-assurance, and also manage their feelings about issues that might trouble them, such as gifted identification, academic mismatches, relationships, or other uncertainties. Getting past self-focus and stretching boundaries enables meaningful engagement with the world.

Going Beyond the Academic Curriculum

"Building character strengths is the mutual responsibility of families, schools, and communities."[17]

Psychologist Eileen Kennedy-Moore discusses how children and adolescents can create rich and fulfilling lives by developing self-esteem, and relinquishing self-doubts.[18] She points to three fundamental keys to making this happen: making connections and caring for others; building upon competencies; and choosing to act in ways that are meaningful and consistent with personal values. Academic learning is important, but helping children acquire a strong moral compass is every bit as critical, if not more so.

Principal Martha Perry is committed to providing a meaningful education for the hundreds of students who attend her school. Here are her thoughts.

A Principal's Commitment

In an ever-changing world, where predictability is far more elusive, the importance of knowing oneself and believing in one's capacity to handle new situations has never been more important. *Learning is about the process, not the product.*

Far beyond acquiring content in specific disciplines, possessing the tools and skills to be responsive to change and the ability to be flexible as one adapts is paramount. As our students learn, it's the core skills of critical thinking, communication, creativity, adaptability, and discernment that will be what enables success. We're committed to ensuring that beyond discipline content, our students' personalized "toolboxes" are filled with the skills that contribute not only to their own success, but to their capacity to contribute to helping others as they work toward solutions to authentic problems.

In addition, schools must not only recognize but highlight the tremendous value of diversity of all kinds and how these contribute

> to learning and growth for all. For any community member to
> be able to achieve their full potential they must truly feel known
> and valued. Imperative to working with others is ensuring our
> schools and, as a result, our students, are culturally competent;
> that equity and inclusion are at the forefront of all we do.

Educational psychologist Michele Borba discusses seven teachable character strengths that she refers to as "superpowers." These superpowers are strengths that would go into the personalized toolboxes Martha Perry describes, and include confidence, empathy, self-control, integrity, curiosity, perseverance, and optimism.[19] Borba explains each of these, and how to foster them through age-appropriate activities, use of suitable resources, and reinforcement from adults who care. Children who embody these seven strengths are "thrivers" and experience greater happiness and accomplishment than others over time.

Other tools for your child's personalized toolkit might be responsibility, resilience, kindness, self-awareness, honesty, forgiveness, and gratitude. It's worth thinking about which strengths your child most needs at this point in time, and then nurturing their development.

Two-Eyed Seeing: Indigenous Perspectives and Gifted Education

"We are gifted and very talented. But you're not going to find out the way you are asking us your questions."[20]

"Recently, my thinking has been heavily influenced by the work I'm doing with my Indigenous colleagues. My efforts with "two-eyed-seeing" have me wrestling with "Western" notions of giftedness as there really is no need for them in Indigenous ways of knowing and being."[21]

"Two-eyed seeing" is a term coined by Mi'kmaw elder Albert Marshall. It means seeing from one eye with the strengths of Indigenous ways of knowing, and seeing from the other eye with the strengths of Western ways of knowing, and to use both of these eyes simultaneously and harmoniously. This concept has been applied to many areas of human activity, including research with Indigenous people,[22] wildlife health,[23] and medicine.[24]

Indigenous students are under-represented in gifted education, from identification through programming.[25] Marcia Gentry, a leading expert in this area, wrote, "A national research agenda focused on gifted/creative/talented Native American students is needed, as this population remains one of the least researched, most overlooked, and most underserved in the field."[26]

The lower participation rates of Indigenous children in gifted education result from a combination of many factors, one of which is the challenging social and economic situation too many Indigenous families experience. Another factor, however, is the Indigenous perspective on teaching and learning, a perspective that's out of sync with the prevailing approach to gifted education, where children's abilities are assessed at one point in time, using a test of IQ or something similar. This leads to children being categorized as either gifted or not gifted, with those labeled gifted getting enriched educational services across school subject areas.

The Indigenous perspective is, however, consistent with the Optimal Match approach that we describe in this book, where each child is given the learning opportunities they can most benefit from at any given time. The Indigenous approach recognizes the importance of being flexible and creative, taking into account the unique and changing nature of each child's interests and abilities, and the complex interacting factors that affect their social, emotional, and cultural development. Indigenous parents and teachers realize that children's abilities unfold dynamically, in response to their interests and life experiences.[27]

Gifted education expert Lannie Kanevsky told us that, based on her work with Indigenous educators, "the whole concept of giftedness is not a good fit within their culture." In a book edited by Bruce Shore, [28] renowned filmmaker Alanis Obomsawin described how conventional gifted education identification and programming is dreadfully mismatched for most Indigenous North Americans. This is also true for so many other children growing up in minority cultures.

Several Canadian schools are having great success applying Indigenous perspectives to teaching and learning processes. They're finding that these perspectives engage all students—Indigenous and others—in the learning process. Education activist Kelly Gallagher-Mackay and innovative school principal Nancy Steinhauer describe dramatic improvements in student success when schools focus on sustaining connection, authentic learning, and problem-finding and problem-solving processes.[29]

Gallagher-Mackay and Steinhauer write, "Effective learning builds on the strengths of the learner rather than focusing only on the gaps." They describe a school in Alberta where problem behavior is dealt with not by a punishment or suspension, but instead by a chat with the principal about the student's goals and career directions. The student is asked to think about how school could be made more meaningful, and that is followed up with changes that take their suggestions into account. By intentionally supporting students' creativity, flexibility, and problem-solving skills, schools are nurturing students in becoming happily productive and informed citizens in a changing world.

We all benefit from practising two-eyed seeing. Supporting gifted learning and development means listening and observing, with patient and thoughtful attention. Be alert to your child's interests, be flexible in encouraging those, and match challenges to their interests and abilities. In this way, you're practising the best of both Indigenous and Western approaches to supporting gifted development, a true example of two-eyed seeing.

Music: Fortifying the Mind, Soul, and Spirit

"Music is a higher revelation than all wisdom and philosophy."[30]

"Where words fail, music speaks."[31]

Music is a universal language that has enriched, soothed, inspired, and invigorated people through centuries, across ages and cultures. It empowers learning, creativity, communication, and connectivity.

You don't have to be a musician to appreciate the countless benefits of music. Music is a multisensory experience, and musical training in early childhood is related to structural brain changes that can facilitate neuroplasticity in children.[32] Author Anne Murphy Paul writes that music helps to improve memory: "Songs and rhymes can be used to remember all kinds of information."[33]

Teachers often use melodies to engage their students, and educators and parents alike use tunes to help children gain knowledge, develop aural and language skills, become active, learn routines, and have fun. Lullabies, campfire chants, rap, marching songs, nursery rhymes, symphonies, ballads—there are endless possibilities for musical expression. Psychologist Mona Delahooke notes, "It's well worth the effort to discover the types of music that bring joy to a child, and listen to, move, and dance with the music together."[34]

There are programs, resources, conservatories, lessons, informal gatherings, play groups, concert series, performance venues, choirs, jam sessions, and other options that enable children to participate in music activities, independently or with others. As we write this, many schools are struggling with cutbacks in educational funding, and this is having a serious impact on music programs. It's vital that parents advocate where necessary for music to be incorporated into the classroom, and ensure their child has opportunities to engage in music, whether as a listener, performer, or creator.

Children who are exceptionally talented in one or more aspects of musical development benefit from adults paying attention to their strengths, differentiating instruction, and providing enrichment options.[35] Nancy Kopman composes music and also leads interactive programs with young children and their parents, grandparents, and caregivers. Her themes include helping little ones understand nature, their "inner voice," transitions, seasons, feelings, motor skills, and more. She emphasizes that adults learn to enjoy music alongside children, co-experiencing it as pleasurable, comforting, stimulating, and validating, from infancy onward.[36]

What kinds of participatory programs are available in your neighborhood? What can you find online? Who do you know who has participated in music programs and who may be able to offer suggestions? What playlists can you create with your family? What instruments might your child like to try? How has music had an impact on your own life?

Composer Hanne Deneire is based in Antwerp, Belgium. Her music programs, House of Music and Children are Composers,[37] take learning and music appreciation to new heights through in-studio and online sessions that encourage children's musicality and hands-on involvement in several different areas—creativity, improvisation, composition, and performance—instrumental as well as vocal. Her nine-year-old son, Lander-Janus (LJ), is equally passionate about music. He plays the guitar, piano, violin, trombone, drums, and baritone (and wants to learn saxophone), plus he reads music fluently, composes songs, and teaches younger children. He also takes weekly art, dance, and theatre classes. LJ has been exposed to music his entire life, and has been encouraged to explore its richness. There's much that parents can learn from this dynamic mother and son duo, and they've each shared their thoughts about the positive effects of music on child development.

Hanne's Words

In Belgian schools, there is almost no creative teaching, no music—nothing. So parents have to arrange to do this outside school hours. My motto, as a mother, composer, educator, and lifelong learner is that children grow through music! That is my primary motivator in raising my son, and I encourage other parents to involve their children in music in all its forms. I believe that music is universal and has the power to connect us all. It is unique, and nothing is as strong. Music is magical. When we sing and create music, we use all parts of the brain. And music moves in many dimensions as it develops over time and in space, and as each performance becomes a new creation and people listen, interpret, and feel it in their own way.

My son started with music when he was born. We have BabyMusic (0-3yrs) at the House of Music, and as soon as he could sit, he was playing the piano and improvising. He knows all the notes now and composes his own music. He loves improvising—we call it "fantasy in the moment." He and others are motivated to learn music through encouragement, instruction, and interactive experiences. It's so great to see their focus and joy!

LJ's Words (Translated from Dutch by Hanne)

I really love the sound of my baritone. It's so beautiful, and it makes me really happy.

I can play music in the morning, so I go to school in a happy mood, and during lunch I come home to "reload," and I also play some music together with my mother. This gives me the power to keep going to school.

I don't like school because the children fight and say bad words. I don/t have many friends there, and I feel like an alien sometimes, but in the House of Music and in all my other activities the children are much nicer, and I do have friends. I feel much more accepted than at school. I cannot understand why there is such a big difference between how people behave, think, and feel in school than in my creative environment. Maybe everyone has to learn music so they can all express themselves and they don't have to fight anymore? Maybe people who are not friendly or who are irritated can feel better through music? Then they will be able to do their best at school, feel happier, and concentrate more.

My friends in music also have other activities in common with me. We like science and Lego, and so we have many different things we can do together and that is fun!

I've always lived in the world of music. From when I was a baby my mother would sing for me, and we play on the piano and other instruments. Now I can play by myself, but I still love it when my mother plays piano for me when I go to sleep. I'm in bed, and one floor lower I hear her playing all the different composers and pieces. That way I always sleep better, and I feel peaceful.

It's unfortunate that LJ experiences his school environment as so harsh. However, it's wonderful that he and his mother have worked together and have found a way to cope with it, through his opportunities for musical growth and self-expression, and his fulfilling connections with other children through their shared interests and activities. It's evident that Hanne and LJ know the value of music—how it can be calming, and also energize both the intellect and the soul.

Hanne's and LJ's stories provide an illustration of the way the Optimal Match perspective works in practice. Observe an interest, support its growth, and it may blossom into a talent. Also, as these stories show, music (like other modes of creative self-expression such as art and writing) can foster the development not only of an individual's interests and abilities, but also their well-being. Music can be an important key to learning, creative expression, and personal growth.

Philosophy: A Sure Path to Thinking and Knowing

James McManamy is a high school philosophy teacher who impresses upon his students that thinking—critical, creative, deductive—is a sure path to knowledge. He's hoping to expand the philosophy program within his school system, predicated on the idea that learning is ongoing and thought is essential. McManamy shared his thoughts on teaching philosophy with us.

The Importance of Philosophy

My senior high school students usually have lots of questions on the day they enter my philosophy class. They have even more questions on the last day of the semester. For most of them it's their first exposure to philosophy. Some do well academically, but many others struggle to learn the "new language" of this subject. One thing they all have in common is that they feel better for having taken philosophy because it makes them think about things they had not previously considered, and it helps them to examine previously held beliefs that they never questioned, but that now seem dubious.

Translated from the Greek, a philosopher is a lover of wisdom. Knowledge, though important, is not necessarily wisdom. The ancient Greeks thought that a wise person was filled with virtue. Some of the world's smartest people (dictators, political leaders, etc.) were brilliant, but lacked a moral sense. I try to inspire my students to ask good, significant, and deep questions so that they can better themselves not only intellectually but morally, so they can fully develop their potential as rational beings and make the world a better place.

Students of philosophy start by posing questions. For example, Are we born good or evil? What's the purpose of life? Can we truly know anything or is everything just opinion? Is there a creator of the universe? Is the universe eternal? What's the best form of government? There's pretty much no question that's beyond the realm of the study of philosophy.

In our media-fed technological age there's great potential for us to improve ourselves and our world, such as using the Internet to alleviate poverty and increase literacy. There's also danger that with sound-bytes and theatrics, people will be satisfied with simplistic answers to complex realities. Philosophy helps people avoid becoming victims of societal and media-generated manipulation. Questioning everything is not negative if its purpose is to uncover truth.

I asked one of my students to say something about his experience of the discipline of philosophy. Jeremy scored 100% in the class, one of the few perfect scores in philosophy that I've ever given. He said that the study of philosophy, when done properly, can lead to personal fulfillment and happiness. Quoting Jeremy:

> *"Philosophy, while both being a tool for the development of critical thinking and a noble pursuit of wisdom, is also a catalyst of self-fulfillment. The very nature of fulfillment makes it a philosophical pursuit, attempting to discover what leads to true happiness...it is in the field of philosophy that one is given the wisdom and skill to pursue fulfillment, to find their own fulfillment and craft it into something truly meaningful."*

McManamy and his student, Jeremy, are both acutely aware that learning is a personal journey, and that what one gains from the experience depends upon how much thought and effort goes into it. McManamy expressed concern that too many people mistakenly consider philosophy to be a useless or impractical course because "contemplating nature doesn't pay the bills." He argues that those committed to the study of philosophy, and especially university philosophy graduates, are in high demand in many places including sports, entertainment, and business and financial sectors. One reason is that employers are looking for problem-solvers who "think outside the box," and philosophers can do that. He points out that philosophy majors include actor Harrison Ford, Super Bowl winning quarterback, John Elway; financial analyst, Mark Hulbert; civil rights activist, Dr. Martin Luther King Jr; Pope John Paul II; and Jeopardy host, Alex Trebeck.

Whether or not your child has the option of taking philosophy at school, you can infuse meaningful inquiry into their daily activities, and can also suggest to amenable teachers that they incorporate philosophical discussions in their classes. Across subject areas, there are questions without clear right or wrong answers, questions students can investigate, and use as topics for lively debates and discourse—all the while sharpening their thinking skills.

Nature: Boundless Benefits and Gifted Learning Opportunities

> *"There is nothing in a caterpillar that tells you it's going to be a butterfly."*[38]

> *"The woods are lovely, dark and deep. But I have promises to keep, and miles to go before I sleep."*[39]

> *"Look deep into nature, and then you will understand everything better."*[40]

The natural world is both healing and invigorating. It can invoke wonder, pleasure, and fear. It contains endless secrets and forces to discover, and they're always in flux. Before there were books, school buildings, or online classes, there was the outside world. A child exploring nature is exposed to infinite authentic and relevant learning experiences that may trigger an explosion of interest that inspires gifted-level development.

The COVID pandemic was an impetus to get kids outdoors, where contagion was less likely. During the pandemic, outdoor education programs sprung up in parks, conservation areas, meadows, forests, campgrounds, and playgrounds. In programs such as Trackers Schools, children participate in hands-on nature studies; collaborate and problem-solve; create bridges and dams; examine flora, fauna, habitats, and wildlife; navigate rocky terrain; and explore streams and marshes. As children learn about their environment, they also learn about each other, and about themselves in relation to the world around them.

Benefits of spending time outdoors[41] include

○ *Health*—fresh air, exercise, vitamin D, better sleep, reduced stress, lower obesity, and enhanced immunity

○ *Fitness*—running, climbing trees, jumping, hiking, canoeing, skipping, sliding, dancing, walking—all leading to stronger bones and muscles, better balance and coordination, and more energy

○ *Well-being*—increased happiness, improved ability to regulate emotions, and stay calm, optimistic, positive, and resilient

○ *Multisensory stimulation*—the scent of grass, mud, or flowers; the feeling of tree bark or rough-sided rock formations; the sight of eagles flying high above or a vast multi-hued ocean; the sound of birds in the springtime or chipmunks scurrying through fallen leaves; the taste of a clover flower or snow as it falls

○ *Learning*—myriad possibilities for stretching boundaries, taking risks, and generating ideas

○ *Cognitive development*—improved attention, focus, problem-solving ability, motivation to learn, and academic achievement

○ *Creativity*—inspiration for imagination leading to making an Inuksuk, drawing, composing music, writing poetry, or building a fort

○ *Play*—a chance to run hard, play tag, blow bubbles, chase butterflies, and skip rocks

○ *Social skills*—flexible and unlimited options for exploring and playing with others

○ *Reflection*—taking time alone to think or relax

○ *Curiosity*—the habits and habitats of birds, animals, and insects; the changing seasons; the effects of humans on nature; and the impacts of climate change

○ *Career springboards*—geologist, zoologist, botanist, farmer, landscape architect, astronomer, oceanographer, photographer, conservation scientist, environmental engineer

○ *Environmental awareness*—interest in renewing and protecting the natural world

Nature enthusiast and poet William Wordsworth perceived relationships with the natural world as integral to intellectual and spiritual development. He wrote, "Come forth into the light of things, let nature be your teacher." Any spot in nature—a park, forest, wilderness, or riverbank—is an ideal place for families to spend time together, learning about life, enlivening the spirit, soothing the soul, and nurturing well-being.

Strengthening Communities and Strengthening Oneself

> *"Community involvement enables engagement, strengthens connections, and offers support, all of which are important for realizing intellectual, creative, and social fulfilment— and the promise of ability."*[42]

How does engaging in building stronger communities support gifted development? Examples include the following:

○ developing friendships, mutual respect, and networks of social support

○ expanding experience with diverse others

○ feeling a sense of belonging

○ building skills in different areas

○ gaining access to a variety of resources

○ contributing to community well-being

○ strengthening competence and confidence

○ fostering global awareness

Community-based outlets and organizations can help children forge productive, collaborative relationships, as well as local and broader awareness through discussions and investigations relating to their interests. There are volunteer groups, mentorships, and youth programs in different domains such as social justice, environmental concerns, science, the arts, entrepreneurship, health and safety, and more.

Community involvements can also promote academic competence and social-emotional capacities. Parents and kids can check out resources and learning opportunities in their communities through local publications, public libraries, parent-teacher associations, cultural organizations, and school news updates. [43]

Responding to Cutbacks in Education

"Focus on needs and services, not labels... a true embrace of equity means that all students get the support they need."[44]

There are many reasons for those interested in giftedness to be concerned about educational cutbacks. There are circumstances— sometimes particular to a certain school district, sometimes having to do with a broader context, or political maneuverings, or unexpected events—that threaten educational provisions for gifted learners. When budget slashing and turbulence intensify, gifted education can get sidelined. This is at least partly because the term "gifted" is plagued by the misconceptions and misunderstandings we discuss in Chapter 1.

And, of course, it's not only gifted education that's affected by budget cutbacks. In times of austerity, there are also slashes to art and music programs, athletic opportunities, field trips, resource librarians, and counselors. Plus, amid increasing concerns about children's mental health, and an escalating need for more psychologists and other clinical specialists in schools, there are not enough professionals on hand to ease children's struggles and support their coping, resilience, and well-being.

When funding cuts are widespread, as they are in so many jurisdictions today, schools are forced to make do with less, and competing agendas arise from different parent or advocacy groups. It's imperative for parents of gifted learners to become informed about the realities and ramifications of cutbacks, to know their rights, and to champion these. In education as in life, the squeaky wheel is most likely to get the oil.

When gifted education is included in the special education budget, it often loses out to exceptionalities that appear more needy. For many decision-makers, the priority funding goes first to children with disabilities, whether learning, sensory, or behavioral, with the assumption (sometimes explicit) that kids with gifted learning needs can get along just fine without any special attention.

What can parents of gifted learners do when times are fiscally turbulent? How can they ensure their child receives an education that matches their learning needs? Here are some practical suggestions:

○ Maintain a focus on the Optimal Match approach, and not on categorical giftedness; that's the most convincing way to explain your child's learning needs to decision-makers.

○ Remain tolerant when scarcity of funding causes emotions to run high and patience to run low, remembering everyone is feeling stressed.

○ Get the facts and take time to reflect upon them. Learn about gifted-related laws, regulations, mandates, and protocols in your district, state, province, or country.

○ Stay informed, and continue to gather information whether things are going smoothly or not.

○ Find out what measures have been taken by others and how they might guide your efforts.

○ Be ready to take the necessary steps as you work to close gaps caused by cutbacks.

○ Build bridges, work cohesively, reinforce alliances, and create new ones.

○ Be attentive to the dynamics of your child's school community including the overall learning environment, priorities, gifted-related actions and activities, and school culture.

○ Maintain a positive, problem-solving attitude.

When there is only so much money to go around, gifted education is sometimes construed as a privilege, as an elitist construct benefitting only those who already have advantages. You're on stronger ground when you make the case that children with gifted learning needs are entitled to the same kind of education that each child is entitled to: one that meets their individual learning needs, and that matches their abilities and interests, so they can keep learning. You'll make the best case possible for funding gifted education if you focus on matching each child's learning needs with the appropriate services.

Changing Realities

"Systems should be designed to be inclusive—to err on the side of letting kids into a service rather than on keeping them out."[45]

"What emerging practices will best address gifted learners' needs across different domains in the years ahead?"[46]

Throughout this book, we address questions about how giftedness develops, and how parents and educators can support that process. We describe the Optimal Match approach, wherein each child receives an education that matches their ever-changing interests and abilities, as the best way to support the development of giftedness over time. For those who wonder if the Optimal Match approach is too challenging to put into practice, we've provided many examples of parents who have successfully advocated for changes toward an optimal match for their children, and educators who have put that approach into practice.

We recently learned about Telra Institute, a school that's implementing the Optimal Match approach for all its learners. Michael Matthews is an expert in gifted education whose work we've cited elsewhere within this book. He's the Board Vice-Chairperson for Telra Institute, and co-wrote this description of the school's approach with Ronak Bhatt, the Founder and Chancellor:

Telra Institute: The Optimal Match in Practice

Telra Institute is a K-5 charter school founded recently in the Charlotte, North Carolina, metropolitan area that has been designed following an approach quite similar to Matthews' and Foster's idea of Optimal Match. As in the Optimal Match approach, Telra students' learning needs are individually identi-fied, and each student is then "matched" into a learning module for each core subject area that delivers an appropriate level of challenge. The school recognizes that learning needs are fluid and as such must be re-evaluated (and students re-matched) on a regular and ongoing basis. Additionally, Telra's instructional and other staff receive ongoing training and coaching that supports their teaching and learning interactions through pedagogy from both gifted education curricula and other aspects of specialized student needs.

Recent research increasingly has drawn attention to the substantial error rates in even the most well-designed approaches to gifted identification and to the limited utility of a general gifted label in designing an optimally-matched educational program across multiple domains. Rather than focusing on identification or labelling, the goal of the Telra Institute approach is to provide a differentiated, rigorous, and accelerated approach to learning that will benefit all advanced learners, regardless of whether or not they have been formally identified as gifted. Through this approach and the school's high expectations, we seek to instill in all students the practices and values of curiosity, tenacity and initiative, and passion for learning.

For readers who wish to explore particular areas further, we've provided hundreds of references to resources that reflect the complexity, richness, and diversity of knowledge about gifted development and education. Leonardo da Vinci said, "The noblest pleasure is the joy of understanding." It *is* a joy—but for parents of gifted learners, under-standing is also a serious responsibility.

In the second edition of this book, we listed five recommendations for future research that were made by gifted education expert Sally Reis:

○ expand conceptions of the multidimensionality of giftedness and talent development

○ eradicate the absence of challenge from too many students' school experience

○ address the needs of underserved populations

○ move from identifying gifted learners to developing competencies instead

○ apply gifted education pedagogy to talent development, with an emphasis on strengths

We're delighted to observe that—thanks to the efforts of Reis and dozens of other gifted education experts, many of whom we've cited in this book—there have been significant advances in the twelve years since then in each of these areas. Matthews' and Bhatt's description of Telra Institute illustrates we're moving closer to an understanding of the importance of creating an optimal match for every learner.

Other key information is emerging from the field of psychology. There's an increasing understanding of the role of extra-cognitive factors in talent development (for example, psychosocial factors and the environmental supports and constraints that can influence the development of giftedness), and links among creativity, competency, and productivity across contexts and domains.[47]

The questions researchers and others continue to explore concern ways to develop a generation of learners who are competent, enthusiastic, resilient, and self-directed, and who can find joy and fulfillment in learning. Children can flourish if we encourage their interests and honor their capabilities. For example, the Raffi Child Honouring Foundation (founded by singer, composer, and child advocate Raffi Cavoukian), emphasizes the importance of entrusting young people to help create a more humane and sustainable world. This involves learning to build community, restore planetary health, and prioritize well-being. There's "an essential code of conduct" with core principles that are integral to respecting "the primacy of early years" so that children will become caring adults.[48]

There's a growing urgency to nurturing a generation of innovators, ready, willing, and able to contribute to finding solutions to the problems of the planet—climate change, systemic racism, increasing environmental devastation, water shortages, a growing wealth gap, radicalization, and terrorism. More than ever, we need to support the development of giftedness as broadly across the population as possible.

Ways to Love a Child

The following advice arrived in the mail from the Kids Help Foundation without author attribution (unfortunately, because we'd very much like to acknowledge the writer):

> *Give your presence. Laugh, dance, and sing together. Listen from a heart space. Encourage. Understand. Allow them to love themselves. Ask their opinions. Learn from them. Say yes as often as possible. Say no when necessary. Honor their no's. Apologize. Touch gently. Build lots of blanket forts. Open up. Fly kites together. Lighten up. Believe in possibilities. Read books out loud. Create a circle of quiet. Teach feelings. Share your dreams. Walk in the rain. Celebrate mistakes. Admit yours. Frame their artwork. Stay up late together. Eliminate comparison. Delight in silliness. Handle with care. Protect them. Cherish their innocence. Giggle. Speak kindly. Go swimming. Splash. Let them help. Let them cry. Don't hide your tears. Brag about them. Answer their questions. Let them go when it's time. Let them come back. Show compassion. Bend down to talk to little children. Smile even when you're tired. Surprise them with a special lunch. Don't judge their friends. Give them enough room to make decisions. Love all that they do. Honor their differences. Respect them. Remember they have not been on earth very long.*

We invite you to consider making additions of your own to this list.

Being Smart about Tomorrow

"The most important task facing us today is how to develop and sustain talent by fostering a love of learning, a zest for challenge, and resilience in the face of setbacks."[49]

Although we inevitably confront challenges and change in our lives, our communities, and globally, every day presents new opportunities to make a difference.

We've given you in these pages tools not only for coping with the challenges of parenting gifted learners, but also for optimizing learning experiences at home and school. We provide evidence-based suggestions for supporting the development of those who are exceptionally capable in one or more domains, and for fostering optimal development in all children. We emphasize that giftedness is domain-specific and highly diverse, and that it's not easily measured or sometimes even recognized. We're especially excited about the paradigm shift we're watching in the field of gifted education, as realization of the importance of matching learner's needs with appropriate provisions gains momentum.

We hope you'll continue being smart about gifted learning, and open to the wealth of opportunities available for encouraging and supporting gifted-level development in those children and adolescents with whom you work, live, and share the richness of life.

Endnotes

Chapter 1

1   Dai, D. 2020 (p. 9) and 2019 (p. 2)

2   Matthews, D. J., Subotnik, & Horowitz, 2009; Subotnik, Olszewski-Kubilius, & Worrell, 2012

3   Peters, Gentry, Whiting, & McBee, 2019

4   Matthews,D. J., & Dai, 2014; Worrell, 2009; Worrell & Dixson, 2018

5   Callahan, 2017; VanTassel-Baska & Brown, 2009

6   Dai, D.Y. (2020). Rethinking Human Potential from a Talent Development Perspective. *Journal for the Education of the Gifted* 43(1):19-37 March, 2020. DOI:10.1177/0162353219897850

7   Tetreault, 2021

8   Marland, 1972

9   Stanley & Benbow, 1983; Stanley, Keating, & Fox, 1974

10   Robinson & Robinson, 1982

11   Nancy Robinson, personal correspondence, January 29, 2021

12   Borland, 1989

13   Howe, 1990

14   E.g., Keating,1991; Feldman, 1991

15   Subotnik, Stoeger, & Olszewski-Kubilius, 2017

16   VanTassel-Baska & Brown, 2009

17   Reis & Peters, 2020; Renzulli & Reis, 2009

18   Assouline, Colangelo, VanTassel-Baska, & Lupkowski-Shoplik, 2015

19   Ericsson, Charness, Feltovich, & Hoffman, 2006

20   Dweck, 2006

21   Dweck, 2009a, 2009b

22   Feldman, 2003, p. 15

23   Belsky, Caspi, Moffitt, & Poulton,,2020; Demetriou & Spanoudis, 2018; Horowitz, 2009; Keating, 2011; Nelson, 1999

24   Howe, 1999; Horowitz, Subotnik, & Matthews,D. J., 2009

25   Simonton, 1994

26   Birren, 2009

27   Bloom, 1985; Howe, 1999; Simonton, 1994

28   Gould, 1981; Guilford, 1967; Spearman, 1927; Thurstone, 1938

29   Gardner, 1983

30   Keating, 2009

31   Matthews,D. J. & Dai, 2014; Worrell, 2009

32   Goertzel & Hansen, 2004

33   Dweck, 2006; Ericsson, 2006

34   Luc Kumps, 2008 (private correspondence)

35   Howe, 1990

36   Winner, 2009

37   Dixson, Makel, Peters, et al. 2020

38   Gardner, 1983

39   Goleman, 2011

40   Subotnik, Olszewski-Kubilius, & Worrell, 2012

41   Amanda Gorman, Youth Poet Laureate, recited at the 2021 Presidential Inaugural Ceremony

42   Terman, 1926-1959

43   Hollingworth, 1926

44   Klein, 2002

45   Marland Report, 1972

46   Assouline, S. G., & Lupkowski-Shoplik, A. (2012)

47   Tetreault, 2021 p. 302

48   New evidence suggests that even those labeled 'mentally retarded' or 'developmentally delayed' can learn a lot more than was ever thought possible. See for example Doidge, 2007.

49   Ontario Ministry of Education, Standards for School Boards' Special Education Plan, 2000, p. 33 (still exists, 2021)

50 New York State, 1982

51 Peters, Rambo-Hernandez, Makel, Matthews, M. S., & Plucker, 2017; Steen-bergen, Makel, & Olszewski-Kubilius, 2016; Subotnik, Olszewski-Kubilius, & Worrell, 2012

Chapter 2

1 Kaufman & Sternberg, 2019

2 Feldman, 1991, p. 45.

3 Toynbee, 1967

4 Merrotsy, 2013

5 Kaufman, J. C. & Sternberg, R., 2019

6 Beghetto, R. A., 2019

7 Keating, 1980

8 Daniel Keating was Dona Matthews' doctoral supervisor. The basis of the Optimal Match perspective, and its juxtaposition with the mystery model, emerged under Dr Keating's guidance. There were many other influences on this idea, including Nancy and Hal Robinson's "optimal match" approach to supporting the development of giftedness.

9 Greene, 2013.

10 Greene, 2013, p. 178

11 Csikszentmihalyi & Wolfe, 2000

12 Csikszentmihalyi, 2019

13 Csikszentmihalyi, 1991, 2019

14 Kaufman & Gregoire, 2016

15 Glaveanu & Kaufman, 2019

16 Balchin, 2009, p. 205

17 Barbot, Hass, & Reiter-Palmon, 2019

18 Plucker, J., Makel, M.C., & Qian, M., 2019

19 Sternberg, R. (Feb. 27, 2018.) What's wrong with creativity testing? Journal of Creative Behavior. https://doi.org/10.1002/jocb.237

20 Balchin, 2009

21 Oreck, Owens, & Baum, 2003

22 Robinson, Shore, & Enersen, 2007 p. 79

23 Other university offerings include The Center for Talent Development at Northwestern University, The Belin-Blank Center at the University of Iowa, and Johns Hopkins Center for Talent Development

24   Future problem solving – www.fpspi.org; Roots and Shoots – (Jane Goodall) – www.rootsandshoots.org; Odyssey of the Mind- www.odysseyofthemind.com; Destination Imagination – www.destinationimagination.org

25   Makerspace info http://www.makerspaceforeducation.com/makerspace.html

26   Worlds of Making https://ny.chalkbeat.org/2020/10/14/21052/island-school-makerspace-lab

27   Birkner, 2020

28   Renzulli & Reis, 2009, p. 90

29   Subotnik, 2009

30   Ericsson, 2006; Weisberg, 2006

31   Lohman, 2005, Worrell, 2009

32   Sternberg, 2006, 2009

33   Sternberg, 2002

34   We discuss Sternberg's points in greater length in Matthews, D.J. & Foster, 2014

35   Check out the scores of articles in Joanne Foster's online column at *The Creativity Post*. Topics include the impact of experience, music, expectations, special needs, mentorships, nature, craftsmanship, confusion, and more. https://www.creativitypost.com/contributor/4998

36   Jett, Taylor Schlitz, Shastid, , & Taylor, 2020

37   Fischer, B. M. (2020). Developing and sustaining creativity: Creative processes in Canadian junior college teachers. *Thinking Skills and Creativity*, Vol 38 https://doi.org/10.1016/j.tsc.2020.100754

38   Keating, 1980

Chapter 3

1   Dixson et al., 2020

2   Dweck, 2009a; Keating, 2009: Peters, Carter, & Plucker, 2020

3   Dixson et al, 2020; Matthews, D. J. & Foster, 2019; Worrell, & Dixson, 2018

4   Peters, Carter, & Plucker, 2020; Renzulli, 2021

5   Worrell & Dixson, 2020

6   The comparison population matters here. If a six-year-old scores at the 99th percentile of a test designed for ten-year-olds, it means extraordinary ability even for ten-year-olds, which is not the same thing as scoring at the 99th percentile for their own age group.

7   If you're a teacher or parent who has received a psychoeducational report, and one of these components is missing, it's reasonable to request that it be supplied.

8   The major relevant scores vary from one jurisdiction to another. In some circumstances, it is IQ; in others it is a combined score comprised of several subject-specific subtest scores, such as mathematical reasoning, computation, and problem-solving.

9   Gottfried, Gottfried, & Guerin, 2009

10   It still may be possible to retest sooner using a different, and equivalent, test, but that depends on jurisdictional policies.

11   VanTassel-Baska, 2000, p. 358; See also Matthews, D. J., 2019

12   Gubbins, 2020; Tirri, 2017

13   Dweck, 2009b

14   Dai & Renzulli, 2008 s

Chapter 4

1   Dixson et al., 2020

2   Borland, 2020

3   Dixson et al., 2020; Matthews, M. S., 2018

4   Fox, 2016

5   Fox, 2016; Matthews, M. S., 2018

6   Matthews, M. S., 2018

7   VanTassel-Baska, 2008, p. 285

8   Parks, 2009

9   Feng & VanTassel-Baska, 2008, p. 130

10   McTighe & Wiggins, 2005

11   The connections between these features of performance assessment and fostering giftedness in minority populations are reviewed in VanTassel-Baska (2008)

12   Gould, 1981

13   Belsky, Caspi, Moffitt, & Poulton, 2020; Gottfried, Gottfried, & Guerin, 2009; Howe, 1999

14   Gardner, 1998; Sternberg, 2009

15   Dweck, 2009b, p. 314

16   Borland, 2020; Hymer, Whitehead, & Huxtable, 2009; Worrell, 2009

17   SPM; Raven, Court, & Raven, 1998

18   NNAT3; Naglieri, 1996

19   UNIT2; Bracken & McCallum, 1998

20   Bracken, 2008; Naglieri, 2008; Naglieri & Ford, 2003

21   Bensen, Kranzler, & Floyd, 2020; Hodges et al., 2018; Lohman & Lakin, 2008

22   Worrell, 2009

23   Barbot, Hass, & Reiter-Palmon, 2019

24   Baer, 2019

25   Amabile, 1996; Czikszentmihalyi, 1996; Gardner, 1993; Piirto, 2003

26   Matthews, D. S., 2015

27   Brookhart et al 2016

28   Lohman & Lakin, 2008, p. 43

29   Lohman 2005a, p. 337

30   Subotnik, Olszewski-Kubilius, & Worrell, 2012

31   Worrell & Dixson, 2018

32   Lakin, 2018; National Association for Gifted Children, 20198

Chapter 5

1   Dweck, 2009b, p. 314

2   ZPD; Vygotsky, 1930/1978

3   Borland, 2020; VanTassel-Baska, 2021

4   National Association for Gifted Children, 2019; VanTassel-Baska, 2021

5   Peters, Carter, and Plucker, 2020

6   Gubbins et al., 2021; National Association for Gifted Children, 2019

7   Ontario Ministry of Education, 1984

8   We have many issues with several of these criteria (e.g., how is creativity measured for this purpose?), but this was the official policy in this jurisdiction at that time.

9   Dweck, 2009a, p. xii

10   Peters, Carter, and Plucker, 2020

11   Dixson et al., 2020; Matthews,D. J. & Dai, 2014; VanTassel-Baska, 2021

12   Borland, 2020; Dixson et al., 2020; Robinson & Robinson, 1982; VanTassel-Baska, 2021; Worrell & Dixson, 2018

13   Dixson et al, 2020

14   Gubbins et al, 2021

15   Borland, 2020; Matthews, D. J. & Foster, 2019; National Association for Gifted Children, 2019

16   Peters, Carter, & Plucker, 2020

17   Borland, 2020; Dixson et al., 2020

18   Borland, 2020; Matthews, D. J. & Foster, 2019

19   Grant & Morrissey, 2021

20   Gottfried, Gottfried, & Guerin, 2009

21   Lohman & Korb, 2006

22   Assouline, et al., 2015

23   Belsky, et al., 2020; Boyce, 2020; Gottfried, Gottfried, & Guerin, 2009

24   Armstrong, 1991, p. 206

25   Matthews, M. S., 2018; VanTassel-Baska, 2021

Chapter 6

1   We're grateful to Karen Rogers for her groundbreaking work in this area. She conducted meta-analyses of academic effect size for different educational options provided for gifted students for the National Research Center on Gifted and Talented, reported on in journal articles as well as her book *Re-Forming Gifted Education: How Parents and Teachers Can Match the Program to the Child*. She describes how to implement the options we discuss here, as well as how to evaluate their effectiveness.

2   Borland, 2020; Dixson, Peters, et al., 2020

3   Wright & Borland, 1993, p. 591

4   NAGC, 2019

5   We discuss this sixth component of the NAGC programming standards in Chapter 11, where we discuss teacher development.

6   Tomlinson, 2017

7   Foster, 2019

8   Tomlinson, 2003

9   Dixson, Peters, et al., 2020

10   Tomlinson, 2021.

11   Jett, et al.,2020 p. 139.

12   George Eliot

13   Riley (2009)

14   Rogers, 2002

15   Renzulli, J. Commentary, January 14, 2021 Assessment *For* Learning: The Missing Element For Identifying High Potential In Low Income And Minority Groups, The University of Connecticut

16   Gallagher, S 2009 in Karnes and Bean, p. 310

17   Renzulli, J. Commentary, Jan. 14, 2021.

18   Online simulations https://www.learn4good.com/kids-games/simulation.htm

19   Malcolm Forbes

20   Hattie et al, 2007 cited in Renzulli, 2021

21   Navan, Joy (2020). *Our gifted elders: Awareness, aspirations, advocacy.* Gifted Unlimited. p. 90

22   Judith Halsted (2009) has written a resource guide titled *Some of My Best Friends Are Books: Guiding Gifted Readers from Pre-School to High School, 3rd Edition.* She offers advice and suggestions for children reading at various levels, as well as annotated bibliographies and foundational references. See also, *Cultivate a Love of Reading,* In *First Time Parent Magazine* http://www.firsttimeparentmagazine.com/cultivate-a-love-of-reading/ By Foster, J. (Jan. 2020)

23   Horowitz-Kraus & Hutton, 2018; Willis, 2016

24   Foster, 2021

25   Tomlinson, 2017, p. 8

26   Olszewski-Kubilius, et al., 2015; Vanderbilt University, n.d. 4

27   Van Tassel-Baska, 1992, p. 681992)

28   Choy, M. & Kaufman, M. B. (2020). *Healthcare heroes: The medical careers guide.* Sigel Press.

29   Price-Mitchell, M. (2019). Future leadership: Lessons from history. At *Roots of Action*, Sept. 4, 2019. https://www.rootsofaction.com/future-leadership /

30   Project I Am. www.officialprojectiam.com

31   Books for Bedtime. www.booksforbedtimenonprofit.org

32   Salmon, 2000, p. 11

33   Amanda Gorman – Youth Poet Laureate - from *The Hill We Climb*, Recited at the 2021 US Presidential Inauguration.

34   Sheppard, 2020

35   Tetreault, 2020.

36   There are great resources, professional development tools, "Brainology" programs, and other learning strategies online at Mindsetworks https://www.mindsetworks.com and elsewhere.

37   Tetreault, n.d.

38   Dixson, Peters, et al., 2020

39 The National Research Center on the Gifted and Talented offers many resources and publications about SEM and other approaches to differentiation through their website at www.gifted.uconn.edu.

40 Renzulli, & Reis, 2014.

41 Renzulli Center for Creativity, Gifted Education and Talent Development https://gifted.uconn.edu/schoolwide-enrichment-model/

42 Teachers will find resources at http://cfge.wm.edu.

43 Swanson, et al., 2020

44 Swanson, 2020

45 Integrated Curriculum Model: https://education.wm.edu/centers/cfge/curriculum/index.php Accessed Jan. 25, 2021; https://education.wm.edu/centers/cfge/curriculum/What%20Works%20CFGE%202013%20Web.pdf

46 Tomlinson, et al. (2008).

47 Subotnik, Worrell, Olszewski-Kubilius, 2018

48 Matthews, D. J. & Foster, 2014

Chapter 7

1 Dixson, et al. 2020

2 Assouline, Colangelo, Lupkowski-Shoplik, Lipscomb, & Forstadt (2009, p. 1

3 Assouline, Colangelo, Lupkowski-Shoplik, Lipscomb, & Forstadt , 2009)

4 McLarty, 2015; Steenbergen-Hu, Makel, & Olszewski-Kubilius, 2016.

5 Colangelo, Assouline, & Gross, 2004

6 Colangelo, Assouline, & Gross, 2004

7 This document is available to schools, the media, and parents, and has been translated into several languages (including Japanese, German, French, Spanish, Arabic, Chinese, and Russian). Research information, personal stories about acceleration, summaries of discussions, questions and answers, findings about educational practices, and a host of resources can be accessed online at www.nationdeceived.org

8 Assouline, Colangelo, Van Tassel-Baska, & Lupkowski-Shoplik, 2016/

9 Becky Hurwitz, gifted advocate

10 Steenbergen et al., 2016; Walsh & Jolly, 2018

11 Robinson & Noble, 1992,p. 23

12 Robinson & Robinson, 1982; University Transition Program, UBC

13 Robinson & Noble, 1992, p. 267

14 Jett, et al., 2020

15   https://www.imdb.com/title/tt11718092/

16   One of the experts interviewed was Dona Matthews.

17   Quart, 2006.

18   Robinson, Shore, & Enersen, 2007, p. 201

19   This Canadian-based resource is an example of a resource that offers families different starting points for investigating private school options, based on children's priorities/needs. "Pathways" includes guidance and insights from education experts. https://www.ourkids.net/school/school-choice-pathways

20   Matthews, D. J. & Foster, 2014. Quiz, pp. 156-157 For more information see the chapter "Decision-Making about Schooling" in *Beyond Intelligence: Secrets for Raising Happily Productive Kids*

21   Jolly, Matthews, M. S. & Nester, 2013

22   Rivero, 2002, p 184

23   Rivero, 2002

24   See GHF online – Gifted Homeschooling Forum for resources, newsletters, discussion groups, and more. https://www.ghflearners.org

25   Kunzman, 2008, p. 258

26   Heitner, 2016p. 217

27   Matthews, M. S., 2019; Ray, 2017

28   Athena's Advanced Academy https.athenasadvancedacademy.com

29   Jolly, Matthews, M. S. & Nester, 2013

30   Whitney & Hirsch, 2007, p. 20

31   Jolly, Matthews, M. S. & Nester, 2013, p. 128.

32   Rivero, 2002, p. 12

33   Renzulli & Reis, 2009, p. 90

34   Rivero, 2002, p. 8

35   Duckworth, 2016, p. 285

36   Rogers, 2002, p. 318

37   Siegle, McCoach, & Wilson, 2009, p. 554

38   Shoemaker, et al., 2016

39   Subotnik, 2009, p. 157

40   Olszewski-Kubilius, et al. (2018); Shoemaker et al., 2016

41   Disney's *Fantasia*

42   Fisher, 2019

43 Estrada, Hernandez, & Schultz, 2018; Young, Young, & Ford, 2019; Yu & Jen, 2019

44 Callahan & Dixson, 2009;Siegle, McCoach, & Wilson, 2009: Subotnik, 2009

45 Estrada, et al., 2018; Young, Young, & Ford, 2019

46 For more on designing and evaluating mentorships, including finding a good match between mentors and mentees, see Siegle, McCoach, & Wilson, 2009

47 Young, Young, & Ford, 2019; Yu & Jen, 2019

48 Juster, N. (1961). *The phantom tollbooth*. Random House. pp. 14-17

49 Matthews, D. J. & Foster, 2014, p. 69

50 Silvertown, n.d., from *Virtuoso, The Travel Network*, 2004

Chapter 8

1 Neihart, 2008, p. 59, quoting William Warren, basketball coach and author

2 Graham, 2009, p. 111

3 Whitney & Hirsch, 2007, p. 25

4 Ryan & Deci, 2016

5 Gottfried, Gottfried, & Guerin, 2009

6 Graham, 2009

7 Haimowitz & Dweck, 2017; Lin-Siegler, Dweck, & Cohen, 2016; Ryan & Deci, 2016

8 Katie Hurley, online communication - Jan 12, 2020.

9 Kaufman, 2019

10 Kaufman, 2019.

11 Duckworth, 2016.

12 Duckworth, 2016, p. 8

13 Information shared by Dr. Michele Foster, Toronto Psychology and Wellness Group., 2020 https://tpwg.ca

14 Csikszentmihalyi, 2014

15 Dweck, 2006

16 Gunderson, et al., 2018; Lee, et al., 2017

17 Amemiya & Wang, 2018

18 Gunderson, et al., 2018

19 Brummelman, Crocker, and Bushman, 2016; Lee, et al., 2017

20 Amemiya & Wang, 2018

21 Brummelman, et al., 2017

22 Lee, et al., 2017

23 Foster, 2021.

24 Dixson, Peters, et al., 2020.

25 Neihart, 2008

26 Lang, 2020; Ledeman, 2017.

27 Leonardo da Vinci

28 Football coach Lou Holtz

29 Mitchell, 2003, p. F1

30 http://www.makerspaceforeducation.com/makerspace.html

31 Whitehead & McNiff, 2006

32 Dixson, Peters, et al., 2020

33 Whitney & Hirsch, 2007, p. 31

34 The research of Sandra Graham (2009), Carol Dweck (2006), and Rena Subotnik (2009) on motivation suggests that there is a distinction between valuing hard work on the one hand, and actual competence on the other. Both valuing hard work and actual competence are intrinsic motivators, but the combination is a lot more potent than just valuing hard work.

35 Foster, 2019

36 McCoach & Siegle, 2008, p. 729

37 Siegle, n.d.

38 Kanevsky & Keighley, 2003.

39 Kanevsky, n.d.

40 Renzulli & Reis, 2009, p. 90

41 Reis, 2009, p. 321

42 In chapter 1, we discussed Carol Dweck's work on mindsets, where she distinguishes between a fixed mindset, and a growth mindset.

43 Piper, 1930

44 Locke, 2020

45 The Raising Entrepreneurs Podcast focuses on helping parents encourage an entrepreneurial mindset in children, and features real-life accounts about these kids—including how they harnessed momentum and used their smarts to make a difference. https://raisingentrepreneurspodcast.com/episodes1/

46 One of the best online resources for some of the skills students discover they need is OWL, the Online Writing Lab at Purdue University: http://owl.english. purdue.edu/

47 Weinman, 2014.

48 Foster, 2016

49 Foster, 2017

50 Many procrastination-related articles and presentations are accessible on the Resources page of Joanne Foster's website at www.joannefoster.ca For example, How to stop procrastinating: Draw on your personal strengths! https://www.rootsofaction.com/how-to-stop-procrastinating/at Roots of Action; Procrastination: realities and remedies. http://www.parentguidenews. com/Articles/Procrastination at Parent Guide News; and several more in Joanne Foster's column at The Creativity Post. https://www.creativitypost. com/contributor/4998

51 Foster, 2017

52 Foster, 2016

53 Goleman, 1995, 2020

54 Schlitz in Jett, et al., 2020

Chapter 9

1 Books like Cradles of Eminence and Smart Girls point out that many children who grow up to be eminent did not adapt well to their school environment or their age peers; the authors argue that this kind of individualism is a necessary characteristic that contributed to their subsequently becoming eminent.

2 Marilyn Price-Mitchell's Roots of Action website, https://www.rootsofaction. com/sociability-how-families-learn-together/

3 Dr. Friendtastic site for kids www.drfriendtastic; Kennedy-Moore, & McLaughlin, 2017, p. 169

4 Matthews, D. J. & Foster, 2014, p. 179

5 Boyce, 2020; Kurcinka, 2020

6 Matthews, D. J. & Foster, 2014, p. 180

7 Kennedy-Moore & McLaughlin, 2017.

8 Some sources of information on Asperger's, and Nonverbal Learning Disabilities, and twice exceptional issues see Cohen, 2006; Bright and Quirky website and summit: https://brightandquirky.com; With Understanding Comes Calm website and resources: https://www.withunderstandingcomescalm.com

9 C.S. Lewis (The Weight of Glory)

10 Steinberg, 2015

11   Pyryt, 2008, p. 599

12   Siegel, & Payne-Bryson, 2016.

13   Harter, 2015, The Construction of the Self, Second Edition: Developmental and Sociocultural Foundations

14   Rinn, 2018

15   Bergold, Wirthwein, & Steinmayr, 2020; Rinn, 2018; Shechtman & Silektor, 2012; Wirthwein, et al., 2019

16   Becker, & Neumann, 2018. 1

17   Kennedy-Moore, 2019, p. 132

18   Matthews, D. J. & Foster, 2014, p. 181

19   Lahey, 2016.

20   Mendaglio, 2007, p. 220

21   Van Gemert, 2019.

22   The Child Mind Institute, Understanding Anxiety in Children and Teens. (2018). https://childmind.org/downloads/CMI_2018CMHR.pdf

23   Kuzujanakis, 2020.

24   Kuzujanakis, 2020

25   Kuzujanakis, 2020

26   Hurley, 2015, p.287

27   Hurley, K. (2019, 2020;Additional resources: The American Academy of Pediatric's Resilience Project (2018) is at https://www.aap.org/en-us/advoca-cy-and-policy/aap-health-initiatives/resilience/Pages/Resilience-Project.aspx; the Association for Children's Mental Health is at http://www.acmh-mi.org

28   The Child Mind Institute,2018, p. 17)

29   Cross, 2008, pp.634 and 637

30   American Academy of Child and Adolescent Psychiatry https://www.aacap.org

31   Webb, Gore, Amend, & DeVries, 2007

32   Hurley, 2021.

33   Webb, 2013.

34   Webb, 2013. p.5

35   Cross, 2013

36   For those in crisis, there are helplines such as the toll-free National Suicide Prevention Lifeline at 1-800-273-TALK (8255), accessible 24/7. Calls are confidential. The website is http://www.suicidepreventionlifeline.org

37   Belsky et al., 2020

38 Lengua, 2020

39 Belsky et al., 2020

40 Belsky et al., 2020

41 https://self-reg.ca/self-reg-101.

42 the National Alliance on Mental Illness offers information on community-based resources and affiliates at https://www.nami.org.

43 Purkey, 2006

44 Webb, et al., 2016.

45 Kang, 2020. pp. 3-4

46 Heitner, 2016.

47 Tetreault, 2019.

48 Kang, 2020, p. 2

49 Kang, 2020, p. 2

50 https://www.joanneorlando.com.au

51 Heitner 2016, p. 4.

52 Belsky, et al., 2020; Matthews, D. J., 2020

53 Guiboult & MacFarlane, 2020. -

54 There are many resources to help parents and educators who wish to support tolerance development in children. For example, the Southern Poverty Law Center provides information, including its publication, *Learning for Justice*. https://www.splcenter.org There are museums of tolerance operated by the Friends of Simon Wiesenthal Foundation, and located in several cities around the world. The New York Tolerance Center is one such facility for training and professional development, and also for teaching children about tolerance, social justice, and the dynamics of hatred. www.wiesenthal.com/newyork

55 Kennedy-Moore, 2019. See also Kennedy-Moore & McLaughlin, 2017, and the website www.drfriendtastic.com

56 See www.bullyingcanada.ca/get-help/ and Making Caring Common at https://mcc.gse.harvard.edu,

57 https://kindly.godaddysites.com/our-solution Kindly Bullying Prevention App

58 Coloroso, 2016. Other resources include work by Joanne Orlando online at https://www.joanneorlando.com.au Heitner, 2016; Kang, 2020; and Marilyn Price-Mitchell, 2013

59 www.cyberbullying.ca

60 Delahooke, 2019, p. 3

61 Delahooke, 2019. You might also find it useful to investigate Mary Sheedy Kurcinka's work with spirited children at https://www.parentchildhelp.com;

62 Delahooke, 2019.

63 Olszewski-Kubilius, 2019

64 Olszewski-Kubilius, 2019 p. 127

65 Additional information about bibliotherapy, its origins, benefits, and processes, as well as recommended book titles for use with gifted learners can be found in Halsted, 2009

66 Boyce, 2020; Kurcinka, 2020

Chapter 10

1   Dai & Renzulli, 2008, p. 119

2   Keating, 2011

3   Horowitz, 2009; Kalbfleisch, 2008: Keating, 2011

4   Horowitz, 2009

5   Bloom, 1985; Feldman & Goldsmith, 1986; Gottfried, Gottfried, & Guerin, 2009; Howe, 1990

6   Keating, 2009

7   Howe, 1990, p. 57

8   Dweck, 2009a, p. xii

9   Horowitz, 2009

10 Gottfried, Gottfried, & Guerin, 2009, p. 50

11 Barbot, 2019

12 Clynes, 2015

13 Lapointe, 2019.

14 Keating, 2011

15 Clynes, 2015

16 Nagle Jackson, American director and playwright

17 Quart, 2006

18 Yogman et al., 2018

19 Yogman, et al., 2018.

20 Keltner, Oatley, & Jenkins, 2018; Resnick, 2018; Yogman, et al., 2018

21 Subotnik, 2009

22 Albert Einstein

23 Tetrault, 2021, p. 298

24 Gruber & Ranganath, 2019

25 Price-Mitchell, 2016.

26 Foster, 2020.

27 Borowitz, 2003, p. 3

28 Dweck, 2009a, p. xiii

29 Jensen, 2015; Steinberg, 2015

30 Jensen, 2015; Steinberg, 2015

31 Moon, 2006; Steinberg, 2015

32 Steinberg, 2015

33 Steinberg, 2015

34 Moon, 2006; Steinberg, 2015

35 Matthews, D. J., 2009; Rinn, 2018

36 Eide & Eide, 2006, p. 447

37 Galambos, 2004, p. 255

38 Kersey, Csumitta, & Cantlon, 2019.

39 Leyva, 2017; Yu, & Jen, 2019.

40 Tarampi, et al., 2016

41 Reilly, Newman, & , Andrews, 2015

42 Ajai, & Imoko, 2015

43 Tarampi, et al., 2016

44 Yu & Jen, 2019

45 Ford, Harris, Byrd, & Walters, 2018; Freeman, & Garces-Bascal, 2015

46 Freeman, 2009, p. 144

47 Michelle Obama

48 Malala Yousafzai's advice to girls

49 Pomerantz & Raby, 2020; Raby & Pomerantz, 2015; Reis, 2009

50 Dweck, 2006a; Freeman, & Garces-Bascal, 2015

51 Freeman, 2009

52 Ford, et al., 2018; Young, Young, & Ford, 2019;

53 Ajai & Imoko, 2015; Freeman Garces-Bascal, 2015; Kersey, Csumitta, & Cantlon, 2019; Leyva, 2017

54 Kerr & Cohn, 2001, p. 106

55   Freeman & Garces-Bascal, 2015

56   Kaufmann, & Matthews, D. J., 2012.

57   Graham, 2009, p. 122

58   Estrada, et al., 2018.

59   Jensen, 2015; Steinberg, 2015

60   Steinberg (2015) and others shows that the best developmental outcomes occur in families where adolescence is characterized by lots of arguments and conflict, in a context of warmth, responsiveness, respect, and solid guidelines and standards. There are many reasons for this: "Authoritative parents encourage children's autonomy and independence appropriate for their age with the result that children develop social competence." (Meece & Daniels, 2008, p. 466)

61   Higgins-Biss, 1995, p. 58

62   Ruch, et al., 2014

63   Christensen et al., 2018

64   Ruch, et al., 2014

65   Wagner, 2019

66   Wagner, 2019

67   Higgins-Biss, 1995

68   Mozart

69   Butterworth, 2006, p. 564

70   Winner, 1996, 2009

71   Butterworth, 2006

72   Mendaglio, 2008

73   Clynes, 2015; Wallace, 2009

74   Subotnik, 2009, p. 162

75   Lubinski & Benbow, 2006, p. 316

76   Dixson, Olszewski-Kubilius, et al., 2020. Ericsson, 2006

77   Dweck, 2006b

78   Clynes, 2015

79   Dixson, et al., 2020

80   Castellano, 2003, p. 76

81   Borland, 2020; Worrell & Dixson, 2018, 2020

82   Ford, 2003a, p. 147

83 Ford, 2003b, p. 507

84 The Javits Act includes those from racial minorities, those who are economically disadvantaged, those who have limited English proficiency, and those with other learning exceptionalities.

85 Borland, 2020; Dixson, Peters, et al., 2020; Gubbins, et al., 2021: Worrell & Dixson, 2020

86 Aguirre, 2003; Worrell, 2009

87 Ford, et al., 2018

88 Davis, 2021

89 Borland, 2020; Worrell &Dixson, 2020

90 Worrell et al., 2019

91 Davis, 2021

92 Dixson, Peters, et al., 2020

93 Dweck, 2009a, p. xii

94 Feldman, 2008, p. 528

95 Gross, 2008, p. 241

96 Clynes, 2015; Matthews, D. J., 2015

97 Winner, 1996

98 Clynes, 2015; Makel, et al., 2016

99 Jackson, 2020

100 Davidson Institute https://www.davidsongifted.org

101 Baum, Schader, & Owen, 2017.

102 Eide & Eide, 2006, p. 463

103 Collins, et al., 2016; Shifrer, 2016);

104 Baum, Schader, & Owen, 2017

105 Baum, Schader, & Owen, 2017; Wang & Neihart, 2015; see also the Twice Exceptional and the Twice Exceptional at Home and at School pages on the NAGC webpage: https://www.nagc.org/resources-publications/resources-parents/twice-exceptional-students; also Bright and Quirky https://brightandquirky.com; With Understanding Comes Calm https://withunderstandingcomescalm.com; and resources at SENG https://sengifted.org

106 For more information on any of these exceptionalities, go to the websites for Children and Adults with Attention Deficit Hyperactivity Disorder (CHADD; www.chadd.org); Council for Exceptional Children (CEC; www.cec.sped.org); or Education Resources Information Center (ERIC; www.eric.ed.gov) E

107 Beckmann & Minnaert, 2018.

108   At the age of three Temple Grandin, Ph.D. was diagnosed with autism and her parents were told she should be institutionalized. She went on to become a professor of Animal Science at Colorado State University, and speaks about autism to audiences around the world.

109   Ritchotte, & Matthews, M. S., 2019. p. 361

110   Webb, et al., 2016

111   Moon, 2011, p. 405

112   VanTassel-Baska, 2000, p. 358

113   Ching-Lan, R. L., & Foley-Nicpon, M. (2019).

114   Vanraalte, et al., 2016

115   Ching-Lan & Foley-Nicpon, 2019

116   Tetreault, 2021

117   Wang, & Neihart, 2015.

118   Robinson, Shore, & Enersen, 2007, p. 208

119   Smith & Wood, 2018.

120   Billings, 2021

121   Robert Frost

122   Hébert & Kelly, 2006; Robinson, Shore, & Enersen (2007);

123   Rivero, 2011

124   Steinberg, 2015

Chapter 11

1   Robinson, Shore & Enersen, 2007, p. 7

2   Dufur, Parcel, & Troutman, 2013; Matthews, M. S. & Jolly, 2020

3   Paul, 2012

4   Matthews, M. S. & Jolly, 2020

5   Lahey, 2016; Pinquart, 2016; Waters, et al., 2019

6   Some examples include the Northwestern Center for Talent Development, Hunter College Center for Gifted Education and Development, and the Center for Gifted Education at the College of William and Mary

7   Delcourt, 2003, p. 27

8   Matthews, M. S. & Jolly, 2020; Stephens, 2020

9   Lewis & Karnes, 2009, p. 697

10   Robinson, Shore, & Enersen, 2007; p. 263

11   Haim Ginott

12   Tirri, 2017

13   NAGC, 2019

14   Ontario College of Teachers, Ethical Standards, 2021

15   NAGC, 2019

16   Ontario College of Teachers, 2021

17   Alter & Foster, 2007

18   Clynes, 2015; Dufur, Parcel, &Troutman, 2013; Waters, Loton, & Jach, 2019

Chapter 12

1   John F. Kennedy

2   Belsky, et al., 2020; Boyce, 2020; Keating, 2011

3   Siegel, & Payne-Bryson, 2012 p. ix and p. xis

4   Satell, 2021

5   Meier, 2002

6   Robinson, Shore, & Enersen, 2007

7   There are several models that can assist educators or parents interested in implementing this kind of collaborative approach, including Barry Hymer and colleagues' living theory approach to gift-creation (Hymer, 2009); Joe Renzulli and colleagues' Schoolwide Enrichment Model (Reis & Peters, 2020), and Renzulli Learning System (Renzulli & Reis, 2009); Don Treffinger and colleagues' Levels of Service model (Treffinger, Nassab, & Selby, 2009); and Belle Wallace and colleagues' Thinking Actively in a Social Context model (Wallace, 2009).

8   Peters, Carter, & Plucker, 2020

9   Some of these include the Belin-Blank Center at the University of Iowa; the Center for Gifted Education at the University of Calgary; the Center for Gifted Education at the College of William and Mary; the Center for Talent Development at Northwestern University in Illinois; the Center for Talented Youth at Johns Hopkins; the Gifted Education Resource Institute at Purdue University; the Hunter College Center for Gifted Studies and Education, City University of New York; and the Neag Center for Gifted Education and Talent Development at the University of Connecticut.

10   Stephen King

11   Ende, 2018

12   Maya Angelou

13   John Quincy Adams

14   Malala Yousafzai and Greta Thunberg come immediately to mind.

15   Gladwell, 2011, p. 151

16   Goleman, 1995, 2020

17   www.rootsofaction.com

18   Kennedy-Moore, E. (2019)

19   Borba, 2021e

20   Alanis Obomsawin, award-winning filmmaker of Abenaki descent.

21   Lannie Kanevsky, personal correspondence, 2021

22   Wright et al., 2019

23   Kutz & Tomaselli, 2019

24   Marshall, Marshall, & Bartlett, 2015

25   Gentry et al., 2014; Peters et al., 2019

26   Gentry et al., 2014

27   Gallagher-Mackay & Steinhauer, 2017; Matthews, D. J., 2013

28   Shore et al., 1981

29   Gallagher-Mackay & Steinhauer, 2017

30   Ludwig Van Beethoven

31   Hans Christian Andersen

32   Hans Christian Andersen, n. d.

33   Paul, 2013

34   Delahooke, 2019, p. 266

35   Abramo, & Natale-Abramo, 2020

36   https://www.nancykopman.com

37   https://www.house-of-music.be, and https://www.childrenarecomposers.com

38   R. Buckminster Fuller

39   Robert Frost

40   Albert Einstein

41   Markham, 2021; Matthews, D. J., 2019

42   Foster, 2020

43   An example of neighborhood publications is *Best Version Media*, which distributes family-friendly magazines to thousands of communities each month (BVM distributed over 33 million locally-based magazines to neighborhoods across North America in 2020.)

44   Peters, et al., 2020

45 Peters, et al., 2020

46 Aida Younis, personal correspondence

47 Olszewski-Kubilius, et al., 2015, 2018; Worrell, et al., 2019

48 The Raffi Foundation for Child Honouring has nine guiding principles: respectful love, diversity, caring community, conscious parenting, emotional intelligence, nonviolence, safe environments, sustainability, and ethical commerce. Information about the Child Honouring course for adults, various resources, and more can be found on the Foundation's website at https://raffifoundation.org/about/

49 Dweck, 2009b, p. 316

References

Abramo, J. M., & Natale-Abramo, M. (2020). Re-examining "gifted and talented" in music education. *Music Educators Journal.* https://doi.org/10.1177/0027432119895304

Aguirre, N. (2003). ESL students in gifted education. In J. A. Castellano (Ed.), *Special populations in gifted education: Working with diverse learners* (pp. 17-28). Allyn & Bacon.

Ajai, J. T., & Imoko, B. I. (2015). Gender differences in mathematics achievement and retention scores: A case of problem-based learning method. *International Journal of Research in Education and Science (1)*1, 45-50.

Alter, S., & Foster, J. F. (2007, November). *A tale of two specialists.* Presentation, National Association for Gifted Children Conference, Minnesota, MN.

Amabile, T. M. (1996). *Creativity in context: Update to the social psychology of creativity.* Boulder, CO: Westview.

Amemiya, J., & Wang, M. T. (2018). Why effort praise can backfire in adolescence. *Child Development Perspectives, 12*(3), 199-203. https://doi.org/10.1111/cdep.12284

American Academy of Child and Adolescent Psychiatry. (2018, June). *Suicide in children and teens.* American Academy of Child and Adolescent Psychiatry. https://www.aacap.org/AACAP/Families_and_Youth/Facts_for_Families/FFF-Guide/Teen-Suicide-010.aspx

American Academy of Pediatrics Resilience Project (2018). https://www.aap.org/en-us/advocacy-and-policy/aap-health-initiatives/resilience/Pages/Resilience-Project.aspx

Armstrong, T. (1991). *Awakening your child's natural genius: Enhancing curiosity, creativity, and learning ability.* Putnam.

Assouline, S., Colangelo, N., & Lupkowski-Shoplik, A. (2009). *Iowa Acceleration Scale Manual,* 3rd ed. Scottsdale, AZ: Great Potential Press.

Assouline, S. G., Colangelo, N., VanTassel-Baska, J., & Lupkowski-Shoplik, A. (2015). *A nation empowered: Evidence trumps the excuses holding back America's brightest students* (Vol. 2). Acceleration Institute at the Belin-Blank Center. http://www.accelerationinstitute.org/nation_empowered/

Assouline, S. G., & Lupkowski-Shoplik, A. (2012). The talent search model of gifted identification. *Journal of Psychoeducational Assessment* 30(1), 45-59. https://doi.org/10.1177/0734282911433946

Assouline, S. G., Colangelo, N., Lupkowski-Shoplik, A. E., Lipscomb, J., & Forstadt, L. (2009). *The Iowa Acceleration Scale manual* (3rd ed.). Great Potential Press.

Baer, J. (2019). Theory in creativity research: The pernicious impact of domain generality. In C. Mullen (Ed.) Creativity under duress in education? Creativity theory and action in education, (vol3., pp. 119-135). Springer. https://doi.org/10.1007/978-3-319-90272-2_7

Balchin, T. (2009). Recognising and fostering creative production. In T. Balchin, B. Hymer, & D. J. Matthews (Eds.) *The Routledge international companion to gifted education* (pp. 203-209). Abingdon, UK: Routledge.

Barbot, B. (2019). Measuring creativity change and development. *Psychology of Aesthetics, Creativity, and the Arts, 13*(2), 203–210. https://doi.org/10.1037/aca0000232

Barbot, B., Hass, R. W., & Reiter-Palmon, R. (2019). Creativity assessment in psychological research: (Re)setting the standards. *Psychology of Aesthetics, Creativity, and the Arts, 13*(2), 233–240. https://doi.org/10.1037/aca0000233

Baum, S. M., Schader, R. M., & Owen, S. V. (2017). *To be gifted and learning disabled* (3rd ed.). Prufrock Press.

Becker, M., & Neumann, M. (2018). Longitudinal big-fish-little-pond effects on academic self-concept development during the transition from elementary to secondary schooling. *Journal of Educational Psychology, 110*(6), 882–897. https://doi.org/10.1037/edu0000233

Beckmann E., & Minnaert, A. (2018). Non-cognitive characteristics of gifted students with learning disabilities: An in-depth systematic review. *Frontiers in Psychology (9)*. DOI=10.3389/fpsyg.2018.00504

Beghetto, R. A. (2019). Creativity in classrooms. In Sternberg, R. & Kaufman, J. C. (Eds.), *The Cambridge handbook of creativity*. Cambridge University Press. (pp. 582-606)). https://doi.org/10.1017/9781316979839

Belsky, J., Caspi, A., Moffitt, T. E., & Poulton, R. (2020). *The origins of you: How childhood shapes later life*. Harvard University Press.

Bensen, N., Kranzler, J. H., & Floyd, R. G. (2020). Exploratory and confirmatory factor analysis of the Universal Nonverbal Intelligence Test–Second Edition: Testing dimensionality and invariance across age, gender, race, and ethnicity. Assessment, 27(5), 996-1006. doi:10.1177/1073191118786584

Bergold, S., Wirthwein, L., & Steinmayr, R. (2020). Similarities and differences between intellectually gifted and average-ability students in school performance, motivation, and subjective well-being. *Gifted Child Quarterly* 64(4), 285-303. https://doi.org/10.1177/0016986220932533

Billings, D. J. (2021). We deserve to be more than one thing. *Puttylike*. https://puttylike.com/we-deserve-to-be-more-than-one-thing.

Birkner, G. (2020, October 14). At a Manhattan school where half the children are homeless, this teacher aims to "make the shame and sadness scatter." Chalkbeat. https://ny.chalkbeat.org/2020/10/14/21517052/island-school-makerspace-lab

Birren, J. E. (2009). *Gifts and talents of elderly people: The persimmon's promise*. In F. D. Horowitz, R. F. Subotnik, & D. J. Matthews (Eds.), *The development of giftedness and talent across the life span* (p. 171–185). American Psychological Association. https://doi.org/10.1037/11867-010

Bloom, B. S. (Ed.). (1985). *Developing talent in young people*. New York: Ballantine.

Borba, M. (2021). *Thrivers: The surprising reasons why some kids struggle and others shine*. Random House.

Borland, J. H. (1989). *Planning and implementing programs for the gifted*. New York: Teachers College Press.

Borland, J. H. (2020). Identification of gifted students. In J. A. Plucker & C. M. Callahan. Giftedness and talent development (3rd ed., pp. 323-342). Prufrock Press.

Borowitz, S. (2003). *When we're out in public pretend you don't know me: Surviving your daughter's adolescence so you don't look like an idiot and she still talks to you.* Warner Books.

Boyce, W. T. (2020). *The orchid and the dandelion: Why some children struggle and how all can thrive.* Vintage.

Bracken, B. A., & Brown, E. F. (2008). Early identification of high-ability students: Clinical assessment of behavior. *Journal for the Education of the Gifted 31*(4), 403-426.

Bracken, B. A., & McCallum, R. S. (1998). *Universal Nonverbal Test of Intelligence* . Itasca, IL: Riverside.

Brookhart, S. M., Guskey, T. R., Bowers, A. J., McMillan, J. H., Smith, J. K., Smith, L. F., Stevens, M. T., & Welsh, M. E. (2016). A century of grading research: Meaning and value in the most common educational measure. *Review of Educational Research, 86*(4), 803–848. https://doi.org/10.3102/0034654316672069

Brummelman, E., Crocker, J., & Bushman, B. J. (2016). The praise paradox: When and why praise backfires with children with low self-esteem. *Child Development Perspectives, 10*(2), 111-115. https://doi.org/10.1111/cdep.12171

Brummelman, E., Nelemans, S. A., Thomaes, S., & Orobio de Castro, B. (2017). When parents' praise inflates, children's self-esteem deflates. *Child Development, 88*(6), 1799-1809. https://doi.org/10.1111/cdev.12936

Butterworth, B. (2006). Mathematical expertise. In K. A. Ericsson, N. Charness, P. J. Feltovich & R. R. Hoffman (Eds.), *The Cambridge Handbook of Expertise and Expert Performance* (pp. 553-568). Cambridge, UK: Cambridge University Press.

Callahan, C. M. (2017). Identification of gifted and talented students. Callahan, C. M., and Hertberg-Davis, H., *Fundamentals of gifted education* (2nd ed., pp. 94-102).

Callahan, C. M., & Dickson, R. K. (2008). Mentoring. In J. A. Plucker & C. M. Callahan (Eds.), *Critical issues and practices in gifted education: What the research says* (pp. 409-423). Waco, TX: Prufrock Press.

Callahan, C. M., Moon, T. R, Oh, S., Azano, A. P., & Hailey, E. P. (2015). What works in gifted education: Documenting the effects of an integrated curricular/instructional model for gifted students. *American Educational Research Journal, 52*(1), 137-167. https://journals.sagepub.com/doi/full/10.3102/0002831214549448

Castellano, J. A. (2003). *The "browning" of American schools. In J. A. Castellano (Ed.), Special populations in gifted education: Working with diverse learners (pp. 29-43).* Allyn & Bacon.

Child Mind Institute (2018). *Understanding Anxiety in Children and Teens.* Child Mind Institute. https://childmind.org/downloads/CMI_2018CMHR.pdf

Ching-Lan, R. L., & Foley-Nicpon, M. (2019). Integrating creativity into career interventions for twice-exceptional students in the United States: A review of recent literature. Gifted and Talented International, 34(1), 91-101 https://doi.org/10.1080/15332276.2019.1704667

Choy, M. & Kaufman, M. B. (2020). *Healthcare heroes: The medical careers guide.* Sigel Press.

Christensen, A. P., Silvia, P. J., Nusbaum, E. C., & Beaty, R. E. (2018). Clever people: Intelligence and humor production ability. *Psychology of Aesthetics, Creativity, and the Arts, 12*(2), 136–143. https://doi.org/10.1037/aca0000109

Clynes, T. (2015). *The boy who played with fusion.* Houghton Mifflin Harcourt.

Cohen, S. (2006). *Targeting autism: What we know, don't know, and can do to help young children with autism spectrum disorders* (3rd ed.). University of California Press.

Colangelo, N., Assouline, S., & Gross, M. (2004). *A nation deceived: How schools hold back America's brightest students.* The Templeton National Report on Acceleration, Vol. 2. (ED535138) University of Iowa.

Coleman, L. J., Micko, K. J., & Cross, T. L. (2015). Twenty-five years of research on the lived experience of being gifted in school: Capturing the students' voices. *Journal for the Education of the Gifted, 38*(4), 358–376. https://doi.org/10.1177/0162353215607322

Collins, K. M., Connor, D., Ferri, B., Gallagher, D., & Samson, J. F. (2016). Dangerous assumptions and unspoken limitations. *Multiple voices for ethnically diverse exceptional learners, 16*(1), 4–16. https://doi.org/10.5555/2158-396X.16.1.4

Coloroso, B. (2016). *The bully, the bullied, and the not-so-innocent bystander: From pre-school to high school and beyond.* William Morrow.

Cross, T. L. (2008). In J. A. Plucker & C. M. Callahan (Eds.), *Critical issues and practices in gifted education: What the research says* (pp. 629-640). Waco, TX: Prufrock Press.

Cross, T. L. (2013). *Suicide among gifted children and adolescents: Understanding the suicidal mind.* Prufrock Press.

Cross, T. (2017). *On the social and emotional lives of gifted children.* 5th Edition. Prufrock.

Csikszentmihalyi, M. (1991). *Flow: The psychology of optimal experience.* New York: Harper Collins.

Csikszentmihalyi, M. (1996). *Creativity: Flow and the psychology of discovery and invention.* New York: Harperperennial.

Csikszentmihalyi, M. (2014). Flow and the foundations of positive psychology. In *The Collected Works of M. Csikszentmihalyi.* Springer. http://biblioteca.univalle.edu.ni/files/original/cb851fc2405f5c05d-3ca12575f49db22dd2d5c4d.pdf

Csikszentmihalyi, M. (2019). Foreword: The rewards of creativity. In Sternberg, R. & Kaufman, J.C. (Eds.) *The Cambridge handbook of creativity* (2nd ed.) Cambridge University Press. https://doi.org/10.1017/9781316979839

Csikszentmihalyi, M., & Wolfe, R. (2000). In K. A., F. J. Monks, R. J. Sternberg, & R. F. Subotnik (Eds.), *International handbook of giftedness and talent* (2nd ed., pp. 81-93). Oxford, UK: Elsevier Science.

Dai, D. Y. (2018). *A history of giftedness: A century of quest for identity.* In Pfeiffer, S. I., Shaunessy-Dedrick, E., & Foley-Nicpon, M. (Eds.), *APA handbook of giftedness and talent* (pp. 3–23). American Psychological Association. https://doi.org/10.1037/0000038-001

Dai, D. Y., & Chen, F. (2013). Three paradigms of gifted education: In search of conceptual clarity in research and practice. *Gifted Child Quarterly, 57* (3), 151-168. https://journals.sagepub.com/doi/full/10.1177/0016986213490020

Dai, D. Y., & Renzulli, J. S. (2008). Snowflakes, living systems, and the mystery of giftedness. *Gifted Child Quarterly, 52,* 114-130.

Dai, D. Y., Swanson, J. A., & Cheng, H. (2011, April). State of research on giftedness and gifted education: A survey of empirical studies published during 1998-2010. *Gifted Child Quarterly, 55* (2), 126-138. doi:10.1177/0016986210397831

Davis, J. L. (2021). *Bright, talented, and black; A guide for families of black gifted learners, 2nd edition.* Gifted Unlimited.

Delahooke, M. (2019). *Beyond behaviors: using brain science and compassion to understand and solve children's behavioral challenges.* PESI.

Delcourt, M. A. B. (2003). Five ingredients for success: Two case studies of advocacy and the state level. *Gifted Child Quarterly, 47(1)*, 27.

Demetriou, A., & Spanoudis, G. (2018). *Growing minds: A developmental theory of intelligence, brain, and education.* Routledge.

Demetriou, H., & Nicholl, B. (2021). Empathy is the mother of invention: Emotion and cognition for creativity in the classroom. *Improving Schools*; 136548022198950 DOI: 10.1177/1365480221989500

Dixson, D.D., Olszewski-Kubilius, P., Subotnik, R.F., & Worrell, F.C. (2020). Developing academic talent as a practicing school psychologist: From potential to expertise. *Psychology in the Schools 57* (10), 1582-1595 https://doi.org/10.1002/pits.22363

Dixson, D., Peters, S. J., Makel, M. C., Jolly, J. L., Matthews, M. S., Miller, E. M., Rambo-Hernandez, K. E., Rinn, A. N., Robins, J. H., & Wilson, H E. (2020). A call to reframe gifted education as maximizing learning. Phi Delta Kappan, 102 (4), 22-25. https://doi.org/10.1177/0031721720978057

Doidge, N. (2007). *The brain that changes itself.* New York: Penguin.

Duckworth, A. (2016). *Grit: The power of passion and perseverance.* Collins.

Dufur, M. J., Parcel, T. L., & Troutman, K. P. (2013). Does capital at home matter more than capital at school? Social capital effects on academic achievement. *Research in Social Stratification and Mobility, 31 1-21.* DOI: 10.1016/j.rssm.2012.08.002

Dweck, C. S. (2006a). Is math a gift? Beliefs that put females at risk. In S. J. Ceci & W. M Williams (Eds.), *Why aren't more women in science? Top researchers debate the evidence* (pp 47-55). Washington, DC: American Psychological Association.

Dweck, C. S. (2006b). *Mindset: The new psychology of success.* New York: Random House.

Dweck, C. S. (2009a). Foreword. In F. D. Horowitz, R. F. Subotnik, & D. J. Matthews (Eds.) *The development of giftedness and talent across the life span* (pp. xi-xiv). Washington, DC: American Psychological Association.

Dweck, C. S. (2009b). Self-theories and lessons for giftedness: A reflective conversation. In T. Balchin, B. Hymer, & D. J. Matthews (Eds.) *The Routledge international companion to gifted education* (pp. 308-316). London: Routledge.

Eide, B., & Eide, F. (2006). *The mislabeled child.* New York: Hyperion.

Ende, F. (2018). What's old is new again. *Smartbrief.* https://www.smartbrief.com/author/fred-ende?page=3

Ericsson, K. A., Charness, N., Feltovich, P. J., & Hoffman, R. R. (Eds.) (2006). *The Cambridge handbook of expertise and expert performance.* New York: Cambridge University Press.

Ericsson, K. A. (2006). The influence of experience and deliberate practice on the development of superior expert performance. In K. A. Ericsson, N. Charness, P. J. Feltovich & R. R. Hoffman (Eds.), *The Cambridge handbook of expertise and expert performance* (pp. 683-703). New York: Cambridge University Press.

Estrada, M., Hernandez, P. R., & Schultz, W. (2018). A longitudinal study of how quality mentorship and research experience integrate underrepresented minorities into stem careers. CBE-Life Sciences Education, 17 (1) https://doi.org/10.1187/cbe.17-04-0066

Feldman, D. H. (1991). Why children can't be creative. *Exceptionality Education Canada, 1(1),* 43-51.

Feldman, D. H. (2003). A developmental, evolutionary perspective on giftedness. In J. H. Borland (Ed.), *Rethinking gifted education* (pp. 9-33). New York: Teachers College Press.

Feldman, D. H. (2008). Prodigies. In J. A. Plucker & C. M. Callahan (Eds.), *Critical issues and practices in gifted education: What the research says* (pp. 523-534). Prufrock Press.

Feldman, D. H., & Goldsmith, L. T. (1986). Nature's gambit: Child prodigies and the development of human potential. Basic Books.

Feng, A. X., & VanTassel-Baska, J. L. (2008). Identifying low-income and minority students for gifted programs: Academic and affective impact of performance-based assessment. In J. L. VanTaska-Baska (Ed.),

Alternative assessments with gifted and talented students (pp. 129-146). Waco, TX: Prufrock Press.

Fischer, B. M. (2020). Developing and sustaining creativity: Creative processes in Canadian junior college teachers. *Thinking Skills and Creativity*, Vol 38 https://doi.org/10.1016/j.tsc.2020.100754

Fisher, M. (2019). A voice of wisdom in creativity quarrel: "Mastery" by Robert Greene. *The Creativity Post*. https://www.creativitypost.com/ philosophy/a-voice-of-wisdom-in-creativity-quarrel-mastery-by-robert-greene

Ford, D. Y. (2003a). Desegregating gifted education: Seeking equity for culturally diverse students. In J. H. Borland (Ed.), *Rethinking gifted education* (pp. 143-158). Teachers College Press.

Ford, D. Y. (2003b). Equity and excellence: Culturally diverse students in gifted education. In N. Colangelo & G. A. Davis (Eds.), *Handbook of gifted education* (pp. 506-520). Allyn & Bacon.

Ford, D. Y., Harris, B. N., Byrd, J. A., & Walters, N. M. (2018). Blacked out and whited out: The double bind of gifted black females who are often a footnote in educational discourse. *International Journal of Educational Reform*, 27(3), 253–268. https://doi.org/ 10.1177/105678791802700302

Ford, D. Y., Dickson, K. T., Davis, J. L., Scott, M. T., & Grantham, T. C. (2018). A Culturally Responsive Equity-Based Bill of Rights for Gifted Students of Color. *Gifted Child Today*, 41(3), 125–129. https://doi. org/10.1177/1076217518769698

Foster, J. (2016). *Not now, maybe later: Helping children overcome procrastination.* Gifted Unlimited.

Foster, J. (2017). *Bust your BUTS: Tips for teens who procrastinate.* Gifted Unlimited.

Foster, J. (2019). How Children Learn: Fit, Fairness, and Flexibility. https:// www.rootsofaction.com/how-children-learn/

Foster, J. (2019). M is for Motivation. In *ABCs of raising smarter kids: Hundreds of ways to inspire your child.* Gifted Unlimited. pp. 92-98.

Foster, J. (2020). The NATURE of creativity: Calling all children. *The Creativity Post*. https://www.creativitypost.com/education/the-nature-of-creativity-calling-all-children

Foster, J. (2020) Why communities matter for children AND adults. *GHF Dialogue Online* https://ghfdialogue.org/why-community-matters-for-children-and-adults/

Foster, J. F. (2021). Curiosity. *First Time Parent Magazine.*

Fox, J. (2016). Using Portfolios for Assessment/Alternative Assessment. In E. Shohamy, I.G. Or, & S. May (Eds.), Language Testing and Assessment. Encyclopedia of Language and Education (3ʳᵈ ed., pp. 135-148). Springer. https://doi.org/10.1007/978-3-319-02326-7_9-ly

Freeman, J. (2009). Morality and giftedness. In T. Balchin, B. Hymer, & D. J. Matthews (Eds.) *The Routledge international companion to gifted education* (pp. 141-148). Abingdon, UK: Routledge.

Freeman, J., & Garces-Bascal, R.M. (2015). Gender differences in gifted children, in M. Neihart, S.I. Pfeiffer & T.L. Cross (Eds.) *The social and emotional development of gifted children: What do we know?* Prufrock Press.

Galambos, N. L. (2004). Gender and gender role development in adolescence. In R. M. Lerner & L. Steinberg (Eds.), *Handbook of Adolescent Psychology* (2nd ed., pp. 233-262). Wiley.

Gallagher, S. (2009). Adapting problem-based learning for gifted students. In F. A. Karnes & S. M. Bean, *Methods and materials for teaching the gifted* (3rd ed., pp. 301-330). Prufrock Press.

Gallagher-Mackay, K., & Steinhauer, N. (2017). *Pushing the limits: How schools can prepare our children today for the challenges of tomorrow.* Penguin Randomhouse.

Gardner, H. (1983). *Frames of mind.* New York: Basic Books

Gardner, H. (1993). *Creating minds: An anatomy of creativity as seen through the lives of Freud, Einstein, Picasso, Stravinsky, Eliot, Graham, and Gandhi.* New York: Basic Books.

Gardner, H. (1998). A multiplicity of intelligences. *Scientific American, 9,* 18-23.

Gentry, M. Fugate, C. M., Wu, J., & Castellano, J. A. (2014). Gifted Native American students. *Gifted Child Quarterly, 58(2),* 98-110. https://doi.org/10.1177/0016986214521660

Gladwell, M. (2011). *Outliers: The story of success.* Back Bay.

Glaveanu, V. P., & Kaufman, J. C. (2019). Creativity: A historical perspective. In *The Cambridge handbook of creativity* (2nd ed.) Cambridge University Press. (pp.9-26). https://doi.org/10.1017/9781316979839

Goertzel, T. G., & Hansen, A. M. W. (2004). *Cradles of eminence* (2nd ed.). Scottsdale, AZ: Great Potential Press.

Goleman, D. (1995). *Emotional intelligence: Why it can matter more than IQ.* Bantam.

Goleman, D. (2011). *The brain and emotional intelligence: New insights.* Simon and Schuster.

Goleman, D. (2020). Emotional intelligence: Anniversary edition. Bantam.

Gorman, A. (2021). The hill we climb. Poem recited at the United States of America Presidential Inauguration.

Gottfried, A.W., Gottfried, A. E., & Guerin, D. W. (2009). Issues in early prediction and identification of intellectual giftedness. In F. D. Horowitz, R. F. Subotnik, & D. J. Matthews (Eds.), *The Development of Giftedness and Talent Across the Life span* (pp. 43-56). Washington: American Psychological Association.

Gould, S. J. (1981). *The mismeasure of man.* New York: W.W. Norton.

Gottfried, A.W., Gottfried, A. E., & Guerin, D. W. (2009). Issues in early prediction and identification of intellectual giftedness. In F. D. Horowitz, R. F. Subotnik, & D. J. Matthews (Eds.), *The Development of Giftedness and Talent Across the Life span* (pp. 43-56). American Psychological Association.

Graham, S. (2009). Giftedness in adolescence: African American gifted youth and their challenges from a motivational perspective. In F. D. Horowitz, R. F. Subotnik, & D. J. Matthews (Eds.), *The Development of Giftedness and Talent Across the Life span* (pp. 43-56). American Psychological Association.

Grant, A., & Morrissey, A. M. (2021). *The young gifted learner: What we know and implications for early educational practice. In S. R. Smith (Ed.), Handbook of Giftedness and Talent Development in the Asia-Pacific.* Springer. https://doi.org/10.1007/978-981-13-3041-4_57

Greene, R. (2013). *Mastery.* Penguin.

Gross, M. U. M. (2008). Highly gifted children and adolescents. In J. A. Plucker & C. M. Callahan (Eds.), *Critical issues and practices in gifted education: What the research says* (pp. 241-251). Prufrock Press.

Gruber, M. J., & Ranganath, C. (2019). How curiosity enhances hippo-campus-dependent memory: The prediction, appraisal, curiosity, and exploration (PACE) framework. Trends in Cognitive Science, 23(12), 1014-1025. https://doi.org/10.1016/j.tics.2019.10.003

Gubbins, E. J. (2020). Professional development for novice and experienced teachers. In J. A. Plucker & C. M. Callahan (Eds.) Critical issues and practices in gifted education: A Survey of Current Research on Giftedness and Talent Development (3rd ed., pp. 505-518). Prufrock Press.

Gubbins, E. J., Siegle, D., Ottone-Cross, K., McCoach, D. B., Langley, S. D., Callahan, C. M., Brodersen, A. V., & Caughey, M. (2021). Identifying and serving gifted and talented students: Are identification and services connected? Gifted Child Quarterly. https://doi.org/10.1177/0016986220988308

Guiboult, K. M., & MacFarlane, B. (2020). Bullying. In Plucker, J. L., & Callahan, C. M. (Eds.) (2020). Critical Issues and Practices in Gifted Education: A Survey of Current Research on Giftedness and Talent Development (3rd ed., pp 75-88). Prufrock.

Guilford, J. P. (1967). *The nature of human intelligence.* New York: McGraw-Hill.

Gunderson, E. A., Sorhagen, N. S., Gripshover, S. J., Dweck, C. S., Goldin-Meadow, S., & Levine, S. C. (2018). Parent praise to toddlers predicts fourth grade academic achievement via children's incremental mindsets. *Developmental Psychology, 54*(3), 397–409. https://doi.org/10.1037/dev0000444

Haier, R. J. (2017). The neuroscience of intelligence. Cambridge University Press.

Haimowitz, K., & Dweck, C. S. (2017). The origins of children's growth and fixed mindsets: New research and a new proposal. Child Development, 88(6), 1849-1859. https://doi.org/10.1111/cdev.12955

Halsted, J. W. (2009). *Some of my best friends are books. Guiding gifted readers* (3rd ed.). Great Potential Press.

Harter, S. (2015). *The construction of the self: Developmental and sociocultural foundations (*2nd ed.). Guilford Press.

Hébert, T. P., & Kelly, K. R. (2006). Identity and career development in gifted students. In F. A. Dixon & S. M. Moon (Eds.), *The handbook of secondary gifted education* (pp.35-63). Prufrock Press.

Heitner, D. (2016). *Screenwise: Helping kids thrive and survive in their digital world.* Routledge.

Higgins-Biss, K. (1995). *The importance of being humorous: The implications for social competence and self-concept in high level cognitive development.* Unpublished masters thesis, Ontario Institute for Studies in Education of the University of Toronto, Toronto, ON.

Hodges, J., Tay, J., Maeda, Y., & Gentry, M. (2018). A Meta-Analysis of Gifted and Talented Identification Practices. Gifted Child Quarterly, 62(2), 147-174. doi:10.1177/0016986217752107

Hollingworth, L. (1926). Gifted children: Their nature and nurture. New York: Macmillan.

Horowitz, F. D. (2009). Introduction. A developmental understanding of giftedness and talent. In F. D. Horowitz, R. F. Subotnik & D. J. Matthews (Eds.), *The development of giftedness and talent across the life span* (pp. 3-20). Washington: American Psychological Association.

Horowitz, F. D., Subotnik, R. F., & Matthews, D. J. (Eds.) (2009). *The development of giftedness and talent across the life span.* Washington, DC: American Psychological Association.

Horowitz-Kraus, T., & Hutton, J. S. (2018). Brain connectivity in children is increased by the time they spend reading books and decreased by the length of exposure to screen-based media. *Acta Paediatrica, 107 (4),* 685-693. https://doi.org/10.1111/apa.14176

Howe, M. J. A. (1990). *The origins of exceptional abilities.* Oxford, UK: Basil Blackwell.

Hurley, K. (2015). *The happy kid handbook: How to raise joyful children in a stressful world.* TarcherPerigee.

Hurley, K. (2019). *The depression workbook for teens: Tools to improve your mood, build self-esteem, and stay motivated.* Althea Press.

Hurley, K. (2020). *A year of positive thinking for kids: Daily motivation to beat stress, inspire happiness, and achieve your goals.* Rockridge Press.

Hurley, K. (2021). Stop telling your kids to be resilient: Do this instead. *Psychology Today https://www.psychologytoday.com/ca/blog/worry-free-kids/202102/stop-telling-your-kids-be-resilient-do-instead*

Hymer, B. (2009). Beyond compare? Thoughts towards an inclusional, fluid, and non-normative understanding of giftedness. In T. Balchin,

B. Hymer, & D. J. Matthews (Eds.) *The Routledge international companion to gifted education* (pp. 299-307). Abingdon, UK: Routledge.

Jackson, P. S. (2020, June 23). Reflections on parenting profoundly gifted children: A (most) surprising territory. The Daimon Institute https://www.daimoninstitute.com.

Jensen, F. (2015). *the teenage brain: A neuroscientist's survival guide to raising adolescents and young adults.* Harper.

Jett, N., Taylor Schlitz, H., Shastid, N., & Taylor, M. (2020). *Turn on the power: How school is limiting your child's potential and what to do about it.* Gifted Unlimited.

Jolly, J. L., & Matthews, M. S. (2020a). Homeschooling and gifted education. In J. L. Plucker & C. M. Callahan (Eds.) *Critical issues and practices in gifted education: A survey of current research on giftedness and talent development (3rd ed., pp. 249-260).* Prufrock.

Jolly, J. L., & Matthews, M. S. (2020b). The shifting landscape of the home-schooling continuum. *Educational Review, 72*(3), 269-280. Doi.org/1 0.1080.00131911.2018.1552661

Jolly, J., Matthews, M., & Nester J. (2013). Homeschooling the Gifted: A Parent's Perspective. *Gifted Child Quarterly, 57*(2) 124-131.

Kalbfleisch, M. L. (2008). Getting to the heart of the brain: Using cognitive neuroscience to explore the nature of human ability and performance. *Roeper Review, 30,* 162-170.

Kanevsky, L. (n.d.) *Possibilities for learning.* http://possibilitiesforlearning.com

Kanevsky, L., & Keighley, T. (2003). To produce or not to produce: Under-standing boredom and the honor in underachievement. *Roeper Review, 26*(1), 20-28.

Kang, S. (2020) *The tech solution: Creating healthy habits for kids living in a digital world.* Viking.

Kaufmann, F. A., & Matthews, D. J. (2012). On becoming themselves: The 1964–1968 presidential scholars 40 years later. Roeper Review, 34, 83–93.

Kaufman, S. B. (2013). *Ungifted: Intelligence redefined.* New York: Basic Books.

Kaufman, S.B. (2019) When does intelligence peak? *Scientific American.* https://blogs.scientificamerican.com/beautiful-minds/when-does-intelligence-peak/

Kaufman, S. B., & Gregoire, C. (2016). *Wired to create: Unraveling the mysteries of the creative mind.* TarcherPerigee.

Kaufman, J. C., & Sternberg, R. (2019). An introduction to the second edition: Divergences and some convergences. In Sternberg, R., & Kaufman, J. C. (Eds.) *The Cambridge handbook of creativity* (pp. 1-4). Cambridge University Press. https://doi.org/10.1017/9781316979839

Keating, D. P. (1980). The four faces of creativity: The continuing plight of the underserved. *Gifted Child Quarterly, 24(2)*, 56-61.

Keating, D. P. (1991). Curriculum options for the developmentally advanced. *Exceptionality Education Canada, 1*, 53-83.

Keating, D. P. (2009). Developmental science and giftedness: An integrated life span framework. In F. D. Horowitz, R. F. Subotnik & D. J. Matthews (Eds.), *The development of giftedness and talent across the life span* (pp. 189-208). Washington: American Psychological Association.

Keating, D. P. (2011). Nature and Nurture in Early Child Development. Cambridge University Press.

Keltner, D., Oatley, K., & Jenkins, J. M. (2018). *Understanding emotions* (4th ed.). Wiley.

Kennedy-Moore, E. (2019). *Kid confidence: Help your child make friends, build resilience, and develop real self-esteem.* New Harbinger.

Kennedy-Moore, E., & McLaughlin, C. (2017). *Growing friendships: A kids' guide to making and keeping friends.* Aladdin.

Kerr, B. A., & Cohn, S. J. (2001). *Smart boys: Talent, manhood, and the search for meaning.* Scottsdale, AZ: Great Potential Press.

Kersey, A. J., Csumitta, K. D,. & Cantlon, J. F. (2019). Gender similarities in the brain during mathematics development. *npj Science of Learning* (4), 19. https://doi.org/10.1038/s41539-019-0057-x

Klein, A. G. (2002). *A forgotten voice: A biography of Leta Stetter Hollingworth.* Scottsdale, AZ: Great Potential Press.

Kunzman, R. (2008). Homeschooling. In J. A. Plucker & C. M. Callahan (Eds.), *Critical issues and practices in gifted education: What the research says* (pp. 253-260). Prufrock Press.

Kurcinka, M. S. (2020). *Raising a spirited child* (3rd ed.). William Morrow.

Kutz, S., & Tomaselli, M. (2019). "Two-eyed seeing" supports wildlife health. *Science, 21,* 1135-1137.

Kuzujanakis, M. (2020). Anxiety in today's children and young adults. *Gifted Education International.* https://doi.org/10.1177/0261429420934445

Lahey, J. (2016.) *The gift of failure: How the best parents learn to let go so their children can succeed.* Harper.

Lakin, J. M. (2018). Making the cut in gifted selection: Score combination rules and their impact on program diversity. *Gifted Child Quarterly, 62*(2), 210-219. https://doi.org/10.1177/0016986217752099

Lang, M. (2020). *Distracted: Why students can't focus and what you can do about it.* Basic Books.

Lapointe, V. (2019). *Parenting right from the start. Laying a healthy foundation in the baby and toddler years.* LifeTree.

Ledeman, D. (2017). Dealing with student distraction *Inside Higher Ed.* https://www.insidehighered.com/digital-learning/article/2020/11/17/author-discusses-strategies-overcoming-natural-student

Lee, H. I., Kim, Y. H., Kesebir, P., & Han, D. E. (2017). Understanding when parental praise leads to optimal child outcomes: Role of perceived praise accuracy. *Social Psychological and Personality Science, 8*(6), 679–688. https://doi.org/10.1177/1948550616683020

Lengua, L. (2020). Adversity can affect child self-regulation and resilience. *Psychology Today.* https://www.psychologytoday.com/us/blog/cultivating-resilience/202003/adversity-can-affect-child-self-regulation-and-resilience

Lewis, J. D., & Karnes, F. A. (2009). Public relations and advocacy for the gifted. In F. A. Karnes & S. M. Bean (Eds.) *Methods and materials for teaching the gifted* (3rd ed., pp 673-716). Prufrock Press.

Leyva, L. A. (2017). Unpacking the male superiority myth and masculinization of mathematics at the intersections: A review of research on gender in mathematics education. *Journal for Research in Mathematics Education (48)*4, 397-433. https://doi.org/10.5951/jresematheduc.48.4.0397

Lin-Siegler, X., Dweck, C. S., & Cohen, G. L. (2016). Instructional interventions that motivate classroom learning. *Journal of Educational Psychology, 108*(3), 295-299. http://dx.doi.org/10.1037/edu0000124

Locke, T. (2020). Sara Blakely's mom on raising two successful CEOs: Let your kids be 'bored" and "figure it out." CNBC *Make It* https://www.cnbc.com/2020/12/27/spanx-founder-sara-blakelys-mother-on-raising-a-successful-ceo.html

Lohman, D. F. (2005). The role of nonverbal ability tests in the identification of academically gifted students: An aptitude perspective. *Gifted Child Quarterly* (49), 111-138.

Lohman, D. F., & Korb, K. (2006). Gifted today but not tomorrow? Longitudinal changes in ITBS and CogAT scores during elementary school. Journal for the Education of the Gifted, 29, 451-484.

Lohman, D. F., & Lakin, J. (2008). Nonverbal test scores as one component of an identification system: Integrating ability, achievement, and teacher ratings. In J. L. VanTassel-Baska (Ed.), *Alternative assessments with gifted and talented students* (pp. 41-66). Prufrock Press.

Lubinski, D., & Benbow, C. P. (2006). Study of Mathematically Precocious Youth after 35 years. *Perspectives on Psychological Science, 1*, 316-345.

Makel, M. C., Kell, H. J., Lubinski, D., Putallaz, M., & Benbow, C. P. (2016). When lightning strikes twice: Profoundly gifted, profoundly accomplished. Psychological Science, 27(7), 1004–1018. https://doi.org/10.1177/0956797616644735

Markham, L. (2021). How nature makes kids calmer, healthier, smarter. Aha Parenting. https://www.ahaparenting.com/parenting-tools/safety/nature

Marland, S. P. (1972). Education of the gifted and talented. (Vol. 1). Report of the Congress of the United States by the U.S. Commissioner of Education. Washington, DC: Government Printing Office.

Marshall, M., Marshall, A., & Bartlett, C. (2015). Two-eyed seeing in medicine. In Determinants of Indigenous peoples' health in Canada, M. Greenwood, S. De Leeuw, N. M. Lindsay, & C. Reading (Eds.) pp 16-24. Canadian Scholars' Press.

Matthews, D. J. (2009). Developmental transitions in giftedness and talent: Childhood to adolescence. In F. D. Horowitz, R. F. Subotnik, & D. J. Matthews (Eds.) *The development of giftedness and talent across the lifespan* (pp. 89-108). Washington, DC: American Psychological Association.

Matthews, D. J. (2013). Canadian Aboriginal students: What they can teach us all about gifted education. https://donamatthews.wordpress.com/2013/11/

Matthews, D. J. (2015). The boy genius and the genius in all of us: A review of The boy who played with fusion, by Tom Clynes. https://www.psychologytoday.com/us/blog/going-beyond-intelligence/201506/the-boy-genius-and-the-genius-in-all-us

Matthews, D. J. (2019). Creative self-expression for health, coping, and resilience. *Psychology Today.* https://www.psychologytoday.com/ca/blog/going-beyond-intelligence/201909/creative-self-expression-health-coping-and-resilience

Matthews, D. J. (2019). Homeschooling: Is it the best option for you and your child? *Psychology Today.* https://www.psychologytoday.com/ca/blog/going-beyond-intelligence/201909/homeschooling-is-it-the-best-option-you-and-your-child

Matthews, D. J. (2019). Go outside! Take a walk, throw a ball, splash in puddles. *Psychology Today.* https://www.psychologytoday.com/us/blog/going-beyond-intelligence/202011/bullying-in-childhood-consequences-and-resiliency-factors

Matthews, D. J. (2020). Bullying in childhood: Consequences and resiliency factors. *Psychology Today.* https://www.psychologytoday.com/ca/blog/going-beyond-intelligence/201904/go-outside-take-walk-throw-ball-splash-in-puddles

Matthews, D. J., & Dai, D. Y. (2014). Gifted education: Changing conceptions, emphases and practice. *Sociology of Education, 24* (4), 335-353. doi/abs/10.1080/09620214.2014.979578

Matthews, D. J., & Foster, J. F. (2014). *Beyond Intelligence: Secrets for Raising Happily Productive Kids.* House of Anansi.

Matthews, D. J., & Foster, J. F. (2019). Intelligence, IQ, tests, and assessments. In K. Nilles, J. L. Jolly, T. F. Inman, and J. F. Smutny (Eds.) *Success strategies for parenting gifted kids.* Prufrock.

Matthews, D. J., Subotnik, R. F., & Horowitz, F. D. (2009). A developmental perspective on giftedness and talent: Implications for research, policy, and practice. In F. D. Horowitz, R. F. Subotnik, & D. J. Matthews (Eds.) *The development of giftedness and talent across the lifespan* (pp. 209-226). Washington, DC: American Psychological Association.

Matthews, M. S. (2015). Creativity and leadership's role in gifted identification and programming in the USA: A pilot study. *Asia Pacific Education Review, 16,* 247-256. doi:10.1007/s12564- 015-9373-x

Matthews, M. S. (2018). Utilizing non-test assessments in identifying gifted learners. In C. M. Callahan & H. L. Hertzberg-Davis (Eds.) *Fundamentals of gifted education: Considering multiple perspectives* (2nd ed., pp. 135-145). Routledge.

Matthews, M. S., & Jolly, J. L. (2020). Parenting gifted children. In J. L. Plucker & C. M. Callahan (Eds.) *Critical issues and practices in gifted education: A survey of current research on giftedness and talent development* (3rd ed., pp. 335-348). Prufrock.

McClarty, K. L. (2015). Life in the fast lane: Effects of early grade acceleration on high school and college outcomes. *Gifted Child Quarterly, 59*(1), 3-13. https://doi.org/10.1177/0016986214559595

McCoach, D. B., & Siegle, D. (2008). Underachievers. In J. A. Plucker & C. M. Callahan (Eds.), *Critical issues and practices in gifted education: What the research says* (pp. 721-734). Prufrock Press.

McTighe, J., & Wiggins, G. P. (2005) *Understanding by design.* Alexandria, VA: Association for Supervision and Curriculum Development.

Meece, J. L., & Daniels, D. H. (2008). *Child and adolescent development for educators* (3rd ed.). New York: McGraw-Hill.

Mendaglio, S. (2007). Should perfectionism be a characteristic of giftedness? *Gifted Education International, 23*(3), 229-230.

Mendaglio, S. (Ed.) (2008). *Dabrowski's theory of positive disintegration.* Great Potential Press.

Merrotsy, P. (2013). A note on Big-C creativity and little-c creativity. *Creativity Research Journal, 25*(4), 474-476. https://doi.org/10.1080/10400419.2013.843921

Mitchell, A. (2003, September 27). Slow schooling: It makes mainstream education look like fast food. *The Globe and Mail,* F1, F10.

Moon, S. M. (2006). On being gifted and adolescent: An overview. In F. A. Dixon & S. M. Moon, *The Handbook of secondary gifted education* (pp. 1-5). Waco, TX: Prufrock Press.

Moon, S. M. (2011). Parenting gifted children with ADHD. In Jolly, J. L.; Treffinger, D.J.; Ford Inman, T.; Franklin Smutny, J. (Eds.). *Parenting gifted children.* NAGC

Naglieri, J. A. (1996). *Naglieri Nonverbal Ability Test.* San Antonio, TX: The Psychological Corporation.

Naglieri, J. A. (1996). *Naglieri Nonverbal Ability Test.* San Antonio, TX: The Psychological Corporation.

Naglieri, J. A,. & Ford, D. Y. (2003). Addressing underrepresentation of gifted minority children using the Naglieri Nonverbal Ability Test (NNAT). *Gifted Child Quarterly, 47,* 155-160.

National Association for Gifted Children. (2019). *National standards in gifted and talented education.* National Association for Gifted Children. http://www.nagc.org/resources-publications/resources/national-standards-gifted-and-talented-education

Navan, J. (2020). *Our gifted elders: Awareness, aspirations, advocacy.* Gifted Unlimited.

Neihart, M. (2008). *Peak performance for smart kids.* Prufrock Press.

Nelson, C. A. (1999). Neural plasticity and human development. *Current Directions in Psychological Science, 8,* 42-45.

Olszewski-Kubilius, P. (2019). Top ten psychosocial skills to cultivate in your gifted child. In K. Nilles; J.L. Jolly; T. Ford Inman; & J. Franklin Smutny (Eds.) *Success strategies for parenting gifted kids.* Prufrock Press. pp 123 – 131.

Olszewski-Kubilius, P., Subotnik, R. F., & Worrell, F. C. (2015). Conceptualizations of giftedness and the development of talent: Implications for counselors. Journal of Counseling and Development 93 (2), 143-152. https://doi.org/10.1002/j.1556-6676.2015.00190.x

Olszewski-Kubilius, P., Subotnik, R. F., & Worrell, F. C. (Eds.) (2018). *Talent development as a framework for gifted education: Implications for best practice and applications in schools.* Prufrock.

Ontario College of Teachers. (2021). *Ethical standards and standards of practice.* Ontario College of Teachers. https://www.oct.ca/public/professional-standards/standards-of-practice 2021

Ontario Ministry of Education. (1984). *Special education handbook.* Toronto, ON: Author.

Ontario Ministry of Education and Training. (2000). *Individual education plans: Standards for development, program planning, and implementation.* Toronto, ON: Author.

Oreck, B. A., Owen, S. V., & Baum, S. M. (2003). Validity, reliability, and equity issues in an observational talent assessment process in the performing arts. (Article includes the *Talent Assessment Process.*) *Journal for the Education of the Gifted, 27(1),* 62-94.

Parks, S. (2009). Teaching analytical and critical thinking skills in gifted education. In F. A. Karnes & S. M. Bean (Eds.) *Methods and materials for teaching the gifted* (3rd ed., pp 261-300). Prufrock Press.

Paul, A. M. (2012, October 24). Why parenting is more important than schools. *Time.* https://ideas.time.com/2012/10/24/the-single-largest-advantage-parents-can-give-their-kids/

Paul, A. M. (2013). Music helps memory. *The Creativity Post* https://www.creativitypost.com/education/music_helps_memory

Peters, S. J., Gentry, M., Whiting, G. W., & McBee, M. T. (2019). Who gets served in gifted education? Demographic representation and a call for action. *Gifted Child Quarterly 63*(4) 273–287. https://journals.sagepub.com/doi/10.1177/0016986219833738

Peters, S. J., Carter, J., & Plucker, J. A. (2020). Rethinking how we identify "gifted" students. *Phi Delta Kappan, 102*(4), 8–13. https://doi.org/10.1177/0031721720978055 https://kappanonline.org/rethinking-how-we-identify-gifted-students-peters-carter-plucker/

Peters, S. J., Rambo-Hernandez, K. E., Makel, M. C., Matthews, M. S., & Plucker, J. A. (2017). Should millions of students take a gap year? Large numbers of students start the school year above grade level. *Gifted Child Quarterly, 61*(3), 229-238.

Piirto, J. (2003). *Understanding creativity.* Scottsdale, AZ: Great Potential Press.

Pinquart, M. 2016). Associations of parenting styles and dimensions with academic achievement in children and adolescents: A meta-analysis. Education Psychology Review 28, 475-493. https://doi.org/10.1007/s10648-015-9338-y

Piper, W. (1930). *The little engine that could.* New York: Platt & Munk.

Plucker, J. L., Makel, M. C., Matthews, M. S., Peters, S. J., & Rambo-Hernandez, K. E. (2017). Blazing new trails: Strengthening policy research in gifted education. *Gifted Child Quarterly, 61* (3), 210-218. https://doi.org/10.1177/0016986217701838

Plucker, J., Makel, M.C., & Qian, M. (2019). Assessment of creativity. In R. Sternberg & J.C. Kaufman (Eds.) The Cambridge handbook of creativity (2nd ed.) Cambridge University Press. (pp. 44-68). https://doi.org/10.1017/9781316979839

Plucker, J. L., & Callahan, C. M. (Eds.) (2020). Critical Issues and Practices in Gifted Education: A Survey of Current Research on Giftedness and Talent Development (3rd ed.). Prufrock.

Plucker, J. L., & Callahan, C. M. (2014). Research on giftedness and gifted education: Status of the field and considerations for the future. *Exceptional Children, 80* (4), 390-406. https://journals.sagepub.com/doi/full/10.1177/0014402914527244

Pomerantz, S., & Raby, R. (2020). Bodies, hoodies, schools, and success: Post-human performativity and smart girlhood, *Gender and Education, 32*(8), 983-1000, DOI: 10.1080/09540253.2018.1533923

Price-Mitchell, M. (2013). Growing up bullied. *Psychology Today* https://www.psychologytoday.com/ca/blog/the-moment-youth/201308/growing-bullied

Price-Mitchell, M. (2015). *Tomorrow's change-makers: reclaiming the power of citizenship for a new generation.* Eagle Harbor Publishing.

Price-Mitchell, M. (2016) Curiosity: How parents foster lifelong learning in children. Roots of Action Online https://www.rootsofaction.com

Price-Mitchell, M. (2019, September 4). Future leadership: Lessons from history. *Roots of Action.* https://www.rootsofaction.com/future-leadership /

Purkey, W. W. (2006). *Teaching class clowns (and what they can teach us).* Corwin Press.

Pyryt, M. C. (2008). Self-concept. In J. A. Plucker & C. M. Callahan (Eds.), *Critical issues and practices in gifted education: What the research says* (pp. 595-602). Prufrock Press.

Quart, A. (2006). *Hothouse kids: The dilemma of the gifted child.* Penguin.

Radcliffe. S. C. (n.d.) www.sarahchanaradcliffe.com

Raby, R., & Pomerantz, S. (2015). Playing it down/playing it up: Girls' strategic negotiations of academic success, *British Journal of Sociology of Education, 36*(4), 507-525, DOI: 10.1080/01425692.2013.836056

Raven, J. C., Court, J. H., & Raven, J. (1998). *Standard Progressive Matrices.* London: Lewis.

Ray, B. D. (2017) A systematic review of the empirical research on selected aspects of homeschooling as a school choice. *Journal of School Choice, 11*(4), 604-621, DOI: 10.1080/15582159.2017.1395638

Reilly, D., Neumann, D. L., & Andrews, G. (2015). Sex differences in mathematics and science achievement: A meta-analysis of National Assessment of Educational Progress assessments. *Journal of Educational Psychology, 107*(3), 645–662. https://doi.org/10.1037/edu0000012

Reis, S. M. (2009). Turning points and future directions in gifted education and talent development. In T. Balchin, B. Hymer, & D. J. Matthews (Eds.), *The Routledge international companion to gifted education* (pp. 317-324). Routledge.

Reis, S. M., & Peters, P. M. (2020). Research on the Schoolwide Enrichment Model: Four decades of insights, innovation, and evolution. *Gifted Education International 1* (33). https://journals.sagepub.com/doi/pdf/10.1177/0261429420963987

Reis, S. M., & Renzulli, J. S. (2010) Is there still a need for gifted education? An examination of current research. *Learning and Individual Differences, 20* (4), 308-317. https://www.sciencedirect.com/science/article/abs/pii/S1041608009000909

Renzulli, J. S. (2021). Assessment for learning: The missing element for identifying high potential in low income and minority groups. *Gifted Education International.* https://doi.org/10.1177/0261429421998304

Renzulli, J., & Reis, S. (2009). *Light up your child's mind. Finding a unique pathway to happiness and success.* Little, Brown and Company.

Renzulli, J., & Reis, S. (2014). *Schoolwide Enrichment Model, 3rd Edition. How-to guide for talent development.* Prufrock Press.

Resnick, M. (2018). *Lifelong kindergarten: Cultivating creativity through projects, passion, peers, and play.* MIT Press.

Riley, T. L. (2009). *Teaching gifted and talented students in regular classrooms.* In F. A. Karnes & S. M. Bean, *Methods and materials for teaching the gifted (3rd ed.,* pp. 631-672). Prufrock Press.

Rinn, A. N. (2018). *Social and emotional considerations for gifted students.* In S. I. Pfeiffer, E. Shaunessy-Dedrick, & M. Foley-Nicpon (Eds.), *APA handbook of giftedness and talent* (p. 453–464). American Psychological Association. https://doi.org/10.1037/0000038-029

Ritchotte, J. A., & Matthews, M. A. (2019*). Gifted and learning disabled: advocating for the needs of your 2e child.* In *Success Strategies for Parenting Gifted Kids.* NAGC

Rivero, L. (2002). *Creative homeschooling: A resource guide for smart families.* Great Potential Press.

Rivero, L. (2011). Multipotentiality; When high ability leads to too many options (The stress and indecisions of being well-rounded). *Psychology Today.*

Robinson, A., Shore, B. M., & Enersen, D. L. (2007). *Best practices in gifted education: An evidence-based guide.* Prufrock Press.

Robinson, N. R., & Noble, K. D. (1992). A radical leap from middle school to college: Can it work? In N. Colangelo, S. G. Assouline, and D. L. Ambrose (Eds.), *Talent Development Proceedings from the Henry B. and Jocelyn Wallace National Research Symposium on Talent Development* (pp. 267-77). Trillium Press.

Robinson, N. M., & Robinson, H. B. (1982). The optimal match: Devising the best compromise for the highly gifted student. New Directions in Child and Adolescent Development, 17, 79-94. https://doi.org/10.1002/cd.23219821708

Rogers, K. B. (2002). *Re-forming gifted education: How parents and teachers can match the program to the child.* Scottsdale, AZ: Great Potential Press.

Ruch, W., Platt, T., & Hoffman, J. (2014). *The character strengths of class clowns. Frontiers in Psychology,* 5. https://doi.org/10.3389/fpsyg.2014.01075

Ryan, R. M., & Deci, E. L. (2016). Facilitating and hindering motivation, learning, and well-being in schools. In K. R. Wentzel & D. B. Miele, *Handbook of motivation at school, 2ⁿᵈ ed.* (96-119). Routledge

Salmon, G. (2000). *E-Moderating: The key to teaching and learning online.* Sterling, VA: Stylus.

Satell, E. (2021). https://www.satellinstitute.org

Shanker, S. (2016). Self-regulation vs self-control. https://www.psychologytoday.com/ca/blog/self-reg/201607/self-regulation-vs-self-control

Shechtman, Z., & Silektor, A. (2012). Social competencies and difficulties of gifted children compared to nongifted peers. *Roeper Review: A Journal on Gifted Education, 34*(1), 63–72. https://doi.org/10.1080/02783193.2012.627555

Sheppard, B. H. (2020). *Ten Years to Midnight: Four Urgent Global Crises and Their Strategic Solutions.* Berrett- Koehler.

Shifrer, D. (2016). Stigma and stratification limiting the math course progression of adolescents labeled with a learning disability. *Learning and Instruction, 42*, 47-57. https://doi.org/10.1016/j.learninstruc.2015.12.001.

Shively, K., Stith, K. M., & Rubenstein, L. D. (2018). Measuring What Matters: Assessing Creativity, Critical Thinking, and the Design Process. *Gifted Child Today, 41*(3), 149–158. https://doi.org/10.1177/1076217518768361

Shoemaker, S. E., Thomas, C., Roberts, T., & Boltz, R. (2016). Building a mentorship-based research program focused on individual interests, curiosity, and professional skills at the North Carolina School of Science and Mathematics. *Gifted Child Today, 39*(4), 191–204. https://doi.org/10.1177/1076217516661591

Shore, B., Gagne, F., Larivee, S., Tali, R., & Tremblay, R. (1981). *Face to face with giftedness.* Trillium Press.

Siegel, D. J., & Bryson, T. P. (2012). *The Whole-brain child: 12 revolutionary strategies to nurture your child's developing mind.* Bantam.

Siegel, D. J., & Bryson, T. P. (2016). *No drama discipline: The whole-brain way to calm the chaos and nurture your child's developing mind.* Bantam.

Siegle, D. (n.d.) *Understanding and Addressing Motivation Issues*, VIMEO presentation

Siegle, D., McCoach, D. B., & Wilson, H. E. (2009). Extending learning through mentorships. In F. A. Karnes & S. M. Bean (Eds.) *Methods and materials for teaching the gifted* (3rd ed., pp. 519-564). Prufrock Press.

Simonton, D. K. (1994). *Greatness: Who makes history and why.* New York: Guilford Press.

Smith, C. K., & Wood, S. M. (2018). Career counseling for the gifted and talented: Alife span development approach. In S. Pfeiffer (Ed).), *Handbook of giftedness in children* (pp. 315-333). Springer. https://doi.org/10.1007/978-3-319-77004-8_18

Spearman, C. (1927). *The abilities of man: Their nature and measurement.* New York: Macmillan.

Stanley, J. C., & Benbow, C. P. (1983). Educating mathematically precocious youths: Twelve policy recommendations. *Educational Researcher, 11(5)*, 4-9.

Stanley, J. C., Keating, D. P., & Fox, L. (1974). *Mathematical talent.* Baltimore: Johns Hopkins Press.

Steenbergen-Hu, S., Makel, M. C., & Olszewski-Kubilius, P. (2016). What one hundred years of research says about the effects of ability grouping and acceleration on K–12 students' academic achievement: Findings of two second-order meta-analyses. *Review of Educational Research, 86,* 849-899. doi:10.3102/0034654316675417

Steinberg, L. (2015). *Age of opportunity: Lessons from the new science of adolescence.* Houghton Mifflin Harcourt.

Stephens, K. R. (2020). Gifted education policy and advocacy: Perspectives for school psychologists. Psychology in the Schools, 57(10), 1640-1651.

Sternberg, R. (2002). Encouraging students to decide for creativity. *Research in the Schools,* 9(2), 61-70. https://sites.google.com/a/sas.edu.sg/creativity-in-the-context-of-education/decide-for-creativity

Sternberg, R. J. (2009). Wisdom, intelligence, creativity, synthesised: A model of giftedness. In T. Balchin, B. Hymer, & D. J. Matthews (Eds.) *The Routledge international companion to gifted education* (pp. 255-264). Abingdon, UK: Routledge.

Sternberg, R. (2018, Feb. 27). What's wrong with creativity testing? *Journal of Creative Behavior.* https://doi.org/10.1002/jocb.237

Subotnik, R. F. (2009). Developmental transitions in giftedness and talent: Adolescence into adulthood. In F. D. Horowitz, R. F. Subotnik & D. J. Matthews (Eds.), *The development of giftedness and talent across the life span* (pp. 155-170). American Psychological Association.

Subotnik, R. F., Olszewski-Kubilius, P., & Worrell, F. C. (2012). A proposed direction forward for gifted education based on psychological science. *Gifted Child Quarterly, 56* (4), 16-188. https://journals.sagepub.com/doi/full/10.1177/0016986212456079

Subotnik, R. F., Stoeger, H., & Olszewski-Kubilius, P. (2017). Talent development research, policy, and practice in Europe and the United States: Outcomes from a summit of international researchers. *Gifted Child Quarterly, 61*(3) 262–269. https://doi.org/10.1177/0016986217701839

Subotnik, R., Worrell, F., & Olszewski-Kubilius, P. (2018). *Talent development as a framework for gifted education.* Prufrock Press.

Swanson, J. D., Brock, L., Van Sickle, M., Gutshall, C. A., Russell, L., & Anderson, L. (2020) A basis for talent development: the integrated curriculum model and evidence-based strategies. *Roeper Review, 42*(3), 165-178. DOI: 10.1080/02783193.2020.1765920

Tarampi, M. R., Heydari, N., & Hegarty, M. (2016). A tale of two types of perspective taking: Sex differences in spatial ability. *Psychological Science, 27*(11), 1507–1516. https://doi.org/10.1177/0956797616667459

Terman, L. M. (Ed.). (1925-1959). *Genetic studies of genius* (Vols. 1-5). Stanford, CA: Stanford University Press.

Tetreault, N. (2019). Our brains on smartphones, (un)social media, and our mental health. https://www.sengifted.org/post/our-brains-on-smartphones-un-social-media-and-our-mental-health

Tetreault, N. (2020). *Brain fingerprints*. www.nicoletetreault.com.

Tetreault, N. (2020). *Accessing the building blocks for positive neural plasticity*. www.nicoletetreault.com

Tetreault, N. (2021). *Insight into a bright mind: A neuroscientist's personal stories of unique thinking*. Gifted Unlimited.

Thurstone, L. L. (1938). *Primary mental abilities*. Chicago: University of Chicago Press.

Tirri, K. (2017). Teacher education is the key to changing the identification and teaching of the gifted. *Roeper Review, 39* (3), 210-212. https://www.tandfonline.com/doi/abs/10.1080/02783193.2017.1318996

Tomlinson, C. A. (2003). *Differentiated instruction: The critical issue of quality*. Paper presented at the annual meeting of the National Association for Gifted Children, Indianapolis, IN.

Tomlinson, C. (2014). Principles of a differentiated classroom. https://sdvaughan.edublogs.org/files/2014/10/differentiation_definitions-1aogy70.pdf Retrieved Jan. 18, 2021.

Tomlinson, C. A. (2017). How to Differentiate Instruction in Academically Diverse Classrooms. https://www.amazon.com/Differentiate-Instruction-Academically-Diverse-Classrooms/dp/1416623302/ref=pd_sbs_2?pd_rd_w=OplWd&pf_rd_p=965b754e-4670-4322-863d-d4929773ec49&pf_rd_r=29WY0GPSBVVDX6M33HS-B&pd_rd_r=970e8391-a3df-4e3c-a123-3e1305c134a6&pd_rd_wg=nq09p&pd_rd_i=1416623302&psc=1

Tomlinson, C. (n.d.) Principles of a differentiated classroom. https://sdvaughan.edublogs.org/files/2014/10/differentiation_defini-tions-1aogy70.pdf Retrieved Jan. 18, 2021.

Tomlinson, C.A., Kaplan, S.N. N., Purcell, J.H.H., Leppien, J.H.H., Burns, D.E.E., Strickland, C.A.A., Imbeau, M.B.B., & Renzulli, J.S.S. (2008).

The parallel curriculum: A design to develop learner potential and challenge advanced learners. Second Edition. Corwin.

Toynbee, A. (1967). Is America neglecting her creative talents? In C. W. Taylor (Ed.), *Creativity across education* (pp. 23-29). Salt Lake City, UT: University of Utah Press.

Treffinger, D., Nassab, C. A., & Selby, E. C. (2009). Programming for talent development: Expanding horizons for gifted education. In T. Balchin, B. Hymer, & D. J. Matthews (Eds.) *The Routledge international companion to gifted education* (pp. 210-217). Routledge.

Van Gemert, L. (2019). Perfectionism: A practical guide to managing "never good enough." Independently published.

Vanderbilt University. (n.d.) *Study of Mathematically Precocious Youth.* https://my.vanderbilt.edu/smpy/

Vanraalte, J. L., Vincent, A., & Brewer, B. (2016, September). Self-talk interventions for athletes: A theoretically grounded approach. *Journal of Sport Psychology in Action, 8*(3), 141-151. DOI: 10.1080/215207 04.2016.1233921

VanTassel-Baska, J. (1992). Educational Decision Making on Acceleration and Grouping. *Gifted Child Quarterly, 36*(2), 68–72. https://doi.org/10.1177/001698629203600203

VanTassel-Baska, J. (2000). Theory and practice in curriculum development for the gifted. In K. A. Heller, F. J. Monks, R. J. Sternberg, & R. F. Subotnik (Eds.), *International handbook of giftedness and talent* (2nd ed., pp. 345-366). Oxford, UK: Elsevier Science.

VanTassel-Baska, J. L. (2008). Using performance-based assessment to document authentic learning. In J. L. VanTassel-Baska (Ed.), *Alternative assessments with gifted and talented students* (pp. 285-308). Prufrock Press.

VanTassel-Baska, J. (2018). American policy in gifted education. *Gifted Child Today, 41*(2), 98-103.

VanTassel-Baska, J. (2021) A conception of giftedness as domain-specific learning: a dynamism fueled by persistence and passion. In R. J. Sternberg & D. Ambrose (Eds) *Conceptions of giftedness and talent.* Palgrave Macmillan. https://doi.org/10.1007/978-3-030-56869-6_25 pp.443-466.

VanTassel-Baska, J. L., & Brown, E. F. (2009). An analysis of gifted education curriculum models. In F. A. Karnes & S. M. Bean (Eds.) *Methods and materials for teaching the gifted* (3rd ed., pp. 75-106). Waco, TX: Prufrock Press.

Vygotsky, L. S. (1978). *Mind in society.* Cambridge, MA: Harvard University Press. (Original work published 1930.)

Wagner, L. (2019). The social life of class clowns: Class clown behavior is associated with more friends but also more aggressive behavior in the classroom. Frontiers in Psychology, 10. https://doi.org/10.3389/fpsyg.2019.00604

Wallace, B. (2009). Developing pupils' problem-solving and thinking skills. In T. Balchin, B. Hymer, & D. J. Matthews (Eds.) *The Routledge international companion to gifted education* (pp. 281-291). Routledge.

Walsh, R. L., & Jolly, J. L. (2018). Gifted Education in the Australian Context. *Gifted Child Today, 41*(2), 81–88. https://doi.org/10.1177/1076217517750702

Wang, C. W., & Neihart, M. (2015). How do supports from parents, teachers, and peers influence academic achievement of twice-exceptional students? *Gifted Child Today, 38*(3), 148–159. https://doi.org/10.1177/1076217515583742

Ward. M. (2017). *Billionaire Bill Gates reveals his deepest regrets and best advice for today's 20-somethings* CNBC Make It. https://www.cnbc.com/2017/05/15/billionaire-bill-gates-reveals-his-deepest-regrets-and-best-advice.html

Waters, L. E., Loton, D., & Jach, H. K. (2019). Does strength-based parenting predict academic achievement? The mediating effects of perseverance and engagement. Journal of Happiness Studies, 20, 1121-1140 https://doi.org/10.1007/s10902-018-9983-1

Webb, J. T. (2013). *Searching for meaning: Idealism, bright minds, disillusionment, and hope.* Gifted Unlimited.

Webb, J. T.; Amend, E.; Webb, N. E.; Kuzujanakis, M.; Olenchak, R.; & Goerss, J. (2016). *Misdiagnosis and dual diagnoses of gifted children and adults: Bipolar, OCD, Asperger's, depression, and other disorders. 2nd Ed.* Gifted Unlimited.

Webb, J. T., Gore, J. L., Amend, E. R., & DeVries, A. R. (2007). *A parent's guide to gifted children.* Great Potential Press.

Weinman, M. (2014). *It's about time: Transforming chaos into calm, A to Z.* iUniverse.

Weisberg, R. W. (2006) Modes of expertise in creative thinking. In K. A. Ericsson, N. Charness, P. J. Feltovich & R. R. Hoffman (Eds.), *The Cambridge handbook of expertise and expert performance* (pp. 761-787). New York: Cambridge University Press.

What Works Newsletter. (n.d.) College of William and Mary. https://education.wm.edu/centers/cfge/curriculum/What%20Works%20CFGE%202013%20Web.pdf

Whitehead, J., & McNiff, J. (2006). *Action research living theory*. Sage.

Whitney, C. S., with G. Hirsch. (2007). *A love for learning: Motivation and the gifted child*. Great Potential Press.

Winner, E. (1996). *Gifted children: Myths and realities*. New York: Basic Books.

Winner, E. (2009). Toward broadening our understanding of giftedness: The spatial domain. In F. D. Horowitz, R. F. Subotnik & D. J. Matthews (Eds.), *The development of giftedness and talent across the life span* (pp. 59-74). Washington: American Psychological Association.

Wiley, K. R. (2020). The social and emotional world of gifted students: Moving beyond the label. *Psychological Science, 57* (10), 1528-1541 https://doi.org/10.1002/pits.22340

Willis, J. A. (2009). *Inspiring middle school minds: Gifted, creative, and challenging*. Scottsdale, AZ: Great Potential Press.

Willis, J. A. 2016, *Teaching the Brain to Read, Strategies for Improving Fluency, Vocabulary, and Comprehension*.

Wirthwein, L., Bergold, S., Preckel, F., & Steinmayr, R. (2019). Personality and school functioning of intellectually gifted and nongifted adolescents: Self-perceptions and parents' assessments. *Learning and Individual Differences, 73*, 16-29. https://doi.org/10.1016/j.lindif.2019.04.003.

Worrell, F. C. (2009). What does gifted mean? Personal and social identity perspectives on giftedness in adolescence. In F. D. Horowitz, R. F. Subotnik, & D. J. Matthews, *The development of giftedness and talent across the life span* (pp. 131-152). Washington: APA Publications.

Worrell, F. C., & Dixson, D. D. (2018). Recruiting and retaining underrepresented gifted students. In S. Pfeiffer (Ed.), *Handbook of giftedness in children* (2nd ed., pp. 209-226). Springer.

Worrell, F. C., & Dixson, D. D. (2020). Diversity and gifted education. In J. L. Plucker & C. M. Callahan (Eds.) *Critical issues and practices in gifted education: A survey of current research on giftedness and talent development (3rd ed.*, pp. 169-184*)*. Prufrock.

Worrell, F. C., Subotnik, R. F., Olszewski-Kubilius, P., & Dixson, D. D. (2019). Gifted students. *Annual Review of Psychology Vol 70*, 551-576.

Wright, A. L., Gabel, C., Ballantyne, M., Jack, S. M., & Wahoush, O. (2019). Using two-eyed seeing in research with indigenous people: An integrative review. *International Journal of Qualitative Methods*. https://doi.org/10.1177/1609406919869695

Wright, L., & Borland, J. H. (1993). Using early childhood developmental portfolios in the identification and education of young, economically disadvantaged, potentially gifted students. *Roeper Review, 15*, 205-210.

Yeager, D.S., Hanselman, P., Walton, G.M. et al. (2019). A national experiment reveals where a growth mindset improves achievement. *Nature* 573, 364–36. https://doi.org/10.1038/s41586-019-1466-y

Yogman, M., Garner, A., Hutchinson, J., Hirsh-Pasek, K., & Golinkoff, R. M. (2018). The power of play: A pediatric role in enhancing development in young children. Pediatrics, 142(3), 2018-2058. DOI: https://doi.org/10.1542/peds.2018-2058

Young, J. L., Jamaal R. Young, J. R., & Ford, D. Y (2019). Culturally relevant STEM out-of-school time: A rationale to support gifted girls of color, *Roeper Review, 41*:1, 8-19, DOI: 10.1080/02783193.2018.1553215

Yu, H. P., & Jen, E. (2019). The gender role and career self-efficacy of gifted girls in STEM areas. *High Ability Studies*, 1-17. https://doi.org/10.1080/13598139.2019.1705767

About the Authors

Dona Matthews, PhD, was the Executive Director of the Millennium Dialogue for Early Child Development at the University of Toronto, and the founding director of the Hunter College Center for Gifted Education and Development, City University of New York. She has taught at universities in Canada and the US, and worked with children, families, and schools, doing assessments, counselling, and consultations. She writes a blog for *Psychology Today*, has written dozens of articles and book chapters, and has given dozens of conference presentations. She has co-authored or co-edited four books: *Being Smart about Gifted Learning*; *Beyond Intelligence*; *The Development of Giftedness and Talent Across the Life Span*; and *The Routledge International Companion to Gifted Education*. She is also author of *Imperfect Parenting: How to Build a Relationship with Your Child to Weather Any Storm* (in press with the American Psychological Association).

Joanne Foster, Ed.D. is a child development and gifted education specialist, and the multi award-winning author of several books. She wrote *ABCs of Raising Smarter Kids*; *Bust Your BUTS: Tips for Teens Who Procrastinate* (IBPA Silver Benjamin Franklin Award); and *Not Now, Maye Later: Helping Children Overcome Procrastination*. She's co-author of *Beyond Intelligence*, and three editions of *Being Smart*, including *Being*

Smart about Gifted Learning. She writes guest blogs and book chapters, and her articles are featured in many publications including *The Creativity Post* and *First Time Parent Magazine.* Dr. Foster taught for several years at the University of Toronto, and continues to work as an educational consultant advising parents, teachers, schoolboards, and advocacy groups. She offers presentations, webinars, and workshops on learning, creativity, motivation, and children's well-being.

CPSIA information can be obtained
at www.ICGtesting.com
Printed in the USA
LVHW081533030522
R17320400001B/R173204PG716925LVX00001B/1

9 781953 360076